Large Animals
and
Wide Horizons

LARGE ANIMALS
and
WIDE HORIZONS

The Autobiography of
RICHARD M. LAWS

JANUS PUBLISHING COMPANY LTD
Cambridge, England

First published in Great Britain 2017
by Janus Publishing Company Ltd
The Studio
High Green
Great Shelford
Cambridge CB22 5EG

www.januspublishing.co.uk

ISBN 978-1-85756-864-6

Cover Design: Janus Publishing
Cover Image: R. M. Laws

Edited by
Ian and Christine Parker and
Arnoldus Schytte Blix
2016

Printed and bound in Great Britain

For Maureen

Contents

Acknowledgements

The editors appreciated comments on Dick Laws' abridged text by John Croxall and, in particular, Geoff Cook, for guidance on Dick's years at St Edmunds. To them and the Janus team of Ken Sewell, Barbara Legg and Tina Brand, our thanks for bringing this book to fruition.

Foreword 1

When Richard M. Laws retired in 1996 after a long watch as seal and whale biologist in Antarctica and elephant and hippo biologist in Africa, director of BAS and finally Master of St Edmund's College in Cambridge, he sat down to write his memoirs. Sadly, however, before this task was completed he suffered several strokes, which, without compromising his mind and memory unduly, rendered him unable to operate computers, and this work ground to a full stop.

At the time of my last sabbatical in Cambridge in 2010 it was quite obvious that nobody in England felt the urge to help my old friend and that his very many years of work was in danger of being lost to the public. So, for the lack of others, and for old times' sake, I took it upon myself to organise the material and get it published. Little did I know that it consisted of an unorganised number of drafts of more than fifty chapters in various stages of completion. In addition the material was written on outdated computers with programs that are now long obsolete and the files were consequently very hard to access. In fact, I doubt if it could have been done without the assistance of a young Norwegian computer wizard called Peter Munch-Ellingsen.

Luckily, with the same assistance, it has been possible to retrieve electronic versions of some of Dick's excellent artistic drawings, which have been included as vignettes in many of the chapters. They are not all relevant to the contents but they certainly show Dick's excellent artistic talent.

I organised the material as best as I could into three parts with altogether fifty-one chapters. In so doing there was bound to be some overlap, but to avoid that would require rewriting of several chapters, which was way beyond the scope of this project. Many times the drafts contained labels saying 'Expand'. Obviously I have not done so, neither have I checked several labels saying 'Check!'

I did a rough 'Windows' spell check of the manuscript. I struggled with English, Celtic, Norwegian and African slang which was used extensively. Hopefully the result is comprehensible, if not perfect, but this has been a rescue and salvage job with little in it for me, except the comfort of having saved what otherwise would have been lost.

Arnoldus Schytte Blix
Tromsø, 4 October 2012

Foreword 2

Dick and Maureen Laws were our close family friends for over fifty years. First meeting in Uganda in 1963, we collaborated extensively during his Africa years and thereafter we visited the Laws whenever in Britain. We corresponded steadily across the years and in 1998 he sent me an extensive synopsis of the autobiography he had started to write. This stopped in 2004 when he could no longer use his word processor. By this point, as indicated by Arnoldus Blix, he had written fifty-one chapters in draft. Other than some simple rearranging, Arnoldus did not edit Dick's writing further, but to ensure that it wasn't lost, he lodged it on the Scott Polar Research Institute's (SPRI) website.

This is where we found and read it. The 757,521 words were heavy going with much duplication. In them one could follow the gradual deterioration of Dick's recall from a chain of mini-strokes before he became unable to use his word processor in 2004. One could also sense that he had been aware of his declining abilities and rising frustration as he raced to get his book finished. As time slid by, he had been unable to remember whether he had already written about an incident, so recorded it a second and sometimes a third time. While the descriptions might have varied in length and sometimes markedly in mood, fortunately the basic facts stayed the same.

Thus with Maureen's and Arnoldus' permission, we have edited Dick's text into an altogether shorter book. Here and there we have filled in blank spots with our own words. Throughout we could refer to the detailed synopsis he produced in 1998. Hopefully this does justice to the record of a remarkable man.

Ian and Chris Parker,
Tolga, Australia, 2016

Introduction

The Concise Oxford Dictionary defines 'Memoir' as an 'essay on learned subject specially studied by the writer'; 'biography' as the 'written life of a person'; and 'autobiography' as the 'written story of one's own life'. This book is a combination of autobiography and memoir. Originally it was planned as a trilogy covering first my childhood, education and working in Antarctica; second my years in Africa and third my return to the Antarctic. This Introduction covers all three phases.

The choice of title needs some introduction. The 'large animals' are the largest of their kind – the elephant seal, the largest whales, the largest 'pig', the hippopotamus – and the largest land animal, the elephant. I studied these huge beasts, not in a preconceived plan, but almost by accident, each element in my career leading to the next.

The 'wide horizons' of the title were both physical and intellectual. Physically they encompassed the endless Antarctic lands and the surrounding great waters, and extensive African savannahs, forests and bushlands. Flying at ten thousand feet over the icefields of the Weddell Sea, or above the polar plateau, there was virtually no horizon, so wide was it; the same was true of East Africa. As well as such limitless vistas I had to confront the wide political horizons of emergent Africa and the multinational stage of Antarctic science.

Physically and mentally, living in the Antarctic and in African wilds was strenuous and exciting. Making new discoveries in biology was mental adventure and exploration.

When I took my degree at Cambridge the relatively new subject of ecology played a very small part, but it became central to my research career. Charles Elton framed the basic principles in his *Animal Ecology* (1937), an influential book which moved the emphasis from research on individuals to that of populations. Ten years after its publication, my career began when I was thrown in 'at the deep end', to studying the biology and ecology of elephant seals on Signy Island. My 'nominal' supervisor was zoologist Sydney Smith, whose field was experimental embryology, not ecology, and who lived ten thousand miles away from me during my field research. Although he was a very important mentor in other ways – he was a polymath *par excellence* – he never had an opportunity to read my PhD thesis until I was about to submit it! Fortunately it turned out to be 'cutting-edge' research leading to deep and comprehensive conclusions.

After those formative early years I studied whales – blue, fin and sperm – on a seven-month voyage on the Southern Ocean as a whaling inspector. At the time the only feasible way to do so was by deduction and extrapolation from their dead bodies. This was very productive and like the elephant seal results led to conservation and management planning – including warnings that whale stocks were being over-exploited. Sadly, because of practical, commercial and international politics my recommendations were not applied.

So it was with some relief that I returned to shore by way of the freshwater hippopotamus, another fascinating but little-known species. I conducted experimental studies of population ecology and biology, then followed by applying this experience to the African elephant and tropical ecosystems in high- and low-rainfall regimes. It involved aerial surveys of East African vegetation and of the growth of bush, woodland and rainforest trees in relation to elephant usage. While the scientific results from both my own work and the teams I now led were very gratifying, the application of these rigorous research results to management were disappointing – frustrated by the tortuous politics of Africa struggling with new independence.

Returning to the Antarctic in the 1970s my personal research was on other seals, especially the crabeater, the world's most abundant seal. With accumulating experience my interests were more and more in ecosystems. It seemed important to draw attention to ecological interactions in the Southern Ocean between the physical environment and the various trophic levels over time, which had probably been set in train by over-exploitation of the large whales.

In due course I became Director of the British Antarctic Survey (BAS), a large multidisciplinary research institute, and needed to understand a whole range of environmental sciences from the smallest micro-organisms to the largest mammals, fish and birds. I had to grasp work being undertaken in geology and geophysics, in palaeontology, glaciology, atmospheric physics, medical research and marine and freshwater biology, as well as botany. I was director when BAS scientists discovered the 'ozone hole', a finding that more than justified the whole expenditure on our science programmes.

With rising seniority I became ever more involved in scientific administration, logistics and widening fields of politics and diplomacy, such as formulating two important international conservation conventions in the 1970s and 1980s – the Convention for the Conservation of Antarctic Seals (CCAS) and the Convention of Antarctic Marine Living Resources (CCAMLR). These were ahead of their time and derived directly from scientific research. Other involvements such as the BAS role in the Falklands War and international treaties concerning the political future of Antarctica went outside my training as a scientist.

Finally, while still contributing to research and organising international scientific programmes I became closely involved in Cambridge academic life. For eleven years this was as Master of the rapidly developing St Edmund's College, which during my tenure expanded both in academic stature and in sport. I also served on Cambridge University's Council of the Senate and a range of other committees, which was gratifying because it was not only my alma mater, but one of the world's five leading universities.

It was my very good fortune to experience such an expansive mix of pure scientific research coupled with research in management and conservation in dramatic environments and circumstances – and to be involved in the upper levels of the scientific civil service and academia. Yet while my primary career satisfaction has come from science, I have also gained great pleasure from painting in watercolour, oils and acrylics, in black-and-white drawings, and in photography – some of which will illustrate this account.

Yet in a career blessed with many successes, my greatest good fortune is given but minor comment: it is my family. Foremost is my lovely wife, Maureen, who for sixty years [when Dick died in 2014] has been a tower of strength and support. She carried the burden of looking after a young family when I travelled. The best part of it was when we could live and work together as a family during the Africa years; then she was my unpaid secretary and often my driver. But this was not possible in the Antarctic. And later when I was travelling to attend far-flung committees she stayed behind to cope with domestic problems. Never did she complain although she is very forthright, so I knew it must be all right! And anyway, 'absence certainly made the heart grow fonder'. But it was tough for her at times particularly in earlier years when communications weren't so good.

My parents and Freda Wood contributed fundamentally to such success that has come my way. Their influence was beyond measurement in mere thanks. Finally there are my colleagues in science and friends too numerous for my faltering memory to list now. As members of the teams of which I was first a junior member and eventually a leader, my gratitude to them all is boundless.

R. M. Laws
3, The Footpath, Coton, Cambridge.
[some time in early 2004]

PART I

Seals' Teeth
and
Whales' Ears

Malcolm and Florence May Laws, née Heslop

1

Northumberland: Boy on the Beach

On 8 June, 1819 a marriage took place in Colombo, Ceylon, 'between William Laws, Schoolmaster Sergeant. H.M. 19th Regiment, Bachelor, and Sarah Dixon, spinster, both residing at Point de Galle in the island aforesaid and professing the Protestant Religion'. William and Sarah were great-grandparents on my father's side of the family. (I don't have any information on my mother's side.) They had two sons, William Laws, a grocer, who founded a chain of stores, still in business in the North East of England, Laws Stores. The other, my grandfather, was Peter Maitland Laws who married Alice Harriet Balls. He was a professional photographer with a studio in Blackett Street, Newcastle, at a time when such photography was in its early stages. The examples of his work that I have are admirable, both technically and artistically, although they are only portraits. However, the only one of my grandparents I remember at all is my maternal grandmother, Alice, who lived with us during my childhood. My grandfather on mother's side was a successful builder and quite well off, living in Tynemouth, and my maternal grandmother was of Scottish descent.

Peter and Alice Laws produced three sons, Albert; Norman and (Percy) Malcolm, (my father) and two daughters, Alice and Florence. Malcolm, born in 1886, was tall and grey eyed, rather reserved, but led an adventurous early life. He was an outstanding athlete in his younger days; he represented the county of Northumberland at cricket, swam for the county and played for a precursor of Newcastle United Football Club. He received a good education at Dame Allan's School, Newcastle, but nonetheless ran away from home, travelling to North

America, where he undertook a series of outdoor jobs – with periods out of work. I remember him telling me, when I was reading W.H. Davies' *Autobiography of a Super-Tramp*, about life on the North American railroads, riding the rails and outwitting the guards. As a lumberjack in Canada, he felled the tall trees with a double-bladed axe and huge cross-cut saw. He also worked on the Trans-Canada railroad as a surveyor and prospected for gold in the Yukon Gold Rush. He told of finding gold and spending it in the saloons, on poker and whisky, using gold dust and the occasional nugget for money. The poems of Robert Service described that hard and demanding life and I regretted both that he did not talk more about those early years of his life and that I did not capture his memories.

On the outbreak of World War I he volunteered for the army in Canada and joined the Canadian Seaforth Highlanders. Expecting to see some fighting he was posted, as he said, 'to guarding a bridge near Ottawa', remote from any possibility of action. Intensely patriotic he wanted to fight against Germany. Given five weeks' compassionate leave, he worked his way across the North Atlantic on a cattle-boat! Reaching Britain he enlisted in the 7th Northumberland Fusiliers in the 50th Division. In 1915 aged 29 he was posted to the trenches. In what was probably the Second Battle of Ypres, April–May 1915 he was shot in the thigh and his leg was amputated high up leaving only a small stump. His artificial leg was a contraption of aluminium alloy and leather, painted near flesh colour, held on to the stump by a massive leather belt and straps. The wound gave constant pain for the rest of his life. The pain was in his mind too, because it confined this physical outdoors man to a desk as clerk, then manager, of a firm of timber importers situated on the quayside at Newcastle.

My mother, Florence May, born in 1896, was large, good looking and remarkably dynamic. She came from Jesmond, one of five children of Richard Heslop, a successful builder, and his wife. Educated at Rutherford College Girls' School, Newcastle, she met my father while serving as a nurse. Her father showed disapproval of her marriage by cutting her off from his resources, though she had a little money of her own.

Despite this unpromising start Malcolm and Florence Laws produced three sons: Peter, born 1918, myself, born 23 April 1926, and Michael, born in 1929. For most of my childhood, we lived at *Strathmore*, 20 Brighton Grove, in Whitley Bay, a well-known holiday resort in Northumberland and a dormitory town for Newcastle. This makes me almost a 'Geordie', a root of which I have always been proud; as I am also of my Scottish ancestry through two of my grandparents. We were a middle-class family, with nannies and maids appropriate to my mother's idea of our family's status.

Florence Laws was a remarkable woman. Much involved in local politics she made her first speech in the year I was born, when she was thirty. Thereafter she was chairman of the local ward committee of the Whitley Bay branch of the Conservative Party. In one address, she bluntly told her audience that if they didn't buy from their fellow countrymen, they could not expect to weather the Depression. She so impressed people that she became the principal Conservative speaker in the North East. I remember a silver salver, among other items that commemorated thanks for her support at 'the battle for Houghton-le-Spring'. She claimed that she was three times asked to stand as a Member of Parliament. Not keen on toeing any party line, she instead stood as an Independent in 1937 in a local ward election, opposing a man and beating him by ninety-seven votes. She owed her success in these fields to her energy, determination and eloquence – an articulate speaker, with the courage of her convictions.

Myself (right) with my two brothers, Peter (left) and Michael

For nine years she was the only woman on the council, becoming Chairman of the Housing Committee and preventing high-rise housing (then the fashion) being built in Whitley Bay. Subsequently as Chairman of the Finance Committee she applied common sense and a shrewd housewife's financial principles to its work. Other commitments were as Secretary of a Special Aid Committee, which helped those in need; as one of the first to start a welfare Housing Association; as President of the British Legion (Women's Section); and as spokesman for Whitley Bay delivering the proofs of evidence at a public enquiry into the proposed unification of Tyneside at a Boundary Commission. She was also the first woman to be Chairman of the Whitley Bay Urban District Council and was later Mayor of Whitley Bay from 1967 to 1968, retiring in 1969. She was awarded the MBE for her twenty-three years' work on area advisory committees, including the Labour Employment Committee, the Ministry of Pensions and National Insurance Committee (which later became the Ministry of Health and Social Security Committee), and served on the Disablement Advisory Committee and the Panel of Registration of Disabled People (matters on which, through my father's suffering, she had deep knowledge).

As children we were steeped in senses of duty and obliged to listen to a great deal of talk and horse trading of a political nature. My mother did quite a bit of entertaining so we boys met adults and learnt at an early age to hold our own in conversation. Dad exacted retribution for wrongdoings by beating us with his leather razor strop (he used a cut-throat), but never unfairly. My mother was concerned about more civilised matters and I was forced to take dancing lessons, which I loathed and was never any good at. I was also taught 'good manners' – to stand when a lady entered a room, to open doors, to be helpful around the house or digging the garden and so on. Together my parents raised three sons all of whom entered Cambridge University. We boys wanted for nothing. I was very fond of my father but, though proud of my mother's achievements, I did not feel loved; there were few warm moments like hugs, cuddles or kisses. A woman of high principle, great integrity and sound common sense, she was also a difficult person to live with and the family had to deal with her outbursts, when (wrongly) she felt herself undervalued. An overall unhappy childhood memory is of the flaming rows between her and my father, who was for a quiet life, with his pressing personal problem of continuous pain.

Peter was tall, handsome, an all-round athlete, victor ludorum at the school games several years running (in the mid-1930s). I remember my awe at his performances: 5 feet 3 inches in the high jump which then (1935) seemed a near impossible attainment – using the new 'western roll'. He was good at discus, putting-the-shot, long and short distances – a god to his two younger brothers. He also won his events in the school swimming sports which we watched in the, to us, splendid atmosphere of the Newcastle Swimming Baths, echoing to the cheers of the supporters. I don't think he was much into cricket, but he excelled on the rugby field as a three-quarter and played for his college, St Catharine's, at Cambridge. He was also academically successful and obtained an 'open exhibition' to the college (less than a scholarship), which at that time was to me an impossible aspiration; he seemed so far ahead and remote.

Michael was also bright, (and was also to get an exhibition to St Catharine's). I saw much more of him as the gap between us was smaller, and later I had the responsibility of looking after him when we were both evacuated during the war. In those days he was a very good-looking, good-natured, gentle chap and looked up to me, as I looked up to Peter.

In the summer the beach was a focus and the family spent quite a bit of time there at weekends. It was a great feeling of triumph the first time I was able to swim unassisted and experience the thrill of being out of my depth. It was also quite a hardy life and we were expected to have a 'dip' every morning, more or less year round, whatever the weather.

We were sometimes able to visit Holy Island (Lindisfarne) a few miles further north, joined to the mainland at low water by a causeway. My fascination with natural history was always present. If we were lucky we would see a few grey seals, usually in the water, bobbing their horse-like heads (or so it seemed to me then – I know better now), as they in turn reflected our curiosity. They were mysterious, rare creatures in those days – large, glossy and smooth. When they came close to the boat one could see their graceful balletic swimming motion through the clear water, in striking contrast to their ungainliness ashore. It was clear to me why they were called 'the people of the sea'. In the air about us we were surrounded by raucous birds – gulls, terns, puffins, guillemots among others, and – sitting on the water – diving puffins, and eider ducks and their more colourful drakes.

Sometime around 1930 we moved for a while to Jesmond, a suburb of Newcastle-upon-Tyne. There we lived in a terraced house of three stories and a basement – 13, Woodbine Avenue. It was then aged 5 that I first went to school: it was the Park Primary School, Monkseaton, within easy walking distance of home, which I attended until I was 9 years old. I can still remember the thrill of acquiring knowledge, particularly of geography.

When the family returned to Whitley Bay in 1935, living again at Strathmore, Brighton Grove, I entered the North Council Junior School, where the Headmistress was a Mrs Veitch. The report at the end of the first year showed that I was third out of forty-seven in the class: 'Good progress shown. Dick is a very reliable worker'! At the age of 10 I started my first term at North Council School, Headmaster H. C. Gray. My report for July 1937 shows me eleventh out of forty-eight in the class – but I was much younger than average.

The local schools, together with my home environment, must have given me a good initial education, because I was successful in getting a scholarship to Dame Allan's School, Newcastle, at the age of 11. I remember the scholarship exam, in April 1937, which I took in my stride, and the interview in the Headmaster's office. The Head complimented me on my vocabulary, which may have been a significant factor in my success. Of course I had picked up a lot of words when my mother had rehearsed her 'political' speeches at home.

I don't remember too much about my early days at Dame Allan's. In my report for the first term I was second out of twenty-nine in the form; 'Biology 1st – Excellent. A thorough and interested worker'; 'Geography 1st – V. good indeed'; 'Drawing 2nd – Excellent'. Other subjects were not so good.

A report from summer 1938 reads: 'Biology 2nd – V. good indeed. He likes this work'; 'Geography -1st – V. good'; 'Drawing 1st – Excellent'. December 1938: 'Biology 1st – V. Good indeed'; 'Geography – 2nd V. good'; 'Drawing 2nd. Excellent'; 'Maths not up to usual mark'. By July 1939 the school reports were not so good: – 'slacking over past year'. 'Biology 4th in term, 10th in exam – good as a rule'; 'Geography – 1st in term; 11th in exam – Exam. Poor for him'; 'Drawing 1st – Excellent'. Clearly I went through a 'bad patch', had my brushes with authority and several painful canings from the Headmaster, though for what transgressions I can't recall. I don't suppose they had any specially good or bad effects upon me and maybe I was slacking.

2

Exploring the Lake District

From the summer of 1938 onwards I was well aware of the events leading up to Munich and the invasion of Czechoslovakia, and that people were getting increasingly concerned and pessimistic about political developments. I helped in Whitley Bay standing behind a trestle table and handing out gas masks; sinister-looking, futuristic contraptions of rubber, with a metal canister in front to hold the filter.

Then suddenly on 1 September 1939 our school was evacuated – travelling by train to Wigton in Cumberland. It was quite an adventure, setting off mid-morning from Manors Station, Newcastle, with our gas masks and labels to identify us. We changed trains at Carlisle and on arrival marched from the station to Nelson School where we were given rations – chocolate, condensed milk, corned beef and biscuits. We formed into parties of fifteen to twenty boys (presumably the same happened to the girls), and walked out into the town with the local billeting officer. He knocked on the doors of the houses where we were to be billeted and the housewives selected from among us however many they had been allocated. It was a lovely late-summer day and all rather novel.

I was placed with the Parkers, a very likeable childless couple who lived in a small cottage in a cobbled yard off the main street, near the southern edge of the town. Their niece, Lily, had a boyfriend with a car and it was on his car radio two days later, as we drove through the countryside, that I heard the Prime Minister announce that war had begun.

My memories of Wigton are limited. The Parkers' house had an outside toilet and the washing place was a stone sink near the front door. On many mornings I washed in the open from a bucket – even on days when it was freezing cold and I had to break the ice on the pail! We shared the Nelson School – the Wigton grammar school – with the local boys, but the two schools didn't meet very much, for we had *our* lessons in the morning, 8 a.m. to 1 p.m. and *they* had the afternoon session, while we played games. By now I was very keen on rugger and we had a good team, perhaps because of the many hours we put into practices. We found that Cumberland rugby was a pretty dirty game compared with the more gentle game we were used to. 'Kick 'im off the ball' and 'Gouge 'is eyes out' were among the least offensive familiar cries. I played in various positions, including hooker which was pretty tough, but I preferred playing in the three-quarters, usually at fly-half or centre. I remember Arthur Bell (later Director of Kew Gardens), Brian Davison (who later became a biochemist and went to the University of the West Indies) and Gwynn Bevan (who got his blue at Cambridge) as three very effective backs. Graham Rose (later gardening correspondent of the *Sunday Times*) was another team mate and I think David Lumsden (later Sir David and Director of the Royal Academy of Music).

I recall we had a school scouts' camp at Slaley above the River Tyne. By then I was patrol leader of the Peewit Patrol and we did all the usual Boy Scout things – learning to pitch tents, set up a camp kitchen and cook 'dampers' over smoky fires, attaining badges. There was wild country fairly close. I remember the beauty and symmetry of young fir trees, wild flowers, the haunting call of the curlews and finding a moorhen's nest with three delicate blue eggs.

In early 1940 we returned to Tyneside; by then the shipyards were the target of German bombing raids. Often the bomb-aiming was wildly out and some large bombs fell on Whitley Bay where they didn't do much damage. However the school was once again evacuated in June 1940 – this time to Windermere.

Again we went by train. Again we were taken to our billets and left to settle in. My friend Bill Harrison and I were billeted at Crossroads House. The occupants didn't take to us so after only a few weeks we moved to Green Gables, a beautiful home, built in 1929 of green Langdale stone and owned by a childless couple, Winifred (Freda) and Cuthbert Woods. She was an invalid with a heart condition, in her early fifties, and had a paid companion, Elsie Craston, who completed the household. I was there for the next four years; an idyllic period that was one of the most formative periods of my life.

Freda Woods came from a Westmorland family, the Brunskills. Her father, Walter, had been a wealthy mill owner, a keen climber and member of the Fell and Rock Climbing Club and the Alpine Club. She was an only child (a younger brother Fred having died at an early age) and had often walked and climbed in the Alps, and there were many mountaineering books in the well-stocked library, to which I had full access.

Freda and Cuthbert were members of the Society of Friends, or Quakers, and they took me to their Meeting Houses where I enjoyed the peace, tranquillity and the opportunity to think, though not necessarily about spiritual matters! At the same time I was required to go to Anglican services and was being prepared for confirmation by Charles Hay, the school chaplain, and was in due course confirmed by the Bishop of Carlisle. Nominally I was 'conventionally religious' for that time and at my age.

Green Gables

Being very well read and with strong opinions, Freda held lengthy discussions with me about life, literature and poetry, religion, beauty, morality and truth, which I had never had in my own family. I think she regarded me as the son she never had and was like a mother to me, very concerned to develop my character and spirituality. One of her precepts, which I have always tried to follow, was 'Don't ever be satisfied with second best'. It would have been difficult to find anyone less like my own mother, which later caused problems with my parents.

Cuthbert Woods had been a Professor of Dentistry at Liverpool University, but retired in his forties to look after his wife. He had a well-developed sense of humour and a fund of funny stories, many of which related to the Liverpool music halls of his student days. He was an expert craftsman in wood and metal and as a hobby made scale model boats and ships for the Liverpool Shipping Museum, complete in every detail. He was very interested in everything to do with the sea. Cuthbert also made clocks – starting from scratch, including their movements, the engraved faces and their walnut or mahogany cases – both grandfather clocks and smaller ones. He collected gold turnip watches beautifully fretted and engraved, some of which he turned into decorative brooches. He was also interested in local history, mainly of the Liverpool area and North Wales; he wrote articles on old lighthouses and various other antiquities. He was quite a good photographer and started me off developing, printing and enlarging. My parents came over for Easter 1941 and gave me a small camera for my birthday, with which I was delighted; it was my first, constructed of Bakelite, and cost 1s 6p from Woolworth's: the store had a slogan then: 'Nothing over sixpence', and the camera came in three parts, each costing sixpence! It took rolls of film of 35mm format.

Mr Woods also improved my skills in carpentry and woodcarving, giving me a set of woodcarving tools, which I still have. And he taught me how to put ships in bottles, usually Haig's Dimple Scotch bottles, although the household was teetotal! Later my first 'published' article (for a Boy Scout handbook) was on how to put a ship in a bottle! I still have an example of that skill.

* * * *

During Dame Allan's second evacuation we combined with Windermere Grammar School, not as in Wigton in separate classes, but completely integrated. We cycled about five miles to school each day – uphill most of the way there and mostly downhill coasting in the evening. The Headmaster of the joint schools was A. K. Wilson, on the surface a bit of a disciplinarian, wielding the cane as necessary – but essentially a decent, kindly man. Later on when I was in the sixth form and a prefect, I led a revolt over the school meals, and had a confrontation with him. It made me realise how difficult his job was, and between us we resolved the problems in discussion and negotiation. I suppose at the time I was equivalent to Head Boy, although there was no such title. Perhaps this was the beginning of a strong-minded approach to authority and readiness to fight for what I felt was right that led me into some difficult situations during my career!

A school report for December 1940 indicates that I was doing particularly well in geography, and I was no longer taking biology or drawing. As it was wartime, our teachers were either women or men older than service age. Mallinson and Miss Joslin were still there and our pretty young Belgian French mistress. Miss Gent taught us Latin. We had a very pretty blonde history mistress (Jean Humble, 'Blondie' to the boys, after a current comic strip). She was the subject of fantasies by us teenagers, and had earlier been engaged to the legendary rugby three-quarter the Prince Obolensky. Later, and much to our surprise, she married the well-liked school chaplain, Charles Hay (The Reverend Canon A. C. de P. Hay). He was also scoutmaster, a keen rugger player and our coach. I cycled across the Pennines to be present at their wedding in Newcastle in April 1944.

The chemistry teacher was Mr McKissock; he had a dry sense of humour and made chemistry interesting; we experimented with 'bangs and smells' and he called his blackboard duster after the Russian Field Marshall who was prominent in the news at the time – 'Chuck me Timoshenko's vest' he would say. Physics was taught by Mr Pennington, a small, wiry, hyperactive and very fit man who enjoyed rugger and fell walking.

Mrs Friend taught us art for School Certificate and I owe much to her influence in stimulating and developing my early interest in drawing and painting. From 1941 I had begun to keep an illustrated nature diary with drawings and do small watercolours of flowers, birds, butterflies and other insects

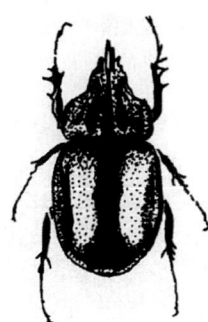

etc. Mrs Friend also taught me calligraphy and in 1943 encouraged me to write a book, *Green Gables: a Nature Diary*, illustrated with my pen-and-ink drawings. I bound it myself in walnut boards, half-calf, with end-papers covered with a repeating pattern of individually drawn roses in pen and ink. Each new flower I saw in the spring – the crocus, hazel catkins and aconite for example – and also some birds were painted. I spent an hour or so most evenings recording and illustrating natural history events – but there was no television in those days!

I had not been seriously taught biology up to this time, but in the fifth form the subject was offered and Mallinson, no biologist, was our teacher. It didn't matter too much at that level, but when I moved into the sixth form and elected to do biology for Higher School Certificate it could have been disastrous.

Examples of my drawing at age 17

Among my biological colleagues were George Knox, Thomas 'Thos' Walker, Brian Davison, Arthur Bell, Bernard Clough and others, who all went on to do well academically. We solved our problem by teaching ourselves, reading the recommended textbooks and other books on the subject, like Wells' *The Science of Life*. I was already collecting books on natural history and we benefitted from the new, semi-popular weekly science journal *Discovery*. Taking it in turns to 'mug up' on a subject we would give seminars to our colleagues. We also visited local biological organisations. I well remember a stimulating visit two of us paid to the Freshwater Biological Association, which occupied Wray Castle on the other side of Lake Windermere. We cycled over there (turning up without any prior contact) and asked to see something of the work of the laboratory.

Two members of staff in particular were most kind and gave us the run of the labs. Dr Winifred Frost was one; she worked on fish and it was she who first made me aware of the use of annuli in scales, opercular bones and otoliths for ageing (a field in which I became professionally involved in my later career). Another research worker there, Dr David Le Cren (who many years later was to be a fellow Director in the Natural Environment Research Council (NERC)), also took an interest and showed us round. I remember the story of developing the wartime perch fishery of the lake, the concomitant decline of the lake's major predator population, the pike, and the knock-on consequences for the ecosystem. For the first time I looked down a proper microscope, and was exposed to the wonders and beauty of phytoplankton architecture and design, learned about the lake's sedimentary history and saw the experimental studies on fish being conducted in a flume race in the basement.

Preparing seminars for one another must have worked because in our small sixth form biology classes, several of us got scholarships to university. One of the essays I wrote on the ecology of Lake Windermere may have tipped the balance for my Open Scholarship to St Catharine's College, Cambridge.

This time self-teaching ourselves in the sixth form was a gentle introduction to the drastic change that occurs when going from school to university and you are expected to work responsibly on your own. It must have significantly influenced my later approach to education, scholarship and research.

* * * *

We had a great school rugby team. We played most of our games on a pitch which was uneven, sloping, usually had a small stream running down its centre and even had slight rocky outcrops in places. Such a playing field would not be considered at all acceptable in today's risk-averse society. My usual position was as hooker and though muddy and cold I was in my element. We played against local schools in matches that were hard and very physical. In one match at Kendal, having been kicked in the head I had to be returned by taxi a bit concussed, very white and faint, but was playing rugby again a week later.

Charles Hay had founded the school's 22nd Newcastle Scout Troop. It was exceptional and I rose to be Troop Leader of some sixty boys. I organised 'wide games' up on Orrest Head above Windermere, where we had the time of our lives. For instance we collected adders, which abounded. Farmers believed they were a hazard to their sheep and paid us a small bounty for the skins – an activity which would certainly be frowned upon now, but was regarded as a public service then!

We also join the school's Combined Cadet Force, and I achieved the illustrious rank of sergeant. We wore the thick, rough and itchy khaki serge battledress, tunic, trousers and puttees wound over heavy black boots; we came to terms with 'blanco and bullshit'.

We 'square-bashed' about once a week in the school playground, had meetings in the local drill hall, where we learned the basic skills of warfare (which seemed apposite in wartime!); and we got to know about rifles and how to strip them down, even fire them.

I was an avid Boy Scout

* * * *

14

I made use of the Green Gables library and developed an abiding interest in mountaineering and polar exploration by reading the classics about the Alps, Himalayas and other mountain adventures as well as the Arctic and Antarctic. One of our set books for School Certificate was Ernest Shackleton's *South: The Endurance Expedition*, a great classic of adventure. I read about Scott and Shackleton and Wilson, whom I greatly admired, and I bought and was given climbing and polar books for my own collection. I began to build up a small personal library (Whymper, Christian Klucker, Younghusband, Scott and Shackleton among many others).

In December 1940, aged 14, I wrote an English essay on 'Mountain Climbing'; it was rather naive, but was marked 87 per cent. Here are some extracts:

> Mountaineering is I think, one of the best, if not the best of outdoor sports ... People think it is dangerous ... This is not true. In mountain climbing, as in other sports there are rules – not so well-defined but they are understood rules ... Why do men climb mountains? – it is a fine sport – develops muscles – not competitive – just as important as the physical side is the spiritual side ... On a mountain, at peace with the world, one can appreciate the beauty of Nature's works – meditate on the beauty of the landscape or perhaps the smallest flower – converse with God ... trust partner completely ... harmony and beauty of surroundings together with scent of pine trees or heather ... thrill of climbing a virgin snow ridge ... spirit of leadership, etc.

Another essay on 'A Reasonable Faith' was given 84 per cent, but it 'did not bring out the relation between Faith and Reason as much as it should'.

Another titled 'One or two paintings I admire' was given 75 per cent:

> My favourite artist is Edward Wilson, the naturalist and scientist, who accompanied R. F. Scott on his fateful journey to the South Pole. He painted many pictures, mostly water colours – I most admire the detail and interest he put into them ... When one takes into consideration that in painting his polar scenes his hands were often very nearly frostbitten one must agree that his work is superb ... He always

portrayed the scene which he saw in front of him and did not ... allow his imagination to stray ... The work which I like most depicts a scene in the Antarctic. It shows the skis arranged in a semicircle casting long shadows over the uneven ice. In the sky is the aurora borealis [sic: I should have written australis, and it is actually a paraselene – mock suns] – a circle of colour with misty beams streaming onto the ice. One can almost feel the stillness of the barrier ice – the absolute silence of it – as one looks at this painting. Another shows a scene in a blizzard, dogs and men almost at their last gasp, trudging through the endless wilderness of snow, thinking no doubt of their homes in England. The snow is whirling in gusts and faintly through the blizzard – the whirling snowflakes – come the rays of the sun outlining the party in a faint luminous glow. One can almost feel the silence broken now and then by the crack of a whip – the grunt of a dog perhaps ...

Clearly, I was already developing a particular interest in polar exploration! I also read with pleasure other books from the shelves, among them novels by Winston Churchill (the novelist, not the politician), Walter Scott, Stevenson, Dickens, Jane Austen, and Fennimore Cooper's *Last of the Mohicans*. Also plays – Shakespeare and Bernard Shaw, poetry – Francis Thompson, Walt Whitman, Robert Browning, Wordsworth and others. I also began to buy books with my pocket money: David Lack's *The Life of the Robin*, which really opened my eyes to animal behaviour, and books on natural history, like those illustrated by Archibald Thorburn, the 'Wayside and Woodland' series, an anthology *A Book of Birds* with Tunnicliffe's engravings, Clare Leighton's *Four Hedges*, Robert Gibbings *Blue Angels and Whales*, set among Pacific coral islands, illustrated with woodcuts of underwater scenes ... all of which influenced my choices later in life.

The Woods had a boathouse on the lakeshore below the house which held a 14 ft clinker-built sailing boat *Daphne*, a comfortable broad-beamed boat with a brown lug sail and centre board. There was also a 10 ft carvel-built dinghy, built by Cuthbert Woods. He taught Bill Harrison and myself to sail and we had numerous excursions to explore the lake and as we became more expert and confident we were allowed to go out on our own. The experience was useful later in the Antarctic, South Georgia, and subsequently in central Africa.

It was as a teenage schoolboy that I developed a deep love of hills and mountains, and particularly the Lakeland Fells and rock climbing, which will remain until I die. The English Lake District is unique, a jewel of great beauty, and I always return to it with a lifting of the heart. I know it better than any other similar-sized piece of the earth and have walked along most of its tracks and climbed most of the hills. Later in life my wife Maureen took to it and walking in the Lake District was probably our favourite leisure pastime.

For Christmas and New Year 1941, the Woods took me to Buttermere, where we stayed in the Fish Hotel. Bill had gone home to Newcastle. The former Buttermere Hotel was then a 'Fell and Rock Climbing Club' Hostel and Freda Woods was a member. She knew some of the older members through her father and introduced me to them. As a result I was taken up my first rock climb – by Bentley Beetham (an Everest climber!), Dr Burnett, A. T. Hargreaves, and E. G. Sutton, all then well-known climbers.

On New Year's Day I went with E. G. Sutton and another Fell and Rock member, Miss Winch, to Fleetwith Gully, where we climbed up a very wet stream course, straddling water, scrambling in the bed of the stream and then climbing up by a chockstone. After this I tried chimney techniques for the first time, and then up to the top. Next day I went to Burtness Coomb again where we did Chockstone Slabs, a face climb ending in a chimney.

Another day I particularly remember, in December 1942, I walked up Birch Hill and over the top to Lingmoor Fell. The views were glorious – cloud shadows chasing across the Helvellyn Range and the shafts of light falling on Wetherlam from a stormy sky – there were storm lights over the fells to the north too. A spider's web at the top was of pearly beauty, beaded with raindrops; I wondered that it could be so strong – enough to hold the heavy raindrops in the wind.

During these years I had many other days on the hills and spent as much time as I could climbing and fell walking. I cycled a great deal on my own, and in April 1943 for instance I cycled home in one day. The distance from Windermere to Whitley Bay was about 110 miles.

* * * *

My life at Windermere and with the Woods was paradise. Yet elsewhere the war was proceeding and we followed its progress on the wireless as it was called then. Rationing and the black-out were with us. We fed well and I seldom felt hungry, despite rationing, although the variety of supplies was limited. The war came closest to me through my elder brother Peter. In December 1943 I cycled home for a fortnight, to see Peter who was home on leave from Africa after three years' active service. Then after the D-Day landings Peter, now a lieutenant in the Durham Light Infantry, was wounded by shrapnel defending a farmhouse in an advanced position near Caen. He had been repatriated to Britain but was not expected to survive. Dad and Mother asked me and Michael to go to Derby to be with them and to visit Peter. We were shocked to see how grey and ill he looked; it was all rather upsetting. We returned to Windermere on 26 June because I had to sit my Higher School Certificate exams next day for which I wasn't in the optimum frame of mind! Fortunately Peter made a complete recovery, although he proved to be allergic to the new wonder drug penicillin. He was awarded the Military Cross.

I took Higher School Certificate in botany and zoology (full subjects), and chemistry and physics (half subjects). I did well, and also took scholarship level in botany and zoology, achieving 'distinction' markings in both. Not really knowing what I wanted to do, I had elected to go in for medicine. The choice was between King's College, Newcastle, then part of Durham University, and Cambridge, where I took the scholarship exams at St. Catharine's and Peterhouse (Peter had been an Exhibitioner at St Catharine's). I travelled down to Cambridge for about three weeks in March 1944, to sit these exams. I felt very unsure of myself socially; for example I didn't know what to do about tipping the gyp (Syd Alderton) who looked after us candidates and I wasn't sure how to handle other things, so probably appeared rather 'wet'. However, I sat the exam and didn't find the papers too bad.

An interview that formed part of it took place in the Master's Lodge I think – or perhaps it was the Senior Combination Room. A vivid picture in my mind is of a glowing open fire and we sat around it in roomy, high-backed chairs. The then Master was Dr Chaytor, who had twinkling eyes and asked me penetrating questions (or so they seemed to me at the time). I met Sydney Smith for the first time; he was the college's Director of Studies in zoology, and was later to become a great friend, mentor and influence in my life. The zoology viva (viva voce or oral exam) was probably the most daunting part of this experience. The examiners were Sydney Smith and L. A. Borradaile, who Sydney told me was nicknamed 'the white rat'. A white-haired old man (a relative term!), he was lead author of the standard invertebrate zoology textbook of the time – known to a generation of zoologists as BEPS (Borradaile, Eastham, Potts and Saunders). Not having been formally taught biology at school, I had had no practice in vivas, and anyway no preparation or wide practical experience of zoology. One question that completely floored me was in the form of a 'spot test'. In these tests candidates were given objects to identify, or asked to look down a microscope at slides and to comment. One of my spot tests was the clavicle of a turtle. For those who haven't seen this it is a bone that has three 'arms', more or less at right angles like an old-fashioned cobbler's last. I'd never seen anything like it, hadn't the faintest idea what it was and couldn't even guess!

By contrast the botany viva went quite well. I was examined by Professor Harry Godwin, Fellow of the Royal Society (FRS), who was very friendly and asked me questions about various plants he produced, which I had no difficulty in answering – fortunately remembering the Latin names. I was a bit stumped when he handed me a mouldy lemon and asked me to comment. But I talked about *penicillium*, which I was familiar with from Peter's operations and as it had recently been in the news as a 'wonder drug'; fortunately it was the required response. In the written exam my brief acquaintance with the work of the Freshwater Biological Association also paid off, as I was able to write a substantial essay on the phytoplankton of Lake Windermere in answering one of the questions!

Then I moved across from St Catharine's to Peterhouse to sit the exam there. I was given a room in the oldest part of the college, on a staircase built about AD1243 and called 'Noah's Ark'. I began the exams, but to my relief after sitting some of the papers, I was told I need not complete them as I had been successful at St Catharine's. I had been awarded an Open Scholarship (value £60 annually; quite a substantial sum in those days). Naturally I was delighted. Later I was also awarded a State Scholarship (about £100) and a Northumberland County Major Scholarship (£60 a year) on the basis of my performance in the Higher School Certificate. These scholarships covered most of the costs of my university education, although there would still be a small call on my parents' limited resources. I returned to Windermere.

My remaining time there went all too quickly. In mid-June I travelled to Cambridge again for a week of exams – for the First MB in chemistry – necessary for registration as a medical student. Then I went home to Whitley Bay. My school days were over.

Sadly there were heated arguments with my parents over my friendship with Freda and Cuthbert Woods, which they wanted me to end. Perhaps it wasn't surprising. They were not happy about the fact that I had picked up pacifist inclinations from them (a feature of the Quakers' faith) questioning the war. This was anathema to my father, coming on top of his own wrecked life and Peter's wounds. But I was unwilling to give up my close friendship with the Woods household after living there for four and a half years as a member of it. So I returned to Green Gables.

I went home again several times in August for further talks, but each time was put under a lot of pressure and returned to Green Gables. They threatened not to support me while at Cambridge. It was a very stressful time for us all and for me tested my senses both of loyalty and of sticking to what I believed right to the utmost.

As it happened the strength of my anti-war feeling was never put to the test. The war in Europe was now drawing to a close and military service was deferred for students until they had taken degrees. In the event my views changed soon after entering Cambridge, and my period of National Service was deferred on graduation in 1947 after the war had ended, so that I could undertake Antarctic work with the Falkland Islands Dependencies Survey. (I was never called for National Service, as the relevant authorities decided that Antarctic service had replaced it!)

Trying to resolve the clash of wills, I went home again in September, but returned to Windermere for a few days at the beginning of October. Soon afterwards I phoned Peter to tell him that I had decided to remain at Green Gables. He came over and put pressure on me but without success. Mr Wilson, my former Headmaster, also had a go at me. Eventually I reached a compromise with my parents and Peter in which they accepted that I would keep in touch with the Woods.

So, a little late for the start of term, I travelled down by train on 12 October to Cambridge to become a member of St Catharine's College, bruised by recent events. A new phase of my life was just beginning.

3

A Cambridge Student

I travelled down to Cambridge for the beginning of the Michaelmas Term 1944.
As a Scholar I was given rooms in college and for the first two years I lived on
J staircase, room 5. The third year I went out to digs on Eltisley Avenue, where
I had a bedroom and a small separate sitting room with a bow window.

Accommodation in college was in sets comprising a sitting room and separate
bedroom, sharing a small 'gyp room' with a gas ring and sink; we weren't
supposed to do any cooking, but could boil a kettle for tea. My gyp (college
servant) was the same Syd Alderton who had looked after me when I came up for
the scholarship exams. I found the Cambridge ambience very much to my liking.
I was independent. It was the first time I had lived in a city: and what a city!

In terms of history, beautiful buildings and environment, it was wonderful. First I got caught up in the freshers' week, with so many possible activities. I joined the University Mountaineering Club, the Bird Club (which had a lovely tie – green with a black redstart embroidered on it), the Natural History Society and the Cambridge University Medical Society as a life member – the tie was quite colourful! I never joined the Union Society, although I attended some of the more interesting debates.

I joined the college Rugby Club and was given a freshers' trial for the university, but didn't get very far. However, I did become a member of the college First Rugby XV from the beginning and remained a member throughout my undergraduate years. I was also elected a member of the prestigious Kittens' Club, which was a social club, mainly if not entirely composed of rugger players, but with a limited membership of about twelve. We had parties in college at which a great deal of beer was consumed and bawdy songs sung. The Kittens also organised parties and dances at places like the Barn (at Fen Ditton), the Golden Lion (at Royston), the Red Lion (at Trumpington), and other venues. I rowed in the rugger boat in the May bump races and am not sure now whether we made *any* bumps. I also played tennis and squash for the college, but was never interested in cricket.

I developed punting skills that have never left me and became quite an expert. On summer afternoons, often with a few girls, we would punt up to the Orchard tea rooms at Grantchester. In May Week we punted down to the Madrigals at Kings. And those days we could still swim in the River Cam, either at the men's bathing place, which had some privacy for changing, or from the grassy banks anywhere. I went bird watching at the local sewage farm and in the Ouse washes, where in the winter terms the migrants were passing through; also out to Madingley Woods at night in summer to hear the nightingales, and to Wicken Fen and Welney Marshes for fenland birds.

The winters were very cold and there was no central heating. The rooms had fireplaces, but coal was rationed to a bucketful a week. My bedroom had a washbasin, but for a shower or bath I had to walk outside across the court to the basement of another building.

The war was closing in Europe and food rationing was with us. One of the features of Cambridge then was the 'Fitzbillie bag'. Fitzbillie's was a cake shop and if one had one of their bags, with a name written on it – it was a passport to relative luxury. On presentation of the bag and the necessary food coupons one could buy a cake; without the bag we went without cakes, because there weren't enough to go round. It took me a year to get such a bag, and then only by inheriting a rather tattered one from a friend 'going down', but this meant that I had 'made it'. My usual choice was the Fitzbillie's date cake because it was filling. We entertained friends, of both sexes, to tea and toasted crumpets before the fire – when we had not run out of coal. I suppose we had a lot of carbohydrate and not very much meat in the college meals, but we were healthy. One food much detested was tinned snoek – shark meat imported from South Africa.

We also ate out when funds ran to it. The curry restaurants were popular. Now we spent many evenings at the pubs near to St Catharine's: the Eagle, the Anchor, the Mill and the Little Rose. Further afield were the Baron of Beef or the Pickerel, which later were put out of bounds, as haunts of prostitutes and American airmen.

In college from time to time I was required to read a lengthy Latin grace before dinner in Hall: a duty shared by the Scholars. We had a competition to see who could read it the fastest and I became quite fluent. I still remember and can reel off the words – '*Oculi omnium aspiciunt et in te sperant, Domine. Tu das iis Escas illorum tempore opportuno …*'

When eating in hall we wore our tattered short gowns and were required to wear them in the streets after dark, otherwise we were likely to be accosted by the Proctors and their 'Bulldogs' and fined for being without a gown – as 'improperly dressed'. The college gates were locked at 10 o'clock and to get inside after this you either had to have a pass from your tutor or pay a fine. So we learnt to climb into college and there was a book, *Night Climbers of Cambridge*, that we all studied, which described all the routes and their degrees of difficulty. Some were very dangerous, so climbing was frowned upon. Students climbed the towers of King's College Chapel and placed chamber pots (which were still in regular use at that time), on the pinnacles; the engineers on at least one occasion dismantled a Morris Seven car and reassembled it on top.

Collegiate society constituted an interesting mix. There were young people like myself and older students who had interrupted their studies to go to war, or put off university until completing their war service. Many of my friends had been in the tank battles in the Western desert, in the navy commanding Motor Torpedo Boats, or flying in the RAF. Some had been captured and incarcerated in prisoner of war camps in Japan or Germany; others had been wounded.

We all got on well, both playing and studying hard. I think the returned warriors were extremely tolerant of naive young 'sprogs', like myself, who had come up straight from school and knew nothing about life.

Among close friends I particularly remember were: Syd Fox, captain of the college and university rugby clubs; Ian Beer, later Headmaster of Harrow and President of the Cambridge University Rugby Football Club; John Haynes (another Headmaster); Arthur Lee, who became Director of the Lowestoft Fisheries Laboratory; Bill Pile, later Sir William and Permanent Secretary at the Home Office; and G. P. Mason, later a High Court Judge – all serious rugger players, several awarded blues. Another was Frank Merritt, a returned war veteran, who had been incarcerated in a Japanese prisoner of war camp; he was now reading and later researching in physical chemistry.

Despite limited funds I managed to live reasonably well. I even bought a suit, tailor-made in Trinity Street, a double-breasted navy blue blazer and eventually a dinner jacket – initially I had to hire one when needed. I also acquired a college rugger colours blazer – maroon, with silver buttons and bearing a rather splendid, colourful shield with a Catharine wheel in gold wire on the breast pocket.

* * * *

In the beginning I was a medical student, having taken my First MB qualification, and was reading for Part I of the Natural Sciences Tripos: anatomy, physiology, zoology and biochemistry. I settled in quickly because of the self-reliance we had had to develop in the sixth form at Dame Allan's School. Some lectures were very dull, others extraordinarily stimulating, if occasionally somewhat bizarre. For example Lord Adrian, a Nobel prize-winner, introduced us to the behaviour of Pavlov's dogs, and demonstrated conditioned reflexes with a cat that had been beheaded. In physiology we experimented on ourselves – for example pouring cold water into our ears to experience the loss of balance as the semi-circular canals were influenced. I also remember impressive lectures and practicals on vision by Roughton, and learning the rudiments of histology from E. N. Wilmer. I was supervised in physiology by W. S. Feldberg, later FRS, who was Reader in Physiology and a very enthusiastic teacher; his research then was at the cutting edge on acetylcholine, a neurotransmitter. D. V. Davies supervised me in anatomy.

In zoology, a subject in which I was very interested, the teaching was rather formal and a major part consisted of morphology and systematics – subjects which are hardly touched upon today. But the practicals were interesting. David Attenborough was a near contemporary, but neither of us now remember meeting at that time.

Among the demonstrators at the practicals was Anna Bidder, later the first President of Lucy Cavendish College, who, when we met again many years later, still remembered the quality of my drawings in the practicals. John Bradfield was ahead of me, and researching the mechanics of animal locomotion (toads I think) for his PhD. Later he became a very successful Senior Bursar of Trinity College, with an annual budget of £20 million or so, and founded the Cambridge Science Park. George Hughes, a year or two my senior, taught us in the practicals and went on to the Chair of Zoology at Bristol. Michael Swann also demonstrated to us and became Professor of Zoology and Vice Chancellor at Edinburgh, Chairman of the BBC and, as Lord Swann, Master of Oriel College, Oxford, for a short time. In zoology I was taught by Sir James Gray, Carl Pantin, George Salt, Hugh Cott, Vincent Wigglesworth, Arthur Ramsay, J. E. Smith, George Carter, Sydney Smith, Laurence Picken, Hugh Whiting, F. R. Parrington, Hans Lissman and Margaret Brown, among others. Most of the lectures I didn't find stimulating, although many of those speaking were then or later Fellows of the Royal Society and very talented. I suppose that my heart was not really in the invertebrate morphology and experimental biology, which were then the department's strengths.

Other department strengths then were in the mechanics of animal locomotion and in insect physiology, which left me cold. My heart was really in vertebrate zoology and my preference was for treating animals as a whole – not for the reductionism then fashionable. Considering that I later became an ecologist I really had very little ecological training. My recollection in that realm is of dry lectures by George Salt, illustrating the principles with flour or borer beetles, wheat sawflies etc.

Carl Pantin's speciality in insect physiology was compensated for by his very broad knowledge of natural history. George Carter (or 'Uncle George') had been on field trips to the Paraguayan swamps in South America – the Chaco – and had practical knowledge of field ecology; lung fishes were a specialty of his. Hugh Cott too was an enthusiastic all-round field naturalist who was also a skilled photographer and illustrator in black and white, as well as a painter. He brought the subject of vertebrate biology to life. During the war he had been engaged on research into camouflage techniques, drawing upon animal camouflage, and illustrating the principles – counter-shading, disruptive camouflage and so on – with his delightful pen-and-ink drawings. His book, *Adaptive Coloration in Animals*, is a classic. He later worked on crocodiles in Africa and Hugh and Carl Pantin were responsible for introducing me to African research many years later.

Hans Lissman was a fish physiologist, who was the first (after Winifred Frost at Windermere) to stimulate my interest in serial growth layers when he invited me to give a seminar to the Part II Zoology course. His major personal research achievement was discovering electrical sensory systems in fish. I was also fortunate to attend lectures on statistics by R. A. Fisher, which were difficult to follow because he assumed a knowledge we didn't have. The course began very simply with us tossing coins as an introduction to probability theory but as the lectures quickly escalated in difficulty attendance on the course rapidly shrank over several weeks until there was only a handful of us left, and few actually finished the course. I signed up for it three times, but never completed it! However I was awarded a first in Part I Zoology and later in Part II.

I also read biochemistry which I quite enjoyed, and the Cambridge department under Baldwin was a centre of excellence in the subject, but I was never much good at it. I only managed a second in Part I of the Tripos.

In my first year as a medical student, anatomy was important. In addition to the lectures, we spent much time in the dissecting room (DR) learning human anatomy. Like many medical students I had wondered what it would be like to dissect human corpses and whether I would be robust enough to cope. Some students had initial problems, though not me, and occasionally one fainted, but we all soon came to terms with it, the women as well if not better than men. We had *Gray's Anatomy* of course, but in the detailed dissection we worked from *Cunningham's Anatomy*, a textbook in several volumes with clear illustrations. It took us step by step through the dissection of each part of the body, starting at a superficial level and 'peeling off' layer by layer of muscles, ligaments, blood vessels and nerves – down to the bones. There was an all-pervading sickly-sweet smell of embalming fluid, formalin based, but there was really no close similarity between the dried up, wizened corpses and living human beings, so it all quickly became very matter-of-fact.

We were paired off in this work and I worked with Gareth Owen, a dark Welshman and Organ Scholar at Downing College. Occasionally I accompanied him at lunchtime to King's College or other college chapels where he practised. At the other extreme we also spent drinking hours together in the pubs. At that time the Cambridge medical students shared the DR with St Bartholomew's Hospital Medical School, London, which had been evacuated to Cambridge. It was clear that the Bart's students had better teaching in dissection than us – practical but adequately academic – rather than the parrot-like learning at Cambridge. The Bart's philosophy was more concerned with function as well as form.

Gareth and I worked well together; we had to get through a 'part' each term in great detail, and we were examined periodically by the 'Demonstrators' who patrolled the DR. At the end of each term we had to get 'signed up' confirming we had indeed done the requisite part to an adequate standard. The two of us started on an arm the first term and went on to do a leg and then, I think, thorax. This proved useful later when working on large animals and understanding medical problems affecting these parts. I would have done more, but at the end of the first year I dropped anatomy, ending my short career in medical science.

The reasons were twofold. First, the anatomy teaching was not good enough. Second, I could not combine anatomy with zoology, because both entailed many hours a week of practical work. However, some elements like the functional anatomy being taught by people like Le Gros Clark, Wood Jones and J. Z. Young were stimulating. In contrast our professor was 'Butcher' Harris, a nickname earned because he had first learned anatomy in his father's butchery. He was intentionally crude, and made the lives of women students miserable by telling jokes and dirty stories at their expense. Yet he was also knowledgeable and interesting. It was in one of his lectures in connection with its polygynous (harem breeding) habits that I first heard of the elephant seal, the species that became the object of my first research some years later.

Like my friends I fervently disliked exams, but I was organised about my work and didn't do much last-minute revision. Nevertheless I remember one morning while walking down King's Parade at about 9.30 a.m., a Porter from St Catharine's came up to me: 'You should be in an examination now, sir, and we've been looking all over for you. You'd better get along there right now.'

I had completely forgotten, and arrived at the examination room more than half an hour late. I did my best with the paper, and did not do too badly. Sydney

Smith swore that the Freudian undertone to this behaviour was that I so disliked exams that my subconscious had made me forget. I was never to make this mistake again.

The Tripos system at Cambridge meant that most students reading natural sciences did Part I in two years; some took three years. It consisted of a mix of three or four related subjects, though there was and still is a wide range of choice. We went on to specialise in one subject for Part II, in my case zoology, in which we could choose several from a number of specialised options; this could be done in one or two years. One had to be 'in residence' three terms a year for three academic years to get a degree. I took two years over Part I and one year over Part II.

For my second year I took up botany in place of anatomy. Having done a lot of self-taught botany at school (which earned me my scholarship) I got a second in Part I Botany in one year without much work.

In St Catharine's my tutors in successive years were the Dean, Canon Christopher Waddams (an Anglican clergyman); Alfred Steers, Professor of Geography; Donald Portway, later to become Master; and Fred Dainton, a chemist, later FRS, Vice Chancellor of Leeds University and a life peer. Red-headed Christopher was always good for a discussion on philosophy, morals or religion. He had us up to his rooms for coffee after lunch or dinner, when we were required to grind the coffee beans in a hand-grinder, an instrument of torture which one clasped between the knees with difficulty. He prided himself on not having a sense of humour, though perhaps this was perverse humour; for he would listen to a funny story and then straight-faced say, 'I don't see what is funny about that. Please explain it to me.' Few funny stories can stand up to that response! Yet, he was a very kind man.

In college my closest friend was Arthur Mansfield, who came from Wimbledon, also reading zoology. Arthur played rugger and we had many interests in common, enjoyed life to the full and talked over many ideas and subjects. This was a friendship that continues today over sixty years later.

* * * *

Sydney Smith was my Director of Studies and supervisor in zoology. He was a very strong influence on my development both as an undergraduate and later in life. By research specialisation he was an experimental embryologist, but had an encyclopaedic knowledge of zoology, and the fine arts in general and Chinese porcelain in particular. He was also very knowledgeable about literature, early biological illustration and Darwin's letters, and was a *bon viveur* and wine steward of the college. Sydney was also a concert standard pianist and proud of having been allowed by Pablo Casals to carry his cello. At his social evenings we were privileged to hear his piano playing and encouraged to listen to his eclectic collection of records and handle his *objets d'art*. We also appreciated his skills as a chef. I learnt much more than zoology from him.

Sydney looked after his students very well, insisting we relax properly before exams. On several occasions he took a group of us camping at Hemingford on the River Ouse over the pre-exam weekend, where we swam, punted and unwound from the tension. He also took some of us to Whipsnade, where I first appreciated larger animals. He developed my photographic skills, the process begun by Cuthbert Woods at Windermere, and with remarkable trust he lent me his expensive equipment, including long-range telephoto lenses. It laid the foundation for whatever skills I later developed in this field.

Sydney introduced me to the Fitzwilliam Museum's diverse collections, and we discussed the paintings in detail. It was my first close encounter with art appreciation and with the impressionists (Degas, Matisse and Renoir were my particular favourites), with the English watercolour school (Blake, Cotman and De Wint made a particular impression) – and with Constable's oils, of which the Fitzwilliam had a representative collection. I recall Sydney pointing out Constable's technical skill where he had loaded his palette knife with more than one colour, and applied it horizontally so that the layers fitted with a vertical church spire; it seemed impossible brilliance. There were many other favourite works including a D. Y. Cameron landscape of Spain, which particularly caught my fancy. (Many years later I looked for it in the collection, but couldn't find it, until I saw it in 1988 on the wall of Vice Chancellor David Williams' office; it was like meeting an old friend.) This exposure to the visual arts was all quite new to me and truly an eye-opener.

Another who influenced me deeply was Laurence Picken, a lecturer in zoology. His formal academic subject was fine structure of the cell, which he studied by light microscope. Yet he had also taught himself Chinese from a dual text and acquired a collection of Chinese books and *objets d'art*; he was a composer and an authority on Balkan and Chinese music. A Fellow of Jesus College, he hosted intellectually stimulating dinners in his rooms where we sampled the products of the Jesus College kitchen, which included their famous crème brûlées. His spacious rooms housed a clavichord, and he was a practised performer on it. Sadly the invention of the electron microscope overtook his light microscopy studies, but he went on to become a Lecturer in Oriental Studies, a measure of his intellectual stature. He made an outstanding contribution to Chinese studies at Cambridge; 'single-handedly reconstructing the court music of the Tang Dynasty'.

I enjoyed the many musical concerts on offer in Cambridge and London and attended my first ballet performance at Sadler's Wells, Schumann's *Papillons*, and was entranced. Later, shortly after the war ended, I became interested in opera starting with a performance of Mozart's *Cosi fan Tutte*, by the Vienna State Opera, at Covent Garden. It was a rich, elegant, joyous, lavish and colourful production enhanced by the sparkling contrast with wartime and post-war greyness and austerity.

In Cambridge there was always something going on, from the 'Footlights' to Shakespeare's or Greek plays, such as Aristophanes' *The Frogs* ('Brekekekex koax' etc.), from jazz concerts to recitals in King's College Chapel. I was a keen member of the CU Film society. I was elected Secretary of the Cath's Junior Common Room (JCR), which meant that I was responsible for ordering the newspapers, redecorating, renewing furniture and curtains, paying the bills and keeping the accounts. On one occasion I invited Marie Stopes, the birth control pioneer, to give a lecture to the JCR and took her out to dinner.

In the 1940s it was still the thing for students to go on 'reading parties' during the Easter vacation. I went twice with Christopher and half a dozen other students as his guests to North Devon. We usually ended the day in the local pub, the Brendon Arms, for a pint or two of cider, before running up the hill to the farm, passing an imaginary rugger ball – for we kept up our rugby training.

Financially I had a State Scholarship, a County Major Scholarship and an Open Scholarship at St Catharine's, but was only allowed to receive cumulative grants from these up to a ceiling of about £200 or so, which was quite low even for those days. (This was equivalent to some £5,000–6,000 fifty years later, based on the Retail Price Index.) My parents were not well off and so I had to be careful. I earned some money during most vacations, which helped, but the system also expected us to spend a significant amount of time studying during the vacations.

My most enjoyable and successful (and lucrative) vacation job was one Christmas when I lived with Professor P. D. F. Murray and his wife, Barbara, in their house on Storey's Way, Cambridge, drawing many of the illustrations for his textbook *Biology*. He was pleased with the results and I made about £100 (now in the 1990s equivalent to nearly £3,000) – not bad for the work of a month or so. This book did quite well, going into several reprints, and I later regretted not having asked for royalties rather than a lump sum! However, it also gave me experience relevant to my courses.

Later David Lack FRS, Director of the Edward Grey Institute of Ornithology, Oxford, whom I had met at an ornithological conference at Wadham College in 1947, invited me to illustrate a children's book he was writing. I took it on and a made a start, but he was very difficult to please and, to my shame, I wasn't able to finish it before I departed for the Antarctic at the end of the year.

In my third year then, I took Part II Zoology. It was very different from Part I, if only because the class numbered only twenty-four and we got to know each other very well. This class, which took finals in 1947, came to be known as the 'golden year' and peer pressure competition may have produced its exceptional results. Of the twenty-four, a third obtained First Class Honours in the exams; in those days, unlike now, the proportion of firsts averaged about 10 per cent. I remember most of the class: Janet Singer, Jane Ramsay, Jane Bidder, Murdo Mitchison, Ray Beverton, John Carthy, John Cloudesley-Thompson, Alan Crompton, Alan Charig, Arthur Mansfield, Norman Holme, Ken Ashby, Alan Cock, Elspeth McConnachie, Ursula Grigg, Fergus O'Rourke, and Geoffrey Matthews. Three of us later became FRSs, and eight, at least, became professors or directors of research of similar seniority. Ray Beverton FRS was the outstanding student of that year and many years later was my 'boss' as Secretary of NERC.

In Part II I specialised in experimental physiology, ecology and vertebrate biology. Hans Lissman (later FRS) was one of our teachers and he persuaded me to give my first seminar to the class, on the subject of serial growth layers in bones and scales.

My boyhood interest in polar matters was further stimulated by Cambridge being the home of the Scott Polar Research Institute, founded in memory of Captain R. F. Scott of the Antarctic. Its archives held the largest single collection of Wilson's watercolours and it had an excellent polar library. The institute was the only centre of research in polar studies in Britain and one of few in the world, so it was a magnet for people interested in or planning expeditions to the polar regions. Naturally I gravitated there.

Towards the end of the final summer term, before the examinations, I had already had offers of several jobs. One was in fisheries research at the Lowestoft Fisheries Laboratory under Michael Graham, who had visited Cambridge looking for recruits and interested me in the possibilities. Another involved research on larval settling at the Plymouth Laboratory under F. S. Russell, the Director, who was building up a world-beating team. A third was research on hippopotamus biology in the Gambia as a member of an Oxford and Cambridge student expedition. Then one day, as I was walking into a lecture, John Carthy asked if I was interested in going to the Antarctic to work on elephant seal biology. A physicist, Gordon Robin (later to become Director of the Scott Polar Research Institute and a good friend), a member of the Falklands Islands Dependencies Survey (FIDS), had reported large numbers of elephant seals at Signy Island, one of the South Orkney Islands (earlier reported by James Marr of Discovery Investigations), and that there was a small breeding population there in the austral spring. Brian Roberts was looking for a biologist to go there to work as a member of FIDS. I was a bit surprised that he hadn't approached me directly, but perhaps he'd put John Carthy up to it.

I expressed interest and was later called to London for interview by Captain Ted Bingham, RN, Brian Roberts and a chap called Hoff representing the Colonial Office. I suppose the latter was what would be called a classics generalist; he was anti-science, or at least strongly conveyed that impression at my interview, and was rather aggressive as I recall, claiming that scientists were uncultured, illiterate philistines etc. Perhaps he was just trying to provoke me, but I disliked him and pointed out in response that in my view scientists – including this one – knew much more about literature and the arts than arts graduates did about science. Despite this rejoinder, I was offered the job, starting at the end of October, when I would have two months to prepare before departure. The job was 'all-found', housing, food and clothing provided, and the salary was £360 a year! This was equivalent to some £8,000 a year today (2004).

Meanwhile, at the end of the summer term, after taking our finals, Alan Wallace, Pete Williams and I went to the Gower Peninsula. While there we received by telegram our results in the final exams; we had all three attained First Class degrees – which was just as well, as it would have been sad had there been an odd one out! We were also informed that we had got college prizes for our performance and later bought some books with the prize money. It was an idyllic summer, one of the hottest in living memory, endless sunshine day after day for several months. Sadly, it had to come to an end. I had to prepare for the next part of my life: my first great adventure, the long journey to the bottom of the world – to the Antarctic, via South America.

4

Falkland Islands Dependencies Survey

The Falkland Islands Dependencies coat of arms

Until my appointment I knew nothing about the Falkland Islands Dependencies Survey or FIDS. (FIDS in capitals refers to the organisation. Fids became a term coined by us for those who worked for FIDS in the Antarctic and which was retained with considerable pride when FIDS became the British Antarctic Survey – BAS. Even today to be a Fid proclaims Antarctic experience, and membership of a unique community. With the expansion of BAS the term has acquired qualifiers – Superfid and Megafid denoting seniority within the service). Indeed I didn't even know where the Falkland Islands were.

In 1923 the British Colonial Office planned a programme of sustained research in the Antarctic which ran from 1925 to 1951 and was known as the Discovery Investigations. It arose from concern about over-exploitation of the large whales and the whaling industry's future (a point worth noting by organisations such as Greenpeace – who through the media appear the first to express such concerns). The research – financed by a British government levy on the whaling industry – focussed on the biology of whales and their place in the ecosystem, but included work on other higher predators, particularly seals and fish.

This British research programme contributed knowledge of the Southern Ocean, which was far in advance of its time. Thirteen extensive voyages by RRS *Discovery* (Scott's old ship) and other vessels between 1925 and 1939 set new standards in oceanographic research, demonstrating the main currents and water masses in the region. A marine biologist, Stanley Kemp, was the first Director (his daughter Belinda, a zoologist, was a contemporary of mine at Cambridge).

A marine biological laboratory was opened at Grytviken on South Georgia in 1925 and work began there under Dr N. A. Mackintosh, continuing during each whaling season until 1931. It provided the first modern understanding of the Antarctic plankton and marine mammals, birds, fish and other krill consumers, and was a hugely important precursor of modern research on large whales and their environment. Among other successes it instituted a tagging programme that provided the best evidence for the long-range migrations of the large rorquals, until modern electronic/satellite tags were employed. Many thousands of biological specimens were amassed in the Discovery Collections, stored in the British Museum (Natural History). The results of their studies were published in an impressive series of monographs, the *Discovery Reports*. In many ways these collections, databases and publications are still unsurpassed. After 1951 the Discovery Programme was incorporated into the newly formed British National Institute of Oceanography (NIO).

The British Graham Land Expedition (BGLE), 1934–1937, was a small privately organised venture in an old French fishing schooner, renamed the *Penola*, captained by R. E. D. Ryder. It further developed methods of polar travel and discovery originated in the Arctic by small private student expeditions led by Gino Watkins, which were very cost-effective. BGLE was led by John Rymill, supported by £10,000 each by the Royal Geographical Society and the Colonial Office. Its members were unpaid and the scientists served as *Penola*'s crew.

Wintering bases were set up off the Antarctic Peninsula on the Argentine Islands and Debenham Islands (in Marguerite Bay), in successive seasons.

**Antarctica with some of the British bases under first the FIDS
and then under BAS during my career.**

Extensive scientific programmes were conducted in meteorology, geology, glaciology and biology. The expedition took a small aircraft, useful for reconnaissance and during dog sledge journeys and flights to the west coast. Off-lying islands of the Antarctic Peninsula were also surveyed as far south as southern Alexander Island. Sledging parties discovered King George VI Sound and travelled as far south as 72° S and across the Antarctic Peninsula to the east.

They established that it was indeed a peninsula, not an island. *Penola* spent the 1936 winter at the Falkland Islands and South Georgia where Brian Roberts made important ornithological investigations. *The efficient methods of travel and field research and results of studies on birds and seals* (my main interest), by Brian Roberts and Colin Bertram, set new standards. The expedition also developed new techniques of polar travel and polar clothing. An expedition planned for 1939–40 was abandoned after the outbreak of World War II.

In January 1943, during World War II, the War Cabinet approved an expedition to the Falkland Islands Dependencies (the Dependencies included South Georgia and all of the Antarctic and sub-Antarctic islands, as well as a large section of the Antarctic continent itself claimed by Britain) to strengthen the British claims to sovereignty in the face of claims by Argentina and Chile; and to deny harbours and oil fuel stocks to enemy shipping. The operation was secret and code-named 'Operation Tabarin' after a famous Paris nightclub.

The expedition was comprised of people with polar expertise under the overall command of the Governor of the Falkland Islands. Biologist Cdr James W. S. Marr, RNVR, who had Antarctic experience under Shackleton (1921–22) and the Discovery Investigations (1927–30), was expedition leader.

In the 1943–44 season bases were established at Port Lockroy and Deception Island. In 1944 another base was established at Hope Bay, with huts erected in the South Orkney Islands at Sandefjord Bay and Coronation Island. February 1945 saw Marr replaced as expedition leader by Captain A. Taylor, Royal Canadian Engineers, and in July Operation Tabarin was renamed the Falkland Islands Dependencies Survey, with the Colonial Office taking control from the Admiralty, which retained responsibility for logistics.

In September 1947 Britain decided to continue FIDS, to reinforce territorial claims and explore the Dependencies' economic potentials. In April 1948 the Governor of the Falkland Islands took over the direction of FIDS, appointing a secretary to head a small administrative staff in Stanley, Falkland Islands. A FIDS Scientific Committee was formally appointed by the Colonial Secretary in London to replace the earlier committee. Crown Agents became responsible for supplies, equipment and recruitment and a FIDS London Office was set up where the Secretary of FIDS spent part of each year. The foregoing is thus a thumbnail sketch of my employers.

* * * *

Towards the end of October 1947, I went down to London to prepare for my Antarctic adventure. Owing to delays in refitting the ship, I had six weeks to define my research programme, read the relevant literature and acquire equipment and materials for two years' work (with just £100). Colin Bertram and Brian Roberts were both extremely helpful. Ted Bingham introduced me to the Naval Dockyard at Chatham where I had equipment made, including branding irons for permanently marking the seals. ICI's Dyestuffs and Paints Divisions advised on colour-marking seals for observations of their behaviour. Tentatively I explored the steps needed to take my PhD degree, with Sydney Smith as my supervisor. In the absence of precedents it was agreed that depending on my progress in the first two years, it would be decided later how much of this time might count towards the university's residence requirements for a PhD.

Selecting a Leica II camera with shutter speeds from 1/500th sec and an f3.4 Summar lens, and buying it from my own resources, meant arranging a bank loan. The British Museum, Natural History (BM) was helpful, giving me books and papers and a course on bird-skinning.

I enjoyed the new sort of life in London as a 'civil servant'! I had access to a shorthand typist and for the first time could dictate my business letters. I saw our ship, at that moment named *AN 76* – she looked seaworthy if a little dirty and rusty and was tiny – with a mere 1,200 tons' displacement. Eventually I received final instructions from the Colonial Office (FIDS) and there appeared to be little likelihood of our leaving England before the end of November, as the ship was still undergoing extensive repairs in London Dock near Tower Bridge.

Then out of the blue, there was mention on the radio that the ship was to be renamed. It would become the RRS *John Biscoe* after an early British Antarctic explorer and an unimpressive ceremony was performed by Mrs Creech-Jones, the wife of the Colonial Secretary. We would sail in a few days, a Thursday. However there were further delays as it transpired that the ship hadn't yet been on sea trials. This was just as well for I still had a great deal to do. A lorry brought my twenty crates and drums of scientific equipment from the BM down to the ship, where I saw it safely stowed.

Everyone told us that the *John Biscoe* was the best Antarctic ship yet, so we concluded that the others must have been exceptionally small and even more crowded! Her decks were by now loaded with gear of every description, including a large stack of timber and a crated aircraft sitting on the foredeck.

On 16 December we all came to the FIDS office as instructed to find that the sailing date had been postponed again, but moved onto the ship that night, with Derek Maling, with whom I had climbed in the Lake District, Michael Green, whom I knew from Cambridge, and Jimmy Knox (a radio operator).

On the 18th, after a busy morning followed by lunch at Favas in Frith Street, I caught a taxi to Fenchurch Street Station where a crowd of us Antarctic types gathered and converged on the 3.25 p.m. train for Tilbury. Arriving at the ship we were interviewed by the press: 'Can we quote you, sir, as saying you are thrilled?'… 'Have you left a girl behind?' etc. Bunks were allotted by drawing numbered slips and I got number 13, which placed me in the port cabin aft. This had been the small ship's laundry in its earlier incarnation but even though there were five other bunks in a tiny space, there was more room than in the midships 'slums'. Access was by a 'manhole cover' and a vertical ladder from the deck. We called it 'the black hole of Calcutta'.

We had several naval blokes in our party and one of them, Lieutenant Commander 'Tanky' Scadding, went on first watch and gave me all the 'gen' when I relieved him. The food was the best I'd had for several years, lashings of it and very well served. Eating space was unfortunately rather cramped and throughout the voyage we had to take our meals in three or four shifts. After all the delays we were now due to sail next day, 19 December. At last the great adventure was to begin.

5

To Sea in a Tub: Voyage on the *John Biscoe*

The skipper of the *John Biscoe*, Captain McFie, had recruited most of the crew from layabouts on the dockside, a motley and unimpressive collection. We expedition members were formally signed on as supernumeraries at one shilling a month! At 5.30 p.m. on 19 December 1947 the ship cast off from Tilbury dock and moved to a buoy in mid-stream. Total souls on board, both crew and expedition members, were forty-six.

Next morning at 9.30 we slipped our mooring and, with the pilot aboard, steamed downstream on one engine, pursuing an erratic course. We were told that this was due to the helmsman not being used to the steering wheel, but suspected it might have been the result of heavy drinking the night before.

That evening we were treated to a very colourful and spectacular sunset. Ranks of low stratus cloud were tinted salmon pink and Derek and I amused ourselves by pointing out various potential climbing routes up buttresses of clouds. Some looked very like climbs we knew – Tower Ridge, Ben Nevis; Kern Knotts – with Sepulchre and Buttonhook, Scafell Central Buttress and so on. By sunset we were off Margate and, with both engines running now, made relatively rapid progress down the Channel.

In the cabin I put some pictures up above my bunk and created a hammock of rope for loose belongings. The weather was beginning to roughen and the ship to roll heavily and pitch violently. Several people were down with seasickness by tea time – and there was a shortage of bread. We passed Sark, Alderney and Guernsey and, after dark, the Isle de Bas light. I was on watch on the bridge from 8 o'clock to midnight. The second officer, Tom Miller, pointed out the various instruments and duties and I took over the wheel for a short time. The swell was quite heavy and I found it difficult to steer a straight course – to an observer the ship would have seemed to be taking evasive measures!

Dr Vivian (Bunny) Fuchs was the leader of the expedition, older than the rest of us and with Arctic and African experience. He was sharing a cabin amidships with Dr Stuart Slessor, who had been down with FIDS already as an expedition leader and had much experience of dog-sledging.

It was very pleasant to stand on the bridge, with lowering clouds thinly veiling the moon. There were very few ships about – in fact I saw only four that watch and time passed very quickly. Next I had a free day, which I spent mainly on the bridge, watching the birds – kittiwakes, skuas, gannets, a lesser black-backed gull and a puffin. The Christmas tree was decorated and I painted a large Christmas card to go on it. The weather became noticeably warmer on Christmas Eve. An appropriate church service was held on the foredeck, and we sang 'For those in peril on the sea' and a carol. The Christmas dinner was up to all expectations. At 10.30 a.m. we had broached several bottles of sherry, gin, vermouth etc. and so by first sitting an hour later all were quite merry. The photographers were leaning at crazy angles from all vantage points trying to catch us off our guard, but we bore up to it admirably. The menu was:

Soup

-

Turkey
Sage and Onion Stuffing
Roast and Mashed Potatoes
Green Peas

-

Christmas Pudding

-

Sherry
Graves, 1943
Macon, 1942

Later Dr Fuchs talked to me about the Polar Medal and told me that I would be in charge of the base at Signy Island. Derek had indicated that he would like to go there also and the chances of our being together appeared quite good.

On Boxing Day afternoon Dr Slessor gave an interesting talk on husky dogs and Eskimo (now known as Inuit). There were three types of husky: the very small Greenland dog used for short journeys with a lightly loaded sledge; the larger Labrador dog; and the very large Newfoundland husky. These were bred with wolves to increase their hardiness. The FIDS dogs were all from Labrador.

I had another long talk with Dr Fuchs who put me wise to the political situation down south. He also showed me the provisional list for base 'H' Signy Island. It included Jim Knox (radio operator) and Ken Pawson (meteorologist), and a Falkland Islander. I said I would prefer to have Derek Maling with me, but Ken was a good fellow and I was sure we would get on very well. In fact there were very few of my companions that I would not have been happy with.

The steering mechanism continued to break down at intervals: apparently the switch on the automatic steering engine had broken. For much of the day the hand-steering apparatus was in use – very hard work.

The Cape Verde islands of St Vincent and Santo Antão came in sight ahead and at 4 o'clock we anchored in Porto Grande the main anchorage, where stood the town of São Vicente. From London we had taken eleven days over a distance of 2,568 miles, an average speed of 9.51 knots.

On New Year's Day I was up at 6 o'clock and climbed up to the crow's nest to demonstrate that I had no hangover and look at the view. Jumbo (Nicols) had put a shark line out, though without catching any. The ship weighed anchor and left Porto Grande at 2 o'clock. January 2nd was very hot and we didn't work, but read and talked. I painted a yellow flower collected in São Vicente. Murky plans for the crossing-the-line ceremony were being formulated by the first mate and others.

In the evening we put on a concert and it was received with much applause. Dudley was most mirth provoking, as Stewart Granger in Rank's *Famous Four*; a close second came Jock with Robbie Burn's soliloquy on the Haggis, 'Chieftain o' the pudden' race'. Our opera '*HMS John Biscoe*' went well, as did *Pyramus and Thisbe* in which I had the part of vile wall! Captain McFie made a speech of thanks, having enjoyed the evening and endorsed a wild party lasting until 2 o'clock.

The main feature of the day, however, had been the crossing-the-line ceremony for which a large canvas bath had been made. The bosun was Neptune and one of the seamen Aphrodite. I was charged that I did 'with cruel branding irons, hurt annoy and insult, with criminal intent our Royal Sea Elephants and did so abuse them that they were sore put to it to find who was Angus and who was Agnes'; sentenced to be 'Shaved with a red-hot razor. Bathed in boiling oil and deprived of the rights of man. Thence to be purged and lustrated.' I gave the polar bears as good as I got and ducked the three of them. Afterwards of course the whole court was thrown in – Barry first, in a splendid struggle. Afterwards we spliced the main brace. By 6 January, seventeen days into the voyage, we were fifty-five miles past the Equator and going 'downhill' with the brakes on, that is rather slowly.

Dr Fuchs now showed me the definitive list for Signy Island. It was Derek Maling (meteorologist), Ralph Lenton (radio operator), both aged 24, a Falkland Islander (general assistant) to be picked up at Port Stanley and myself as Base Leader. It couldn't have been better.

That night the lights of Rio were visible on the starboard bow, followed later by Cape Frio light. During the evening there was a continuous spectacular display of summer lightning over the hills behind Rio.

Jock, the ship's electrician, had a very painful abscess at the base of a fingernail and David Dalgliesh (an RN surgeon-lieutenant and our ship's doctor, who was to become a great friend over the years; he was about six years older than myself) decided to operate. We found that the only three syringes in the medical kit were of 2 cc capacity and the anaesthetic – pentathol – required about 10 cc to take effect. After much tinkering a rubber-tubing feed was fixed up so that the syringes could be interchanged. It was difficult to get Jock under with this quite inadequate equipment and Derek, who was also assisting, fainted while I was filling a syringe from a phial he held. Jock burst out singing and quoting Robbie Burns, and the operation was completed. He told us later that he felt no pain – but during the treatment his body appeared to be writhing in agony. I viewed it all quite objectively; who knows but I might have made a good doctor!

The captain reported a minke whale in the afternoon, brown from the film of diatoms on its skin. At 6 o'clock, while on watch, I saw seven or eight whales blowing about a mile or so dead ahead and as we came up to them their backs and dorsal fins were visible when they came up to blow. One of them sounded only twenty yards from our starboard beam, throwing up its massive black tail flukes and plunging almost vertically downwards.

The following morning's watch was quite uneventful. In the afternoon I assisted in the pulling of two teeth from 'Greaser' Cox, a lower right molar and a wisdom tooth – part of my dental training! Dr Slessor talked to us Base Leaders about the medical stores.

Next day as I woke, Lobos Island – breeding ground of fur seals – was abeam to starboard, with the long grey line of the Uruguayan coast on the horizon. In the early morning, uniform grey light, it was uninspiring. We passed the Banco Ingles lightship at 10.36 a.m., the pilot boarded at 1.15 p.m. and at 1.50 p.m. we entered the harbour. At 2.20 p.m. we moored alongside; 16 days 2 hours and 13 minutes from St Vincent, having travelled 3,717 nautical miles. In Montevideo we spent several days, memorable more for the parties we attended than anything else.

A fresh breeze blew as we left port at 6 o'clock accompanied by Dominican and Patagonian black-headed gulls; it was to be more than two years before I was again in a city environment.

At 12 noon (31°51' S; 56°27' W) one seal was seen off the starboard bow and at 6 o'clock several seals and penguins – the penguins porpoising (probably rockhoppers?). One seal was only ten yards from the ship, a southern sea lion I thought, but it was difficult to be sure. During the afternoon numbers of black-capped and dusky petrels, sooty shearwaters (or great-winged petrels?) and some Schlegel's petrels, accompanied us. We were also followed by what I took to be a sooty albatross.

Next day I was woken at 7.45 a.m. by David, who was on the dog-watch, to see two blue whales on the starboard quarter – my first sighting of this species. Although they were not close they were huge and very impressive, moving majestically and seemingly in slow motion. At 11 o'clock thick brown patches of seaweed – kelp – began to appear and we passed them throughout the day. I read most of the day and David did his mending. At midday a Wilson's petrel appeared and was in evidence for a while. There was also what we took to be a giant petrel; also black-capped petrels and an odd-looking petrel with black head and body (white-chinned?). At 6.15 p.m. a large albatross with wing span of about 10 feet was seen from the bridge; it was probably a wandering albatross in juvenile plumage. So passed a typical day of our passage to Port Stanley.

Then at 4.45 a.m. the Falklands came into view on the southern horizon as the sun appeared over the banks of grey cloud in a glorious burst of colour – making the fluffy strato-cumulus look like flames. As we drew closer the various hills began to stand out. The general impression was reminiscent of Scotland's west coast. There was a short coastal plain from which rose the brownish hills, broken here and there by tumbled crags of greyish rock. Mount Vernet and Mount Kent were at first the dominating hills but as we drew nearer they were supplanted by Mount Low. We rounded Volunteer Point, keeping well out in order to avoid the rocks indicated by the breakers. A skua flew across the bows, three neat little Commerson's dolphins, immaculate black and white, raced alongside occasionally jumping – 'swish-thump' – and showing as green shapeless forms beneath the waves and foam, at times looking like torpedoes as their dorsal fins finely cut the surface and left a white wake. The sky was by now free of all but long cirrus bands. There was a definite nip in the air and a scent of peat smoke and wild thyme as we drew near the shore, which reminded me of Scotland and England.

At 9.30 a.m. we passed through the Narrows, which are one cable (200 yards) wide but always seem much less; in fact the navigable channel is nearer 60 yards across because of the kelp-covered rocks which stretch out under water from either shore. The ship was moored to the public jetty by 9.45 a.m. and we prepared for the Governor's inspection. Since the frigate HMS *Snipe* bearing His Excellency Miles Clifford back from the Antarctic had not yet returned, Mrs Clifford came on board instead and we dutifully shook hands with her before she disappeared into the wardroom for cocktails.

As soon as we were able, Derek extracted 120 ft of rope from the bosun's locker and we prepared to go climbing on Mount William with Ken Pawson and Dave Golton. Taking the road along the side of the loch, our view of Port Stanley was a town of red corrugated-iron roofs, boasting the most southerly cathedral in the world.

At the foot of Mt William were masses of ferns, like compound harts-tongues. The mountain's quartzite rocks dipped to the north so that the ridge on which we started to climb was overhanging on its southern side. As the wind and rain came from the north-west, we were in exposed positions most of the way. It was delightful gritty rock to climb on and we followed the ridge in a terrific wind until it became necessary either to leave it or to rope up. So we left it for a short distance and did some more botanising.

On 27 January we all met at Government House in the morning for a stern talk by Fuchs on 'fraternising with the crew'. Last night there had been trouble – two barrels of rum smuggled ashore by the crew. The bosun was again unmanageable and abusive to the chief engineer. He was discharged – which was a very good thing.

Next day the frigate HMS *Snipe* arrived, bearing the Governor. On 29 January we spent the early part of the morning tidying up for HE's (the Governor's) inspection. I had an appointment with HE at 3:30 p.m. when he told me formally that I would be Base Leader at Signy Island. We had a chat. I then picked up Derek and went on to the Hallets' home – where we hoped to use their darkroom. As we developed several cassettes and Dennis Hallet had asked us to develop some of his films, we were late in finishing and stayed to supper and drinks afterwards and didn't escape until after midnight.

It was a cold and windy night and we reached the pier to find that no launch had been sent from the *Snipe*, and a lighter from the *Gold Ranger* was there but wasn't going out until 4:30 a.m. The lights of *Snipe*, *Gold Ranger* and *John Biscoe* were all plainly visible and we flashed a message in Morse code which *John Biscoe* picked up and replied to. We asked her to pass it on to the *Snipe*, which gave no response to our repeated flashes. The first officer of *Snipe* was also waiting on the pier as were numbers of ratings, also the first officer from *Gold Ranger* and several Trinidadians who were obviously feeling the cold.

It was not until 2:30 a.m., after much flashing of lights, that a launch from *Snipe* came alongside, tossing like a cork in the heavy seas. The more drunken of the sailors were taken off in it and eventually we were able to get away in the third boat, thanks to the *Snipe*'s first officer. The first officer of *Gold Ranger* was rather mad that no boat had put ashore from his ship. Leaving behind several *Biscoe* chaps to be picked up next time with the *Snipe*'s chief officer we nosed out from the jetty into the darkness and considerable swell. The small boat was tossed about quite violently and shipped a lot of water. Fortunately we made it to *Snipe* and then pushed upwind to *John Biscoe* where a ladder was lowered. Jock lost his cap and in trying to get up I had my fingers crushed between the launch and the *John Biscoe*, but managed to climb the ladder. At 3 a.m. I turned in after a hurried snack of fried potatoes in pitch darkness. The officer on watch of *Snipe* was not willing to risk a further trip, as the launch's engine was 'dicky', so ordered it to tie up behind the *Snipe*. I suppose we were lucky to get back when we did.

On 30 January we went along to Government House where HE gave us a pep talk. The Base Leaders were made Magistrates. At 1.30 p.m. on the 31st we weighed anchor again and left Stanley. In the open water outside we were tossed about violently and the swell was terrific, so when we began to ship water over the bows the captain became rather anxious about the deck cargo. He attempted to turn around almost losing way in the mountainous seas and rolling through 90 degrees, a manoeuvre accompanied by noises of much smashing of crockery. But fortunately being lucky at the first attempt, we were able to put into Sparrow Cove and anchored there. There were several penguins huddled near the ship and the wrecked and stranded hulk of Brunel's *Great Britain* was only 200 yards away from us, where it had been beached since 1937. This was the world's first ocean liner built of iron, and launched in Bristol in 1843, 322 ft long with a tonnage of 3,270. It was covered with a dense population of mussels, some of which we collected later for supper. There was a thick mist, which reduced visibility and cut off the top of Mount Low. While we were there people fished and read: I made up for lost sleep.

The weather brightened that evening and we were again under way at 6 o'clock. Some of us stood on the monkey island as the ship, rolling heavily, and escorted by gulls, penguins, terns and giant petrels, slowly drew away from the Falklands. The view we had of the hills around Stanley was quite unforgettable. From heavy black storm clouds a curtain of sunlight pleated into rays, cast a glow over all the crags and fells, leaving each new horizon to form a darker edge so as to be gently silhouetted. To the north the incandescent yellow merged into the purple of Mount Vernet. Fuchs talked to the Base Leaders at 7 o'clock and gave us our political instructions.

By 3 February it was definitely colder, but still no bergs. The temperature at noon was about 46°F telling us that we had not yet crossed the Antarctic Convergence, where the colder Antarctic water meets the warmer temperate waters. The sea had assumed more of a grey-blue cast and the sky was for the most part grey and overcast. In the morning several fin whale blows showed to port and in the late afternoon two blue whales came quite close.

Next day the sea was smoother, but the swell greater. It was markedly colder with the air temperature 37°F at noon. Evidently we were now south of the Antarctic Convergence. In the morning five fin whales passed close to the ship, travelling in a north-easterly direction. Their spouts were about 12 feet high and the wind blew them out of vertical. The small, curved dorsal fin was diagnostic and they showed a lot of their backs when surfacing – leaving an oily slick on the surface at that point.

At 3:45 p.m. I saw my first iceberg – initially a white spot on the horizon, which assumed an architectural shape under the binoculars; but it turned out to be only a small bergy bit. There were lots of 'growlers' (small icebergs that show little above the water) about later and the first real berg at 5 o'clock. A few hours later a wonderfully sculptured glacier berg passed to our starboard side. Its shape and colouring were exquisite, as only ice can produce, but it was still rather far away for us to see at all well and was swallowed up in a sea fog that closed down on us.

On the 5th I was up at 6:30 a.m., to see many large tabular bergs around us – in fresh green translucent shades and great variation in form and structure. Some were breaking up, pieces falling off into the sea. We were by now in the Bransfield Strait separating the Antarctic Peninsula from the South Shetland Islands. While I was on galley duty the precipitous rocks and ice slopes of Smith Island (6,600 ft) came partly into view through a rift in the sea fog and leaden clouds, while delicate fluffy snowflakes drifted about us. This was a mystical setting for my first sight of Antarctic land. There were very many ringed and some macaroni penguins near, cape pigeons, terns, and giant petrels; mature wandering albatrosses flew very near the ship among the large bergs with fantastic fretted towers and miniature mountain peaks. It was very calm with a slight swell. At 8:30 a.m. Castle Rock (a volcanic plug) off Smith Island came into view dead ahead as we emerged from a bank of fog and we quickly altered course. Then the low-lying Snow Island, with its ice cliffs and outlying rocky islets showed up when the weather cleared for a short while. Smith Island was visible again later, with the snow peak of Mount Bartlett on Livingston Island rising behind it to 5,280 feet.

Next Deception Island appeared, cloud-capped and sombre, with less snow than the other islands. It is volcanic and there are hot springs in places along its shore. In shape it is roughly a horseshoe, with an excellent natural harbour in the centre. It is bounded by cliffs of black basalt, red and black larva ash, and rugged outlying rocks. Rounding the coast to the west, we entered Whalers' Bay through the narrow and impressive passage called Neptune's Bellows and dropped anchor in Pendulum Cove, in 36 fathoms, after a total passage time from Stanley of 3 days, 18 hours and 50 minutes, and a distance of 746 miles.

The Norwegian whalers built a shore station here in 1912–13, which had fallen into disuse since the whalers began to use factory ships in the 1920s. There was talk of them reopening it again. The wrecked whaling station installations straggled along the shore and to its west was the wooden fourteen-roomed FIDS base hut. We were surrounded by dirty snow slopes, with black ash like slag-heaps sloping down to the shore. In the natural harbour was an Argentine gunboat, the size of a small tug.

Two large crates containing the de Havilland Hornet Moth aircraft were loaded onto a large raft made from the ship's life rafts and empty drums. Then, precariously perched, the plane was taken ashore. Sadly, the skis for the plane still had to come from Canada. On her second cruise *Snipe* brought in a case thought to contain the skis, but when opened it held only stove pipes. Without skis the Hornet Moth remained in its crates on the beach until it was returned to Stanley a year later!

Then the rest of the cargo was landed. We didn't explore the island, even in the vicinity of the base, and after a hectic three days we left Deception at 10.30 a.m., on 8 February, passing under the huge basalt cliffs of Neptune's Bellows and heading for Signy Island at last. We saw the outer side of the island now – black beaches, caves and grotesque rock formations and bizarre colouring. Livingston Island was visible to the south-west. Then we passed the rugged, snow- and ice-covered Elephant and Clarence Islands. It was on inhospitable Elephant Island that Ernest Shackleton's expedition had spent some months in 1916 living under boats while Shackleton and five others sailed 1,450km to South Georgia in a modified whaleboat to organise a rescue.

We passed through many icebergs of all shapes and sizes. I have never since seen such a concentration and the initial novelty soon wore off, but they remain among the most beautiful sights of the Antarctic. It is only in midsummer when some begin to get dirty and decayed that one no longer appreciates their beauty.

The Inaccessible Islands, the most westerly land in the South Orkneys, came into view that day at 3 o'clock and we were heading for them when someone switched on the fathometer and was shocked to get a sounding of only 8 fathoms. Panic stations and we altered course! Then Signy Island came into view at last, a long, low, dark shape, contrasting markedly with the mountainous, ice-covered Coronation Island to the north. The weather deteriorated and it was very gloomy, raining steadily, as we arrived at Borge Bay, Signy Island, on the southern shore where the base was sited.

6

Signy Island

Two sealers, a Briton, George Powell, aboard the *Dove* from London, and the American Nathaniel Palmer, on the *James Monroe* from Stonington, USA, discovered and charted the South Orkney Islands archipelago in 1821. Powell recounts how on 6 December he landed on the eastern end of the largest of the isles and took possession in the name of King George IV and 'as I imagined it to be the first land discovered since the coronation of our most gracious sovereign', he named it Coronation Isle. Shortly afterwards Matthew Brisbane charted Coronation Isle's south coast, discovering but not naming Signy Island.

During 1912–13 a Norwegian whaler – Petter Sörlle – working for A. S. Rethval of Oslo, charted the Orkneys and named Signy Island after his wife, Signy Sörlle. In 1921 Tönsberg Hvalfangeri established a shore whaling station at Signy Island's Factory Cove. It ran for four years but ceased to operate in 1925–26, about the time that the British Discovery Investigations began. In 1927 their research ship, the original *Discovery* (of Captain Scott's 1901–04 expedition), visited Signy. She was replaced by RRS *Discovery II*, which visited the islands several times during 1929–1937. In 1931–32 she surveyed the South Orkney Islands and in 1935 James Marr reported on them. During the Second World War HMS *Carnavon Castle* visited Signy Island in 1943 and hoisted the Union Jack.

On 17 March 1947 Gordon Robin and his FIDS team erected a hut above Factory Cove, near Berntsen Point. A Nissen hut transferred from Cape Geddes was also erected and meteorological and generator huts were put up in April, using materials from the derelict nearby whalers' living quarters. Reflecting the political challenges by Argentina and Chile to British ownership, three 'British Crown Land' notices were erected on Signy at Knife Point, Waterpipe Beach and near the base on Berntsen Point. This was to be home for two years.

When I arrived, some of the old whaling station still remained. The collapsed whalers' living quarters were still there on the slope above. There were five steam tanks (shaped like large jars standing on end 'digesters' for processing whales), enclosed in a wooden structure with a ramp leading up to a wooden deck to provide access to their mouths. There was also a boiler and its collapsed chimney, winches and a tank. A small wooden whaling 'plan' (deck) and a stock of loose coal could be seen on the shore. Near it were several steel barges and wooden barges, including a derelict 28 ft wooden-hulled steam launch, and a number of empty oil drums. Also on the shore under Berntsen Point was a dry, well-constructed explosives store, containing detonators, shells, black powder and harpoon heads for the whaling guns. Other relics of the whalers were heavy mooring shackles and chains let into the rocks.

Signy Island is low-lying, roughly triangular (7.2 x 4.8 km) with the triangle base being its south coast, and 34 km² in area. It lies off the middle of the south coast of Coronation Island from which it is separated by the Normanna Strait, about two miles wide. Robin Peak (858 ft) towers over North Point and Stygian Cove. (I have used the official place names in this account; in my time some of the features had different names.) It had a thin permanent ice cap, crevassed in places, which covered the interior of the island area with miniature peaks and ridges and a central ice cap., rising to a height of 922 ft at Tioga Hill as the McLeod Glacier, which reached the sea at the ice cliffs about 400 yards from our hut. The centre of the island formed an icy plateau with sharply defined edges and steep slopes, surrounding the high ground on nearly every side. Flat or slightly rounded 'tops' rose from the plateau and were connected by shallow cols. In summer much of the island was snow- and ice-free, particularly in the low-lying coastal areas to east and south-east, which were rocky, with peat bogs, glacial drift and frost shattered debris.

Signy's climate is maritime, determined by a succession of depressions travelling around the Antarctic from west to east. It lies in a zone with the highest annual average cloud cover in the world, also the strongest winds at sea producing the highest waves, and a mean annual temperature is -3.8°C. At least one

summer month has a mean sea-level air temperature above freezing point, usually only by a degree or so and very rarely above 11°C. The mean for the coldest winter month is below -12°C, with temperatures frequently below -20°C and sometimes below -40°C. In terms of human susceptibility it is effectively colder if the wind chill factor is applied. An air temperature of -40°C with a wind of only 25 knots is equivalent to a wind chill of -60°C. Gales in excess of 60 knots are not rare and occur throughout the year, and as the depression fronts pass through with monotonous regularity, the day-to-day weather is extremely variable with very abrupt changes taking place within a day. In an example in my diary the temperature fell from -1°C one morning to -21.3°C at night; over 20° in just 11 hours! Signy's environment is also strongly influenced by being within the Antarctic pack ice zone. When the sea freezes to form fast ice the temperature plummets, but rises when the ice breaks up and moves away. Such fluctuations may happen many times during the summer and occasionally during the winter, under the influence of sea swell, tide and wind sheer. Another diary entry during a gale: 'Next day the sea was high and increasing and the bay ice was breaking up in a great swell; all day there was the noise of ice blocks crashing and grinding, one against another.'

As the South Orkneys are north of the Antarctic Circle, the sun doesn't completely leave them during the winter as it does further south, though the days were very short. Also, when the sun was low in the north the high curtain wall of Coronation Island mountains cast us into shadow, so on Signy the direct light of the sun, even in the absence of cloud, is lost for a number of days around midwinter.

* * * *

Signy was also known as the FIDS Base H. On our arrival Dr Fuchs went ashore at 6 a.m. and approaching the beach he had seen a pile of apparently dead elephant seals below the base – and wondered what on earth the Fids had been up to. On landing he was relieved to discover that they were alive, noisy and smelly. I landed after him at 7:00 am, arriving on Signy for the first time: it was 11 February 1948, a dull day with a fresh breeze with the base barely visible through the mist and rain. I met Gordon Robin, the outgoing Base Leader, for the first time. He was an Australian physicist, employed as a meteorologist, who had intended to do research using radar mapping techniques. But the previous year his radar equipment didn't arrive and so he turned his hand to plane-table mapping of the island and making various observations on its biology and geology. His companions were three Falkland Islanders. During the day we took time off the heavy work of landing our stores equipment and Gordon officially handed the base over to me.

In all we had about six hours, discontinuously, for this task. This involved passing on local knowledge, taking over the post office business (stamps and cash) and reconciling accounts, receiving the stores inventories – food, clothing, fuel and the few items of scientific equipment, among other things. Derek and Ralph took over their respective 'departments', meteorology and radio communications, from the men they were relieving. The time was not nearly long enough, considering that we three newcomers had no Antarctic experience.

The outgoing team moved onto the ship and we moved our personal belongings into the tiny hut where we slept that night. We were woken at 4 o'clock by two blasts on the *John Biscoe*'s siren as she left, leaving the three of us in sole possession of the island. We expected the ship back later in the season to land the fourth member of our winter party (a Falkland Islander) – but in the event a heavy concentration of pack ice and bergs closed in early and we didn't see another ship for ten months, that is in November 1948.

The three of us were Derek Maling, ex-RAF, Ralph Lenton, ex-naval radio operator, and myself. Derek had begun a degree course in geography at Durham University; he was the meteorological officer and was able to do some glaciology and geology in addition. Ralph had been apprenticed as a cooper; he had been in the building trade before joining the navy as a petty officer, and had other experience like running a transport café on the A1. His practical skills were to prove most useful over the months ahead. I was biologist, Magistrate and Base Leader. Both Derek and Ralph were three years older than me and had more experience of life; I understood that I had been put in charge, not for any perceived leadership qualities, but to ensure my research received support.

Base H (Signy Island) with the Laws Glacier in the background

Our communications with the outside world from now on was by wireless. We had three radio schedules a day – at 9 o'clock, 3 o'clock and 8 o'clock local time. They were primarily for official communications and for reporting the regular three times a day Meteorological Observations (Met. Obs.).

In December 1948 Ralph was transferred to Deception Island (Base G) and we acquired newcomers John Kendall and Charlie Skilling. John was a Yorkshireman, grey haired and older than the rest of us, with few interests other than his work. He had been a nurse in a mental home, a quiet man, with some gruesome stories to tell. He was now our radio operator.

Charlie was a slim, dark-haired 19-year-old Falkland Islander, with a lively, questioning mind. He fitted in very well and was always willing to help others with whatever tasks were going. He was particularly helpful to Derek and myself in our fieldwork. And he learnt a lot, enjoyed the outside activities and took to skiing like a natural. Having an extra man was to make all the difference to the routine work.

Base Commander aged 22, Base H

* * * *

The living hut was a 20 ft x 14 ft single-storey frame building with double wooden walls, no insulation and three small windows, only one of which opened. It was on a peninsula and had fine views of the mountainous south coast of Coronation Island and north-east Signy. The walls didn't reach normal ceiling height, so the ceiling was angled where the roof sloped down to meet the walls. In the month after arrival we constructed a laboratory extension and in the second summer we added a new 'wing' which was to be used as an extra store room, more weatherproof than the Nissen hut.

There was little free floor space in the living hut. The rest was occupied by an Esse cooking stove plus another stove (Esse 'Fairy' for winter heating), a kitchen bench and cupboards, four beds, bookshelves, medicine chest, dining table and four folding wood and canvas 'director' chairs, the meteorological table and the radio bench. All the wall space of the living hut was taken up by shelves for books, records and personal gear, instruments, crockery, wireless equipment and so on. There was little in the way of decoration. I framed a picture of the Yorkshire Dales and hung it on the north wall. Other posters went up on the oblique top of the walls and there was a picture of Snowdon over the laboratory doorway.

The two coal-burning stoves heated the hut and the cooking stove glowed red hot some mornings after a gale, even though the regulator setting was at 'minimum heat'. It was a most changeable beast and might well burn out. We then had to relight it, a job made easy only if it was possible to use embers from the other fire.

Light was provided by paraffin-burning Tilley pressure lamps, with asbestos mantles. They involved a daily evening routine and once we learnt their idiosyncrasies they were little trouble and gave reasonably bright light. Occasionally we started up a generator for electric lighting and for photographic enlarging, but fuel supplies were so limited that we were very parsimonious over its use. During our second year the original small generators were on their last legs and eventually packed up altogether. Unfortunately the larger replacements proved so thirsty that electric light was even more of a luxury. Dr Fuchs at Stonington (Base E) tried using diesel oil in lamps and sent a message claiming their supply would last '25 years 16 days 13 mins!' I replied: 'We have enough elephant seal blubber to keep us in lighting for 275 years 29 days 11 hrs 27 mins 11 secs. Hope to be relieved before then.' Fuchs's reply: 'Oh what a glorious thing, for you to be a blubber-king!'

We slept comfortably in wooden bunks with mattresses and sheets. It was quite difficult keeping the sheets white as we couldn't send them to a laundry and had no facilities – no washing machine or mangle – and there were no detergents, only soap and soap flakes. We cut a petrol drum in half and it made a passable washtub, heated over a primus in the Nissen hut. Our best opportunity to do a wash came on our weeks on cook's duty, which came round every three weeks (once a month in the second year when there were four of us). Water had either to be fetched 200 yards from the stream (when it flowed) or produced by melting snow in a metal tank that stood near the cooking stove. Drying was the main difficulty to be overcome as, except for a very few days in midsummer, the washing froze. We scrubbed out the kitchen weekly as the rough wooden floor quickly became soiled with coal dust.

Our infrequent baths were usually taken in the evening. Having ensured that there was plenty of water in the tank we had to heat it up by the kettle-full on the stove. A galvanised hip bath was a silly little contraption and only held part of me at a time, then overflowed! Still it was usually a pleasant relaxation to have a bath, though not so pleasant in a cold spell, when icy draughts came up through the floor boards. In winter if we spilt any water on the floor it froze. With outside air temperatures between -18°C and -15°C, the hut was very cold and a thermometer placed on the floor 8 inches (20 cm) from the Esse cooker read -8°C. Another reading taken beside the medical chest was -11°C and the surface water in the snow water tank by the stove was frozen. Higher in the hut the temperature was usually over 20°C.

The other buildings were a shed divided into generator room and meteorological store, where hydrogen was chemically generated for the met balloons (a dangerous activity; fortunately in the second year we had cylinders of hydrogen gas, but heavy to move around). We built a two-seater privy. There was a standard Nissen hut, rather the worse for wear and painted red, where we kept our food and chandlery stores, ropes, blocks etc., sledges, skis, clothing and spare bedding, and all sorts of other stuff. It was like a cross between a very primitive and untidy general store in a small village and a junk store. Because the base was undermanned we 'rather let it go'.

On the shore in the explosives store, we opened one of the tins to see whether the powder had deteriorated, laid a train and had quite a reasonable puff. It must have lain there over twenty years and was still effective. This hut was very well constructed, more weatherproof than our base, and would serve well as an emergency hut if necessary (in the case of fire or other damage to our main hut). The explosives were of no use to us, so in the second year Charlie and I cut a hole in the ice some way offshore, and dumped them in the sea.

Clothing for our first year was inadequate. For general wear about the base we had khaki battledress (serge and tropical action rig – the latter was windproof), naval work suits (as overalls), sea boot stockings and socks, long winter drawers and vests, string vests (knitted from real string), striped pyjamas, scratchy army shirts which improved with washing, etc. No handkerchiefs, and during the second year I found myself just about out of them. Towels were provided. For winter wear there were Labrador-pattern anoraks (windproof outer and blanket inner with puppy skin trimmings to the hood), windproof overtrousers, 'Scapa scanties' (a naval term for heavy knitted woollen long john drawers), sealskin boots, stiff leather boots, duffel slippers and leather gloves with duffel inners. None were waterproof, except heavy oilskins and sou'westers (oilskin fishermen's hats).

A major problem was that when we first went down, FIDS' policy was to hold stocks of clothing on each base, and issue items to base members as needed. Unfortunately the stocks of clothing at Signy when we arrived were minimal, particularly the large sizes. Trousers were in especially short supply and, in a message sent out within two weeks of arriving, I requested Dr Fuchs to send two large battledresses and four large shirts. They did not arrive and I was reduced to wearing trousers I had brought with me for the voyage out – and eventually those of my grey chalk-stripe suit, tailor-made in student days by Shephards in Trinity Street, Cambridge! The only 'issue' outer clothing I had in the first year that fitted me was naval fatigues (work-suit garments like prisoners used to wear – navy blue button-up cotton jacket and boiler-suit trousers). Fortunately there were some white woollen RN jerseys and sea boot stockings. Boots were also a serious problem. We were issued with RBLTs (rubber-bottoms-leather-tops) manufactured in Canada, suitable in summer, but too cold for winter wear, even though they had thick felt inners. Initially for winter we had no Eskimo mukluks, a more practical winter footwear.

The warmest footwear we had were sealskin boots with duffel inners which we soaked and put on wet to make them flexible, then wore them till they dried. Not ideal in our circumstances and still too small for my large feet. Chewing to soften them was suggested ('Oh! for a helpful Eskimo,' I cried).

In February 1949 when we unpacked the incoming stores – surprise, surprise! In response to our pleas for better boots FIDS had sent some beautiful pairs made by Lawrie: size 14, with a warm fleece lining which was detachable. New windproof clothing had been specially designed by Colonel Ken Butler and was excellent. The anoraks had pockets, drawstrings to pull the hood close around the throat and face, and other drawstrings around the waist and thighs. Moreover they were ventile cloth, windproof and more or less waterproof. The gloves had also been specially designed and were warm. Other clothing was now supplied in appropriate sizes, but the trouser problem was unresolved; they 'were sending some trousers with the next ship'! After a trouserless year that would be a good thing. There were also oilskins and rubber thigh boots (which unfortunately leaked and as we had no repair outfit we seldom used them).

We had long narrow cross-country skis with Kandahar bindings but no metal edges. We also had a primitive six-foot army sledge with wooden runners, a bivvy tent with inadequate flimsy bamboo poles, and a mosquito netting ventilator. The standard of equipment supplied at our first relief in December 1948 was also much better than that we found on our arrival. We had a small boat – a Newfoundland 'dory'. In my first year's equipment requests I put in for an outboard motor for coastal journeys and it actually arrived.

Our armoury (just a rack in one corner) held both .303 and .22 rifles, a 12-bore shotgun and two .45 revolvers. We had three ice chisels for testing the safety of the sea ice and for digging fishing and sounding holes in the sea ice. They were six-foot poles with a chisel-like piece of iron attached to one end.

In April 1948 there was a message from Dr Fuchs about rations, a request for our demands to be in by 7 May. London had indicated a cut in the budget and wanted the food scale reduced. At least we were having some say in the matter rather than suffer arbitrary cuts decided by the London Office.

One of my official duties was to act as Postmaster, responding to philatelists' orders. Ralph helped me by typing terse notes about the 'regulations' to send to importunate stamp collectors. To one chap who said, as a civil servant, that regulations could easily be circumvented I wrote a stiff letter. Others who had sent magazines etc. or were decent enough to write a pleasant letter I also sent a covering note. This kept Ralph and me at work until 3 a.m. some nights.

As the 'civil authority', I also received a diverse post-bag of letters that in a larger community would have gone to the local council. There were enquiries about the population (reply '3 men and 100,000 penguins'), public health ('inadequate'), local industries ('arts and crafts') and so on.

Checking fuel drums we found that size, shape and markings were no guarantee of contents.

For a period during the winter Derek placed thermographs inside the hut at floor level and at ceiling height. The traces showed it was not unusual for the temperature at ceiling height to be +25°C and at floor level -10°C. This environmental gradient encouraged the bad habit of sitting with our feet resting on a bunk or chair off the floor, muffled in duffel boot linings. We had some really violent howling gales up to and above Force 12 (hurricane strength) which rocked the hut and lowered the temperature outside to a wind chill equivalent of perhaps -50°C or so, therefore affecting the indoor temperature too. Some mornings we would find that the stove had burnt out overnight due to the wind, but we cooked breakfast on the primuses.

Days passed quickly just doing odd jobs. At the end of June the chimney of the cooking stove collapsed due to rusting. Ralph and I spent a morning on top of the whaling digesters, taking it in turn to saw through a length of old 6 inch iron piping. After knocking the accumulated moss and rubbish of twenty years from it, we erected it with Derek's help, and though crooked it was a great improvement. Another day we took the water tank outside to clean it, quite a job for the three of us, as it required careful manoeuvring to shift it at all. In July we received a message from Dr Fuchs about the coal sacks – they were valuable at 5/6d each – and should be carefully husbanded!

In November we made several trips to Gourlay Point to collect penguin eggs for eating, bringing back about a hundred eggs each time, which were stored in flour, but we lost a large proportion from their freezing and cracking. My birthday came around again and Derek shot a Dominican gull for dinner – its stomach full of bacon rind! Charlie spent some time trying to get another, but although one was circling around he had no luck; I drew a cartoon to mark the occasion. Derek prepared a fine dinner of five courses: soup, asparagus, roast gull, carrots, chips, apple sauce, stuffing; fruit salad and cream gateaux. We had beer (one bottle), sherry, gin, whisky and rum to choose from by then, an advance on our first year. Remembering my last birthday we took it easily and then sat around and talked, feeling very full.

Early in November I began the annual report with the compilation of tables of data and over the next two or three weeks we were all occupied on writing reports and other papers to be ready for when the relief vessel arrived. Derek worked on his survey report. I was preparing graphs etc. for the elephant seal report and writing and typing it. I also wrote a bird report and catalogue of paintings and sketches. Then we worked several evenings on stores inventories etc. in the Nissen hut until supper. I helped Ralph with the Nissen hut clean-up and we had a bonfire. Ralph was working on the canteen stores and bills and typing stores lists. My twenty-two personal telegrams cost £8.3.0. Writing reports went on until 3 December when the ship arrived.

Among the items delivered was the outboard motor. A classic 'Seagull', it was uncomplicated and, apart from hiccups in the first few days that we corrected by tinkering, it ran well and was much appreciated. Charlie and I made a frame to attach it to the boat. On 11 December, we went to Gourlay by boat. The outboard's performance was excellent and we returned in thick fog, steering by compass across Paal Harbour.

Our coal supply for the forthcoming season had been dumped on the beach. On 15 December we started carrying it from the beach where the ship had left it up to the hut. We moved the 3.25 tons in three days! On Christmas Day 1948 we went out to Bare Rock where Derek took a round of angles by theodolite from the cairn, also from near the ammunition hut, and I did some sketching. We had a pleasant but quiet day, consuming an excellent Christmas cake, and played the gramophone.

Avalanche Corrie, Coronation Island

Six months after my arrival I had a haircut and shaved off my beard. Result – unrecognisable! Incidentally we made a practice of growing our beards for about six months and then remaining clean-shaven for the next six months; that way we introduced some variety into our small society in the form of new faces!

On 23 April 1948 it was my birthday and I was 22 years old, and according to my thinking at that time, with only eight more years to live. But if the next two were as eventful as 1948 I should have no grouse! Derek gave me a pair of slippers that he had made – white with leather sole and black pom-poms so that I felt a bit like a circus clown when wearing them. Ralph produced a chocolate and cream sponge cake for tea but better was to follow. For dinner we had seal liver, peas and potatoes followed by trifle and then a large iced birthday cake with six Met. balloon candles and the inscription in chocolate: 'Many Happy Returns, Dick', a letter H on one side and a penguin on the other: definitely a culinary masterpiece. I blew out the candles and Derek photographed the festive scene.

We had a bit of a celebration which included the others filling up a water jug, in which there was by accident a little waste Bouin's fluid (a biological fixative based on picric acid). When added to their drinks it tasted bitter and when we identified its origin I was accused of 'fixing' them! Later, as the evening progressed, we went out determined to have an explosion for a bit of excitement. This did have some point, as I wanted to blast a hole in the rocks so that I could study colonisation of a shore pool. In the howling blizzard we set up two charges (of the black powder for harpoon guns) with detonators, all from the old whalers' explosives store, and fired at the detonators from a safe distance using a .303 rifle. Sadly the wind deflected our shots and we had no explosion.

On 8 May it was Derek's birthday, and I busied myself cooking and preparing special dishes. I made some marzipan icing for the cake from butter, sugar, flour and almond essence, icing sugar on top and a sponge cake model of Napes Needle (Lake District), coated with chocolate on top; there was a figure with an ice axe on top and four candles at the corners. I put chocolate eyes and mouth on my one successful meringue (made from penguin egg whites). The cakes went down well – especially the marzipan icing – and Ralph took photographs of the two of us.

The next year we celebrated Derek's birthday a little late. Again I made the cake decorated it with sledging scenes cut out in silver paper. Also baked scores of éclairs, finished baking the bread and made some cream. For dinner there was roast gull and stuffing, apple sauce, green peas and mashed potato, followed by trifle.

There were, inevitably I suppose, occasional mishaps. For example, one morning towards the end of March we lost the outboard overboard! We fished for it but without success. It was late by then so we went back to the hut and I got on with the cooking. A few days later we lost our dory in a storm – a catastrophe. We had gone over to Drying Point to kill and post mortem some seals for my research and a heavy sea arose quickly making it unsafe to return by boat. Unfortunately there was no suitable beach on which to haul up the heavy boat so we left her moored in a sheltered cove on the north side of the point. The heavy sea didn't subside for several days and our boat was smashed to pieces; by the third day it had been reduced to one plank, which was still tied onto the mooring rope! On 27 March we found a few more bits and one oar intact. It was bad luck and truly a disaster for us. I had to prepare a report on the loss of course, but the Governor was very decent about it.

So it went on over the two years, punctuated by a few winter sledging trips (camping) and very occasional visits from ships when we experienced professional cooking in civilised surroundings aboard, and received fresh fruit and vegetables and sheep carcasses from the Falkland Islands.

We spent a great deal of time outdoors, but on some days we were confined to the hut by the weather. Paperwork was more of an evening activity; after supper we usually sat writing up the day's work, and any diaries that we kept. Specimens I had collected were dealt with or put into jars or trays for attention next morning. Frequently one was too tired to do more than sit and listen to the gramophone or radio, or perhaps read a little. On our first winter Ralph made exquisite model furniture from hardwood packing cases; I painted from my sketches and Derek read, wrote or translated. Photography filled many long evenings. That autumn I read a number of Bernard Shaw's plays, for relaxation. My diary notes that 'Shaw does write a lot of tripe about vivisection & biology in general. He has all the superstitions and cant of an uninformed bricklayer, and judged on this work is as far behind the times now as he was ahead in the 1890s.' How pompous I was! Other books that left impressions were *Madame Bovary*, Pater's *Marius the Epicurean*, Ruskin on mountain form; Janet Whitney's biography *Elizabeth Fry*; G. W. Young's *Mountain Craft*; *The Horse's Mouth* by Joyce Carey – very good; *Journey without maps* (but my diary doesn't state the author); and *Anna Karenina*. Also read were a batch of biological works: F. S. Russell's *Behaviour of animals*; Charles Darwin on sexual selection and polygamy; Scholander's diving experiments on seals, whales and penguins, and others.

Our gramophone was an HMV wind-up model, 78 rpm, and the selection of records supplied was eclectic, ranging from chamber music (string quartets) to orchestral music (symphonies and concertos), to what we thought of as Falkland Islands music (pop, cowboy and country music etc.). Some of my most evocative memories are of Joan Hammond singing 'Oh my beloved Father'.

On a typical bad weather day in February 1948, I painted my first two 'full works', as opposed to sketches: a snowy petrel on its nest in a rock fissure, and one of a Wilson's storm petrel paddling near an iceberg – plenty of blues and greens in the reflections. It was in the Antarctic that my painting really began to take off. Edward Wilson, the biologist with Captain Scott's expeditions, who was a role model for me at that time, had produced an amazing amount of high-quality work. Like Wilson I made rapid pencil sketches in the open, with detailed shorthand notes of colour effects, working up the sketches into finished watercolour paintings during the winter evenings, often months later. We had no electricity during the first winter and so the illumination was provided by Tilley oil lamps and had a yellow hue. My earliest paintings reflect this and the snow shadows tend to be green, but I soon learnt to compensate. I also learnt that the impression of snow can be created by leaving areas of white paper untouched – what you leave out is as important as what is put in. Of interest were sunsets, fuzzy pack fog and cloud effects. The other work I produced consisted of more detailed drawings and paintings of biological subjects – the freshwater crustaceans, marine fauna such as nudibranchs and their egg masses, crustaceans, polyps, worms, fish, and a squid that I captured, terrestrial animals and lichens. In spring and summer I painted elephant seals, Weddell seals and their pups, and birds. I was also collecting and preparing study skins of birds for the Natural History Museum in London, and both drew and painted them.

Weather permitting I sometimes went out at night. I recall occasions when the snowies (snow petrels) were in. They flew back and forth outside their nests along the face of the forbidding black crags, sometimes provoking the occupants of another nest to chatter at them for coming too close, but usually quite silent. If I sat still near the nests they might land at my side, as the prions often did, mistaking me for a rock. Usually they appeared quite suddenly like ghosts and disappeared just as quickly. Sometimes they were outlined against the moon for a moment and its light shone through the feathers of their wings and they might hover for a second framed by the lunar halo – incredibly beautiful and spiritual. These clear nights (and days) were one of the bonuses of the winter period.

All the drawings were supposed to be the property of the Colonial Office as were the negatives of my photographs. My agreement with the Colonial Office provided for me to retain the drawings for my own use 'for a reasonable time after my return to England'. I sent one to Brian Roberts so that he would be aware of their quality, ensuring that they would send me more materials when I ordered them!

Snow petrel at nest

At the beginning of April we decided to go skiing on the ice slopes at the head of Moraine Valley. This was my first day's skiing ever and I enjoyed it very much, but took some hard tumbles and was stiff next day. We continued skiing on suitable days and gradually built up some proficiency, if not style.

Skiing was a means to get about, providing exercise and entertainment. I made a four-foot snow jump by banking up snow behind some wooden boxes. I did half a dozen runs over the jump, covering about 10 ft or more horizontally. I landed well four times and carried on down the slope, but on two other occasions the skis shot forward and I sat down with a bump! Ralph tried it and landed with a crash so wasn't keen to try again. Looking back we were very foolhardy, but in the flush of youth didn't consider the likelihood of accidents. A broken leg would have set us back pretty badly.

* * * *

While Signy Island was the focus our research, we also collected data as and when we could on the larger Coronation Island to the north, from which Signy was separated by the three-mile-wide Normanna Strait. We rowed across when the water was calm enough and clear of ice, or skied over when it was frozen.

On 22 March 1948, some five weeks after landing on Signy, we woke to find the sun streaming into the hut from a cloudless sky. I roused the other two and cooked an early breakfast, as we were going over to Coronation for the day. (We had to snatch at any fine day that presented itself as they came so infrequently.) We put together food for two weeks (a rule even for day trips away from our island), tent, primus, sleeping bags, four gallons of kerosene, matches and so on, in addition to the scientific and climbing kit. I asked Ralph to tell Terry Randall at Base E (Stonington) that we intended going over to Coronation Island and that there would be no 6 o'clock Met. Ob.

About twenty yards from our landing on Coronation was a 9 ft seal with coat in very good post-moult condition. Dorsally it was dark-grey, almost black, and the flanks and belly were flecked with silver grey. Its head was disproportionately small and the neck similarly slender, mounted on rather powerful shoulders behind which the barrel-like body tailed off. The tail itself was quite long for a seal. The vibrissae (whiskers) were very long and its teeth looked rather vicious. Derek went up to it and stroked its muzzle! It made no effort to attack him but backed away. Derek photographed it and then as I wished to see it swimming we prodded it with an ice axe to encourage it to take to the water. Making its way across the bay it hauled out on an islet where, with the aid of binoculars, I could see three other similar seals. They were the first Weddell seals I had seen.

We cut up the hillside after counting the elephant seals in sight, mostly at the head of the bay on a boulder beach – thirty-two, all small ones. There were penguin tracks in the snow and some nesting areas with the red excreta characteristic of the Adélie penguin rookeries.

Scrambling higher, on top of a ridge I came across the cairn marked on the Discovery chart as Δ 270 ft, which offered a superb view of the ice cliffs of Iceberg Bay, which is aptly named. It also showed me that the next bay was probably the best place for a depot as it had a good gravelly beach. Returning to the boat we rowed (this was before the outboard arrived) along the precipitous rocky coast to this cove. The beach shelved gradually and then steepened up to high-tide mark after which it eased off. We had to haul the boat up above to avoid an incoming tide carrying it away or its being damaged by large bits of brash floating in with it.

Derek built a cairn 20 ft above sea level and fixed its position by compass bearings, while Ralph and I established a stores depot near it. After lunch we left for the interior. In the rocks of the old moraine were a few patches of grass (*Deschampsia caespitose*) which also occurred on Signy. Pressing on westwards up the ice slopes towards the saddle, we had to don snow goggles against the intense glare. This glacier was quite small, having a lunar shaped snout, and appeared to be regressing; indeed from what I had now seen of Signy Island, Iceberg Bay and Marshall Bay, I thought that probably most glaciers in the South Orkneys were regressing.

We had noticed some ominous black clouds bearing in from the south-west and now the wind hit us on the top whipping up the fine surface snow into devilish flurries and whorls. It was not sensible to continue, so while Derek took the height by aneroid barometer (560 ft uncorrected), I could see the coast of Marshall Bay, and an island (later named Lynch Island after a 19th-century American sealer) which had been separate from Coronation on the 1933 Discovery map was now joined to the mainland by thick landfast glacier ice. Here, at least, the ice had increased.

Walking back to the dory we watched two Weddell seals on a small rock islet thirty yards out. We left tent, food, primus, 4 galls kerosene and other items in a dump near the 20 ft cairn and placed flat stones over all to weight it down. Then we pushed off the dory and with Ralph and me at the oars headed for Signy. The wind was whipping up the sea in the Normanna Strait and I had visions of us spending two or three nights on Coronation, but as there were no white tops yet, kept going. Derek relieved Ralph at the oars and heading south-west – half into the wind so as to take the seas for the most part head-on – and by making allowance for the wind, we managed the shortest distance to Stygian Cove on Signy after forty hectic minutes' rowing. We then worked our way round the Signy coast, with the wind coming in squalls, which tended to push us round, shipping quite a bit of water as the waves increased. The dory sat high in the water so that the windage made it difficult to steer. Ralph recalled he had read that Newfoundland cod fishermen in these conditions used to take out the plug and allow in some water, whereafter the boat should then lie lower in the water and be more manageable. We did this and now rowed with our feet in several inches of water, but it seemed to work! It was all a bit frightening and the adrenalin flowed, for had we missed our landing, we would have been blown out into the vast Southern Ocean.

At Balin Point Ralph took over and gave me a spell and we were back at base by 5.20 p.m. having taken about one and half hours. Thawing out, we sent a report to Dr Fuchs, had dinner and export gin – to celebrate David's birthday – and then early to bed. It had been one of the best days ever!

Our longest visit to Coronation was much later, on 21 July 1949, when Derek, Charlie and I man-hauled all supplies and equipment on two seven-foot sledges over the frozen sea. On that day the air temperature was -29°C. The days were so short that we pitched camp before 4.30 p.m. It took us about five minutes to erect the pyramid tent and throw snow on the valance around the bottom, and pass the sleeping bags and other kit inside to the cook. Then, while two of us tidied up outside, whoever was cook prepared the evening meal. As he did so the two on the outside would crawl into the tent through a sleeve opening, which was then closed (there was a tubular hosepipe ventilator at the top of the pyramid). We then changed socks and duffel slippers and hung them to dry, together with our gloves and sealskin boots, at the apex of the tent. The meal was very nourishing and at the beginning of the trip very filling. It consisted of 5.6 oz pemmican, 3 oz pea flour, 1 oz potato powder, some dried onion and occasionally a rasher of bacon (per man). This was eaten with a 'dog biscuit', plenty of butter, 1 oz chocolate and 1 oz mint cake. We had a mug of tea and milk with about eight lumps of sugar. Equal shares were ensured by one of us turning his back and saying a name, while the cook pointed to each dish.

The meal was generally sufficient to warm us up and then one by one we climbed into our sleeping bags – a bit of a struggle as the small tent was only meant for two people and the bags were made of very heavy materials. The cook washed up, not very conscientiously, and after this the primus was turned up for half an hour or so to dry out the duffels and socks hanging at the top of the tent. Then once the primus was turned out we snuggled down into our bags as quickly as possible, for despite the tent being double-walled the temperature inside dropped rapidly to almost outside temperature. All that was then to be seen before the candle was extinguished were three brown sacks with three noses peeping out. The temperature fell and the vapour in the tent condensed on the walls as feathers of hoar frost.

In the morning we woke to the alarm clock, gazed up at the roof, which was thickly coated with frost feathers, and knew we had another day of low temperatures. One of us got up and lit the primus stove, fingers getting slightly frostbitten if they accidentally touched the cold metal. The stove was placed on the bag of the person lying in the centre and allowed to burn away for half an hour to dry off and warm the tent; only then did the first riser cook breakfast using snow brought in the night before. The meal consisted of 3 oz oatmeal, 8 lumps of sugar, some butter (amounting to about 5 oz per day) and milk. This was washed down with orange juice and hot water. Lunch was prepared: a small thermos of hot cocoa, three biscuits plus butter and marmite for each. While this was being done the others packed the kit, emerged, scraped the sledge runners and loaded them as the cook passed items outside and finally untied the floor cloth and climbed out himself.

Because it was difficult to haul sledges over Coronation Island's rough terrain, we moved around it on the sea ice, but camping on land. And so it went for three weeks. I kept records on the seals and birds we saw, but for the main part we were engaged in plane-table surveying. Derek concentrated on geology, collecting samples. Unfortunately he tore one of his sealskin boots on sharp rocks and in the course of an hour or so, snow entered the boot and froze his foot, and by the time he appreciated the problem it was well advanced. He rejoined us and thawed out his foot, but large blisters developed. He had no choice but to walk back to base with us as we couldn't pull him on the sledges, and this didn't help his feet. He retired to bed after I had lanced the blisters but it took several days before he was able to walk again.

We enjoyed our three-week winter journey although it had been cold and with our primitive equipment – particularly the inadequate footwear – had been hard work. We had not travelled far, but had experienced to some small degree the hardships that the pioneers in the heroic era had coped with.

Three in a tent

* * * *

Throughout my service with FIDS it had been apparent that our diplomatic relationships with Chile, and particularly with Argentina, over territorial claims in the Antarctic were tense. For example we heard *BBC Overseas News* announce that Ernest Bevin, the Foreign Minister, had stated: 'British officials in command of bases in the Falkland Islands Dependencies have been given instructions for dealing with Argentine and Chilean intruders.' In a poem taken from *Punch*, and entitled 'The King Penguin', the distinctive jingoistic flavour of those times comes through, and is worth quoting:-

The King Penguin

On a desolate rock of the outer isles the lord of the penguins stood
And he looked his last on the stormy blast and a world that was not good
For the Nicaraguan Navy swept the rim of the icy seas
And the Guatemalan flag flew high on the rude Antarctic breeze
And he folded his flippers about his breast and he murmured 'Was it vain
The fight for trade that the sea-dogs made with the towering ships of Spain?
I have grown too old to be consoled, too old to shout hurrah
At the threats of war from Ecuador and the sloops of Panama:
Little by little they break away from the breed that gave me birth
The lordliest empire ever seen by the sun that tours the earth
(For a Briton's hand upon British land as soon as his face was wet
Would wave him on before he was gone, he had no time to set).
But now the Yugo-Slavian types can mock at the power I knew,
And the Falkland gulls salute the hulls of the squadrons of Peru;
I have seen the days when the guns would blaze
And the whole sea surge with foam
Or ever they let some alien set his foot on my island home.
I have lived too long to see the wrong of a Patagonian peace
Imposed on the grebe and the albatross and the kelp and the upland geese.'
He folded his flippers about his breast, and he paced his piece of rock,
He saw the Bolivian Admiral land and he could not stand the shock;
He dived for ever beneath the waves, but as he plunged he said
'I will not bow to a stranger's rule, I am English born and bred,
They have taken the splendour away from the world, and now
they have laid their ban
On the University graduate vote – and I was a Balliol man.'

We also heard that 'the cruiser HMS *Nigeria* has sailed for the southern Dependencies with Mr Miles Clifford, the Governor of the Falkland Islands, on board. He will make his annual tour of the Dependencies.'

Commander Waterhouse the Captain of HMS *Sparrow* said when he visited Signy with supplies that the purpose of his trip was also a show of force to impress the Argentines and Chileans that Britain meant business. The only Argentine warship I had seen up to now was small, like a Tyne tugboat, which had been in Deception Island harbour when we arrived there on our way to Signy. There was an Argentine base about fifty miles from Signy Island, on Laurie Island, but we never saw them.

We also heard that the cruiser HMS *Glasgow* was on her way south to make a show of force for the benefit of the Argentines, but we wouldn't be seeing her at Signy, as there was a gentleman's agreement not to send any heavy stuff further south than 60°S. If the Argentines had sent a gunboat or a cruiser down to us, as Magistrate I would have had to deliver a formal note of protest.

It all foretold events to come!

* * * *

At the beginning of 1949 I was certainly looking forward to another year at Signy. Despite the occasional irritations of living both in isolation and close proximity with my companions, we basically got on very well with one another and the quality of our life took a lot of beating.

At about 10 o'clock on 20 March 1949, the *Biscoe* arrived and the Governor came ashore to inspect the base. He seemed quite pleased with everything. Among the equipment delivered to us was the Norwegian pram dinghy – very heavy and about 18 ft long – to replace the lost dory, and two new Coventry Climax generators of larger capacity to take the place of the old machines, which took a load off my mind. There was a decent tent, ski sticks, etc. The FIDS auditor came ashore to examine the accounts of the post office. This was one of my chief bugbears as there were hundreds of letters from stamp collectors in each mail and it was surprising how much work that entailed (a peculiarity of FIDS was that its bases issued stamps that because of their isolation were very much sought after by philatelists around the world – and were a source of useful revenue). Although my accounts weren't quite correct the error was at least on the credit side!

Aboard the *Biscoe* I went through our yearly reports with the Governor and we discussed a number of specific points. I said that I should like a third year if possible in order to complete my work. This had been affected last season by:

(a) The abnormal ice conditions that year and the understaffing of the base, which resulted in my being unable to do all the seal work I planned, and

(b) half the seal breeding population had been carried away on the ice.

Personally, I liked the life immensely, but at £360 a year I was underpaid and should have liked a little more in the bank. The question then arose as to whether it would be better to remain at Signy for my third year or go to South Georgia. There were points in favour of both options but on the whole I felt that South Georgia was the better place for a further year. It would provide an opportunity to study a very large established elephant seal population – probably the largest of them all – and to apply my research findings to reviewing the management of the sealing industry there. The Governor said that he was not in favour of people staying for longer than two years, but that in my case as I had my teeth into a job of work he was all in favour of it.

He told me that next year he intended to turn Signy into a five-man base, agreeing with me that the present base was too small, got awfully draughty in winter and was difficult to keep clean; so next year a new hut was to be erected.

The mail brought me a letter from Christopher Waddams in Cambridge (formerly my tutor) in which he hinted at my being offered a Fellowship by St Catharine's. He said obliquely that he 'would like my residence in Cambridge to be more permanent' and that he would do all he could at that end. Of course that is what I wanted myself, provided that I could get away occasionally on expeditions. I thought I had ample material to submit for a PhD thesis (although I was not yet registered for it).

I sought Bunny Fuchs' views, and on 24 August he sent a message saying opinion at Cambridge was divided as to whether I should go directly to South Georgia for a third year. Would I not prefer a break of six months at Cambridge before South Georgia? In September a signal came in saying Professor James Gray (zoology) recommended my return to Cambridge provided I could go to South Georgia in October 1950. I proposed returning to Cambridge. On 15 September a message from Sydney Smith said there would be accommodation for me in

Cambridge and confirmed the South Georgia move. Thus my course was set: I would return to Cambridge for six months, then come back to FIDS and South Georgia. So at the end of February 1950 just over two enjoyable and exciting years after we had first landed on Signy I departed for the Falkland Islands on the *Biscoe*, thinking I might never see the island again.

* * * *

Despite millions of seals having been commercially harvested in the Southern Ocean from late in the 19th century and far into the 20th century – to the point of bringing some species close to extinction – very little was known about their biology. The main subject of my research at Signy was the southern elephant seal (*Mirounga leonina*) which was the most common seal. It is an ugly monster. At all but the youngest ages, the male has a proboscis and this together with the animal's great size (up to 20 ft long and 4 tons or more in weight) is the reason for its name. Except as pups, when fur-covered (and with a bark like a Pekinese dog), they are gross in appearance and rather ugly. In the southern spring, September to November, elephants, as we called them, hauled out onto land in limited numbers to give birth and mate. They came ashore again between January and April for between four and six weeks to moult. For the rest of the year they were at sea – although there were always a few on Signy's beaches. August 1948 was the only month when elephants had been completely absent from the Island.

To establish how many elephants used Signy I had had to make regular visual counts, mapping where they were seen (all my companions on Signy helped me with these counts as and when they could). The coasts of the island are rocky and much indented and censuses involved thoroughly checking all beaches and isolated coves. In every potential landing site there might be some elephant seals even towards the end of the summer. Initially, counting involved laboriously checking all possible places, either walking and clambering round the shores, or skiing around the island on the ice surrounding it, or by boat when there was sufficient ice-free water to do so.

With experience I established where the majority of elephant seals congregated and where to concentrate counting, and which areas they avoided. I divided the island into naturally defined areas for studying movements between beaches and whether individuals stayed in specific areas. Borge Bay on the north-east part of the island became my main study area. Conveniently, it was near our base. I made frequent and intensive counts in that area backed up by fewer extensive counts over the whole coastline of the island. At their peak in my first summer there were 3,200 elephant seals in the main study area.

During counting I endeavoured to not merely establish overall numbers, but record males separately from females and put both into rough size/age classes. Initially this was very difficult, particularly when they were congregated into 'pods' where they lie touching, side by side or even on top of one another. I also found it hard to tell the sexes apart. Nevertheless my skills were honed by experience and I came to know my subjects.

In the denser concentrations, moulting elephant seals lay in stinking wallows away from the sea, bunched together like sardines in oil – actually their own shit. In the larger pods they lay two and sometimes three deep, roaring, snorting, writhing masses of blubber wafting a revolting smell into the wind; it was in fact 'visible' on cold days, because clouds of ammonia vapour emanated from them. Dante would have got good ideas for describing another pit in hell.

* * * *

Four other species of seals were resident around or visited Signy Island during my stay. The most abundant was the Weddell seal, *Leptonycotes weddellii*, a species that occupies a niche mainly in Antarctic coastal waters, breeding on the fast ice as far south as 80°S, but is present as a small land-breeding colony at South Georgia. In areas of fast ice it has to make and maintain breathing holes, using its teeth to bite out chunks of ice. It spends the non-breeding season mainly in the pack ice. We frequently saw leopard seals, *Hydrurga leptonyx*, and crabeater seals, *Lobodon carcinophagus*, both of which are pack ice residents, and given the abundance of leads and cracks giving access to the air that characterise this environment, neither has to make or keep breathing holes open in the ice. The Ross seal, *Ommatophoca rossii*, a fast-ice species, has the most southerly distribution and, while it has been recorded from the South Orkneys, we didn't see one. Finally, there was the Antarctic or southern fur seal, *Arctocephalus gazella*, essentially a sub-Antarctic species, with a large breeding population at South Georgia. I was pleased to report that one individual was seen on Signy during our stay: the first record since the days of the commercial sealers in the 1800s who exterminated them from the island. I photographed his tracks but left him undisturbed.

A Weddell seal

As with the elephants, I shot samples of the other seals, collecting ovaries, uteri, fallopian tube sections, stomach contents, parasites and skulls. For our own consumption we took some liver and flesh.

One evening, about 18 September, I designed a metal clip for marking seals. It was made from the strips of monel metal provided for bird ringing and I stamped it with: '*Inform FIDS Colonial Office London*'. I planned to make a hole in the web of a seal's hind flipper at an appropriate distance from the free edge, and insert one end; it would then be bent to form an overlapping clip and closed with a pair of pliers. I tried to affix a clip to one pup, whose mother moved away, but her persistent efforts to return after getting over her initial surprise made marking impossible. Clearly two people at least were necessary – one to hold off the mother while the other attached the clip. Several of the mothers made straight for me on sight – one when I was still thirty yards away. They would not move far from the pups and usually advanced up to five yards before returning to their pup. Its movement and cries stimulated an aggressive maternal instinct. Young pups snapped viciously when handled but became more docile as they grew older; the large ones were incredibly strong though.

The tag could be further improved by shaping the end of the strip to be threaded through the flipper web, so as to give it a taper, and next morning I modified the tags accordingly and sharpened my scalpel. At a time when few seal species had been lastingly tagged for identification, these 'handmade' tags proved to be very effective (in fact some were still being recorded on the Signy Island seals up to twenty-two years later!).

A day in early April 1949 was a red-letter day for seal observations. I noticed a very dark seal of unexpected shape which, when I came up to it, proved to be a bull Antarctic fur seal lying with hind flippers tucked under his abdomen. His hair was dark sooty-brown with light tips, vibrissae, ears a light sandy colour and flippers grey-black. The head was very pointed and the matted fur gave him a hedgehog-like look! He lay near the shore on a grounded ice-floe and was not at all disturbed, even when I walked up close to have a look and experience his musky smell.

This was exciting as it was probably the first recorded sighting of a fur seal in the South Orkneys since commercial sealing brought the species near to extinction in the 19th century. (Little did I think then that in the 1980s and 1990s thousands of fur seals would haul out at Signy during the summer and a small number of pups would be born. This was to pose a conservation problem as the seals' trampling destroyed the natural vegetation over large areas of low-lying ground). However, in the distant past before the sealers had arrived, they had numbered in their many thousands and must have had the same influence then and the phenomenon was nothing new.

7

Cambridge and Falklands Fur Seals

After a smooth straightforward voyage from Signy we arrived at Port Stanley and, after the limited Antarctic smells, experienced the peat smoke and plant aromas. While waiting for a ship to take us north and home, we were accommodated in a boarding house run by the local sausage maker. Here I met Ray Adie for the first time. A South African geologist, he was one of the 'lost eleven' from Stonington where he had spent three winters. Ray and I were put to work in the Treasury counting Falkland's currency notes and checking their numbers before they were destroyed. Daily we were locked in a room in the Treasury building for lengthy periods and the currency was passed to us through a hatch. We went through about £80,000 in a week, the largest amount that has, literally, ever physically passed through my hands in so short a time.

Other days we walked in the surrounding country, or went trout fishing on the Murray River. We visited various houses for 'smokoe' (morning tea) and sometimes for lunch or dinner, a change from the sausages! We were also entertained to drinks and dinners by various officials, such as the Colonial Secretary and his wife, who were glad of company from outside the limited society of Stanley.

We Fids were also welcomed to Government House by the Governor, Miles Clifford, and his wife. He had ginger hair and moustache reminiscent of Adolf Hitler – and among ourselves we referred to him as 'Ginger Geoff'. He had been Deputy Governor of Nigeria, where he had met my brother Peter, then a District Commissioner. Their dinners were formal black-tie affairs.

I spent a morning with the Governor, briefing him on my research, and he seemed impressed. We also discussed my future plans. I would spend six months in Cambridge and return at the end of the year to continue my research at South Georgia. When I put it to him, he agreed to increase my salary from £360 to £400 a year, for this second 'tour'. In my experience Miles Clifford was one of the more effective governors of the Falkland Islands.

I also saw a good deal of 'Ham', or 'Shag' Hamilton, the government naturalist, and his wife, Rose, who hailed from my county of birth, Northumberland, and was charming. Ham had been in the Discovery Investigations, and had written several papers on the Falkland sea lions and leopard seals. In 1936 he carried out a survey of the sea lions, concluding, from detailed counts in the breeding season, that the population numbered $c.379,000$. He had also made observations on their biology, including age and growth, from the rate of development of their skulls.

Now approaching retirement, his main interest when I knew him was in a hatchery for brown trout, which he had established to introduce the species to the Falklands rivers for sport fishing. He took me to his hatchery on the pillion of his motorbike – an adventurous ride – and we caught trout at will on bent hooks baited with worms – very unsporting! It was good, though, to have a fellow biologist to talk shop with after two years out of circulation in 'the ice'.

Ten of us were taken to the port of Santos in Brazil on the RN frigate HMS *Bigbury Bay* crammed in as supernumeraries. From Santos we went to Rio to join RMS *Andes* which called in at Las Palmas and then Lisbon.

Sitting at a table in a small saloon while having a drink with some of the others, I noticed a pretty girl in a fur coat and an orchid corsage walk gracefully by. She was with her parents and younger sister and had just embarked. Later I met her: she was called Maureen. We talked and danced the time away; Maureen was a very graceful natural dancer and of course my skills improved enormously. Captivated by her delightful personality, adventurous character and charming nature, I spent as much time as I could with her during the three days sailing to Southampton. On arrival Maureen gave me her address in London and we resolved to meet again.

Running ahead of my tale, in due course I invited her to my college, for the St. Catharine's May Ball, and we met quite often both in Cambridge (punting on the Cam and other diversions) and London, going to ballets, operas, concerts and plays – usually in the 'gods' – and dining out. Throughout this time in Cambridge before going to South Georgia, and having decided that she was the girl for me, I courted Maureen.

Arriving at Southampton I first travelled north to see my parents and then, at the end of April, went up to Cambridge. I found digs in Hills Road and renewed my acquaintance with St Catharine's and the Zoology Department. PhDs based on extensive fieldwork were unusual and I had to formally make firm arrangements to meet the 'residence' requirement. With Sydney Smith's support the Degree Committee agreed that I could register and count my fieldwork towards the time requirement. All my Antarctic field work (which would eventually amount to some three years) was deemed as only equivalent to three terms of residence in Cambridge! This meant that I would have to put in a minimum of six terms' residence in order to qualify for my doctorate.

I could fit in one term's residence now, Easter term, April–June 1950 and the long vacation, and then would need an additional four terms of residence in 1952–53, to complete the laboratory work and writing-up, after my fieldwork at South Georgia. This meant that it would take at least three years from registration in April 1950 to complete my PhD degree. In effect my thesis would be based on my field work of two summers at Signy Island and one summer at South Georgia. It was agreed that my thesis would be provisionally entitled 'The reproductive cycle of the southern elephant seal', and limited to not more than 80,000 words. Thus I had to be selective in what I included in this thesis. Consequently, most of my detailed work on growth and age, behaviour and population dynamics could not be included in my thesis, but would have to be published separately.

It would be understatement to say that I was kept extremely busy. I was given a large, dark room to myself on the ground floor of the old Museum of Zoology, where I was able to spread myself once my specimens arrived on the *John Biscoe*. In the 1950s there were no mechanical calculators, let alone electronic calculators or computers. Everything had to be done by hand by myself without assistance.

Much of the summer term was spent catching up on the relevant scientific literature. Teeth, seal ovaries and other collected tissues had to be sectioned, stained and photo-micrographed for histological examination and description. The vast volume of observations made from two years in the field had to be analysed. In addition, as I was still an employee of FIDS, I had to provide two papers for a new series of FIDS scientific reports that Dr Fuchs had established. They constituted my first two scientific papers – one on the methods I had developed for marking seals, and the other on my new method for determining seal age from the growth layers I had found in their teeth. I had no option but to 'burn the midnight oil'. In addition I was re-adjusting to civilised life and pleasures, such as tennis, squash, punting and, of even greater importance, pressing my case with Maureen.

Between 1953 and 1956 I had published five substantial papers/monographs on age determination, growth and age, reproductive and social behaviour, reproductive physiology and population dynamics and management. A great deal of the initial work for these publications was done in that summer of 1950 in conjunction with commencing my PhD thesis (in all I published some fifteen papers arising from my PhD work).

A great companion at this time was Ray Adie who was in Cambridge working on his PhD on the geology of the Antarctic Peninsula in the Department of Geology. He had spent three continuous years in the field working out from Hope Bay (Base D) and Stonington (Base E), where he stayed a year longer than planned, due to the relief being prevented in 1948–49 by adverse ice conditions. We saw a lot of each other as his laboratory was just across the street from me. With our common Antarctic experiences we often met up at the Bun Shop for morning coffee, lunch or afternoon tea, and spent many convivial evenings in Cambridge's numerous pubs.

In March 1949 the Treasury had given approval for setting up a FIDS Scientific Bureau and in 1950 it came into being, provisionally for three years. The Colonial Office provided two offices in Queen Anne's Chambers, Dean Farrar Street, London. Dr Fuchs, now 42 years old, was appointed Principal Scientific Officer in charge of the Bureau, with direct responsibility to the Colonial Secretary, a member of the Cabinet. With some exceptions the Bureau was charged with the custody of all specimens and records and with the responsibility for their analysis and publication. (Topography and mapping were the responsibility of the Directorate of Colonial Surveys; hydrography came under the Admiralty Hydrographic Department; and meteorology was the responsibility of the Met. Office). Dr Fuchs recommended that staff returning from the Antarctic should be given an automatic three-month extension to their contract to write up their scientific work. Quarterly reports were to be provided by the Bureau to the Colonial Office. It was intended that FIDS scientific reports would be published through the BM.

Bunny Fuchs, whose home was in Cambridge, spent his week in London and visited Ray and me in our laboratories most Friday mornings, either separately or together, and we discussed progress and plans.

Disappointingly, there were few active biologists in Cambridge sharing my particular interests. Colin Bertram was now Director of the Scott Polar Research Institute, which I often visited mainly to use the library. Brian Roberts, who had recruited me to Antarctic work, was still Head of the Colonial Office Research Department and visited Cambridge (where he had a flat) at weekends. He was a mentor and a fount of information and stimulating ideas. In the Zoology Department the research student with the nearest interests to mine was Barry Cross (later FRS) (doing a PhD in veterinary physiology). Sydney Smith and Lawrence Picken again provided intellectual and artistic stimulation and gastronomic treats. The zoologist Donald Parry was doing a PhD on cetacean locomotion, having spent a season as a whaling inspector/biologist in the Antarctic – as I was to do a few years later. Michael Swann was very helpful with advice on microscopy and photo-micrography in connection with my studies on tooth structure. Hugh Cott, another vertebrate biologist who had taught me as an undergraduate, was still there as were others from my undergraduate days. Janet Singer, now married, was doing a PhD on hydroid nerve nets with Carl Pantin. Geoffrey Matthews, a contemporary on the Part II Zoology course, was in the middle of a PhD on navigation in birds, conducting experimental work using pigeons.

Maureen had met Bunny Fuchs on the *Andes* and we spent a number of Sunday afternoons with him and his charming wife, Joyce, helping to keep their large garden on Barton Road under control, and enjoying the occasional lunch and many sumptuous teas. I learnt to wield a large scythe, developing a proficiency which later came in useful when I had a garden of my own. I knew that I was serious about sharing my life with Maureen, but she was only nineteen and wasn't in a hurry, so I bided my time, mostly very happy but occasionally downhearted at the thought that she didn't yet share my aspirations.

Bunny Fuchs was always very ready with help, guidance and good advice, a true friend and mentor at that time. His work undoubtedly influenced the policy decision by the Colonial Office to increase FIDS activities and provide funding for the additional requirements – to the benefit of us all. He was taking the first tentative steps towards setting up a professional scientific organisation.

* * * *

I was now planning to leave for South Georgia in October. King Edward Point, South Georgia, was to be FIDS Base M, and set up in Falkland Islands government buildings, originally built for the Discovery Investigations in 1925. The Falkland Islands Dependencies Meteorological Service would be located and accommodated there. I was to be the Base Leader and responsible for a dozen men, including meteorologists and a weather forecaster for the whaling industry operating from the island. The Magistrate was to be Ken Pierce-Butler (earlier Secretary to FIDS) with his own establishment of a police officer, two Customs officers, a radio operator and engineer, a handyman and a cook, some of whom would mess in the new FIDS Base M. The Magistrate had a palatial bungalow and there were houses for some of the other staff. Other structures to be maintained were a Customs House, post office, gaol, radio station, with generators providing electricity for the small community, storage sheds, and a billiards/table tennis room for recreation. Unfortunately, I was unable to leave as planned. Miles Clifford, the Falklands Governor, reneged on his agreement to increase my salary. At stake was only £40 a year (equivalent to around £800 in the year 2004), but a principle was involved and I stood my ground. I knew that I had more than proved myself and given good value by the work I had already accomplished. Letters and telegrams were exchanged; it was bureaucracy gone mad! Eventually the Colonial Secretary, Creech-Jones, intervened, sending a curt telegram to the Governor instructing him to make up his mind on the matter. I suspected that Brian Roberts had something to do with this. Most of the simple scientific equipment and stores that I had been purchasing during the summer had already gone south on the *John Biscoe* by the time the issue was resolved in my favour.

Before departing I had a week or two with my parents in Northumberland and bid farewell to my lovely Maureen. Departing in mid-December 1950 I flew with BOAC in an Argonaut, four-engined and propeller-driven in those pre-jet days, and took three long days to reach Montevideo in Uruguay. After a day or two there we boarded the SS *Fitzroy*, captained by Freddie White, and sailed to Stanley, Falkland Islands, arriving there in early January. I could not expect to leave the Falkland Islands for South Georgia until the end of February when the Governor was to make his annual trip there and the other bases. This would further erode the time I had for research at South Georgia, already reduced due to the unfortunate hassle over my salary.

I had anticipated a stormy interview with the Governor over the increase in my salary, but to the contrary we had a friendly talk. When I got up to go he said, 'Oh, by the way, Dick, you should know that I don't like having a pistol held to my head.' Nevertheless thereafter we always got on well and he had used my Christian name for the first time. Much later I came to know him quite well, as Sir Miles and then Miles, and when he died he left me a memento of those times. He had confirmed that I was to be Base Leader of a team of five, but also responsible for the messing arrangements for others at King Edward Point. He agreed that we should have a permanent cook at South Georgia and mentioned that there was a clubroom with billiard table etc.; also there was a cinema at the nearby whaling station, home to hundreds of whalers (hence the presence of a policeman and two Customs officers), and it was quite different from any of the other bases.

In the interim the Governor asked me to carry out a survey of the local fur seal population in the Falkland Islands. The South Atlantic Sealing Company that was licensed to take a quota of sea lions for their oil was foundering financially, and had asked for a licence to take fur seals as well. He wanted my advice on whether or not to grant it.

The company had expected to make profits by killing sea lions for their oil. In this they had been encouraged by a report, apparently written by a desk-bound 'scientist' in Whitehall, who had never been near the islands and had no knowledge of seals. The best information available was in Hamilton's 20-plus-year-old reports from the Discovery Investigations in 1936 and 1939. He had counted sea lion pup production and, relating the results to the apparent age structure of the population, had estimated a total population of almost 400,000. It was thought such a population could sustain a small industry. However, the population seemed to have declined as the sealers' catches had not come up to expectations. This is why Tilbury had approached the Governor and Colonial Secretary for a licence to take a quota of fur seals. The government was interested, as the licences would provide revenue in the form of royalties, as was the case with the elephant seals at South Georgia.

* * * *

The plan was that Peter Tilbury, Manager of the South Atlantic Sealing Company, would conduct me and the government's Sealing Inspector, Johnny Browning, around the coast off West Falkland to make a census, although it was somewhat late in the season for best results. I had been happy to take up the offer, because it was an opportunity to see different seals in the field. Initially we were to fly to Port Albemarle on West Falkland then tour the islets by local boat. However the weather had been bad and the aircraft was well behind its schedules, and eventually we went by sea.

We set off for Port Albemarle in the South Atlantic Sealing Company's wooden ship the *Protector*, an ex-minesweeper. This was no penalty for me, given my love of the sea and immunity from seasickness. Along East Falkland's north coast we had passed some two thousand fur seals. Because of the mist, though, we saw very little of the shore until we were almost at Cape Dolphin. Turning south into Falkland Sound, which separates East and West Falkland, I kept a sharp lookout through binoculars, but saw no seals.

At Ajax Bay, our first port of call, we put ashore some equipment and stores for the local sheep abattoir and freezing project: an ambitious Colonial Development Corporation (CDC) scheme, financed by the British taxpayers, to provide a mutton processing facility that would cut out the need to send sheep to Patagonia. In the evening sunshine, the rolling green uplands and blue mountains were a perfect setting for a settlement. It was rudely spoilt by the shambles of rusting machinery, timber and empty drums. We spent the evening ashore, drinking and talking with the station staff, and I had a long chat with young Charlie Skilling, my Falkland Island friend who had wintered with me on Signy in 1949 and now had a job at Ajax Bay. A reliable observer, he had seen a few seals there, including a leopard seal and an elephant seal.

Next day we didn't get up until 7.45 a.m. and had an idle morning while crushed stone was loaded. We were not able to get away until early afternoon as it was decided to take some barrels of cement as well. It was then that I realised that this was a general-purpose cruise, and Peter Tilbury was using the ship to make money and not to count seals! Understandable as this was, given the company's financial circumstances, my needs would have to take distant second place, with many places that I would like to have surveyed being missed out because they didn't fit the planned commercial itinerary.

Yet my scientific disappointment was counter-balanced by a cruise among the many islands and islets off West Falkland that few would ever have the good fortune to experience. Listing those we passed not chronologically but alphabetically – Arch, Calista, Cat, Carcass, Christmas, Barren, Beauchene, Bird, Dyke, Gibraltar, George, Great, Jack's, Jason, Jason South, Jason Elephant, New, Fur Seal North, Fur Seal South, North, Passage 1, 2, 3 and 4, Sandbar, Sea Lion, Speedwell, Stop, Swan, Swan North, Swan West, Tussock, Tyssen, Weddell, Wedge, West and West Point – they were too many for any tourist brochure.

With the climate, very rough seas and the many dangerous reefs and rocks, these were exciting waters. In the south-westerly swells, the troughs of the waves were often twenty feet below the crests – very large in relation to the size of our vessel. There seemed to be reefs and tide rips in every direction and on looking up the *South America Pilot* I found the area described in frightening terms. The scenery was as grand as it was varied; rolling downs juxtaposed with jagged peaks and cliffs and violent seascapes all added greatly to my visual pleasure. Of continual interest was the wildlife, particularly the birds that were always present. While the variety of species may not have been great, there was always abundance: penguins, skuas, blue-eyed shags, petrels and albatrosses (mollymauks of several species).

The economy of West Falkland and its isles is dominated overwhelmingly by sheep. Thus as part of making the ship pay its way we picked up and dropped off sheep as we went. At Port Howard we took on thirty of which some were dropped off on Jack's Island near a large sea lion harem. On Weddell Island we loaded four human passengers, plus three hundred sheep and dogs. The humans and their dogs were dropped off on the First Passage Island, while the sheep were rowed ashore, 18–20 at a time to Second Passage Island.

On Arch Island, I saw a few sea lions, and on Sandbar Island there were hundreds of them. Besides the dominant bull I could initially see four others (called 'jaspers' in the Falklands, after the old sealers' terminology), eighteen cows and about thirty black pups. Several cows – 'clapmatches' – were in the water, and many more came out of the tussock as we approached. The difference in colour between sea lion cows and bulls was most noticeable – the cows light tawny and the bulls dark chocolate, against which the bright pink of the mouth showed up startlingly. As the sheep scurried off they caused pandemonium among the sea lions, which took to the water, cows, pups and all bulls but two who just backed away from the sheep.

Bird Island reputedly held one of the main fur seal colonies in the islands. I was keen to get ashore, but it was too rough to land. Nevertheless we passed along a shore of high cliffs in which there were large caves reputedly used by fur seals. We saw about thirty of them on ledges thirty or forty feet above sea level, at first sight apparently having scaled a vertical rock face. However, having passed them and looking back, I saw a series of rocky ledges that gave them access. Morris McGill, the Weddell Island manager, recalled that in the past men used to climb down rope ladders to the caves in the Bird Island cliffs, kill and skin the fur seals and carry the skins up on their backs. He had interesting stories about the old sealing days in the Falklands and in Tierra del Fuego. He had often seen fur seals near the First Passage Island and thought they bred in caves on its south side.

Cape Meredith came abeam, a low, shelving, rocky headland, where there was reputedly a sea lion rookery (originally a term for a colony of rooks, it had been expanded to cover such colonies of penguins, seals and turtles), but we saw none. We did, however, see a few fur seals on the shelving rocky terrace, which forms the cape's western extremity. En route up the west shore of Weddell Island the ship was rolling so badly that we lost a sheep overboard; immediately the following giant petrels attacked it and it didn't last long. At last on the most westerly, and smallest, of the islets off Elephant Jason, with great excitement I saw it was packed with fur seals. I estimated with difficulty, for they were closely packed and many must have been out of sight in gullies and depressions, that they numbered about three thousand. It was too rough to land though, and after this tantalising glimpse we carried on up the south coast of Elephant Jason looking for more accessible spots. I saw a few hundred sea lions on the shore; the pups looked smaller than those on Jack's Island (suggesting they were younger).

Both North and South Fur Seal Islands, despite their names, were devoid of fur seals. At New Island there was a harbour. Going ashore we could walk to a fur seal rookery on shelving rocks on which lay over five hundred fur seals of all ages. It was wonderful for me to see these animals at close quarters. There were one or two sea lions amongst them. The old 'wig' fur seals were very large and looked like old jaspers. Many had silvery fur. There were several large pups in view and doubtless others among the rocks. The slopes above were black with oil and filth, showing that the seals had often climbed one or two hundred feet up from the sea. I found two dead pups and obtained two teeth and measurements. These fur seals were very tame and it was only when we dislodged a couple of sea lion clapmatches, which plunged into the sea, that they took fright and rushed for the water. Once there they played about just offshore, displaying no fear.

Fur seal harem

Leaving this rookery we climbed Landsend Bluff where lying down and looking over the edge, which was an overhang, I was amazed. On a ledge, which jutted out from the foot of the cliffs, both below us and around the small island, were thousands of fur seals looking like wasps around a jam pot. Smaller narrower ledges higher up were also packed tight and the seals were even lying in shallow recesses cut in the rock by the waves. Other seals were playing in the water. Not counting these, there were over seven thousand in the area we could see; I was sure that ten thousand was a moderate estimate for the numbers on this part of the coast. Our guide, Cracker, told me that there were more on North Island from which he thought the seals here at New were an overflow.

The ground we walked over was riddled with holes made by the diving petrels, and the remains of the skuas' feasts were liberally strewn about; the skuas dive-bombed us a number of times. We walked through a colony of rockhopper penguins and smaller colonies of mollymauk and shag. The mollymauk young are odd creatures; they rock backwards and forwards on their feet and snap their bills together with loud claps. In going through the rookery, we stumbled over a large stand of tussock, disturbing a jasper which was lying some hundreds of feet above sea level; he made off in a great rage.

The only time I spent any real time ashore was when I visited Arch Island with Johnny Browning while the *Protector* and Tilbury were ashore at their Albemarle base. We left in a pram dinghy on 3 March prepared to camp for several nights. Having rowed to Arch, we hauled the pram up above the high-tide mark and put our gear in the main wooden hut.

A ridge forms the island's backbone and climbing up to it took us to the top of the island behind the huts. Initially we had to force our way through dense tussock, up to ten feet high and then suddenly emerged onto open moorland, with diddle-dee, strawberries and very luscious grass. We enjoyed excellent views of the other islands and watched a herd of sea lions, looking just like a moving patch of kelp, fishing and playing in the surf. Descending to the south coast, back through tussock, we came to the first of the sea lion rookeries, disturbing a clapmatch which bounded out of the tussock, roared defiantly and went down the hill. A jasper followed her into the sea. We walked on around the coast, meeting families of grey duck, kelp geese, upland geese, some penguins, but very few more seals. We picked up a number of skulls and teeth and found two dead sea lions.

The next day we returned with a rifle and collecting materials, took teeth and measurements from the two jasper carcasses seen the previous night, and collected several sea lions and an elephant seal for biological specimens. Later we walked along the beach beneath nests of shags placed on overhanging brackets of tussock, and ran the gauntlet of their droppings. Following a track into the tussock about twenty yards in from the beach, we came upon an amazing scene.

A large hole, about fifteen yards long and ten yards wide, was filled with noisome, black, oily mud. At first it looked empty, but as we watched we heard an animal breathing and, looking closely in the direction of the sound, we saw a bump on the surface of the mud. A well-aimed stone and the black, glistening body of a large bull elephant seal jerked up, and roared at us. The seal, when we disturbed it to encourage it to go into a patch of sunlight for a photograph, stirred other carcasses and bones up to the surface. In the surrounding tussock there were several other smaller pools and they, too, contained dead seals. Some were in the first stage of decomposition.

Starting from depressions in the ground that filled with rainwater, they were found by seals to be comfortable places to lie up. With time they were churned peaty and black by the seals' movements and gradually deepened as the seals carried coatings of mud away with them. Eventually, while seals could still exit them when their water levels were high, this became impossible in a dry year when the water evaporated and its level fell. They were traps which, easily entered, became impossible to climb out of and seals thus caught died. It was obvious to us that the tussock was no place to be on a dark night!

We measured the depth of several holes (seven feet at the edges, but deeper in the middles) and photographed them. I added several birds to my list (an owl, a Johnny rook, some caranchos (crested caracaras) and a peregrine falcon).

We were packed and ready to leave at 3 a.m. next morning, expecting to be picked up by the *Protector*. It never came and after filling time for a while we decided to row back to Albemarle. Leaving mid-morning and taking turns at rowing we made quite good progress. It was quite rough crossing the tide rip off Sandbar Island where the sea lions were roaring, but the clouds cleared and the wind dropped a bit. The next tide rip, near Jack's Island, was not so difficult to negotiate and from there it was just a long hard row, with the wind behind us. It took about an hour and a half. Johnny and I killed seven geese to take back to Stanley when the *Protector* left the following morning.

I had had a most enjoyable and interesting trip, although the original objectives of the voyage had not been seriously addressed because Tilbury had been preoccupied with taking on miscellaneous contracts in order to raise money. This was perhaps not surprising. The sealing venture was not founded in reality. Our voyage had shown me that neither the sea lions nor the fur seals were as abundant as people had thought. With considerable extrapolation, I estimated a total fur seal population of 14,000, and I did recommend that the Governor should *not* issue a licence to the company. It was to be some thirty years before another fur seal census was undertaken by Ian Strange, the then government naturalist, using aircraft. He came up with a total of 14,000 fur seals, exactly the number I had estimated in 1951, but a mere 3,000 sea lions, less than 1 per cent of Hamilton's estimate made in the 1930s.

I left Stanley on the *John Biscoe* on 9 March, heading for South Georgia and very conscious that I had lost nearly two months of my original programme.

8

South Georgia

Captain James Cook claimed the Isle of Georgia for Britain in 1775. Known subsequently as South Georgia, it lies in the South Atlantic Ocean between latitudes 53° 50' and 55° S and longitudes 35° 50' and 38° 15' W. The island is about 120 miles long from north-west to south-east and its greatest breadth is under 30 miles: it is heavily glaciered with an indented coastline and a backbone of high mountains rising to some 10,000ft.

Throughout the 19th century the island sustained a sealing industry which expanded into shore-based whaling very early in the 20th century. Britain asserted its rule in 1843 under the governorship of the Falkland Islands as a dependency of those islands. Sealers and shore-based whalers were licensed by the Falklands Governor. The first permanent settlement on South Georgia was Grytviken, established by the Norwegian whaler Carl A. Larsen, operating it through his Argentine Fishing Company. Other bases appeared at Prince Olaf Harbour, Leith Harbour, Stromness, Husvik, Godthul and Ocean Harbour.

With the growth of these settlements came the need for the physical presence of British authority. Thus a base was established in Cumberland Bay at King Edward Point (KEP) in 1909, across King Edward's cove from the whaling station of Grytviken. KEP thus became the 'capital' of South Georgia. The officer in charge on the ground was deemed the Magistrate with responsibility for asserting official British presence, enforcing British law and regulating all economic, scientific and other activities on the island. In due course a policeman and Customs officials were added to the station. However, governance as such was nominal with the various sealing and whaling concerns largely managing themselves.

Chronologically, the Magistrate was under the Governor of the Falklands until 1949, and it was in this period that the Discovery Committee used KEP as its base and built its Marine Biological Laboratory which was active between 1925 and 1931. In 1950–1951 it became the FIDS South Georgia Base (during my tenure). Between 1952 and 1969 it was primarily a government meteorological station. In 1970 its operation was taken over as a BAS (the successor to FIDS) Research Base until the Argentine War in 1982. In 1985, as a consequence of that war, South Georgia and the other territories that had formerly been governed as Falklands Dependencies were detached from the Falklands and became British Overseas Territories. In 2001 it was returned to BAS after a period of military control in the wake of the Argentine War.

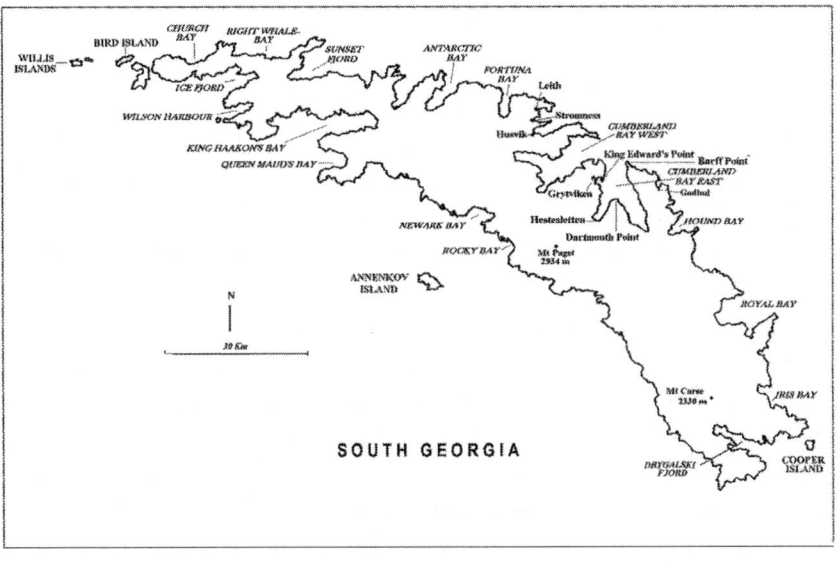

* * * *

On 14 March 1951 at 9:30 a.m. the *John Biscoe* tied up alongside the FF *Southern Venturer* at Leith Harbour, in Stromness Bay, South Georgia, and I set foot on South Georgia for the first time. We were at Leith for only a short time and my overwhelming impression was of the noise of machinery, smell, steam and smoke, ramshackle buildings of rough construction – wood, rusty corrugated iron, peeling paint – and hard working men. There were jetties at which whale catchers were tied up – small, purpose-built vessels.

**King Edward Point, South Georgia, with Grytviken,
the old whaling station, across the bay**

Then *Biscoe* moved on down a rugged coastline, backed by glaciers and high mountains, to Cumberland Bay and the government station and capital of South Georgia at KEP, where I was to spend a year as Base Leader and biologist.

Entering Cumberland Bay we headed for its eastern arm. A strong warm wind was blowing off the land, and as we rounded Sappho Point, we were enveloped by a powerful sickly sweet, oily smell. It was compounded of whale oil and blood, and diesel oil fumes, borne on the wind in a cloud of black smuts and glowing red hot particles. They came from Grytviken, the whaling station half a mile away across the King Edward Cove from KEP. As we approached we could see the whaling factory, owned by Larsen's Compaña Argentina de Pesca, known as Pesca for short, lit by a red glow and emitting clouds of steam and smoke – a scene from Dante's Inferno. Its purpose was to make money from whales. Hunted and killed with catcher boats, using explosive harpoons, the carcasses were towed back to the station and rendered into commercial products, primarily whale oil, but also meat, bone meal and other by-products. An annual quota of elephant seals was also taken from the beaches around the island and rendered in the same plant. The company had been in continuous operation since 1904 when it was founded and, while registered as an Argentinian Company, it was still managed by Norwegians.

* * * *

Our base at KEP was surrounded by beautiful scenery. On top of the cliffs commanding the entrance to the cove, just before Penguin River was reached, stood a gun mounted in the First World War. Behind the gun emplacement rose Brown Mountain (330m). A long curving shingle beach, backed by tussock grass, led south-east from Penguin River to Discovery Point at the mouth of Moraine Fjord. On fine days a superb view opened up behind Hestesletten of Mt Paget (2,915m) and Mt Sugartop (2,325m.) in the Allardyce Range.

In fine weather from April/May to September/October it was an idyllic place but during the whaling and sealing season, October to April, particularly when whales were aplenty, the factory belched smoke and steam, and noxious smells that we became accustomed to. Then it was a hellish place with whale oil droplets and sooty particles born in the steam in the air, flames belching from the smithy and the water in the cove surfaced with noisome oil, blood and grax (remaining contents of the cookers – solid fragments of the blubber, soluble proteins and some oil). Standing at the factory slipway one's surroundings were a few whale carcasses floating at the buoys, pecked at by the black and white Dominican gulls, and a line of battered old catchers moored to the jetty until they set off again after whales. The beautiful surrounding environment was often hidden from sight and mechanical sounds drowned out the bird calls.

The government station was built on KEP, a low tussock-covered promontory near the entrance of the cove, opposite Pesca, the land running roughly east to west at the north-east side of King Edward Cove. Grytviken means pot cove in Norwegian, from the many old cast iron trypots left by the early elephant sealers. At other times there was a beautiful view including Mount Paget rising to nearly 10, 000 feet. It was very lovely and not really polar at all, for there was an abundance of green vegetation.

At the western end was a strong jetty of wooden piles where the bottom shelved steeply into deep water. The post office stood on the shore just south of the jetty and alongside it two boathouses. A track led eastwards through the middle of the settlement. On the shore side was first the Meteorological Building (built in 1907 by the Argentines), near it a store (1925), to which a truck railway led from the jetty. Discovery House (1925) came next, an attractive building erected to house the Discovery Investigations staff and containing living accommodation, offices, and dry and wet laboratories. Then came the Magistrate's house (1925) a Customs house and tennis court (1947). Opposite the tennis court was a brick-built gaol (1913) which had housed only a few prisoners over the years; east of it was the police house (1950). Westwards down the track from here stood the radio room and residence and store (1925), then the power house and a cylindrical fuel tank on the shore. The radio station was established in 1925 when the use of radio by whaling ships was already well developed. Because of atmospherics and the remote location, two high aerial towers were built in a steel lattice construction like miniature Eiffel Towers. The call sign was 'ZBH' and it was a registered coastal station for ships' communications.

Completing the establishment, there was a boat store and general store on the shore between the power house and the jetty. Finally KEP is bounded to the east by Hope Point, the northern entrance of King Edward Cove marked by a cairn and white cross in memory of Sir Ernest Shackleton. Between the cross and the rest of the Point was a full-size rifle range, for Falkland Islanders are great marksmen.

In addition to myself, the other Fids in our group were: Ian Biggs (meteorologist), Danny Borland (outgoing Base Leader; Met. forecaster), A. I. 'Mac' Macarthur (Met.), Arthur Mansfield (meteorologist) and Jack Newing (radio operator, meteorologist). We also had a cook, Andy, whose surname I forget. Arthur was a close friend from Cambridge days, with a degree in zoology, and had joined FIDS at my suggestion for the experience. He was employed as a meteorologist because he had spent his national service in the Education Branch of the navy specialising in meteorology. He had been at KEP for some months already. It was good to have his company for the year ahead. Apart from periodic home leaves, Danny stayed on South Georgia for another twenty years. (He eventually became Director of the Arctic Biological Unit based near Quebec, Canada.)

The other members of the community on KEP were Ken Pierce-Butler (Magistrate) who was a Fid who had been leader at Stonington and lived in a well-appointed bungalow, near Discovery House; his cook, who was our cook Andy's wife; Bill Bonner (policeman), Henry Luxton, (Customs officer), and Charlie (whose surname I forget, engineer) and his wife.

In my first few days I put the laboratory and my rooms in order, including some posters on the walls to add a little colour. At the first opportunity we rowed in our small 10–12ft dinghy across the cove to the whaling station. We could also walk round the shore of King Edward's Cove to Grytviken about 800 yards away. There was a cinema at the whaling station – Grytviken *Kino* – with showings twice weekly and whenever there were more than three whale catchers tied up. We more usually walked round the north shore of King Edward's Cove to Grytviken about once a week. There were facilities for table tennis and badminton that all too often ended up at 1 a.m. after a big drinking session. On the Point too we had table tennis, darts and billiards and there was little chance of anyone getting bored.

We had plenty of fresh meat (pork or whale meat) from the whaling station and occasional fresh fruit and vegetables whenever a ship came in during the summer. I couldn't help thinking how different it was from the peaceful, unspoiled environment of Signy Island.

At the time the impact of the whaling station seemed dreadful. Yet twenty-five years later, after it had closed down, biochemical studies of the sediments in the cove showed that bacteria had broken down the oil and organic matter in the cove, and organisms were recolonising the sea floor. Kelp was growing back, although the shoreline was still covered in a dense layer of thick oil and tar. The same studies showed that the extent of serious pollution was limited to the environs of the cove itself. Outside of it the enormous impact of the whaling operations appeared to be largely reversible in a few decades.

* * * *

Grytviken was the first station to be established in the Antarctic, when Captain C. A. Larsen arrived on 16 November 1904, with about sixty other Norwegians on three ships, *Louise, Rolf* and *Fortuna*. The first whale, a humpback, was taken on 22 December and the factory, operational in about a month, produced the first oil on 24 December. The station they established was the forerunner of the immense and extensive Antarctic whaling industry that developed later. It had accommodation for 300 men and was designed to produce whale oil (from baleen whales), sperm oil, whale meat meal and bone meal. A few years after my time there it also began producing protein solubles, whale-meat extract and frozen whale meat. It was an efficient factory and could process some twenty-four fin whales, each 60–70ft long, in 24 hrs (as many as the floating factory *Balaena* could process in the same time in 1954). An additional 100 men worked on the catcher boats in the whaling season and the total winter complement was about 200. There were three other stations on the island, an hour by sea up the coast to the north in Stromness Bay. These were Husvik (Norwegian owned) and Leith Harbour and Stromness (both owned by a British company, Christian Salvesen). Husvik and Leith Harbour were active whaling stations, Stromness, with a floating dock, was used for major engineering repairs.

Grytviken's primary function was processing the whales that were caught by Pesca. In the two seasons I was there (1950–51 and 1951–52) almost identical numbers of whales were caught by Pesca: 796 and 798 respectively! Nineteen blue whales were taken in 1950–51, by far the largest number in any recent season. In these two seasons respectively 515 and 567 fin whales were caught, 165 and 155 sei whales, a mere 2 and 5 humpbacks and 95 and 65 sperm. The combined catches of all species at Grytviken, Husvik and Leith Harbour were 2,662 and 2,333 respectively in 1950–51 and 1951–52, so the Grytviken catch was roughly a third of the total caught in these years.

Central to the operations was the wooden flensing plan, raised on piles. It lay between the two main jetties of the station and was about 75m long by 45m across (roughly an acre). The dead whales were towed into the cove by a 'buoy boat' (or the catcher involved) from where they had been killed and flagged, up to 300–400 miles away. Usually they were attached to one of a number of buoys in the cove until they were ready to be processed. Then one of the station motor boats collected them and moored them at the foot of a slipway that led up from the sea onto the plan. On a signal from the head flenser, a whale would be manoeuvred to the slip and a wire strop passed around its tail just in front of the flukes. A heavy hawser was heaved down from the steam winch (45 ton pull) mounted at the other end of the plan, which was kept slippery with water and with blood and oil from previously dismembered whales. Steam winches on either side ripped off two sheets of blubber, progressively freed by the knives of the flensers, shaped like a giant hockey stick. Whale blubber is not flabby like the fat on overweight humans but firm, a network of dense fibrous tissue in which the oil is stored. Winches at the side of the plan rolled the whale over to remove the lower strip of blubber. The whole process was rather like peeling a banana on a grand scale!

On the northern side of the plan was the blubber cookery. Strips of blubber were drawn over to it and cut into smaller pieces which were carried in conveyor buckets up to the top of the blubber cookery, the 'blubber loft', where they were fed into a dozen huge digesters or pressure cookers. The oil was separated from the blubber by blowing steam in at the bottom until the oil separated. Each cooker would hold up to 24 tons of blubber that was cooked for about five hours at 60 lbs/per square inch of steam pressure. The oil separated from the water and was 'blown off' to the separator house, behind the main winch, for a final separation by centrifuge. The remaining contents of the cooker and grax were also sent to the separator house. After this purification the oil was pumped for storage in whale oil tanks to the north and west of the station. With a good supply of whales to provide the raw material, the station could produce 1,000 barrels (six barrels to the ton) of oil a day.

On the other side of the plan was the meat cookery, to which the remnants of the whales – the meat and offal – were drawn by winches. This raw material was pulled up a steel slip to the top platform or 'meat loft', where guts, tongues and belly blubber were fed through circular iron hatches, like drain covers, into special rotating Kværner cookers for cooking. A perforated inner drum rotated under steam pressure in the cooker and the heat and attrition broke down the tissues, releasing the oil. The flippers and ribs were cut up by ten-foot long steam saws and treated the same way. The meat cookery and blubber cookery each had their own boiler house to provide steam power.

At the back of the meat cookery the huge back fillets of meat – up to ten tons or more each – were cut up and the chunks were loaded into a bucket conveyor and taken to a cutter for chopping up. The minced meat was then slowly cooked, to coagulate the proteins, as it was conveyed through treatment tubes and emerged at the end onto a vibrating screen. Liquid passed through the screen to a battery of horizontal centrifuges or de-sludgers, which removed the fine particles of solids and sent the liquor to the separator house for recovery of oil. Two large screw presses squeezed the remaining liquid out of the meat and sent it for oil recovery. The press cake emerging then travelled to a cutter on the deck above to be broken up and loaded into huge cylindrical dryers to have the moisture removed. One of these was used for bone meal, the others for meat. An oil-fired flame was blown down the drier to evaporate the moisture.

At the head of the plan, farthest from the sea, was the bone cookery where the heads and backbones of the whales were drawn up to the 'bone loft'. Four huge steam-powered bone saws cut them up into chunks small enough to be fed into many bone pressure cookers and one huge Kværner cooker. Cooked bone was unloaded into a skip, wheeled into the meat factory and tipped onto the floor, where the larger chunks were cut up with axes and fed into the breaker. Bone took longer to cook than blubber but yielded as much as a third of a whale's oil. The dried meat and bone meal was milled and bagged in 50kg bags. The factory could produce 150 tons of meal in a day and the huge shed behind the dryers, the guano store, would be filled to its capacity of 7,500 tons by the end of the season. The storage capacity for these products gave the land station one great advantage over the floating factories, where space was at a premium.

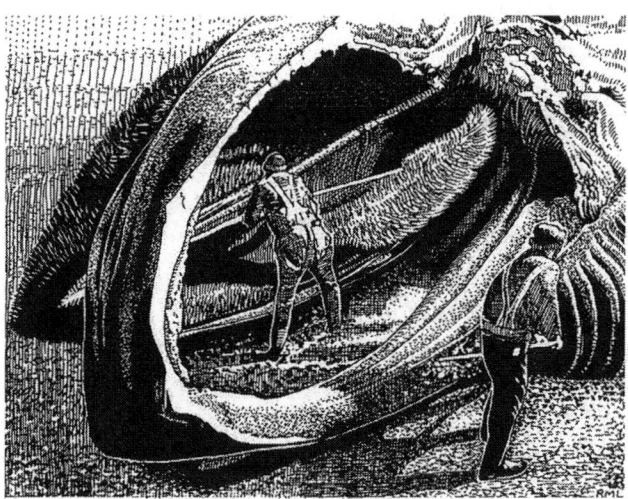

Flensing a great whale

The production part of the factory depended on various boiler houses, generating plants, machine shops, electrician's workshop, smithy, carpenter's workshop, barracks, hospital and stores, a laboratory, various stores, a 'slop chest' for clothing, a bakery, a manager's house or 'villa' and barracks and bath house for the men. A large galley/dining room served for the men. Pigs and hens were kept for meat and eggs and there was a butcher's. The entire factory area was crisscrossed with pipes carrying water, steam, and oil, some running across an alley a foot above the ground. One pipe, underground, led around the shore to provide a water supply for KEP.

Much of the equipment in the factory was manufactured at Grytviken and the staff included engineers and other tradesmen with the appropriate skills. The station was for the six winter months of the year a self-sufficient community, reliant in summer on tankers and cargo–passenger ships to bring down fuel and stores and carry away the whale oil and meat and bone meal – as well as men.

Of the two main jetties the larger to the north took large vessels, tankers and store ships alongside, and the manager's villa stood opposite it across an open square. Two other buildings were the church, which was originally built in Strömmen, Norway, dismantled and re-erected at Grytviken in 1913, and the cinema, the Grytviken *Kino*. We each had a season ticket, proclaiming it the southernmost cinema in the world.

The smaller jetty to the south was associated with the catchers' stores – each vessel had its own small lock-up in a long building. The mechanical and engineering, machine shop, electrical workshop, smithy and plater's shop also provided the facilities for overhauling the catchers during the winter months and carrying out repairs during the whaling and sealing seasons. These facilities were extensive, capable of ship and heavy machinery repairs, as well as straightening the heavy iron harpoons and making hooks in the smithy. Most of the catchers were tied up at the station for the winter.

Across the water to the south-east lay the hulk *Louise*, a wooden barque, one of the first three ships to arrive in 1904. Built in 1869 she was dismantled shortly after arrival and used for coal storage into the 1920s. Half way around the shore track from Grytviken to KEP was an explosives store. A small dam to the north provided domestic water and Gull Lake, also man made, was a reliable source of fresh water on a large scale for the factory and it provided water for a very efficient hydroelectric power plant.

I spent hours observing the whaling operations on the plan and in the factory. After conducting post-mortems on elephant seals I was used to large mammals, but the whales were on a vastly different scale. I observed the anatomy of a number of fin, sei and sperm whales, and was privileged to see at least one blue whale and one or two humpbacks cut up, after they had been measured using a tape measure

– the largest was about 85ft long. I particularly noted the streamlined body form of the rorquals (baleens), their flippers and flukes, the unusually large eyes, the large baleen plates, and the ungainly shape and black and white colouration of the humpbacks, the barnacles and lice on their prominent callosities. Some of these corpses were females and it was saddening to see the foetuses, perfect in distinctive whale form – to the flippers/flukes and the throat grooves along the belly – as they lay on the deck in all the blood and oil. I also saw my first sperm whales close-to and investigated the complicated head, with only one nostril, the other evolved into the 'case' containing spermaceti, which we now know plays a functional role in sound production and echolocation. I was able to follow the processing of the carcasses through the factory. One got used to the smells, except when a long dead whale was brought in, known as a *dauhval*, which was bloated from decomposition and had meat dripping off the bones and a vile smell as it was processed. Even grade 3 oil had some value! However, my own elephant seal research was to leave me little time for studying whales at the shore stations on South Georgia.

The first modern whale research had been carried out by the biologists of Discovery Investigations, starting in 1925, when Discovery House was built. The first whale biologists to work there were Mackintosh (leader), followed by Wheeler, Harrison Matthews and others. They began work on 5 February and by the time the station closed down for that winter had already examined the carcasses of 241 whales, a remarkable achievement. An outstanding study published in *Discovery Reports* by Mackintosh and Wheeler on 'Southern blue and fin whales' (1929) was many years ahead of its time and based on hundreds of whales examined on the Grytviken plan. They set new standards in the study of whales, examining some 1,208 whales at Pesca as well as another 454 at Saldanha Bay in South Africa. This publication comprising 283 pages covers external characters, baleen, food, blubber, external parasites, reproductive organs, breeding and growth (sexual maturity, breeding season, sexual cycle, ages and growth) and conclusions on the stock of whales and its composition. Their work helped to provide the beginnings of a solid foundation for the regulation of whaling. In due course in 1954 I was to start work under Dr Mackintosh at the UK NIO on some of their material and was staggered to see its quality, for its time, given the difficulties that had to be overcome.

* * * *

The pattern of my life at South Georgia became fairly settled. I was usually out every other day, depending on the weather, and busiest during the summer before the seals began leaving for their winter foraging at sea. My field day began by rowing across the bay in the morning to Hestesletten where sealing was prohibited. It is a very flat, low-lying moraine plain, bounded by a high ridge to the north and by a low-lying moraine ridge to the south, beyond which lies Discovery Point and Moraine Fjord. To the west are two glacier lakes and then the land climbs steeply to a hanging glacier and thence to Mt Sugartop. Behind the beach there is a strip of tussock grass of varying width, but on average about twenty yards wide, dotted with wallows and pools caused by elephant seals during the moulting season. A small hut stood between two small but conspicuous crags at the north end of this beach and near it Penguin River entered the sea. The beach itself was of boulders and pebbles and landing was usually difficult because of the surf.

I visited Hestesletten for the first time on 17 March 1951, rowing there with Arthur Mansfield. That day we shot three cows and made collections. In one I found a tiny embryo in the uterus; another, when shot, rolled into the surf and we had the devil of a job to collect the essential data and specimens; by the time we were finished we were soaked in cold, bloody sea water. We also collected teeth for ageing from four other carcasses, including a bull we found with a bullet wound in the head, killed no more than a day or so before. This was disturbing, for it meant that someone from Pesca had shot it and I reported the crime to the Magistrate after we had rowed back to base.

Next day the specimens were stored for further examination. Later I drew up large-scale maps on which to plot the locations (numbered stations) of the collections I would make during the year. The evening was spent sorting out 'canteen' stores – toothpaste, brushes, soap, sweets, cigarettes and tobacco, etc. – which were supplied free to members of the base. Two Norwegians from the station looked in. They were Egil Undrum and Johan Holte Larsen, who worked in the office. We particularly liked Johan, who was to become a good friend and attempted to teach us Norwegian during the coming winter; he was a blond Viking about 6 ft 4 in tall.

A pattern developed as Hestesletten was my nearest seal study area. The field work – counting and classifying seals and collecting research material – was done in the mornings, the afternoon spent writing, or examining and analysing material collected, and time passed all too quickly. And in the evenings more writing or drawing, or perhaps dissecting specimens and occasionally painting.

When not out in the field my usual day was spent in the laboratory, making up various reagents and fixatives to preserve collected material, dealing with specimens and preparing clean data sheets copied from the field sheets, which were often bloodstained, and carrying out the light administrative duties of a Base Leader. While I was thus occupied, the others went about their various duties. On Signy we lived in cramped conditions and were in sight of one another most of the time. Here it was very different from the other bases further south, because at KEP work places and duties were dispersed and one often saw little of people except at mealtimes and in the evenings

Hestesletten, South Georgia

* * * *

At the end of March I went on the sealer *Albatros* to the west coast. Introducing myself to Captain Hauge, I was installed in the chart room below the bridge, where I was to sleep on the floor. Our route was initially north-west along the rugged coast, past Stromness Bay and the smoke of Leith Harbour, Fortuna Bay, and the high and heavily crevassed Fortuna Glacier, which was very conspicuous from the sea. All along this coast were traces of a raised beach, about thirty to forty feet above the present sea level. We could see little of the coast after leaving Fortuna Bay, for the wind increased to gale force and the light snow developed into a blizzard.

We took time off to inspect the wreck of the *Ernesto Tornquist*, a former supply ship for Pesca, which lay about 200 yards east of Cape Constance. A 6,620 ton ship 138 metres long, she had run aground the previous year during a gale. Fortunately crew and passengers, some 260 people, were rescued. Captain Hauge took the *Albatros* right in to the wreck, which lay on a rock ledge at the foot of high cliffs in a small bay. Three masts stuck up out of the water and the bows were still showing. Behind were several caves, in one of which the survivors had spent the night, and a ship's lifeboat lying on the rocks emphasised the calamity.

The blizzard persisted as we resumed our course and I joined the 'funnel parliament', next to the funnel being the warmest place on the ship where everyone gathered except the captain. I had chatted with a Pole who was peeling potatoes; he had lived two years in Britain at Chester and Aberdeen after the war, before moving to the Argentine.

Soon the light of Prince Olaf Harbour entrance was to port and through driving snow we saw the buildings of the now disused whaling station. Anchoring in an inner arm of the fjord we waited out the blizzard. Facilities were primitive; the loo was an open shelter over the side of the deck. It was colder now and the snow froze on the decks, while the wind screamed incessantly. Despite the weather we went ashore to the old whaling station. There were two whale catchers there, the *Stora* and *Southern Gambler*, both Salvesen's boats from Leith who, like us, were waiting out the storm. We tied up alongside *Gambler* and pottered about among the flapping rusty corrugated iron. The engineer, who went on ahead, had worked at this station before it closed in 1931; it now belonged to Salvesen (formerly Lever Bros.). In this melancholy scene our steps rang hollow in the empty mess room, once so full of life. Returning to the boats, we saw their crews were fishing from the sterns with conspicuous success, bringing up large *Notothenia*, South Georgia cod, one after the other, using a lead weight with two unbaited hooks.

Sealing gangs took everything they could: clubbing young seals, lancing bigger animals and with full-grown bulls, firing a musket ball through the palate into the brain. Periodically the shallops loaded with skins and blubber returned to their parent ship, to anchor in one of the bays. There the blubber was rendered (tried) to separate the oil.

In the early days in the more inaccessible parts, sealing gangs lived ashore in rough huts, sometimes throughout the winter, and boiled down the blubber on land. Their old, rusting trypots were still visible in various parts of the island.

The following account of sealing at South Georgia in the 1940s and 50s is condensed from the three trips I made in 1951 on board the *Albatros*, Ole Hauge the master. The *Albatros* was steel-built, 107 ft long, 210 tons, and retained traces of her former occupation as a whale catcher, such as the gun pillar in the bows; she had oil-fired steam engines, and carried a motor boat and pram dinghy.

The crew, excluding the captain, numbered about sixteen, comprising an engineer, two firemen, one motor boat man (who occasionally helped in the engine room), a mate (who was also gunner ashore), two seamen (one of whom was in charge of the pram dinghy), a cook, a mess boy and seven sealers. The captain, mate, engineer, motor boat man and cook lived aft; the crew's quarters were forward of the hold. Men of five or six different nationalities might work in the *Albatros*, and the language in general use was a mixture of Spanish and Norwegian, although most of the sealers were expatriate Poles. The majority spent the winter in Argentina, returning to South Georgia each spring.

As in the whaling industry, a system of quota and bonus prevailed. The seal quota on which the bonus was based was arrived at by taking the average number of barrels of oil produced in the previous three years, and a bonus was paid for each barrel obtained. If the set quota was exceeded, an increased bonus was paid. In December, January and February and at other times when they weren't sealing, the sealers worked at the whaling station at Grytviken. Sealing trips were seldom more than a week at a time.

Most of the charts of South Georgia were inaccurate and several sealing captains had compiled their own. In general, their knowledge of this stormy, rocky and treacherous, and frequently fog-bound, coast was so intimate that they dispensed with charts and compasses. They were without means of communication, but fuel depots were placed round the coast, so that, in the event of a vessel being wrecked, her motor boat could fetch help. This happened later in that 1951 season.

When sealing, the *Albatros* spent the night in a sheltered anchorage close to the beach to be worked the next day. Work usually began at about five thirty in the morning when both motor boat and pram were lowered. The sealing party of seven and the gunner jumped into the heavy pram dinghy and were towed to the beach by the motor boat, which ran in as far as possible before casting off the towrope. The pram was then rowed in, often through very heavy surf, and the party jumped ashore. Usually the pram then waited just outside the line of breakers, though occasionally, if there was little or no surf, it might be hauled higher up the beach.

The sealers, who frequently worked up to the waist in water, wore overalls, rubber thigh boots and, over the boots, rubber or oilskin trousers tied below the knee with string. Waterproof jackets and sou'westers were usually worn, or, if the weather was fine, a peaked leather cap. Their equipment consisted of iron hooks on a three-foot shaft, long rope strops of about 10 ft with a loop spliced in each end, and a long *spekk* (blubber) line. The gunner carried a Krag-Jorgensen rifle (.458 calibre) and a small canvas satchel containing the soft-nosed bullets. Swedish Eskilstuna knives for flensing were housed in wooden sheaths, made in South Georgia, with a sharpening steel and a small hook attached. These knives were washed frequently in the sea and kept razor sharp with the steel. I acquired such a set of equipment for my own use. A whetstone for coarse sharpening of the knives was usually carried by one of the flensers, and they were honed with the steel. One man carried two or three metal tubes about 10 ft long and of 1 inch diameter (condenser tubes from a defunct boiler at the whaling station).

The seven sealers had three separate tasks: beating, flensing, and hauling. A beater selected a bull and drove it backwards to the water's edge, by tapping it on the proboscis with one of the rods and shouting 'Ush-aaaaa' or 'Oh-ho-ho', or some other taunt, sometimes striking the rod with a stone to make more noise. At the water's edge the gunner shot it in the head – they were never shot through the palate as the old books record. When the bull slumped down the eyes, by relaxation of the pupils, turned a brilliant emerald green as the reflective tapetum was exposed.

Flensers immediately started cutting off the blubber. A series of cuts was made in the skin: (i) round the base of each fore flipper so that the flipper could later be pulled through inside the skin, (ii) transversely around the head behind the eyes and in front of the tail and finally (iii) a median dorsal cut connected the transverse head and tail cuts. Working with their hooks and deft sweeps of their knives the flensers freed the skin together with its underlying layer of blubber, rolling the carcass over as necessary. Skin and blubber (which varied between one and six inches in thickness) came off in one piece; the whole process took on average three to four minutes. If several seals had been killed, one or two skilled flensers went ahead, making the initial cuts and freeing the blubber from the back and sides, while a third followed with the three haulers and completed the flensing.

The haulers put a strap through one of the holes created and, if several seals were killed close together, the pieces were dragged into the sea and the *spekk* line was threaded through the loops in the strops. The pram came in as close as possible and the *spekk* line was thrown to it and made fast. The pram was then rowed out to the waiting motor boat which towed the skins to the parent vessel where they were winched aboard and stowed.

On the sealing beach the gunner was responsible for seeing that the work was done safely and efficiently and he decided which seals were too small to kill. He was usually last into and first out of the pram. A sealing captain and his gunner customarily worked together for many years and developed their own system of signs for communication between ship and shore.

The work continued as long as there were seals to be taken, the vessel moving between beaches where necessary, or until the vessel had the maximum cargo it could stow. There were no fixed meal times and food was often snatched while the vessel moved from one bay to the next. The working day usually ended about seven in the evening and sometimes much later, although at the beginning and end of the season it was shorter, due to the reduced day length. Despite the weather, days when work was impossible were rare; though this relied on the sealers' strong constitutions and determination.

* * * *

I planned to repeat and greatly extend my Signy Island research on the elephant seal's breeding cycle and behaviour in South Georgia with an intense study in the Dartmouth Point Seal Reserve in East Cumberland Bay. This involved camping on site for over a month. Fortunately, Dartmouth Point was within a couple of hours' rowing from our base at KEP, so that I could keep up to date on events and those there could contact me. Here I must again record my indebtedness to Arthur Mansfield, my close friend from Cambridge days. He came over to where I was at Dartmouth Point whenever he could and not only was principal link with KEP, but an enormous help with my field work.

My adventure began on 18 September to be in place when the first seal pups were born. Arthur and I loaded the camp equipment into the clapped-out government launch *Stella* before breakfast and we headed for Dartmouth Point towing a dinghy. It was a perfect day, with hardly a breath of wind and the sea mirror calm. The anchor was dropped thirty yards offshore near the conspicuous bluff south of the Point and taking several trips my equipment was ferried ashore in the dinghy. For the next four weeks, regardless of the weather – which was particularly bad at times – I usually skied more than ten miles a day, counting and observing seals, painting them for identification purposes, and killing and examining some individuals in connection with my studies.

I drew a rough map of this coast and divided it into numbered areas, 1–12. Seals would be recorded by area on a census sheet with positions recorded on my map. In addition to counting, I marked as many individuals as possible – each with a colour and pattern so as to be identifiable. This enabled me to record date of arrival and follow their movements and changing behaviour. On my first trip out I noticed several cows showed orange pustules, looking like a fungus, on their face and back. It was more noticeable when the cows were wet, but not so apparent when they dried. They appeared to be of all age groups, perhaps more young than old. It was an infection I hadn't seen at Signy Island.

On 21 September there were three new pups – the beginning of a steadily increasing number. I marked the cows with a red O to serve as identification of date of birth.

Sheathbills, scavengers of the Antarctic, were in close attendance to take advantage of the placentas as the seal cows give birth and any calf deaths. They are daring rogues, pecking the cows' hindquarters, also the pups' fore and hind flippers. The seals have no effective retaliation, for when they swing around roaring, the cause of the trouble walks off sedately, just out of range. These sheathbills were clearly a major cause of disturbance in the harems and at times the cows went quite berserk, fought with each other, and even temporarily left their pups.

As at Signy, elephants of all ages and both sexes use their fore flippers to throw whatever the substrate on which they lay – snow, water, pebbles etc. – onto their backs. With the bigger animals this odd behaviour creates great holes on either side of them. Some shot the stones with great force, five or six feet into the air. I assumed that this flipping to be an aspect of displacement behaviour.

At the outset bulls were setting out harem territories, but somewhat half-heartedly. A pattern was beginning to emerge in the social organisation of the breeding areas. From my observations it was obvious that the cows are gregarious and stay close until they give birth. I noted that no cows pupped except in the company of other cows. Up to this point while they are close together a single bull can keep them as his harem. Thus one bull had a phenomenal fifty-eight cows. After pupping they don't tolerate other cows very near and the harem tends to spread out and take up more room. This makes it impossible for one bull to control large harems and so others step in.

Elephant seals

As hauling out and giving birth are closely synchronised, the oestrus period is similarly synchronised, and as it develops the competition between males to secure harems of potential mates hots up. Thus all through my time at Dartmouth Point, there was a rising frenzy of males fighting one another, roaring, trying to take over established harems or splitting them into units that they could take over for themselves. By 11 October there were fifty-two harems in my study area and bulls were now trying to mate in earnest. By the end of my intensive Point Dartmouth study the female breeding cycle was clear. As early as seven days post-partum some cows showed larger follicles in the active ovary (developing for the next oestrus cycle), and the corpus luteum in the other ovary was much smaller. After ten days post-partum activity was general and at around nineteen days after giving birth the cow elephant seal ovulates and mates. At that time elephant seal society is anything but peaceable; cows with new pups are snapping at their neighbours and pups other than their own; bulls are trying to round up cows and keep them in controllable harems, roaring and fighting one another. Mortality of new pups is high; many are crushed by adults and yet others fall into melt holes in the snow from which they cannot get out.

Getting my biological samples was not without incident as it involved going among the animals in harems, which protective bulls resented. I needed two dated cows for reproductive material, members of the same harem. I tried to move the bull away, but couldn't, so I killed and examined the first cow within a few yards of him. Eventually, I did move this bull and another cow, to get at the second date-marked cow. On another occasion I went to a different harem where I had a lively time killing and trying to examine a date-marked cow. The bull chased me repeatedly, and I was forced to give up, before obtaining all the material I needed. In one area I slipped on the ice while dodging a bull, and managed to cut myself rather badly, falling down with the heavy collecting box on top of me. I scrambled clear just in time, when the three-ton bull was about a foot away! I hurried back to camp to bind the cut, which was rather deep, to stop the bleeding. Such incidents made the point of how much safer it would have been with a helper.

In fact I was not completely out of touch with KEP. Arthur came over whenever he could to help with data collection. There were social visits from Larsen and the Skuseths from Grytviken. When the generator and lighting system in my camp failed, Charlie came over and installed a new system and in addition set up radio communication between my camp and KEP. Ken Butler had suggested that the factory should take the skins and blubber from the animals I shot, a good idea for it meant that they were not wasted. Larsen had agreed, so boats from the factory came across irregularly.

All was not smooth running at KEP in my absence as Base Leader. Ken Butler had been somewhat high handed and refused others access to the motor launch *Stella*. Thus, for example, to get to me Arthur had to row in a dinghy. It had led to a rebellion against him by the small community on the Point. It gave rise to a scurrilous cartoon, graffiti on Discovery House and the barricading of Bill Bonner's house: all rather childish, but diverting! Nevertheless I asked Arthur to tell Ken that I took a dim view of his decision and that it was going to mess up the seal work. Man management was an essential attribute when communities of isolated people make molehills into mountains too easily.

Promptly at 3.30 p.m. on 13 October the Pesca boat appeared and without much difficulty we loaded my equipment and specimens and left for KEP. I had been twenty-five days camping at Dartmouth Point and had achieved all my objectives.

* * * *

Having returned to KEP, I now extended the Dartmouth Point work on a less intensive scale at Hestesletten, Discovery Point and Maiviken. However, not being camped on the spot, each day's work required skiing or walking along the beaches to Grytviken with my equipment, and then along the coast, past Horse Head and Penguin River to Hestesletten and beyond. This covered up to ten miles and kept me very fit. Arthur kindly made some of these counts when I was away on sealing voyages.

For the remainder of this breeding season, when I was not accompanying the sealers on their commercial operations, I continued to collect data from Maiviken, Discovery Point and more extensive information from Hestesletten, which was the closest. The results complemented those from Dartmouth Point.

At the end of October our residents at KEP increased by twenty people, among them three women and three children. Arthur moved in with me to make more space. Of the twenty, six comprised the South Georgia Survey, an independent expedition led by Duncan Carse that we housed in the gaol at KEP. The leader had a separate room. His project interested me because their mapping work was similar to that Derek Maling and I had done in the South Orkneys a few years previously. When I showed the members my photos of South Georgia it changed their plans rather, because they had not realised how difficult it was to travel over. Theirs was the first of four expeditions between 1951–52 and 1956–57.

* * * *

Not long afterwards I was again on board *Albatros* for more than a week in heavy seas. *Don Samuel*, another of the four sealing boats, captained by Hammarstadt (formerly mate of the *Albatros*), had been wrecked a few days earlier. This confirmed just how dangerous these waters were, for the hydrographic charts were inaccurate and the sealers relied to a considerable extent on their own hand-drawn maps, or used no maps at all (having the knowledge in their heads). The *Don Samuel* had been steaming 'full fart' – full speed – heading for an anchorage for the night, when, in deep water, it hit uncharted rocks and sank in a couple of minutes. Although it happened very quickly, all the crew survived because of their professional seamanship, experience in handling boats and fast reactions. They boarded the motor boat and made a remarkable journey round the coast. The first anyone knew of the event was when we steamed around a headland near the mouth of King Haakon Bay in *Albatros* and saw some figures among the tussock behind the beach waving to us. It was the *Don Samuel* crew. They had been living under an upturned boat for a week, eating albatross chicks and elephant seal meat. They seemed to have thrived on the experience! At the time the sealing boats had no radio communication, but as a result of this shipwreck, from the next season onwards they were fitted with radio transmitters. Ironically the rocks were later charted and named Samuel Islands in 1958.

On this trip, anchored in Wilson Harbour, we were surrounded by glaciers that were calving continuously and sounding like heavy guns. The water in these fjords was incredibly clear and blue-green. I had never seen anything quite like it – the nearest concept is liquid ice. Off the glacier fronts, particularly the bigger ones, the sea is a milky green-blue and opaque, due to 'glacier flour' – the dust carried down by the glaciers – and sharply demarcated from the clear water of the open sea.

Next morning we went ashore at 4:30 a.m. to work a long beach. It was an incredible place, and, even though I had been there before I was surprised. Sailing below miles of high forbidding cliffs, the ship turned abruptly and headed straight for them as though the man at the wheel was drunk. But, suddenly a narrow channel opened and passing through we found ourselves in a pleasant bay with rolling hills behind and two glaciers – everything green: the water, the ice and the tussock-covered land. There are several such spots on this coast. Later we worked for six to seven hours in torrential rain, most unpleasant. Arne Bogen, the gunner, said in his quaint English, 'Ef I your place, I no work – I stay in bed all day, go sleeps.'

There was a minor happening in the afternoon. It was very rough and the heavy motor boat capsized and sank; fortunately, it was attached to the *Albatros* by a strong rope. It took an hour or so to raise it and get it on board: a remarkable achievement given the limited equipment available. These men were very practical and adaptable, proving yet again that they were *extremely* good seamen.

I got on very well with these sealers, whom I liked and respected – nearly all Polish with a Dane, some Norwegians, a Swede and a Finn. One day I lost my pipe, so they presented me with one (together with two pipe-cleaners) with many words and deprecating shrugs. It was *not* a sweet pipe, being cheaply made from relatively soft wood – *not* briar – but it was a kind gesture and I smoked it occasionally to show my appreciation. Often now they would ask me down to the fo'c'sle for a drink – which meant polishing off a whole bottle of aquavit at a sitting. In the evening returning from the fo'c'sle, my steps were sometimes a little unsteady and clambering over the blubber heaped on the decks was difficult, particularly if there was a swell.

I enjoyed my evenings with the sealers at play. Spending most of their day up to the waist in bloody seawater and handling oily blubber and so on, they made a special point of being very clean when work was over. We had games of cards with continuous rollicking commentaries in Spanish, Polish, Norwegian and English and it was great fun. One of the men, Pilat, was just like Chico Marx and I had to smile every time I saw him, when he smiled back shyly. Another was a former Polish university professor.

In contrast, when landing on a beach they looked like a bunch of pirates. They had a quaint way of shouting to the seals. '*Oh huh! lobo, scapage scapay, oh ho! look out lobo ehuh!*' and so on. Then to a cry of '*arriba*' all leaped out of the pram, brandishing their long blubber hooks and knives like small swords and with lengths of rope swathed round their torsos, and crying '*lobo querido*' (dear seal) proceeded to kill all the mature bulls they could find!

It was nearly the end of the elephants' breeding season and on the beaches now were mainly pups, lying together as sardines in a tin. Like most young animals they are charming – with large brown, wondering – and watering – eyes, and immaculate silvery-grey coats. They like to lie in the fresh-water streams – occasionally having mock battles, when they try to imitate the big bulls, and raising up their bodies on their fore flippers they thump each other on the neck and half-heartedly bite. One of them did a double backward somersault when I tickled his ribs!

Back at Grytviken on 20 November after an interesting trip I was feeling very fit after all those days in the open. I really enjoyed this hard life among hard men. Naturally, after a trip it was rather cramping to sit in my study typing. However, the time for my departure was approaching and I spent most days working on a seal management plan and writing up some of my thesis.

As things turned out, *John Biscoe*'s arrival was delayed and I had to spend Christmas in South Georgia and not in Port Stanley as planned. This meant resisting Eskedal, the hardest drinker of a very hard-drinking lot, whose ambition was to drink me under the table! As my days on South Georgia drew to a close, we heard that an Argentine cruiser was coming down our way so there would probably be one or two British warships arriving before too long. It had been well worthwhile, my field time in South Georgia, and I hoped that when my results were published they would cause a stir in zoological circles.

A small elephant seal harem

120

9

New Ideas for Managing and Conserving Elephant Seals

The sealing industry began soon after Captain James Cook rediscovered South Georgia in 1775. It was lucrative but the sealers killed indiscriminately all the seals they found and the beaches were soon depopulated. In the early days southern fur seals were taken as well as the elephant seals, but the fur seals were quickly exterminated owing to their greater value and by 1822 were commercially extinct.

Sealing reached a peak early in the 19th century, but the stock of elephant seals was so depleted that by 1880 it had become unprofitable to hunt them. South Georgia was then deserted until the turn of the century, when the species was found to have increased sufficiently to make hunting profitable again. To prevent a recurrence of the previous indiscriminate slaughter the Falklands Islands government in 1899 introduced a Seal Fishery Ordinance, as a first step towards putting the industry on a rational basis. The position was revised by further ordinances in 1904, 1909 and 1921.

As a result of this legislation the coastline of South Georgia was divided into four divisions. The first extended from Cape Nuñez to Cape North, the second from Cape Buller to Cape Saunders, the third from Larsen Point to Cape Disappointment and the fourth from there to Cape Nuñez. Several seal reserves where no hunting was permitted were designated. The divisions were worked in rotation; each year the seals in one division were undisturbed. Licences for taking a stipulated number of adult male elephant seals were issued annually to the sealing company by the Magistrate. It was forbidden to hunt fur seals and, since 1916, Weddell seals because the latter species is confined to a small relict colony in Larsen harbour at the southern end of the island. Leopard seals could be taken until 1927, but yielded a negligible fraction of the total oil output of the sealing industry.

The four reserves where no hunting was permitted were Willis Island and Bird Island, the coastlines from Cape North to Cape Buller, from Cape Sounders to Larsen Point, and in the vicinity of Dartmouth Point in East Cumberland Bay.

Policy for restricting offtake to males only rested on the biological fact that with so highly polygynous a species, a single male could serve a large number of cows. As the sexes are nearly equal in numbers at birth, just as with domestic livestock, a large surplus of males can therefore be harvested without affecting the herd's reproductive potential. Further, the enormous sexual disparity in size, an adult male being around eight times the weight of the average adult female, gave economic reason to harvest males only and leave the maximum number of females to breed.

Southern elephant seals didn't lend themselves to pelagic hunting as some northern seals did, and they could only be taken when on land. This happened twice a year: when they came ashore – September early November – to breed, then again to moult – females in January and February, males from March to May. These limited periods when accessible on land greatly assisted supervision of sealing and law enforcement.

The first licence was issued in 1910 to the oldest established whaling company at South Georgia, Pesca, who monopolised the sealing industry until within a few years of its demise in 1964. The Magistrate, as the senior civil authority on the island, issued annual licences. At first only the divisions nearest to the station were worked, and 1 October to 31 December was a close period. Later, September was also included in the close season, although September sealing was allowed in certain war years (1914, 1916–1918). The seals were therefore virtually unmolested in the breeding season. The close season was altered in subsequent years.

The Magistrates' reports provided a record of annual seal catches at South Georgia over the period 1910 to 1951. The total number taken up to 1951 was 193,328 mainly adult male elephant seals, which produced 299,000 barrels of oil or 1.6 barrels per seal (several times the return from the 19th-century uncontrolled slaughter of males, females and pups).

The number of seals that could be taken was revised annually. For many years it was fixed at 6,000 – by 'rule of thumb' – but in 1948 and 1949 it was raised to 7,500 on the Magistrate's (Fleuret's) recommendation, and in 1950 to 9,000. The 1948–1950 quotas were not achieved, a warning sign. In 1951 the quota was set at 8,000, but in spite of extending the season to 25 November, the company was only able to take 7,877, the highest annual catch under the regulations. Until 1952 the quota was divided equally among the three divisions worked each year although their stocks were probably always unequal in size.

Following my work, quotas were allocated in proportion to my estimated size of the stocks within each division and certain other conditions were enforced. Until my work in 1951 sealing regulations had been predominantly ad hoc. The South Georgia sealing industry was under government control from the beginning of the 20th century until it ceased in 1964 with the end of the whaling industry at South Georgia, to which it had been subsidiary. Despite its arbitrary regulation until my results were available, it was probably the most successfully managed of all marine 'fisheries' industries.

The final years of whaling and sealing were in the hands of a new company, Albion Star (South Georgia) Ltd, which took over the sealing licence from Pesca in June 1960. However, it suspended sealing in 1962 because 'the decision was bound up with the falling price of both whale and seal oil and the company's increasing difficulty in obtaining a viable whale catch'.

In 1963 the company sub-let its lease to the International Fishery Company (IFC), a consortium of three Japanese whaling companies that applied to the Falkland Islands government for a sealing licence, which was granted. However there was no resumption of sealing and in 1964 the industry closed.

* * * *

The Magistrate's annual report for 1936 stated that although there was no sign of diminution of numbers, the animals were vacating the large open beaches for smaller beaches often inaccessible to sealers. The reports for 1939 and 1945 also remarked on the increase in the size of the colonies on these smaller beaches. In 1951 when comparing photographs taken in earlier years with what I could then see, it was evident that many of the large, best beaches were under-populated. I interpreted this declining use of the prime beaches as being to avoid seal catchers. Again, while on its own this did not confirm overall decline, it suggested a level of stress that complemented lower catcher's day's work (CDW), the differences in harem sizes and breeding bulls' ages.

From my research I had sex ratios at birth (estimated from detailed sexed samples of newborn calves and foetuses) and had developed accurate ageing criteria (from growth rings in the teeth). Now able to age animals, I had established average growth rates, longevity and ages of the sexes at sexual maturity. In addition the post-mortem material allowed me to estimate annual pregnancy rates (82 per cent of mature females). From the close study on sample beaches – Dartmouth Point, Hestesletten, Maiviken and Discovery Point – I had established mortality of the young between birth and weaning was 2 per cent. Combined with the accumulated counts of both sexes coming ashore to breed and moult and the ratios of bulls to cows, I could estimate not just overall numbers, but the population's basic age class components. On top of all this we had the size of commercial catches in previous years and the age composition of animals taken in 1951.

This substantial body of information invited comparison with our own demography. Human life tables present a tabular numerical representation of mortality and survivorship of a cohort at birth at each subsequent year of life. It comprises an array of measures, including probabilities of death, probabilities of survival and life expectancies at various ages. The original data are to be found in archives of births, deaths and marriages, etc. In 1951 life tables were well established for people, but novel for wild animals, particularly large mammals. A paper by E. S. Deevey (1947) is now a 'citation classic' (if ages of wild animals – alive, found dead or extinct – are known, 'fates of oysters and song birds can be quantitatively compared with the fates of people and fruit flies'). I had been fortunate to come across it when in Cambridge in 1950 after my first two-year Antarctic sojourn. Life table notation had not previously been used in field ecology. Yet it guided my thoughts when analysing the population dynamics, management and conservation of the world's largest elephant seal population. After all, I now had the information to do so.

* * * *

124

My data allowed me to make the first population model (in terms of both numbers and biomass at age) for the South Georgia elephant seal population (and possibly the first for any large mammal).

I now had sufficient material to present the Governor of the Falkland Islands with a programme for the future of the elephant sealing industry. I advocated continuing the policy of protecting females from the sealers, to produce as large a pup crop as possible, and limiting offtakes to males only.

I recommended that the stock of breeding bulls should equal one twelfth of the estimated stock of adult cows, and by promoting an average harem size of twelve, and raising the average age of bulls on the beaches from 4.5 to 7.5 years by only allowing 6,000 bulls above a certain size to be taken, the quota would be sustainable indefinitely. The reduced quota would be compensated for by the higher yields from these older animals as well as taking as much as possible during the beginning of the breeding season when bulls coming ashore are in their best condition. The highest blubber oil production per animal was 2.3 barrels per seal in August–September at the beginning of the breeding season, which progressively declined to 2.1 barrels through October, and by November to 1.8. In the March–April moult the yield remained low at this level.

I also recommended that teeth be routinely collected, the catch correctly aged, and that the government should employ a seal inspector to monitor numbers and catches. I stressed that these proposals were only a first step and that as their results became apparent and in the light of unpredictable influences that might arise, they should be open to appropriate modification.

While my scientific findings were greatly rewarding in themselves, incorporating them into new legislation and putting a small industry on a managed and sustainable basis was, I believe, the most important practical result of my work in 1951.

* * * *

One area in which my suggestions came to nothing was in changing the way sealing was carried out. Taking only blubber and leaving the carcasses to rot on the beaches was wasteful. At best the blubber and skin accounted for some 40 per cent of the body weight. As early as 1926 – the year of my birth – it had been demonstrated that the remaining 60 per cent of the carcass could increase the oil yield by as much as 26 per cent and the rest could be rendered into meat and bone meal. In 1954 the company estimated that full-use carcasses should produce 16 per cent more oil and 316 kg of meal. Further experiments in 1956 and 1957 confirmed a 16 per cent increase in oil produced and an average of about 250 kg of meal per seal.

At 1951 prices, such higher yields would have increased the value of a season's sealing from about £109,000 (£2,006,000 in 2004) to some £182,000 (£3,350,000 in 2004). The biggest drawback to achieving these better returns was the small size of the sealing vessels, which limited the volume of product per trip. The only feasible solution seemed to be to have a small factory ship, with a fleet of smaller vessels to capture and deliver the seals to it for processing. I explored this possibility in 1951 with a senior executive of Pesca (Mr Holland) and it was considered again in 1957 but rejected on economic grounds.

The sealing industry at that time was very economical and as seal oil was equivalent to the highest grade of whale oil, the product value was high. In terms of capital investment the costs were low because they were met from the whale catch. The sealing vessels were obsolete old whale catchers, the cost of which had already been written off. Their running expenses were low. Their equipment was unsophisticated, manpower was in monetary terms unskilled, though rich in experience. In a nutshell, as conducted, the companies were getting a valuable product with equipment that had already been paid for by whaling. Putting a factory on the water would call for a substantial new investment at a time when doubts about the future of whaling were already being voiced.

* * * *

When my recommendations turned out to be succeeding, a full-time sealing inspector was appointed in 1956, the additional safeguard of sample counts introduced and marking experiments begun. Although it steps outside the chronological progression of my life that this memoir has been following, it is appropriate here to briefly review the consequences of my recommendations until the sealing industry ended in 1964. By 1958 the size and composition of the catch came close to fulfilling the conditions necessary for obtaining the maximum sustained yield of males. By reducing the time in which seals could be taken, focussing it on the breeding season and ensuring all bulls taken were above the size limit, CDW levels rose from 27.6 seals in 1949–52, to 34.3 seals/CDW in 1955–58 – that was by 26.1 per cent. – the oil yield rose by 33 per cent (to 2.2 barrels per seal), and by 1961 the average age of the catch rose from 6.7 years to 7.7 – in the order of my target of 7.5.

Long after my work in 1948–51, Carrick and Ingham (1960) published a paper that confirmed the accuracy of my age data and population models. Their work was greatly enhanced through being able to compare ages estimated from teeth layers of known-age animals, branded as pups and collected later in life. They also analysed data from Heard Island on elephant seal long-term survival, estimating total recruitment at birth at Macquarie and Heard Island was 110,000 pups and finding the overall population was 3.5 times this. This was the same as my estimate (3.5 – range 3.2–3.8) for an unexploited herd at South Georgia. They also concluded that there was a 27 per cent survival rate for 6-year-old females at Macquarie Island, amazingly close to my figure of 27.5 per cent for the 6-year-old female cohort at South Georgia. Their findings were very gratifying!

In 1973, intensive counts of the whole coastline of South Georgia in 1985 and 1995, showed pup numbers were 102,000 in 1985 and 110,000 in 1995! The elephant seal population seemed stable between the 1950s and 2004.

Lest my writing suggest that no one else has contributed to this satisfactory state, my research has been followed by others, notably the sealing inspectors, and in particular Nigel Bonner, who refined and expanded the body of my work. It was merely my good fortune to have been first in a queue of very competent scientists who have worked on South Georgia and in the Antarctic.

10

Cambridge and the Arctic

Later in 1952, I returned to Europe, on *John Biscoe* from South Georgia to Stanley, then to Montevideo aboard *Fitzroy*, sleeping in the day cabin of Captain Freddie White; it was difficult to obtain a normal berth! (Freddie, who was also from Tyneside, and his Falkland Island wife Nel, were by now good friends.) We went via Rio Gallegos in Patagonia, with a cargo of 250 sheep. Our course was over the Falklands Shelf's shallow waters which are notoriously rough. The sheep were loose on the foredeck and in the storm we lost all but twenty. The diversion to Rio Gallegos was to deliver the sheep for slaughter at a freezer plant, so the journey was not profitable for their owner!

From Patagonia we went on to Montevideo where I boarded the RMS *Alcantara*, calling at Rio, Las Palmas and Madeira, before stopping off at Lisbon where I had arranged to stay with Maureen and her family in Estoril – 'Spring in Portugal' was the currently popular *fado* song.

We had a very agreeable fortnight together. I got to know Maureen's father, Leonard, and mother, Bonnie, (her maiden name was Dundee!). From Portugal I returned to Cambridge to finish my PhD research, but knowing that Maureen would soon be coming over to London.

My younger brother Michael was now an undergraduate, having come up to Cambridge in 1949 as an exhibitioner of St Catharine's college reading natural sciences, making him the third Laws brother to do so. Registered for a PhD, still with Sydney Smith as my mentor and supervisor, I was awarded a research scholarship, then worth about £800 a year (£13,400 now). Entitled to a set of free rooms in college just off the main court, I got all my meals free. I was also appointed a university demonstrator in Part I Zoology, working in the zoology practicals with Anna Bidder (later first President of Lucy Cavendish College) and George Hughes (later Professor of Zoology at Bristol University). In addition I had my salary from FIDS (a princely £400 a year, equivalent to £6,030 now) and was sufficiently 'well off' to contribute £75 a year to my brother Michael's costs as a student as a way of repaying my parents.

At that time Cath's had only about ten PhD students. They included Donald Ramsay and Norman Sheppard, Doug Wilkinson, Leo Wolfe and Frank Merrett – the first two later becoming FRSs. We all got on well and I was fortunate in joining my brother Mike's social circle, which included Gordon Lowther reading anthropology and archaeology (who was later to be a close colleague in Kenya in the 1960s), Colin McLean, who became Ambassador in Oslo, and Bob Heron, later Director of the Duke of Edinburgh's Award Scheme. It also contained Margaret, who married Peter Raftery (the First Secretary at the British High Commission in Nairobi who became a close friend) and Peter Hall (to become a Cambridge architect) among others.

Our social life was good, when I could drag myself away from my research. I still knew many people in Cambridge, including the FIDS geologist Ray Adie now nearing the end of his PhD; we spent a lot of time together and regularly met up for morning coffee, at the Bun Shop or Copper Kettle to compare notes. We saw Bunny Fuchs when he came up from his London office on Friday mornings to discuss our progress.

I was allocated a large room on the ground floor of the Museum of Zoology with plenty of space to unpack and lay out my specimens (having consigned seventy-three elephant seal skulls to the BM in London). The material to get through without assistance included sectioning seals teeth, and preparing sections and slides for studying histology of reproductive organs, including ovaries, uterus and vagina, pituitary, testis and epididymis, and photo-micrographing them. The volume of results was too long for my thesis ('The Reproduction of the Southern Elephant Seal') and I was writing several papers in parallel for separate publication.

As my field work counted as only one year (three academic terms), and having done two terms in 1951, I had a minimum of four more terms of formal residence to put in before I could submit my dissertation.

Later in the summer Maureen and her parents came up to Cambridge for a few days to be shown around. She was twenty-one that year and had come over to the UK to get a job as an air hostess, but it didn't work because she was too tall. So she took a secretarial job in a small family fashion store called Heyworth's in Cambridge, and lodged in a house run by Danuta Smaczny and her Polish ex-RAF husband. Danuta had lost her family during the war. Sophisticated and charming, she is still a good friend fifty years on.

**Maureen Holmes,
my wife-to-be**

* * * *

My Cambridge period was interrupted when a friend from student days, Arthur Lee, now an oceanographer at the Fisheries Laboratory, Lowestoft, invited me to join his team doing a hydrographic survey in the Arctic and to carry out experimental fishing off Greenland. I jumped at the chance and in August 1952 took five weeks' leave. Our ship was the RV *Ernest Holt*. She was no bigger than a commercial trawler, but I shared a luxurious cabin with Arthur; we had a huge en-suite bathroom, but water had to be rationed. The wardroom was comfortable and the skipper, Captain Aldiss, was a very good chap.

On the very rough voyage north we crossed the Arctic Circle on 22 August and arrived off Bear Island on the 25th. The island had a weather station on its north side, but its claim to fame was said to be a horse which lived only on polar bear meat, and two mad Norwegians who spent their days shovelling coal out of one hole into another then back again – and their nights boozing!

On our arrival the sun came out and the waves smoothed so we had a glorious morning trawling for fish about 22 miles south but in sight of the island at nearly 75° N. We shot the trawl in 80 fathoms for the 'breakfast haul' and got about five baskets of fish, not much but including cod and tiger catfish. From this we could each select a fish to be cooked by the steward, a Newfoundlander ('Newfy' naturally) for our breakfast.

Various other trawlers and a long liner were in our vicinity, but reported worse catches than ours. At noon we came up to the position of our first planned scientific sampling station, with Bear Island astern and east of us. I helped Philip Tallantyre (another friend from undergraduate days, now a research officer in

Arthur's team) with plankton hauling on the first two stations. At each the ship was stopped and the depth measured. If it was deep enough we sent down two series of Nansen water bottles to 1,200 m (off Greenland we hoped to get down to 3,000 m). These bottles have thermometers affixed to them and by an ingenious mechanism, first developed by the Norwegian explorer Nansen, samples of water are taken at specified depth intervals. These were analysed for saltiness, dissolved oxygen and temperature. Next we lowered an instrument called a bathy-thermograph that drew a graph of the temperatures on a smoked glass slide, to a depth of 140 m. While this was going on two others made plankton hauls, sending a special net down to 600 m and hauling it up slowly. The plankton samples captured were bottled in fixative solution for later microscopic analysis.

Next day in bad weather I was up at 5 a.m. to help Arthur at the next sampling station where again water was collected from different depths. While moving between stations, I spent time on the bridge talking with Captain Aldiss. Asking about seals I was told that they (from his description harp seals) were often caught in the trawls. The weather improved and we found ourselves sailing into the sun. The sea was becoming calmer all the time and interesting cloud shapes on the horizon relieved the seascapes. We saw a number of fin whales in the mirror-calm sea, blowing and splashing. The day's last bathy-thermograph and plankton hauls were made at 9 p.m. after which the weather again deteriorated.

It was very rough during the night and with an overcast sky and low visibility we sighted Jan Mayen Island at 10 a.m., first a low cape and then higher land, cloud-capped, but with snow patches visible. Blue sky appeared and the clouds cleared progressively throughout the day, so that we had a fine view of Beerenberg, the mountain named after a Dutch admiral and nearly 8,000 ft high. It had a truncated volcanic cone covered in snow and ice, with glaciers flowing down the sides like streams of molten white lava. The position and size of the moraines indicated a great regression of the former icecap had taken place. The strange cliff rock formations were reminiscent of Deception Island in the Antarctic. Though there was a Norwegian weather station on the island we saw no one, but did three bottom temperature casts and bathy-thermographs and two trawls. The hauls consisted mainly of *Chlamys* (clams or 'queens'), capelins, with other fish, starfish, urchins and some large, very tasty, prawns (*Sclerocrangon*).

The trawl was torn during the second haul and we fixed the position of the rock, and then with the island glowing orange in the evening sun, and Beerenberg

Minke whale (*Balaenoptera acutorostris*) breaching

towering majestically above, we headed south for Iceland. Next day the weather cleared until in the afternoon the sky was cloudless and the bright sunshine glittered and sparkled on the sea surface. An American plane flew over from the south-west and buzzed us several times; it was probably curious because there was little shipping in these waters. The skipper put up the ensign, but the halyard broke and a tattered rag hung from the flagstaff!

On 30 August Iceland came in sight looking forbidding in the grey light and battered by heavy seas. Along the west coast we passed the mouths of numerous fjords that indented a flat-topped table land with scattered snow patches. This plateau ended abruptly in precipitous high cliffs exposing layered strata of both lava and ash.

We anchored late, in the middle of the approaches to Reykjavik, and tried to attract a pilot, but didn't get alongside the quay until about 1 a.m. The day dawned fine. The ship's agent, Geir Zoega, took a party of us to see the sights: the pool where criminals used to be drowned, the world's first parliament – the Althing – the Reykir geysers and the greenhouses around them where carnations, tomatoes, lettuce, and even bananas grew, and the hydroelectric plant at Irafoss. It gave an amazing impression of controlled power with its massive, humming turbo generators. As we were leaving, the man in charge – only one was needed because of the nature of the controls – asked if we would like to see a waterfall. He turned a handle and opened one of the sluice gates in the wall of the dam so that a torrent of foaming white water rushed over the bare rocks beneath us as we gazed from the observation window. It was awe-inspiring. Then touching the control again he cut off the water and the rocks below appeared once more. It was an impressive demonstration of man's power over nature that nearly swept away an unfortunate fly fisherman in the flood!

Throughout, the scenery was impressive: barren lava plains and flows; rolling country dotted with dwarf willows and birch trees, craggy mountains with the active volcano Hekla away to our east. Altogether it was an interesting and enjoyable interlude.

Leaving Reykjavik in the early evening in bright sunshine we travelled westward under a beautiful moon, planning to spend the next seventeen days off south and south-eastern Greenland, before returning to Grimsby via Reykjavik and Aberdeen.

The routine hydrographic work, collecting water and plankton samples at different depths and deploying the bathy-thermograph, was interspersed with trawling for fish, and continued throughout our time in Greenland waters. We measured 385 cod, taking otoliths from 100 (for age determination), stomach contents and other collections. We also weighed a sample of fish to establish liver weight in relation to body weight; a cod of 7–8 lbs has a liver of only 4–5 oz, at this time of year. Then a succession of accidents occurred – trouble with the bathy-thermograph winch, breaking the trawl headline and sideline, tearing the net on rocks, or through overloading with heavy loads of sponges from these relatively untrawled banks. It gave me a good apprenticeship in the realities of the trawlerman's life.

The weather on the whole was very good, including some splendidly clear days with wonderful views. The coastal mountains were bare, rocky and pinnacled, typical glaciered country, a mountaineer's paradise, with sheer walls, serrated knife-edge ridges and extensive aiguille formations. The hills were very varied in shape and colour and the watery atmosphere lent depth and an air of grandeur to the scene. It was a distinctive and beautiful coast, but dangerous on account of the off-lying islands and grounded bergs. We counted seventy of these, one carrying a block of rock the size of a cottage. The icebergs made navigation difficult, particularly at night. Everywhere the landscape pointed to a recent history of glaciation. Our farthest north position was the aptly named Cape Desolation. We saw many icebergs and one night an extensive and colourful auroral display. I made several sketches with compass bearings to conspicuous navigational features of parts of the coastline – Cape Desolation area, Sermersok and Cape Farewell – for the Admiralty's *Arctic Pilot*, which contained no illustrations of the west coast.

By 11 September we had moved down to the Cape Farewell region again – in *flatta* calm as the Icelanders would say – and found sixteen trawlers working in the lee of Eggers Island, trawling in territorial waters. There was a temperature inversion layer where the smoke from the trawlers spread out in a thin black band and was visible from miles away. In the cold layer below the inversion were startling mirage effects – floating islands, icebergs looking huge, and a trawler that appeared to be a full-rigged sailing ship. Later we went in among the trawlers. They were making fairly good catches, going round and round in circles, one behind another.

In due course we turned and headed for Reykjavik. I stood on the bridge and watched a most impressive display of the Northern Lights – huge curtains of green rippling in the sky. We had been having a beard contest, for which the captain had offered a bottle of whisky as a prize. Beards to be judged by length, thickness, curliness, colour and sex appeal! In Reykjavik the steward and I had been neck and neck for first place; his was black, mine blond but already with grey streaks! It was time to judge the results: Scottie one, Newfy runner-up (only one vote behind).

We left Iceland on 18 September, called in at Aberdeen where we sold our catch, then on to Grimsby to sign off. I now had Arctic experience to compare with the Antarctic and, as always, had thoroughly enjoyed time in the field. I took a very large Greenland halibut with me back to Cambridge, where I presented it to the High Table at St Catharine's College and settled down to completing my PhD thesis. Maureen was still in Cambridge and life was good.

* * * *

I had been admitted to the Degree of Master of Arts (MA), University of Cambridge. This degree was awarded for a small fee (five years after being awarded a first degree). Importantly it meant that, as a senior member of the university, one could now be out at night without having to wear a gown – a regulation that otherwise applied to undergraduates and recent graduates.

In January 1953, Maureen and I took a ship to Norway to ski. We stayed at the youth hostel or *Ungdomsherberge*, in Lillehammer (where Gwen and Maureen had stayed in 1951 when they were hitch hiking around Scandinavia). We had thirteen days' holiday, inclusive of everything from Newcastle to Oslo return by ship, train to Lillehammer, the stay in the youth hostel and a hotel one night, for £23 each! (The equivalent after inflation is £385 today). It was an interesting and enjoyable holiday though the snow could have been better for skiing, especially because of Maureen's limited skill. We did a bit of ice skating, which neither of us had done for years, and she told me that I almost went off with a beautiful Norwegian girl who skated like an angel! Of course I don't remember that.

In July, Ray Adie, who Maureen had also known for some time, and Aileen, were married at St. John's College and I was best man. Bunny and Joyce Fuchs and their daughter Hilary were also at the wedding as were other FIDS friends.

Near Lillehammer, Norway

Later that month I took Maureen to the Lake District for the first time and we stayed with my elderly Quaker friends, Freda and Cuthbert Woods, who had looked after me during the war years when my school was evacuated from Whitley

136

Bay. I had loved my time there and knew the entire district very well indeed. The Woods' house and garden were beautiful and overlooked Lake Windermere. They had a small sailing dinghy, which we used; I had sailed her many times in my younger days. Maureen's first long walk was up Fairfield, near Grasmere: this was a horseshoe ridge walk that went on and up, on and up, on and then down and down, all day and without water. Maureen passed this test and we did become engaged! It was superb swimming in the cool rocky pools of the lovely river flowing from Langstrath, near Stonethwaite, in Borrowdale, where we later came to camp. There were little waterfalls to cool off under as well. She certainly fell in love with the Lake District.

After six months or so working at Heyworth's, she decided to try fashion modelling and went for an interview at Majorie Molyneaux's agency. It was a wet day so she was in boots and raincoat. All the other hopefuls were in very high heels and little black dresses! In spite of her boots she was told that she walked very well and yes, they would take her for training. So she moved to London, having found a small, newly finished flat at 5, Emperor's Gate, Gloucester Road. Eventually she also found a flat-mate, Heather Watty, whose parents lived in Portugal, and for the next year modelled in various fashion houses including Harvey Nichols. She quite enjoyed it and she loved to put on the attractive clothes, but it was boring much of the time, so in Harvey Nichols she used to help sell the clothes. She enjoyed doing that and was enthusiastic and honest in her opinions! I would come down to visit, usually at weekends. I supervised her when she was trying to cook a roast in the oven for lunch and I bought her a first cookery book, the *Penguin Cookery Book*, which she still uses though now in 2004 it is very tattered!

At that time FIDS had no future jobs to offer and I had been looking around. My success was well known to the FIDS Scientific Committee and some members like Colin Bertram and Brian Roberts and of course Bunny were thinking about my future. As it happened Dr Neill Mackintosh, who had done classic studies on the large whales from South Georgia and who was now Deputy Director of the NIO, was a member of this committee. He offered me a permanent appointment at the NIO in the small group of three comprising the Whale Biology Section. The laboratories were located at Wormley in Surrey and the starting salary was reasonable, though not munificent. Maureen and I discussed this prospect in depth. I had no doubt that I could obtain an academic research post elsewhere, perhaps in Cambridge, where I was known. But whale research sounded interesting and had a practical purpose – to work much as I had done on seals – towards understanding the biology of the larger whales and to contribute to their sustainable management and conservation. It would also be my first permanent and pensionable job. We decided that I should take up this appointment as a senior scientific officer at the NIO and this meant being part of the Royal Navy Scientific Service.

As at least nine tenths of a large whale's life is spent under the surface in the vast remote reaches of the world's oceans, it was not then possible to study their population ecology by direct observation. However, there were three main ways of doing this indirectly. First, inferences about distribution and abundance could be made from sightings of their conspicuous blows at the surface. Secondly, by firing whale tags into their blubber, (hopefully recovered later when they were killed by whalers) other inferences could be drawn – about their migrations between the Antarctic feeding grounds in summer and breeding areas in winter, and perhaps over time about their age and abundance. Thirdly, the most promising method, the basis of Mackintosh's classic studies with Wheeler in the 1920s and 1930s, was to examine the carcasses of whales killed in the whaling industry – either on shore stations or in pelagic whaling factories on the high seas. The observations and measurements of the dead whales and collection of organs for subsequent study of feeding, growth, reproduction and age could be a primary source of information, and would provide validation for later non-invasive research methods. I had gained much experience of this approach in my elephant seal research and had already seen whales being processed at the whaling stations on South Georgia.

Such material could best be obtained by joining a commercial expedition where a fleet of whale catchers caught whales of several species and delivered them to a mother ship – a floating factory – for rendering to oil, bone meal and meat meal, frozen meat and other by-products such as meat extract. The floating factories were just that, contained within a large hull designed with a stern slipway leading to decks where the whales were dismembered and sent into the factory below. While these operations were taking place it was possible for a biologist to collect research material. But space was at a premium; every berth had to be filled by a worker with no room for supernumeraries. However, the International Whaling Commission (IWC) called for each factory ship to accommodate two government whaling inspectors. Their duties were to record and ensure that whaling was carried out in accordance with the regulations on the whaling season, minimum lengths, prohibition on catching protected species or lactating or 'milk whales' of any species. They also imposed fines for infringements, set by the IWC.

I started my new job as a Junior Whaling Inspector, employed by the Ministry of Agriculture, Fisheries and Food (MAFF) for a 6–7 month whaling voyage on a British registered factory ship, the 23,000 ton *Balaena*. I received briefings from the MAFF and the NIO, and read up some of the relevant literature.

I also submitted my PhD thesis, and the oral examination was conducted in October 1953 by Colin Bertram (Director of the Scott Polar Research Institute) and Leo Harrison Matthews FRS (Director of Science, Zoological Society of London). They gave me a good grilling but recommended that I had reached the required standard. Now I was ready for the next big adventure in my life.

11

Whaling on *Balaena*

Towards the end of October 1953 Maureen and I travelled up to Newcastle and Whitley Bay by train and a few days later Maureen and Dad saw me off at the quayside on MS *Blenheim* to Oslo. I was going to join the floating factory ship FF *Balaena* and would be away at sea for seven months. When I got back Maureen and I were to be married in Portugal.

The trip across was uneventful. I read a little, slept a bit and talked with Commander Henry Buckle, RN ret., a very agreeable chap, who was to be the Senior Whaling Inspector and already had several years of experience on the *Balaena*. We arrived at Oslo in the early morning of 29 October to be met by the secretary of the *Balaena*, Ole Ness-Jensen, who took us to Tönsberg and the ship, owned by Hector Whaling, a British company. I found it tidier than I had expected. She was lying in deep water close inshore, moored to rocks on the beach. A small motor boat ran between ship and shore.

My cabin was aft, to one side of the slipway at the stern up which the whales were hauled. It was small and I was to share it until Cape Town with the young Third Chemist James Clifton, after which I might get a cabin to myself. I had some space allocated to me in the chemical laboratory, near the stern and one deck down from the main deck – the after-plan.

We left on Guy Fawkes Day, 5 November 1953, after seven hours' swinging the compass and testing the direction-finding and other radio equipment. Meals were at unaccustomed times: breakfast 7:30 a.m., lunch 11:30 a.m., coffee

3.00 p.m. and supper 6:00 pm. I was to fall into a regular routine of working until near supper time, then cleaning up and showering. Each day I got the ship's position from the bridge and certain other information and wrote it up in my journal. On the 9 November at noon we were in the middle of the Bay of Biscay – the sea quite calm for a large ship like us, but other ships were bucking about. The *Balaena* was so long and so huge (23,000 tons) that it took a big sea to make her move at all. I walked about on deck in the afternoons, watching the crew splicing wire strops, making wooden toggles, painting and doing other jobs. They also laid the false deck (a wooden deck that covered the real deck to protect it from the heavy wear and staining with blood and oil during the whaling season).

I had a cable from home saying that I had been awarded my PhD degree and threw a little party on the strength of it. Seven of us got through a bottle of gin in half an hour – as with the whalers at South Georgia, it was a hard-drinking community. The wardrobe in my cabin now contained two cases of gin and one of whisky, with two cases of gin under the washbasin, and a bottle presented by the captain to each of the officers. At duty-free prices the spirits were ridiculously cheap – as I recall gin was 8s/6d and whisky 10s/6d!

Now let me introduce the people I lived with on this long voyage. Commander Buckle, already mentioned, was a charming 64-year-old rascal. Christopher Ash (Chris), was the Chief Chemist – a degree from Cambridge, about 35 years old and a very good chap. Alec Robertson, a little older, was the meat expert who selected the whale meat suitable for freezing (for pet food) and rejected meat which had deteriorated. He had spent six years at Smithfield Market in London, originally came from Newcastle and drank like the proverbial fish but could take it. He also knew Portugal well. Richard Sheppard (Shep) was the radar man and chief technician or boffin concerned with all radio, electrical and electronic work and projected the films on film nights – but he was more than a mere technician as we were to discover later in the voyage. Mitchell (Mitch) was a freezer engineer who provided the cold for freezing meat. He spoke Norwegian well and drank too much, but was a pleasant chap. Ole Ness-Jensen did all the office work and administration; he was very capable and had an English wife. Jim Clifton, the third chemist with whom I was sharing a cabin, was not as insufferable as I had thought at first but was still a bit of a nuisance. Our Captain Virik was a very good sort, a bit reticent but friendly; he served in the Royal Navy during the war, as did many of the Norwegians, and he also had an English wife. Finally there was Hugh Simons, the Second Chemist who joined us at Cape Town, and Harry Weeks, the winchman who hauled whales aboard. I didn't get to know Harry until whales were being taken in the Southern Ocean, but he was interested in my work and went out of his way to notify me when specimens he knew I was interested in were coming aboard.

We had lifeboat drill, which involved mustering at the lifeboat stations, while the boats were launched. But it took over three-quarters of an hour before the first boat was in the water; then the engines of the motor boats wouldn't start! This inefficiency didn't augur very well for a real emergency, particularly in the Southern Ocean.

Our last landfall would be Cape Town. Each day I was writing up my two journals – an official one for NIO and a private one for myself. The most interesting happening those days was a school of killer whales – about thirty of them. They passed by the ship during the afternoon, moving quite leisurely, and all one could see was the sharp fin – like a shark's. They are said to attack and kill other whales and seals like a pack of wolves. One was seen to breach. The Norwegians call them *spekkhogger* – blubber chopper – because they feed on the blubber and especially the tongues of other whales. One afternoon the steering gear broke down and the ship's course became very erratic; the engineers used the two engines to steer until the mechanism was repaired. Cdr Buckle gave a little party to introduce me to the doctor's wife – so he said! There were several wives on board: the captain's, the doctor's and the secretary's.

It was a lot cooler when there was a good breeze and one afternoon I worked on a painting in the lab – from a sketch I did at Lillehammer in the snow with Maureen. I spent quite a time sitting in the commander's cabin writing and listening to the BBC; it was more comfortable than my own.

The day before we reached Cape Town, we saw the first of the Antarctic birds, a wandering albatross with a wing span of about ten feet – flying ever so gracefully in the wake of the ship. These birds would be with us all the time further south. Fortunately, although there were a lot of people on deck practising shooting with air rifles, nobody shot it so we didn't expect to have the trouble that beset the Ancient Mariner!

On 30 November we had wonderful distant blue-tinged views of the Cape Peninsula – Table Mountain, flat-topped, the Devil's Peak, Twelve Apostles and the Lion's Head – a hazy blue in the distance. Cape Town undulated over the slopes surrounding the mountain. To the east of us, on the far side of the enormous bay, was a low-lying sandy coast which looked rather interesting – probably in the vicinity of Saldanha Bay (where there was a shore whaling station). The water was muddy grey-brown instead of the deep-sea blue to which we had become accustomed and the shallow water made the swell more noticeable. Coastal birds flew to and from their fishing grounds – the shags in long lines low over the water and the black and white boobies very gracefully but seemingly aimlessly. Small schools of penguins were in the water – Cape penguin or jackass – and a number of fur seals porpoised away from the bows of the ship; I had one under close observation beside a piece of kelp. The sun was shining, the wind blowing and all was right with the world.

Balaena came into the harbour that afternoon and tied up. When Customs formalities were completed, the whale catchers came alongside and began to load up with stores and take on fuel oil. Hugh Symons, Second Chemist, came aboard, sporting a huge black beard. He had been on the *Balaena* the previous season in my position (Junior Whaling Inspector), stayed in South Africa during the off season and was coming down again, now working for the company. He was a zoologist and a student at Queens' College, Cambridge. He invited me ashore to a party arranged for some of the others – Chris Ash, Shep, Alec, Hugh and myself. We were joined by four attractive girls. We danced and drank champagne on the terrace until the place closed at midnight. It was really very romantic, but I wished that Maureen could have been there instead.

On Tuesday 2 December, after two days in Cape Town, we were off to the Antarctic. On Thursday the catchers reported ice 100 miles ahead. On 5 December we were at 50° S latitude and it was thought probable that the first whale would be caught the next day. In fact three sperm whales were caught, inflated with compressed air and brought to *Balaena*, where they were tied up astern to be worked up when more had been caught. Our position was now about 56° S, 19° E, and we passed the first iceberg that afternoon. It was massive, about 120 ft high, with three gleaming white pinnacles rising from the sea. A fairy-tale castle may be cliché but is the best way to describe it. All day we were in thick fog and steaming at reduced speed. I entertained in my cabin and we drank to the first whales. The following day work began in earnest.

* * * *

Commercial whaling came under the International Convention for the Regulation of Whaling (ICRW) and the schedule to the Convention was amended as necessary at meetings of the IWC. In that 1953–54 season, sperm whales could be caught at any time and there was no catch quota for them. The baleen whaling season began on 2 January, but there were further restrictions on blue and humpback whales. The blue whale season began on 16 January and humpback whaling was limited to a specific four days from 1–4 February. There was an overall catch quota for baleen whales of 15,000 blue whale units (BWU); one BWU was equivalent to one blue whale, two fin whales, four humpback whales or six sei whales. At that time the other baleen whale species, the small minke whale, was not hunted, because it was not considered commercially valuable. The Bureau of International Whaling Statistics (BIWS) based in Sandefjord, Norway, kept records of the whales caught as they were sent in by radio from the individual expeditions. As the baleen whales quota in BWUs was approached towards the end of the season, the BIWS made a daily revision of the expected date of the attainment of the quota as it was approached. Then a few days before it estimated the quota would be reached, the bureau notified all expeditions by radio of the date of the end of the season. This was usually in early April, so we could expect a whaling season of about four to four and a half months of unremitting toil.

FF *Balaena*

Each expedition had two whaling inspectors, appointed by the respective governments, to see that the rules were obeyed. These included areas closed to whaling, the minimum size limit for whales caught and the prohibition on catching lactating females. Work went on continuously over the 24 hours, except when there were no whales to be processed, due either to bad weather or lack of whales. Apart from the ship's officers and crew, who worked normal seagoing watches, everyone else on board worked a system of two 12-hour shifts.

On 7 December I examined my first whale! During the night there were sundry clanking and rattling noises and I looked out of my cabin port at 2:30 a.m. and saw one sperm whale lying on deck. I looked out again at 5:30 a.m. to see whether I should get up and saw three sperm whales in the slipway, just below my porthole. Strange bedfellows! After breakfast at 8 o'clock, one of these was worked up, and I followed all the operations on deck in a blizzard. It was a male, pulled up the slipway by a winch attached to a grab or 'tongs' that clasped the tail flukes. Virtually all sperm whales in the Antarctic are males, which migrate in the southern summer from tropical and subtropical waters to feed on Antarctic squid. (Females remain year round in warmer waters in family groups.)

First the flensers stripped off the blubber by attaching a hook, and by means of a winch and a wire cable peeled off a long strip as they cut with their flensing knives – large curved blades fitted to wooden handles about five feet long, which are continually sharpened by whetstones. I noted the sex, measured the length and the thickness of the blubber and made notes on the colour and external appearance, the presence of parasites and so on. When the blubber had been removed another cable was attached to the tail and it was hauled from the after-plan to the fore-plan, through an arch in the superstructure of the ship, called 'Hell's Gate'. On the fore-plan the meat was stripped off in similar fashion, and the head severed from the backbone and sawed up by the ten-foot steam saws. The backbone was cut up in the same way and all parts except the intestines and other offal cut into sizeable blocks, which went down through round holes in the deck for processing in the steam pressure boilers.

I collected some specimens, including two teeth from the lower jaw. In 80–90 minutes there was nothing left of a prehistoric monster which was 54 ft long and had weighed probably 70–80 tons. When there were more whales each one was processed in about half an hour, but this initial one was more leisurely and provided a good chance for me to see for the first time how it was all done.

Although I had seen the whaling operations at the shore stations at South Georgia, work on the floating factories is faster and much more hectic. I spent the rest of the day working on specimens and got my laboratory refrigerator going.

The following morning, although no whales had been caught I was up at 5:30 a.m., just to get into the hang of the routine. The two 12-hour shifts began and ended at midnight and noon, and I wondered how I would stand up to this working day, or longer, for four months.

From then on we often had bad weather – blizzards, strong winds and very rough seas, with low visibility – when catching rates slowed or stopped. At noon on 9 December we were at latitude 57°21' S, longitude 32 °48' E and the catchers ahead told us the fringe of the pack ice was about a hundred miles south. We were steaming on course 080 degrees, almost due east and parallel with the ice edge. There was a large tabular iceberg that day, the first real berg we had yet seen. It was about half a mile long and seemed about 200 ft high with a flat top like a table and caves cut in the cliffs by the waves – which I termed the whale hangars! There was no colour though, because it was such a dull day.

The following day was fine and sunny with little wind. I worked in the lab during the morning because no whales were coming in. They hauled the first ones up the slipway at about 1:30 p.m., and I worked on them until 5:30 pm. Then I had drinks with Shep in his cabin and listened to a gunner on the radio telling how he'd shot a whale with an experimental electric harpoon (there's only one) and had not been able to kill it. They were still putting current into it after half an hour, and it recovered every time they shut off the current. This was horrifying. If only it worked to plan, it would be such a blessing for it would kill the whale instantaneously and save much pain. It had been designed and built by a British firm of gunsmiths, Wesley-Richards, and the 'cannon' was a spigot-gun: instead of fitting inside the barrel of a gun as in a conventional whaling cannon, the harpoon shaft fitted over the gun barrel or spigot. It was supposed to have a flatter trajectory and thus be more accurate. The main problem was conducting the electricity to the whale, once the harpoon had struck. A flexible copper mesh conductor within the harpoon line was intended to be relatively elastic, but it often snapped when the tension came on the more elastic forerunner – the 'fishing line'. The Norwegians were conservative against the new technique, wishing to revert to the well-tried Svend Foyn gun.

There was good news on 12 December. I was working on deck examining whales when Mitch came along and told me there was a catcher, *Setter 3* going to Cape Town for repairs to the propeller. Naturally she would be taking mail and I had about half an hour to write to Maureen in order to catch it.

A few days later, on 14 December, at 50° S, 45 ° E. we were steaming along the fringe of the pack ice. There was great excitement for me, because I saw my first seals of the voyage – seven beautiful crabeaters – lying out on the floes. I thought then that seals would always be my first love in the animal world. There were great numbers of birds, which were really attractive, although not brightly coloured. The Antarctic petrels are brown and white. The cape pigeons are brown and white too, but in a different pattern and the blue petrel has slaty-blue wings, a bright cobalt-blue beak and legs the same colours with bright yellow webs. It is very smart, distinguished from the prions by a white tip to the tail feathers. The all-white snow petrel was my favourite though. White against white against snow, all one sees is the black bill and eye, looking just like an exclamation mark lying on its side. Similarly, in the dark of night, the sooty albatross has just the small white ring around the eye visible.

* * * *

On 16 December we had our first taste of real Antarctic weather. Outside there was a howling gale with the wind screaming past the ship (we were now in the 'shrieking sixties') blowing the tops off huge grey waves about 10–15 m (30–45 ft) high from trough to crest. It was much rougher than it should have been at that time of year and the rolling was just beginning to get unpleasant. Even so Ellefsen, the expedition's top gunner, caught one whale. At supper time we had to hang on to plates and other items in order to prevent them sliding off the table and then, as it got worse, we held onto our chairs to remain seated in them. All this on a very large ship.

Normally I would write up my log and diary for the day, then read a little. Hugh would knock on the wall and I'd go next door for a nightcap, or I would knock and he would come to my cabin. The drinks would probably be Benedictine or Van der Hum or Scotch whisky. There was still a *vestige* of civilisation!

But it was offset by reality. On a typical evening, outside my portholes would lie, side by side in the slipway, two very large, very dead, very ugly whales, so I kept my curtains drawn! Possibly during the night another whale would be hauled up the slipway and I might be rudely awakened as the whale claws, jockeying for position around the tail flukes, might slip and crash against the bulkhead near my head, with a deafening clang.

The weather continued rough. We received heavy snow, and passed through plenty of drift ice – small pieces of ice about six feet across which bobbed about in the water like so many apples in a tub. They do damp down the swell though and some nights it was comparatively calm.

We continued to move west and though expecting some we hadn't caught any whales for six days. If only I'd known there would be a gap of six days, I could have made an effort to do all kinds of things, but time had flown by just in talk and conviviality. I read a couple of books and did a little work on a paper for FIDS.

December 19 brought news that RRS *Bransfield* (the meat freezer ship with the expedition) with thirty-three bags of mail was expected alongside that night. At 11 p.m. the mail from *Bransfield* finally arrived and I collected mine in the commander's cabin. There were many letters from home and all sorts of people, but none from Maureen.

On 22 December we were heading east. The sea was calm, several catchers were near us, their lights reflected in the water, and the *Bransfield* also was in sight as well as the Norwegian factory ship *Abraham Larsen*.

The following day we moved eastwards at full speed almost at 30° E neither seeing nor catching sperm whales, with the catchers forming a line in front of us covering a broad transect across the endless ocean. In fact it looked as though there wouldn't be much activity until the long whale (baleen) season began on 2 January. That day we had a Christmas present from the company. I received a bottle of Haig Scotch, one of Norwegian brandy, four bottles of South African beer, five bottles of soda water and a bag containing nuts, figs, chocolate, a packet of cigarettes and a cigar. It seemed rather a nice gesture! It reminded me of the year before when I had been on a skiing holiday in Norway with Maureen and bought some chocolate with orange filling.

That night Jahre and Norheim, the day-shift foremen of the after-plan and fore-plan, came to my cabin for drinks after supper and I gave them each a bottle of whisky for Christmas; it should help to make my work move more smoothly! Christmas had begun on Christmas Eve when I had a bath at about 5 o'clock and changed into suit, collar and tie – very distinguished with beard! Then I went over the way for a drink with Hugh, Mitch and Frank Day (the electric harpoon expert). Christmas Dinner followed at 7 o'clock. It was very good: turkey and all the trimmings, and Christmas pudding, wines and crackers and flickering candles, paper hats in the crackers of course. Also, we each received a very fine leather cigarette case from the company with a picture of the *Balaena* embossed upon it. Things began to get uproarious and we had small booklets with carols in Norwegian and English, which the Norwegians began to sing – we joined in. Later we went to Frank's cabin and returned to the smoke room for coffee and liqueurs. Then we all visited Alex's cabin where Jim Clifton (who had just got up to start the night shift) fell fast asleep after two whiskies – like the dormouse in *Alice*. I must have been the Mad Hatter because later, returning to the smoke room with a guitarist and an accordion player, I kept asking for the record 'Spring in Portugal' – and finally got it. Back to another cabin and I left at midnight, but just as I was getting into bed Frank came along and said he had been deputed to bring me back. Well, I didn't get to bed until 3 o'clock, but it was a good evening.

On Boxing Day we were at 63° S; 44° E when our catchers radioed in that they had taken thirty whales before breakfast. It looked as though I would be rather busy. I was up at 5 o'clock and worked on deck all day until 8 o'clock in the evening, when *Setter 9* – the new diesel-engined catcher – arrived with mail from Cape Town, including a sixth letter for me from Maureen. I was so glad to get it only two weeks after she'd posted it.

The following day was beautiful, calm and clear. I worked on eleven whales and wrote up notes, cleaned specimens and so on. I took several photographs and finished the first reel of cine film on shots of *Setter 8* and *Terje 4* delivering whales at the stern of the *Balaena*, and of sperm whales being flensed and cut up. Our whale catchers were called *Setter* or *Terje* (after the dogs, setters and terriers) with a number. At sunset there was a glorious riot of colour along the horizon. Hugh and I stood on the poop and talked as the ship ploughed through the calm water with several whales towed from the stern. One was hauled aboard every twenty minutes, cut up and put into the factory, coming out as oil, meat meal and meat extract. The contrast with the living animals in their environment is immense and one forgets that side of it – the killing – in the hustle and bustle (one has to, for peace of mind).

On 28 December the whalers had found a large lump of ambergris in a sperm whale, weighing about 50 kilos – so at 35/- an ounce it was very valuable. I took a small a chunk of it – about an ounce – for a souvenir. It smelt like cow-dung (it is in fact a form of whale dung!), coming from the intestines of the sperm whale. It is thought to form by irritation set up by the hard beaks of the squid on which the whale feeds. I'm not so sure about that though, and think it may be caused by something quite different. In a year or two, if I kept it, it should have matured to a pleasant smell; it's used as a base for fixing the scent of the most expensive perfumes.

Setter 3 (which took the last mail out) would be back from Cape Town in a few days with another mail. Then *Biscoe*, an oil tanker (and not the *John Biscoe* I knew so well from FIDS days), would join us shortly afterwards. We were moving eastwards quite rapidly and it now seemed that we'd be fishing near the Ross Sea after all, just east of the Balleny Islands I expected. So we would probably return to Cape Town. I worked on seven sperm whales and my friend Harry Weeks, the British winchman on the after-plan, came in for a drink before supper – and to show me a whale carved from a sperm whale tooth.

New Year's Eve went off reasonably well, but I was glad when it was over. I had Hugh and Mitch in for drinks before the celebrations began. There were only three of us English there – Hugh, Mitch and myself – and the Norwegians were rather stodgy. The cocktail was quite good – rather like Bunny Fuchs' 'special', and roast pork for dinner. Tio Pepe sherry, white and red wine, coffee and liqueurs. Songs afterwards. The evening finished about 1.30 a.m. Hugh couldn't remember getting to bed – actually it was quite early. It was one of the more unusual of the many times I had seen in the New Year.

The ship seemed deserted on New Year's Day. There was no hangover for me but apparently everyone else had one (except Commander Buckle). As there were no whales to be worked up I read most of the day. Later we saw a film called *Wedding Bells* – which augured well for 1954! *Setter 3* returned from Cape Town. I'd gone to bed when, at 11:30 p.m., Mitch dropped a couple of letters inside my door: one from Maureen and a wonderful surprise and a good start for the year in which we would be married! The other letter was from NIO, as from November (when I became a senior scientific officer) my salary had increased to £875 a year, and next November it would go up by £50 (equal to at least £1,000 in 2004).

The baleen whale season began at midnight on 1–2 January, when twenty-two fin whales were caught. Mitch gave a 'by-products party' to mark the start of the frozen meat production. We drank black velvet – South African champagne and Guinness. Next day there was fog, snow and very heavy seas so that no whales were caught. Everyone was idle – which was perhaps appropriate as it was a Sunday.

The expedition and the factory were now working at full speed catching and processing whales over the next few days and this kept me very busy. There were two beautiful days of clear skies and blue seas with a few magical-looking icebergs around us. The whale catchers had been doing very well and on each of the fine days they stopped catching at 10 a.m., because the factory was at 'full cook' and couldn't handle more. It clearly showed how dependent the whole operation was on the weather. It changed again on 8 January and the work rate slackened off because of this; the boats caught only ten whales. That night was 'tot' night – a bottle of gin appeared on each table as an incentive or 'thank you' from the company for every 10,000 barrels of oil, and yesterday the expedition 'take' reached 20,000 barrels. We were now at about 84° E.

I was most interested in the mature females and because I couldn't examine every whale in detail usually left the males alone. The foreman, whose English was none too good, called them 'boys' and 'girls' so when I went along to the poop deck, where his office is, I asked, 'Any girls about today?' There were many more boys than girls, so I was often heard to say regretfully in the lab, 'Damn! – sixteen boys astern and not a single girl.'

While flensing was going on my job was to record the species and sex of each whale, measure its length, make external observations of diatom film, parasites, scars, and if a female check whether it was lactating, by examining the mammary glands on the underside.

Without its blubber each whale was then attached to the main winch and pulled through Hell's Gate to the fore-plan and rapidly dismembered. Flesh of good quality went to the freezing units, the rest of the carcass – meat, bone, liver and offal – went into designated cookers where they were cooked under pressurised steam. In half an hour nothing remained of a monster eighty or more feet long; the largest I measured was a blue whale of thirty metres.

The biologist's job was potentially one of the most dangerous in the whole operation. Disorientated and bathed in clouds of steam, one had to keep one's wits about one, to be looking around all the time for wires and hooks. A harmless cable lying in innocent curves on the deck would suddenly become a taut wire 6–8 feet above the deck as winch power was suddenly applied by turning on the steam pressure. It often seemed that the whalers, whose sense of humour was primitive, delighted to try to catch me out in this way. In escaping such disasters it would have been easy to step into one of the open digesters and fall fifteen feet to its bottom – if it was still empty. The biologist inspector was the *only* person on the ship who, in the course of his job, ran the gauntlet of every one of the specialised operations I have just described, from the time the whale appeared at the top of the slipway, until the little unusable offal disappeared over the side. The most dangerous element was ripping the backbone when a huge sharpened hook on the end of a hawser under a tension of 70 tons ripped through the neural arches. When the sharpened hook sometimes came adrift it snaked and on one occasion hit me as it flew through the air, fortunately a glancing blow, otherwise it would have killed me. As I needed to examine a number of vertebrae to check whether their epiphyses (disks joined at each end of a vertebra) were fused to the centrum (the 'cylinder' of the vertebra) or not, I had to work close to this hawser. The information was needed to work out the progress, with age, of fusion and when physical maturity was attained, that is when growth in length stopped.

I also had to collect internal organs for my research, such as the ovaries and testes, adrenal, thyroid or other organs and check on the stomach contents. The ovaries were a particular difficulty, because the whalers' work went on at an inexorable pace – they would not stop for me – time was money. So often I found myself chasing and clambering over a huge pile of slippery offal trying to 'excavate' the second of a pair of ovaries from the heap, right up to the last moment when the guts were about to slip into a digester or over the side. Either would have been a quick ending. One would have lasted a few minutes at most in the cold Antarctic waters, for the ship was moving and the lifeboat drill at St Vincent many weeks earlier had shown the futility of lowering a boat to save a man overboard.

A week later it was still very rough but we were heading south to where the weather was usually better and where we could expect more blue whales. Such heavy seas had made delivering whales very difficult. Several ships of our fleet were in sight, disappearing from time to time in wave troughs so that only their crow's nests were visible. The total first-week catch for the whole fleet had been 1,700 BWUs.

By 13 January we had a tot for 30,000 barrels. A week later it was a lovely day. We were at 63°56' S, 86°16' E – the sea mirror calm, temperature 8°C with occasional sunshine. *Biscoe* came alongside in the morning and refuelled us. That day was also very notable because I found a huge pair of blue whale ovaries with a combined weight of 131 lbs – 58 kg (73 and 58 lbs). I froze them for later examination, but they must easily be the heaviest mammalian ovaries on record! I later reported on them in the scientific journal *Nature*.

The blue whale (*Balaenoptera musculus*) season had begun on 16 January. Once again we were among dense pack ice and some fantastically carved icebergs in the most perfect egg-green (or blue) colours. It is impossible to do them justice in a description. Standing on the poop deck that afternoon I saw my first blue whale spouting. There was a heavy sea running and crashing against the blue walls of an iceberg, and just by the iceberg a flock of birds on the surface of the water. Suddenly the whale blew and all the birds flew off. I don't know why it's called a blue whale because it isn't really blue but a lovely slate-grey with lighter patches. They really are magnificent beasts and I'm extremely impressed by them – they beat all the other species into a cocked hat.

Six blue whales were caught that first day and I was on deck throughout. For a change the weather was pleasant – occasional bursts of sunshine and a temperature of 3°C, which felt quite warm. At the end of the shift the commander, who had recovered from a painful bout of shingles, was better and took over the next twelve-hour shift. On their own the inspectors' duties are the easiest job on the ship and involved me in perhaps two hours' work a day. It gave me ample time for my research, but signing on as an inspector was the only way for a biologist to get a berth on the ship.

A very full day and particularly interesting was 22 January. I found a pair of twin foetuses and one whale which had just finished lactating – a landmark in the breeding cycle. Now I had examined all except three pairs of the ovaries I had collected and written up my notes for the day – whale log, specimen log, lab notes and journal. I was sitting in the quiet of my cabin with a long *pjolter* (whisky and water) at my elbow writing to my darling Maureen!

By 25 January we had turned westwards and were still travelling that way, catching plenty of whales. I had discovered a source of a kind of cartilage for a plastic surgeon who had asked me for some. Apparently whale cartilage was better than any other (including human cartilage) for certain kinds of surgery and small amounts had been collected before by the whaling ships. However, I had found a part of the whale's skull which yields a uniform piece about ten feet long by one foot in diameter! We took a section that day and cut it up into small slabs – which I understood might keep all Britain's plastic surgeons happy for five years! Stored in a mild antiseptic Cetavlon, what I collected that day might be a hundred times the current stocks in England.

Another tot night came up – marking 60,000 barrels. The crews' pay bonuses depended on this and as it didn't affect me, I was the only man on the ship who didn't know for sure!

Everything about the whale is fantastic. The largest we'd hauled on board so far was a 92 ft-long blue whale; we'd had several 89–90 ft long. They really are huge – the biggest animals that have ever lived. It was a terrible shame to see them being slaughtered at all, but even more so in such an irrational and unsustainable manner that they were becoming progressively scarcer. Yet money speaks: a big one produces say 150 barrels of oil worth about £2,000 and meat meal, meat extract and liver oil to the value of about £1,500 (equivalent to between £70,000 and £105,000 in 2004). So it was a very valuable animal in economic terms. Blue whale scarcity meant that fin whales had become the backbone of the industry, each fetching around £2,000 (£40,000–£60,000 in 2004 terms) on average.

Whale catcher *Setter 9*

At the end of January *Balaena* was off Enderby Land, part of the Antarctic continent, the first land we had seen for many a day – since leaving Cape Town in fact. *Biscoe* came alongside to bunker us and take away our whale oil. As soon as she finished loading she would be leaving for the Cape and England.

On the night of 3 February there was a serious operation on a man from one of the *Setter* boats, for a mechanically obstructed intestine, which lasted five hours (and was successful). I was asked to be the blood donor so I waited up but in the end they didn't require any – perhaps they found my blood had too high an alcohol content!

As the middle of the season drew near (6 February was the day when the day shift changed to night and vice versa), I had now done post-mortem examinations on some 230 whales. I had collected a mass of material including a thyroid gland (about 2 yards long!) and parathyroids for a surgeon in London; I was feeling rather pleased with myself because the scientists last year couldn't find it! I think my earlier labours on elephant seals had been a good introduction to whale post-mortems.

February 16 was a wonderful day. The mail arrived on *Powell* during the afternoon and when I went along to supper at 6 o'clock there was a big pile of letters by my plate and most importantly seven from Maureen. Then I must have dozed a little because at 1:15 a.m. the light went on and one of the sick bay attendants wanted to know if I'd give them some of my blood for an operation, so I put on my dressing gown and toddled over to the hospital. A man had been working in the steering flat of one of the catchers (*Setter1*) and was still inside the guard rail. The gunner suddenly began chasing a whale, twisting and turning of course, and when the wheel was put hard over, the heavy metal quadrant (which engaged cogs and turned the rudder) caught the man, who was kneeling, and pinned him to the wall for a moment. His pelvis was crushed and he was in a very bad way by the time he was brought aboard. The Danish doctor from *Bransfield* came over and he and our own doctor decided to operate. There was a lot of internal damage and they had to amputate a leg. In fact the man's injuries were so serious that he didn't survive. It was a terrible business.

A few days later I was due to go for a trip on a catcher, but the captain of *Setter 8* who had promised to let me know next time he came in for bunkering forgot, so the first I knew was seeing her leaving. Catchers are fast boats (16 knots), about 230 ft long with the harpoon gun in the bows, and a catwalk so that the gunner can walk from bridge to bows without getting his feet wet. I was keen to experience what actually took place hunting whales.

February 26 was another lovely day and I decided to go over to the *Bransfield*, the refrigerator ship, to help Hugh with some experiments he was carrying out on preserving meat in formic acid, plus gelatin, and trying the effect of coating it with chlorophyll before and after freezing. We left about 9:15 a.m. First we had to get ourselves and our gear onto *Kai*, the small vessel that ferried the meat between *Balaena* and *Bransfield*. This entailed being lowered from the stern of *Balaena* onto *Kai*, while both ships moved about with the heavy swell. It was interesting.

On *Bransfield*, after a rough crossing, we carried out the first part of the experiments. I was due to go back in *Kai* when she returned two hours later, but decided to stay for lunch. A storm came up and it became too rough to transfer from ship to ship so we carried on with the work. By tea time it seemed obvious that we would be unable to return that night and were given a cabin and a bottle of Haig's Gold Label whisky with which to console ourselves. However at 12:30 am we were woken because the sea had settled very quickly – actually we'd steamed into better weather – and *Kai* was alongside again. We had a long and very cold trip back on the bridge of *Kai* – at first in bright moonlight and then a lovely sunset-dawn which we watched changing until it was almost full daylight by the time we got back to *Balaena*. After being away all day it was quite a shock to see all the steam and smoke and smell the shocking stinks coming from her. Living on board we had become so used to it that we no longer noticed these things. My nose took some time to settle down again! Also I got some photos of *Balaena* from the sea which turned out quite well.

On 1 March *Powell*, which had taken over from *Biscoe*, was bunkering us, but the weather deteriorated and she had to break off at 7 o'clock in the evening. I worked in the lab until Hugh came along with the news that *Setter 9* was bunkering. The commander agreed to request the gunner, Hem, to take me out so at about 10 o'clock, I went over in a sling to *Setter 9*. That's a sort of breeches buoy, with a wire loop through which one puts a leg and is then hauled over. As we left the weather was really very bad, with driving snow, strong winds and heavy seas. *Balaena* was pitching violently and the stern would sink deep, then as it rose the water poured over the sill of the slip way like a miniature Niagara, and the floodlights at the stern made a jade-green pool in the blackness of the sea. She looked immense and squat viewed from the stern with a whale in the slipway.

Captain Hem, the gunner, was a huge, 6 ft 3 in, red-bearded Norwegian probably weighing 16 stone. A very likeable fellow, he offered me a bunk in his day cabin (a settee, fitted with side boards to prevent falling out) which was very comfortable. We were now heading south to the ice. Our position was 64°50' S, 54° 06' E. *Setter 9* was the most up-to-date catcher in the Antarctic at that time. She had diesel engines and a variable-pitch propeller so the speed could be controlled directly from the bridge by altering its pitch. She was also equipped with 'Asdic' whose ultra-sonic signals made it possible to follow a whale underwater (and out of sight). The specially trained operator, Barnett, was English.

Some whales were about, including a fin whale mother and calf, but we headed west for better weather. The crew was working to knock ice out of the rigging and de-icing the gun and forerunners (the rope attached to the harpoon). The first day we caught five fin whales and the other boats only caught three between them. The following day we caught two large fins before breakfast and by 2 o'clock had taken five, all quite large.

After they had been harpooned and killed, they were pumped up with air to prevent them sinking and marked by a radar reflector and a red flag carrying the catcher's number. If we didn't deliver our catches to *Balaena* ourselves, a buoy boat later picked them up and took them in to the factory. On this occasion we would make delivery, but the weather was so bad that we only found one, made it fast and began towing it in to the factory ship sixteen miles away.

The wind rose to above Force 12 and the seas became threatening. It was impossible to sleep and I paid frequent visits to the wheelhouse to see what was happening, but could see nothing in the dark but the white tops of waves towering above us. *Balaena* came in sight – a blaze of lights and pitching heavily; *Setter 6* had three whales to deliver, so we had to wait. However, before we could deliver our whale it broke loose in the very heavy and confused seas. Each roll seemed to be our last. We were particularly worried, because Hem told me that he had had trouble with this new ship's stability in much lighter seas than this. In fact, he had been instructed to ensure that his oil bunkers did not fall too low, for the weight of the oil low down promoted stability. Unfortunately the storm hit us when his fuel supplies were getting low and dropped even lower as he needed full power to keep the ship headed into the wind. So we became very concerned about 'turning turtle'; for this had occasionally happened to other whale catchers.

I fell asleep for a couple of hours and was woken for breakfast by one of the ABs '*God mor'n! god mor'n! frokost er ferdig.*' (Good morning, good morning! Breakfast is ready); I wished I hadn't woken. Hem suggested it would be safer to remain on the bridge – in case the ship foundered – which sounded a bit ominous. The catcher was moving about excessively and mountainous seas were rushing down upon us; each roll seemed likely to be the last one. From the bridge we looked up the long slopes through the spinning Kent 'Clear view' screen to see waves breaking on the crests. Occasional small bergy bits swept down the slope towards us narrowly missing the ship. The catwalk, gun and rigging – in fact everything forward of the bridge – were thickly crusted with grey ice at least three inches thick. From time to time pieces broke off in the wind and crashed against the wheelhouse windows. Everyone was very subdued. They said it was the worst weather they'd ever experienced – including Captain Hem. The wave height was estimated at 60 feet (25 m) at times. Certainly it was the worst storm I had been in at sea and had me really worried. Fortunately I had never in my life had a problem with seasickness – though that was the least of our worries. We heard over the radio that *Balaena*'s wheelhouse – 14 m (45 ft) above sea level – had been flooded! Nearby *Thule* was drifting down wind upon *Willem Barentz* (a huge Dutch factory ship) which had already lost a whale overboard from the plan, taking bulwarks with it. Altogether during these few days our expedition lost twenty-three whales, including five blues, in the storm, representing in total value over £50,000 (more than £1 million in 2004 terms).

The storm continued during 4 March and if anything worsened. The seas were like mountains and white with foam. Huge 12–15 m (40–50 ft) waves were breaking over us, and every so often the ship was punched and shuddered to a stop in the middle of a roll. I've never experienced anything like it. The chief engineer confessed that he was seasick. Hem said he wasn't very happy about our chances; the coating of ice thickened; the gun mounting buckled under the force of the waves and we had lost the harpoon and forerunners. Luckily, however, at 5:30 p.m. we managed to run into an ice pack and were in calmer water, but with heavy thuds as we continued to hit bergy bits and ice floes.

Next day the wind was still measured at Force 11 – but we were in calmer water in the lee of ice packs. I worked with the crew on deck in the morning chipping ice from the rigging and from the winches and deck fittings – what was left of it, that is! We were then in position 66°58' S, 45° 33' E. We could now see the full extent of the damage: the bow rails had been bent to an angle of 45° and there was a big piece torn from the catwalk.

Yet the whaling continued; passing south of the Antarctic Circle, we chased a blue whale later that day – from 7 to 9 o'clock – along the edge of a tabular iceberg 25 miles long, but didn't catch it. Hem had one '*bom*' (miss) and the second mate had one too. We saw one crabeater seal and six Adélie penguins, a few snow petrels, silver-grey fulmars, Antarctic petrels, terns and several of the small minke whales. That night it was clear and moonless with a glorious display of the *Aurora australis*, flashing across the sky – predominantly a green curtain, but shot with reds, blues and yellows. I wished Maureen had been there to see it – but perhaps best not?

After the fifth whale of the day, Hem came in to the cabin and as he so often did, insisted on my having a 'liten drink' – in other words half a tumbler of neat gin, or 'yin' as he called it! Later, when we were on the bridge looking for whales, he sent down again for the gin and we repeated the dose. It was appropriately warming.

Next day we had taken four fin and two humpbacks; we were now in the very limited 4-day humpback season. The humpbacks are very tame and so ugly that they are beautiful. Our expedition caught and processed about 200 in the four days but as I was on the catcher I had no opportunity to study this new species. However, since one was dismembered and disappeared into the factory every half hour any opportunities would have been limited. I had seen some during my year at South Georgia in 1951. Humpbacks are ungainly compared with the faster rorquals. They measure up to their name really having a hunched-looking back, with a small fin and series of bumps on the spine. They also have longer flippers, are coloured more starkly white and black, with large bosses of barnacles infested with the large whale lice. They are slower swimmers, but breach more often, leaping out of the water and subsiding with a great splash. Some gunners claimed that they had shot humpbacks in the air – one even claiming that he had shot two at once 'as they were flying'. But this was probably an exaggeration for the gullible.

At sunset the 'capital ships' of our fleet, *Balaena*, *Bransfield* and *Thule*, were silhouetted against an appropriately blood-red sky, with clouds of steam and smells arising – obviously on 'full cook'. Later I had a radio message from Hugh telling me that the laboratory on *Balaena* had been flooded during the storm, with serious consequences.

We went down to the ice again looking for blue whales, but had no luck. It was a lovely morning, but the weather was unsettled. We caught two fin and took them in to the factory. Then we caught two more in very bad weather, in which Hem was predominantly under water for an hour or so on the gun platform. The other boats did better, mainly because, having gone to the ice and being unsuccessful there, we were late in arriving among the fins.

In one of the bights in the pack ice four humpbacks appeared ahead, rolling lazily about in the flat-calm water, flapping their long, grotesque flippers and throwing their flukes up into the air. We took two – a huge female and a smaller male. Both lines were out at the same time. The first of them was really huge, encrusted with many barnacles. We flagged them and left them at the ice edge. The other two we could not take because the day's quota of six was filled. We saw several fins, which we chased and lost and were chasing two blues at 3 o'clock, when the signal for '*stopp fangst*' (stop hunting) came. So we went back to pick up the humpbacks and took them in to *Balaena*.

It was '*fri fangst*' (start hunting) again from 6 a.m. and we again went down to the ice. A signal came saying that each boat could take two more and we got our two very easily from among the hundreds about us. Hem decided to go in to the factory for more harpoons and also needed fuel, and I went back on board *Balaena* – back to the smell and dirt after a really wonderful, adventurous week on *Setter 9*.

I had enjoyed it all – even the storm, though that probably more in retrospect than at the time. It was an experience not to be missed, although it had its downsides, not least the deaths of these magnificent animals.

They were still talking about the storm on the factory ship. I found most of my books 'soggo', instruments thick with rust and everything higgledy-piggledy! Even so I never saw it at its worst because my good friend Harry Weeks (the AB winchman) had cleaned up most of the damage. It was very kind of him. With a friend of his (Leo, the Irishman – the one he planned to go into partnership with at home) he'd worked like a slave all night mopping up the water and clearing up the broken glassware. Most important – and what took most of the time, he washed all my photographic negatives (including micro-photographs of elephant seal tissues that I needed for my FIDS scientific reports) and hung them up, in order, to dry. Unfortunately, a jar of iodine-crystals had been smashed in the general upheaval and that had ruined many of the recent negatives taken on

Balaena. But for Harry's efforts, the whole lot would have been ruined. He was a sterling character.

She's a big ship, as described, but *Balaena* was tossed around and at one time did a 37-degree roll! That was when everything came off the shelves in the labs. Books, glassware, records, specimen jars, chemicals, including a gallon of concentrated sulphuric acid, made a grand jamboree on the deck. Nor was that all, for water came in through the ventilating system and lay about six inches deep on the floor. 'Lay' was not the right word because they told me that it slopped from side to side and halfway up the walls, repeatedly wetting almost everything. Barrels were careering about and on the factory deck heavy iron harpoons (160 lbs) were hurled about. Fortunately, the only casualty was one man who had his foot crushed.

Water swamped the bridge 14 m (45 ft) above the waterline and a wave broke into the chief officer's cabin on the deck below – breaking through the armour plate glass in the porthole it swamped him – then cascaded down the stairs to the saloon. The forward-facing windows imploded and splinters of glass were embedded in the wooden furniture. Oh! It was a storm! The waves buckled the foredeck – of heavy steel plates – and this caused some apprentices who were near the bows to be trapped below when the doors jammed, and they were very panicky and shouted out until released.   Of course no work was possible; it was a matter of sitting it out and surviving. One of the lifeboats was carried away and an 80 ton whale (very dead!) was careering around the fore-plan wrapping itself around the deck fittings, as a gang of seamen chased after, trying to get ropes attached to it to tie it down. Eventually it was swept overboard, carrying a stretch of bulwarks with it.

When the storm struck, seven whale carcasses had been hauled up into the slipway, but these were lost together with others being towed astern. Harry Weeks said it was far and away the worst storm he'd experienced in seventeen years at sea, seven of them in the Southern Ocean. Henry Buckle agreed and he had been at sea for forty-five years – fifteen of them in the Antarctic. So you see I hadn't been exaggerating about the position on *Setter 9* during the storm! As if to atone for the trouble it had caused, the sea was now flat calm and the sun shining. I spent a whole day trying to clear up the remaining mess. *Bransfield*, back again from her trip to England, was to depart on the night of 10 March and I wrote some more letters as it was probably the last chance for some time.

The Antarctic whaling season ended on 18 March that year and we finished working up the last whales the following day. It was such a relief, because life had become so monotonous, especially after the excitement of the catcher trip. I was finding getting up at 5:30 each morning, with large bloody whales on deck and everything rather dirty, was dispiriting.

We had an unfortunate accident on the final day of the season. One of the catcher mates was disarming the harpoon gun on his boat for the last time when it went off and decapitated him. It was tragic and more so coming at the very end of the season. We had a burial at sea from the fore-plan deck.

On the way to Cape Town, the false deck, impregnated with whale oil and blood, was ripped up and thrown overboard and the remaining decks and superstructure were all scraped and washed with caustic soda to remove the oil and dirt. It was quite dangerous to go on deck because the seamen were spraying caustic everywhere. I scrubbed out my lab and washed my implements and it looked a very different place. So we headed north again with an occasional diversion. One day, at 10 a.m. when I was down in the lab, the ship suddenly heeled over. I ran up on deck to find *Balaena* had changed course, steaming in a large circle, and there were some lifebelts in the water and what appeared to be a bloated corpse. It transpired that one of the Norwegians – a nephew of two directors of the company and uncle of another – in a fit of melancholia, had jumped overboard. It took 15–20 minutes to lower a lifeboat and nearly an hour to get the 'body' on board. Fortunately he survived his experience and ate a hearty lunch! Approaching Liverpool another member of the crew jumped over the stern and drowned. The day before, one of the doctor's patients had died. Three others had died during the voyage, so what with those already noted, it had been an unfortunate season for deaths and serious accidents.

We docked in Liverpool on Easter Monday and I got home the same day to have about five days with my parents before travelling to London to start work.

* * * *

As a biologist my work was successful. It substantially revised the Discovery Investigations of Mackintosh and Wheeler twenty-five years earlier. Further, I had produced substantial new ideas about whale reproduction, growth and age and didn't feel my time had been wasted. Indeed with the optimism of youth I hoped they might earn me quicker promotion! It also meant that I could begin to plan my work for the next three or four years. The scientific results were incorporated in two large, 28-page and 160-page, monographs that were published in the *Discovery Reports* series in 1958 and 1961.

12

Marriage, Surrey Idyll, and Work at the NIO

Some of the NIO's biological staff had remained at the Natural History Museum, South Kensington, where the Discovery Collections were housed and whale material was examined. On my return from the whaling voyage on *Balaena* I worked there for about two months, examining my collections in 'the hut', a large wooden hut located behind the main museum, with rather limited facilities. I spent most of my time at a desk in the museum's 'Whale Basement'. This was a large and dark storage area, the only windows near the ceiling at ground level, and with a silent 'rain' of dust from the specimens housed there on ranks of stout shelves. These included complete skeletons of giant whales and dolphins, individual skulls and other bones. It was filled with the pervading smell of such places – musty, oily and slightly sweet. I can't say that I enjoyed it as a workplace, but most of the time I was alone and there were no distractions, except when I went over to the hut for a cup of coffee. So I got quite a lot done.

Dr Helene Bargmann, who was in charge of the small group, had been working for Discovery Investigations for years and was responsible for curating the Discovery Collections, a huge number of jars and tanks full of specimens collected in Antarctic waters. She was an intelligent, attractive woman with a keen sense of humour, and stimulating company. There were two assistants, John Smoughton and Miss Doris Wilson. John was a general handyman/assistant, who was later to help me examine the material I collected. Doris was working on an extensive index of the large series of published *Discovery Reports*. During this strange-seeming hiatus, a period in limbo, I stayed at 13 Ashfield Place, South Kensington, where Bunny Fuchs had rooms.

At the beginning of June I found myself on a train from Waterloo heading for *Gare du Nord*, Paris, and then to Portugal to marry my darling Maureen. She drove into Lisbon (for the first time) to meet me. Monday 7 June was the day of our civil marriage performed by the British Consul, a lady. It was not very impressive, except that the rules provided for the Consulate door to be left open so that if necessary an objection could be made! That evening we had a reception (cocktail party) for about eighty people. Our church wedding in the small English church, St Pauls, in Alto Estoril two days later was followed by a small lunch party. It went off well: marrying her was the best thing that ever happened to me. Maureen drove me off in her mother's Triumph Mayflower car, to the old walled town of Obidos, about an hour's drive away. I still hadn't a driving licence! We stayed in Portugal until the end of the month, enjoying every day to the full. In due course we boarded the Blue Star Line's cargo/passenger ship RMS *Uruguay Star*, returning from South America, taking passage to Southampton.

And so we came to our first home in Wormley, Surrey, near Godalming: it was a tiny wooden cottage that I had found with the help of the NIO, with a small garden full of flowers, fruit trees and a minute lawn. We called it 'the base hut' as it looked and was

Properly married, 1954

primitive, like a small Antarctic field hut. Appropriately only one rather small bed was provided for the two of us! At the end of July we collected a 7-week-old male cocker spaniel – a copper-coloured bundle of mischief whom we called Brandy. Then in September we moved into an Admiralty prefab bungalow in Hatchett's Drive, in a very pretty situation on top of Woolmer Hill, outside Haslemere. December came with deep snow and we travelled up to Edinburgh where I received the Bruce Medal for my Antarctic work from the Royal Society of Edinburgh.

So life assumed a new pattern as I became a commuter, taking a daily train to Witley station and the NIO where I now worked. We enjoyed the long evenings and the weekends, when we explored the surrounding countryside. The area around our home was really beautiful and we did plenty of cycling to explore it. All the while we were looking around for a house of our own. Eventually we settled on a site in Braemar Close, up a hill from the town of Godalming and only a few miles from the NIO at Wormley. With help from Maureen's parents and Freda Woods, and a mortgage, we bought the plot and built a house on it. So in June 1955, we moved in to Arrabida, 13 Braemar Close, Godalming, named after our favourite beach in Portugal. Or should I say, Maureen did, for I happened to be away for a month, working in Norway at a whaling station!

In the summer of 1957 our son, Richard Anthony, was born on 9 July, followed by a second son, Christopher Peter, on 23 December 1958. And so the years passed happily and busily for us both, immersed in marriage and domesticity.

* * * *

A brief recap of the NIO is perhaps in place here. It was a newly created government institute, first mooted at a meeting of the Scientific Advisory Committee of the War Cabinet in 1944, when the Hydrographer of the Navy pointed out that Britain had fallen seriously behind many other countries in its contribution to research in oceanography. In view of our traditional interest in the oceans of the world, a British oceanographical institute was called for. The Royal Society, to which the question was referred, was strongly in favour of setting up such an institute to advance the science of *physical* oceanography in all its aspects. The Scientific Advisory Committee supported its proposals, but recommended that the work should also embrace *biological* oceanography.

On joining NIO in 1954 I was one of five senior scientific officers – physicists and biologists – in a scientific and technical staff then numbering only forty-one. The headquarters building had just been completed at Wormley, Surrey, about thirty-eight miles south-west of London. An ugly building, it had been built for the Admiralty as an extension of the Signal and Radar Research Establishment at Haslemere. As well as large shared laboratories it had workshops, a library, a canteen and other facilities. By 1955 the staff had increased to forty-eight and in 1958, when I was promoted to Principal Scientific Officer, there were still only fifty-three scientific and technical staff, which advanced to fifty-nine in 1960.

Of most interest to me as a biologist, was that in 1946 the Colonial Office had raised the question of the future of the Discovery Investigations, which it had been running since 1925 for the government of the Falkland Islands Dependencies. They had been financed by a fund fed by the revenues from whaling and controlled two specially constructed research vessels – RRS *Discovery II* and RRS *William Scoresby*.

The NIO was run by a council in which, because of the navy's great interest, the Admiralty assumed a leading responsibility. The first chairman of the council was the Chief of the Royal Naval Scientific Service. Under the council, a director (Dr G. E. R. Deacon FRS) and secretary of the new institute were appointed. The two ships, *Discovery II* and the *William Scoresby*, were purchased by the Admiralty from the Falkland Islands Dependencies government and presented to the institute. The remaining scientific staff of Discovery Investigations, headed by Dr N. A. Mackintosh, were taken over by the NIO, and other existing groups of physical oceanographers were added.

Thus, the origins of the physical and biological groups within the institute were separate: some scientists coming from FIDS and others coming more directly from the Discovery Investigations. From the beginning there were tensions, not least between Mackintosh and Deacon. Mackintosh who had headed Discovery may have felt that he should have been the NIO Director and not Deacon (who had also served with Discovery Investigations). Possibly their antipathy had its roots in the past. At the time biology was mainly concerned with whales (the original *raison d'être* of Discovery Investigations), with associated studies on krill (*Euphausia superba*, a shoaling crustacean 6–7 cm long, the staple food of whales, and many seals, birds and fish, in the Antarctic) and other zooplankton. While responsibility for the Discovery Investigation collections (housed in the

Natural History Museum) passed to the NIO, publication of the prestigious *Discovery Reports* by Cambridge University Press continued under the editorial eye of Dr Mackintosh.

At the same time, by arrangement with the Colonial Office, the NIO assumed responsibility for the data and collections accumulated by FIDS, pending the establishment of a scientific bureau for these purposes in London. While I had submitted a dissertation and been awarded a PhD by the University of Cambridge, I still had to write up and publish much of my work on the southern elephant seal for the Falkland Islands Scientific Reports Series. In the early years of our marriage I spent many evenings at home completing two more scientific monographs on the southern elephant seal, which were published in the Falkland Islands Scientific Reports Series under the editorship of Evelyn (known to all as 'Anne' – after the film star) Todd who had the burden of the editing and production of the series. I thus had feet in both NIO roots.

My boss was the institute's Deputy Director Dr Mackintosh, who was distinguished for his work on blue and fin whales in the 1920s. Other colleagues in biology included James Marr, famous as 'Scout' Marr on Shackleton's last expedition and field leader of FIDS (1945–46) who was working on Antarctic krill. John Hart, a distinguished botanist and phytoplankton expert, had several Antarctic voyages to his credit on *Discovery II*. Ron Currie was particularly interested in oceanic primary production (and later to become Director of the Scottish Marine Biological Station at Dunstaffnage). Peter David worked on arrow worms (Chaetognaths), particularly *Sagitta gazellae*; he was an Oxford graduate, a sophist who, sadly, delighted in cruelly interrogating junior colleagues who were less articulate, but was an outstanding photographer of marine life. Peter Foxton, a popular colleague with a great sense of humour, studied the 'standing crop' distribution of Antarctic zooplankton and later on salps, jelly-like creatures that have a strange biology and life history (many years later he took a post in NERC HQ and was liaison officer with BAS). Arthur Baker worked on another krill species, *Euphausia triacantha*, and on the copepod, *Calanus acutus*.

Also with me in the Whales Research Unit (WRU) were Robert Clarke and Sidney Brown. Robert was an Oxford graduate turned whale biologist who had specialised on sperm whales in the Azores, and the open-boat whaling methods practised there. Sidney was a mine of information and later mastermind of the international whale-marking project, particularly on dispersal of blue and fin whales. He worked with Dr Mackintosh on whale sightings surveys in the Southern Ocean. Arthur Fisher was my assistant in the whale ovary work and assumed responsibility for NIO's ships in the 1970s.

There were twenty-two other scientists on the staff forming an eclectic and interesting group with which to be involved; eight of us were in due course appointed Fellows of the Royal Society for our work. We biologists all worked in a large, square, open-plan laboratory with windows on three sides. We occupied desks along the sides, separated by free-standing bookcases. Centrally were cupboards, tables and chart tables. I also had access to a small laboratory next door in a store room, which I set up for histological preparation of whale tissues. This was hardly ideal. There were two elderly scientists (i.e. in their sixties!). James Marr, when in the throes of composing his *magnum opus* on krill, was wont to declaim passages of prose like an actor, or to recite dirty limericks he had just composed, or to belch loudly and disgustingly. John Hart, phytoplankton expert, was reclusive; he spent quite a bit of time during the day doing his football pools, but was quiet as a mouse.

Robert Clarke was an admirer of Ernest Hemingway – he wore broad-brimmed felt hats and string ties, and waxed lyrical in a sonorous manner about the aphrodisiacal properties of ambergris, on which he was an authority. An old-fashioned 'actor-manager' came to mind. One day a visiting group descended on us – an inquisition on the research work. It came to each of us in turn and we could all hear the questions and answers as it progressed around the room. Robert was the first to be seen, and as he was then in his ambergris phase (the open-boat whaling phase had faded by then), he gave an impassioned account of ambergris in ancient history. This involved cuisine, love potions, word descriptions of its smell – 'like bat's shit in an old sea cave', a fungus that was supposed to be found only in association with ambergris, etc. The visitors listened, evidently fascinated by the performance; Robert completed his final peroration and a distinguished professor (the famous J. Z. Young, FRS) said: 'Ah yes, Mr Clarke, but what precisely has this to do with basic research on the biology of whales – for which you are paid your salary?' There was a deathly hush, but we never did hear Robert's explanation. (It was said that Young, a neuro-anatomist/physiologist, had been invited to serve on the committee by mistake; a minion at HQ had been told to invite 'Professor Yonge' to serve; much more appropriate since Professor C. M. Yonge was a distinguished marine biologist! The mistake was partly rectified by inviting C. M. Yonge onto the committee as well!) Naturally all these aspects of our environment, although entertaining, disturbed our concentration!

* * * *

At the request of Dr Francis Fraser FRS, Keeper of Zoology at the Natural History Museum, I had brought back from my *Balaena* voyage, deep-frozen, a large chunk of fin whale skull, containing the auditory meatus and middle and inner ear. It included the so-called wax plug (described by Lillie in 1911). Fraser's assistant, Peter Purves, had examined the wax plug collected by Lillie and held in the museum collections and, after sectioning it, drawn attention to the presence of discrete layers that he observed. A paper on it was in proof, due for publication under Purves' name in the *Discovery Reports* in July 1955. Credit for this initial discovery is unquestionably Peter's and was the reason why Fraser had asked me to collect further material on my *Balaena* trip.

Given my discovery of such layering in seal and sperm whale teeth that had been such a breakthrough in ageing these animals, this naturally caught my attention. If such layering in the ear plugs of the toothless baleen whales could provide the same information on ageing, it would be a huge advance in our ability to analyse their population dynamics and manage their stocks. However, Fraser and Purves faced a major problem: direct access to sources of whale data. They could only get ear plugs, establish the sexes and species of whales that they came from, together with reproductive status and measurements of size etc. that were necessary to develop ageing keys, from those who had that access. This is where I enter the scene.

One of the nearest shore-based whaling stations to the UK was in Norway. However, for someone such as Peter, who had no experience of handling large animal carcasses, let alone familiarity with dissecting whales, or knowing where to locate the auditory meatus and middle and inner ear within a whale's skull, collecting such material was impractical. It was proposed that given my familiarity with dissecting whales, I should go in 1955 with Peter Purves to Steinshamn. Our object was to find the best way to extract whale ear plugs and develop a method for large-scale sampling the age composition of whale catches. We agreed that the scientific results would be published jointly. In June and July 1955 Peter and

I were at Steinshamn together and achieved our objective, albeit with not nearly as much raw material as we would have liked.

As the NIO scientist dealing with whale research, I was able to greatly extend the supply of data by requesting our whaling inspectors to routinely collect ear plugs from the factory ship catches in the southern oceans. Hugh Symons, a Cambridge biologist, now Second Chemist on the *Balaena*, published a short paper on some ear plugs, but the first major collection made at my request was by Whaling Inspector Malcolm Clarke.

Treating this as part of our collaborative study, I sent the collection to Peter Purves, giving him first crack at bisecting the plugs longitudinally and then grinding them down on wet-and-dry paper on a band-sanding machine to bring out the finer structure, when the layers could be counted and ages determined. I also then aged the plug collection and married it with other data – growth and reproductive data – most from my own time on the *Balaena*. With our joint paper now in sight, Purves dropped a bombshell, he wanted to be the sole author of the paper on the Clarke material, notwithstanding that it had been collected by NIO under my supervision and, with good faith in our collaboration, I had also given him access to the supporting whale data.

Seemingly, Peter was upset that papers resulting from his earlier work on baleen whale hearing had always come out with Fraser, his chief at the Natural History Museum, as senior author. Correctly, the volume material I was contributing coming from my own research, he saw himself as again emerging as junior author. Instead of discussing his problem with me face to face, he arbitrarily broke our agreement and compromised more than a year of my own work geared to joint publication. In the end, unable to handle the statistical aspects himself, he had to publish jointly with a statistician – Malcolm Mountfort.

Purves and the ear plug controversy unpleasantly illustrated of one of modern science's competitive and less attractive aspects. It fed tensions between scientists who should collaborate and not compete. Another instance where the tension was reflected in the quality of scientific output concerned James Marr, already mentioned. His 'great work' was on krill. Originally quite a tight monograph, it had with slack research discipline become diffuse and wandering. Over several decades hypotheses became theories/axioms, scientific argument got lost in hyperbole, and the whole work needed tightening up. Mackintosh, as editor of the Discovery publications, tried to do this and make it less discursive – as was his right and as a biologist he was well suited to do so. Marr objected, appealed to his old shipmate and Deacon, in his position as Director of NIO, overruled Mackintosh. The contretemps brought in other personalities, and Mackintosh, a real gentleman, gave in. Significantly, however, when the paper was published in 1962 it contained the disclaimer 'This report is a comprehensive study of an important organism in relation to its environment and the *treatment and interpretation of the data are those of the author*' (my emphasis). No other report in the series had such an editor's note.

Notwithstanding my criticisms, James Marr's report was a significant contribution to Antarctic biology. It comprised 463 pages including 157 figures, 64 tables and a bibliography of about 750 titles. However, due to its size, I suspect that only a handful of biologists have read it thoroughly; it would be too daunting! It was in such unnecessarily strained conditions that we pursued our research. Sadly I was not immune.

* * * *

Discontinuing my promising work on ear plugs I concentrated on completing my major monograph on fin whale reproduction, growth and age that was published in 1962. However, one way or another I was getting a bit fed up with my professional life at the NIO and the internal political strains common to deskbound bureaucracies. The Purves setback was an acute irritation, but a more important contributory reason was difficulty keeping up with the cutting edge of my field. From far back in childhood I had been encouraged to lead and be at the forefront of my field. Freda Wood's precept: 'Don't ever be satisfied with second best' (Chapter 1), has stayed with me down the years, and contributed to my being very ambitious. To be at the cutting edge of biology I needed to travel. No doubt funds were rather limited, but the NIO provided little support for foreign travel, which was frustrating.

Nevertheless, in 1955 I participated for the first time as a member of the IWC Scientific Committee, on which I served until I left the NIO in 1961. In 1955 I became involved as a member of the International Biological Programme's Committee on Marine Mammals, also serving until 1961. In 1959 I was appointed to the MAFF Consultative Committee on Grey Seals and Fisheries as one of two independent members, remaining a member until 1966. At the 1960

British Ecological Society Symposium on 'The exploitation of Natural Animal Populations', in Durham, I gave a paper on 'Some effects of whaling on the southern stocks of whalebone whales'. In 1960 too I was an invited speaker at the 25th North American Wildlife Conference, Dallas, Texas, where I gave a paper entitled: 'Problems of whale conservation'. Of course I attended a number of other meetings in the UK, but my point is that over the eight years I worked for the NIO, this was a very small number of significant meetings.

* * * *

As a member of the MAFF Consultative Committee on Grey Seals I met Dr John Morton Boyd (later Director for Scotland, Nature Conservancy Council) – also a member. Through this association, in 1959 I joined a Nature Conservancy Council (NCC) Expedition to North Rona, organised by Morton.

At the time he was the regional officer of the Nature Conservancy for the West of Scotland and the Hebrides, about my age and very lively. Our goals were to count the grey seal population, to brand as many pups as we could for long-term study and make other observations. There were four members of the expedition: myself, Morton, Malcolm Douglas – a tall, dark, dour highlander, warden of a nature conservancy at Braemar who knew much about red deer but little about seals – and Jim McGeogh. Jim was a detective inspector in the Inverness-shire Police. He was a specialist at taking photographs at crime scenes and a fingerprint expert. Cheerful, and very Scottish in character, he was the Honorary Warden of North Rona and Sula Sgeir [a tiny island to the west of Rona] Reserve and had spent his annual holidays for the past 6–8 years mostly on Sula Sgeir.

Rona is beautiful, about 120 ha in extent, with varied scenery. The island is roughly triangular in shape and rising to 116 m at Toa Rona. There is a central grassy ridge running north-west to south-east bounded by sheer precipices and rocky cliffs. A low-lying, narrow rocky peninsula about half a mile long, called Fiannuis, extends northwards. On the west coast huge cliffs of pink rock marked with white veins of quartz fall sheer to the water. The island is riddled with caves and one could hear the deep boom of the surf in them and the 'singing' of the seals. A few sheep grazed and there were many black-backed gulls, some kittiwakes, and puffins in the nesting season; migrants pass through and we saw some snow buntings. But seals are the main attraction, the largest breeding colony of the grey seal, *Halichoerus grypus*, in the world; the species that had brought us there.

There had been five households of about thirty people in the 17th century who lived in stone houses, sunk into the ground and covered with peat. They must have had an unusually hard life, but no one had resided on Rona since 1844. The island first came to public attention when the Scottish naturalist Dr Frank Fraser Darling erected a simple hut and lived there for a year with his wife and family in the 1930s. He wrote a successful book, *A Naturalist on Rona*, about the experience, published in 1936. According to Darling the village is the site of a Stone Age settlement.

* * * *

We were landed with our supplies by Fishery cruiser *Brenda*, lived in a prehistoric stone hut, got water from a well on the cliff and kept in touch by radio telephone with the outside world through Archie MacEochran, keeper of the Butt of Lewis Lighthouse. We took over one of the abandoned houses, known ironically as 'the Manse', open to the sky and about 18 by 8 ft in size. We fitted a ridge-pole – an old ship's spar – roofed it with tarpaulins and stuffed turf and moss into the cracks in the walls. Although it was draughty and damp, it made a secure home for our stay. The weather was characterised by frequent North Atlantic gales and huge waves, but ameliorated by an esoteric selection of malt whiskies.

It was on the northern, low-lying Fiannuis that the seal herds hauled out and by the end of the breeding season turned it into a sea of mud, dotted with dead calves. Leac Mor, a great slab where it is easy for the seals to get ashore, lies on the east side of Fiannuis and two gullies run across inland from it – the centre of calf production.

It was absorbing to make the acquaintance of the grey seal and compare it with the others I knew. The pups are born with white, or rather cream-coloured fur coats and are lovely. They are soon weaned and then moult to lose the birth coats to become a glossy silver and black – truly handsome. The adults were rather timid, and difficult to approach without causing disturbance – a huge contrast to the Antarctic seals, which are very tame. The bulls were great cowards, much more so than the cows, which remained to defend their pups when we approached. Part of the programme was to brand and tag as many pups as we could.

This was strenuous as it meant catching and wrestling with the pups which were very strong. I made a frame for the hot branding irons out of Dexion and tins. The procedure involved shearing a small patch of fur off the back, then applying the hot iron (the letter R) to the sheared patch for about twenty seconds. The brand showed initially as a shiny, slightly crinkly surface, which was then brushed with hot Stockholm tar to minimise infection.

If the brand was not held firmly in one place and slipped, it blurred the shape of the R, and after a morning trying to hold wriggling victims still, I made a Dexion frame to hold pups while the hot iron was applied or a tail tag attached, the wounds again smeared with Stockholm tar. With this equipment we branded over 200 pups with a letter R and affixed a further 250 with plastic tags.

As the whole seal population was not on land simultaneously, we used pups-of-the-year as a basis for estimating the overall herd size and marked them with dye to preclude double counting. We made three censuses and found that there were about 2,400 calves born – indicating a herd of 8,000–10,000; they have since increased.

Unfortunately about 25–30 per cent of the pups died within a few weeks of birth. Adults crushed some, others from bites by adults and wounds which had become septic. An unknown number was washed away by high seas which sweep the rocks; others fell over cliffs to their death.

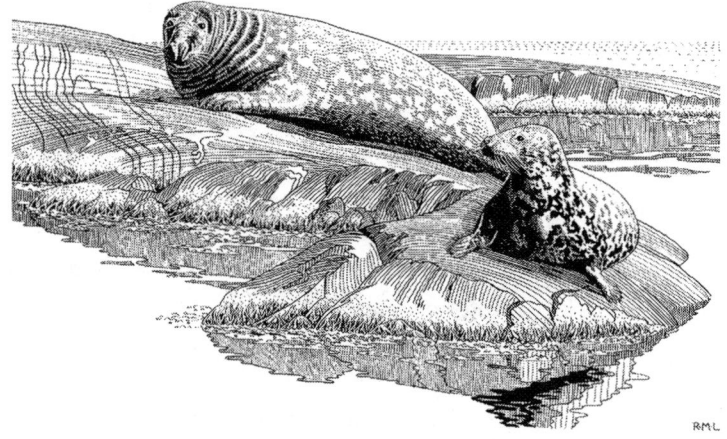

Grey seals on Rona

After three weeks of gales and rain we got off the island and arrived in Stornoway at 10 o'clock on 6 November, took the steamer to the mainland at 12:15 a.m. and caught the train to Mallaig at 7:42 a.m., to Glasgow, then to Edinburgh and London. I got home at 1:00 a.m. after over 24 hours' travelling.

I was now far fitter than at the outset of three weeks' really rough living and very strenuous work in the field. Apart from my work on whales on the *Balaena* voyage it was the only real field research I was able to carry out at the NIO in eight years, and it brought home to me what I had been missing. My formative years in the Lake District and Antarctic experiences made the point that my metier was the outdoors and field research. I missed a strenuous outdoor life that tested the body as well as the intellect, and even more the humour, and camaraderie of tough, hardworking, hard-drinking companions (not that I have ever been a drinker!), who were prepared to pitch in and help one another, regardless of specialisations and qualifications. Looking back, it is surprising that I stood the largely desk- or lab-bound life at the NIO and the politics of the IWC for so long. The Rona expedition made it clear that the time had come to move back into the field.

PART II

Hippos' Tears
and
Elephants' Tusks

Uganda and the two national parks where I worked until 1967

13

First Visit to East Africa

I was becoming increasingly concerned about the miasma surrounding the IWC and its ineffectiveness, the second-tier position of biology at the NIO, the lack of support for my own work and limited opportunities to conduct field work, or even to attend scientific meetings overseas. So I began to think about another job. The Food and Agriculture Organization of the United Nations (FAO) offered me an appointment to set up a cooperative scheme of whale research in the waters of the Eastern Pacific, based at Lima, Peru that also involved Chile and Ecuador. It was extremely well paid, non-taxable and with a very large expense account, but it did not particularly appeal.

Then, in June 1961, the Director of NIO, George Deacon FRS, asked me to represent the institute at a Symposium on Underwater Photography to be held at the Royal Geographical Society. He pressed me to take it on despite my protests that I knew nothing about the subject, but there was no one else available at the time and a briefing would ensure that I gave a reasonable talk. So I agreed and was briefed, given a set of slides and duly presented my lecture. It included some excellent underwater flash photos of the deep-sea floor and others of oceanic squids being caught on hooks and attacked by their fellows – stirring stuff.

When leaving one of the sessions to walk out into Kensington Gardens, Hugh Cott (who had taught me as an undergraduate) approached: 'Hello, Dick. How would you like to work in Africa?'

It transpired that the University of Cambridge was involved in a plan to set up a ten-year research programme, funded with £80,000 by the Nuffield Foundation, and was looking for a biologist to head a small team to work on tropical animal ecology, based in the Queen Elizabeth National Park (QENP) in western Uganda. It was to become widely known by its acronym NUTAE (Nuffield Unit of Tropical Animal Ecology). Hugh was the Secretary to the Management Committee, of which Professor Carl Pantin FRS was the Chairman. I said that I would like to hear more and so Pantin invited me up to Cambridge for a lunch at Trinity College. Afterwards we talked, sitting in the sun in the walled Fellows' Garden, about the objectives of the research and the support for it. I had a number of questions, which he dealt with, and he then offered me the job; I said I would like to think about it for a few days.

Maureen and I talked it over and agreed that, in the light of the recent events in the Congo following Independence, the rapid departure of the Belgian administration and the upheaval which followed, Central Africa was not a good place to take our family. So I told Pantin that I had decided not to take up his offer and promptly forgot about it. A few days later I had a call from Barton Worthington, whom I had known for a few years as Chairman of the Consultative Committee on Grey Seals and Fisheries. He had much African experience and urged that I should think again and that he would be happy to fill me in on the practicalities and the opportunities as he saw them. So Maureen and I went down to his old farmhouse in Sussex. He had been delegated to persuade me to see for myself what East Africa was like, to participate in the forthcoming 'milestone' Arusha Conference, where I would meet many of the scientists and administrators involved in African wildlife research, and visit various national parks. I could take some leave, go for as long as I wished and then decide whether to take up the job; there was no obligation and there would be no hard feelings if I turned it down. It seemed too good an opportunity to miss, so I accepted.

* * * *

Taking five weeks' leave from the NIO, I flew from London Airport on Wednesday 23 August 1961. After a ten-hour flight we landed at Entebbe Airport at 7:15 a.m., to be hit by the moist tropical heat, and I was met by Alan Brooks, the Game Department biologist. We drove to his house in Entebbe for breakfast and then visited the Game Department where Alan worked. I met Ron Rhodes, a Fisheries Officer, and Dick Newton, Resident Game Warden, before Alan showed me his laboratory and the department's menagerie.

That afternoon we drove through very green vegetation, with red earth, tall anthills and banana trees, to Kampala to meet Colonel 'Bombo' Trimmer, the Director of National Parks. He then took me to Makerere University campus to meet Ralph Dreschfield, Uganda's Deputy Governor and Chairman of Trustees of the Uganda National Parks, and Professor Leonard Beadle (a member of the NUTAE Committee). After a night with the Beadles, I spent the next day meeting the staff and members of the Zoology Department. It was like a small, well-equipped UK University unit.

Bombo Trimmer collected me at 8:30 a.m. next morning, and his driver drove me to Mweya, the HQ of the QENP 260 miles away. It was a pleasant, enjoyable drive through lovely country, becoming progressively more beautiful and the people I saw by the roadside more attractive as we drove west. It was all much greener than I had expected, through stretches of dense forest and papyrus swamp and with the occasional patch of brilliant colour from a tree in blossom or lilac water lilies. Grass fires were burning and the smoke prevented distant views, but there were lovely hazy blues, with little hills popping up all over the place. The best scenery was from the top of the eastern wall of the western Rift Valley, looking down to the west over the QENP, some 770 square miles (1,978 km^2).

The plains stretched out below, dotted with trees and shrubs, but on the whole open and less arid than I had been led to expect. At the gate a letter awaited me from the warden, Frank Poppleton, inviting me to stay in his home.

There I met him and his Danish wife Inge, and we had tea on their veranda. I immediately liked them; Frank was Kenya born, about 45 years old and exceptionally fit, Inge about 27, dark and attractive, and they had a small son, John. We got on well. I felt sure that it would be a good place to live; the setting was perfect and the Poppletons' house was about a hundred yards from that which would be ours, if I took the job. Both houses overlooked Katwe Bay and when it was clear they had a wonderful view of the Ruwenzori Range and the Congo, with the volcanoes of Rwanda to the south. The houses were attractively constructed in local materials (makindu-palm logs with cemented joints and papyrus-thatch roof). The partitions between the rooms, also palm logs, didn't reach the roof, so assuring coolness, and the rooms were spacious and had character. I had a quick look around the house we would occupy. It was more than up to expectation and I had no doubts that Maureen would like it. The garden was laid out with a big lawn and shrubs and flowers, although periodically the elephants came through and 'beat it up'. The insects weren't at all troublesome, although there were some cockroaches, and sprightly, colourful lizards. No one was bothered about snakes, although they kept a snake-bite anti-venin kit, just in case.

Frank showed me around the 'camp' too and the rather primitive makindu and papyrus research facility (but nonetheless better than expected). I met the manager of the park tourist lodge, McLennan, and Bert Cottingham the works manager. Next day I met Mr Roussos, a Greek entrepreneur, at Kabitoro outside the park gates who had a finger in many local pies, there and in the Congo – road transport, hotel, hippo cropping, fishing, cotton, coffee, etc. We had a beer with him in his hotel and I asked him to look out for a Belgian-trained cook for us. (Clearly, I had already decided to accept the Uganda appointment!). I wrote that night to Maureen to tell her how marvellous it all was. The Parks would provide two garden boys free and the unit would have a driver, a clerk-cum-lab assistant and two rangers assigned to help. Ralph Dreschfield had told me in Kampala that 'the entire staff' was 'at my disposal for any work'. Everyone was extremely cooperative and helpful.

On my return to Kampala by train, Bombo Trimmer met me and took me home for breakfast. Certain of accepting the offered post, I ordered a grey Land Rover, long-wheelbase estate wagon, with a roof hatch, front winch, spotlight, spare jerricans. Later, after seeing John Locke at Makerere, I went on to Entebbe for dinner with Ralph Dreschfield, where I spent the night.

After a morning in the Game Department where I met John Blower, the Chief Game Warden, I returned to Kampala, visited the Uganda Society and then had lunch and further talk with Dreschfield. Later I went back to Alan Brooks' place where I met Bill Longhurst, a pleasant American Fulbright Scholar who had worked on hippo in the Queen Elizabeth Park.

* * * *

At this point and given the QENP would be so central to NUTAE, I shall digress with a few dry facts about this park. Prior to 1926, the land in Uganda's western Rift Valley around Lake Edward's eastern, shores was populated by Batoro farmers.

A varied fauna included a wide spectrum of large mammals (elephant, hippo, wart hog, bush pig, giant forest hog, kob, waterbuck, topi, bushbuck, several duiker species, buffalo, lion, leopard and spotted hyena among them). The presence of the local people and the fact that they hunted this wildlife will have undoubtedly depressed numbers. Temple-Perkins of the Uganda Game Department estimated that hippo were being killed for meat at about ten a day (somewhat under 4,000 a year).

In 1926 Kazinga village and the population of the area was evacuated to prevent the spread of sleeping sickness. By separating the humans from the areas around the lake that were infested with the tsetse fly carriers of the disease, it was believed (correctly as it turned out) that the particular trypanosomes that caused it in humans would die out. As a legal device to keep the people out of the area as well as for conservation reasons, the evacuated land was declared the Kazinga Game Reserve. Coincidentally, it met up along the Uganda–Belgian Congo border with the Congo's Albert National Park that ran along Lake Edward's western shore and beyond, to include much of the Ruwenzori mountain range. The removal of people led to rapid increases in wildlife and within five years (that is by 1931) the Game Department noted that this was particularly the case with hippo.

In 1952 the Kazinga Game Reserve was proclaimed the Kazinga National Park and renamed in 1954 as the Queen Elizabeth National Park. It contained varied habitats ranging from open grasslands to the tall closed-canopy Maramagambo forest. In addition to large mammals there were 545 bird species on the checklist, at that time greater than had been published for any national park anywhere. The small vertebrates and invertebrates were little known, and there were 57 ecologically distinct plant communities and 966 vascular plants on the incomplete checklists.

By 1952 when national park status was proclaimed, there were thought to be about 15,000 hippo, and though the national park trustees may all have been laymen, they were disturbed by the widespread soil erosion associated with hippo grazing. In the mid-1950s four American biologist Fulbright Scholars came to work in Uganda – Bill Longhurst, Wendell Swank, George Petrides and Hal Buechner. They worked in QENP (though not exclusively) and reported exceptionally high large-mammal biomass of over 20,000 kg/km^2, with hippo contributing a high proportion. The Fulbright men agreed with the trustees that hippo were excessive and supported a decision to reduce hippo numbers.

The flexible Uganda National Park Act gave discretion to manage animals and plants for the general benefit of both wildlife and people. The park trustees saw their goal as maximising diversity and acting against influences that might diminish it, including reducing animal numbers if their excess reduced diversity – as was the apparent case with hippo. The trustees were fundamentally pragmatic, felt conservation was not well served by doctrinaire attitudes and recognised their need to be guided by good science.

In 1957 the trustees initiated a hippo-management culling programme, the first such management for any species in African national parks. About 1,000 hippos were shot annually over five years, males being selectively taken, and the meat was sold to local people. This, then, was how QENP appeared to me on completing my first visit.

* * * *

To resume my narrative, next day Bombo, Alan and I left by Land Rover for Arusha in Tanganyika (which became Tanzania in 1964), for the international wildlife conference that was scheduled there. The route took us through Kenya, where the Africans seemed noticeably more sullen and cowed than in Uganda and less well dressed. (When I next wrote to Maureen I noted that although Kenya was beautiful, I would prefer to live in Uganda, because the people were more cheerful and friendly.) The route was through pleasant rolling country in the 'White Highlands', and climbing steadily we passed a sign on the Equator at 9,320 feet above sea level. With the overcast sky, rain and muddy roads one might have been in northern Scotland, not equatorial Africa. The farms looked very English and the whole countryside appeared somehow European rather than what I expected of Africa.

The road led gradually down through attractive country, to a superb view across the Rift Valley to the Aberdare Mountains and Mount Kenya. Nakuru town and lake came in sight and we could see the pink flush of myriads of flamingos along the shores. We had several glasses of Scotch before a good dinner at the Stag's Head Hotel, where we stayed the night. After a day at Lake Nakuru to see the estimated million flamingos, we went on to night stop in Nairobi. Leaving early for Arusha, the route was over vast plains dotted with scrub, and animals new to me: Grant's and Thomson's gazelles, giraffe, zebra and, in acacia woodland, gerenuk. The gerenuk (Waller's gazelle), eight of them, were slim and wonderfully coloured in various coffee shades; one typically standing on its hind legs browsing.

Arusha stands on the lower slopes of Mt Meru and was a centre for professional hunters and their clients; it was normally full of tourists, but our conference had taken up all the accommodation. On Tuesday 5 September 1961 the Arusha Conference was seen as a seminal point in African wildlife conservation. Historically, from the outset of British rule in East Africa, preserving the abundant wildlife had been given high priority. In the words of Lord Salisbury, Prime Minister between 1895 and 1902, Britain would not allow a repeat of the disappearance of this wildlife as had happened to the American bison and the immense game herds of South Africa. However, Britain was relinquishing colonial control of its African territories and great apprehension was felt about independent Africa's commitment to conservation. The Arusha Conference was organised to impress upon emergent Africa the immense prestige it would gain through continuing to conserve wildlife, the commercial benefits that this would bring, and how the world would judge its commitment to civilised governance, of which conserving flora and fauna were yardsticks. It was a very political event that would result in a new phase for African wildlife research. To emphasise the international importance given to the conference, many big names in wildlife conservation would be there.

Two lions

I sat next to Julian Huxley and Max Nicholson from England; Frank Fraser-Darling from Scotland was there, as was Leonard Beadle from Makerere; John Owen, Director of Tanganyika National Parks; Mervyn Cowie, Director of Kenya National Parks; Rocco Knobel, Director of South Africa's National Parks, Captain Charles Pitman, long-time game warden of Uganda now retired; Vesey Fitzgerald – a naturalist with long experience in Tanganyika; Lee and Marty Talbot from the USA working on wildebeest; Bill Longhurst and George Petrides, both American Fulbright Scholars who, as already mentioned, had investigated hippo in QENP, and many, many others.

All next day there were meetings, including some quite interesting papers and discussion – although not much of the latter. Most of the ground was covered more than once. A number of Africans spoke about their wildlife heritage, including a harangue from a Masai Chief. The 14,000 ft Mount Meru appeared from behind the cloud, looking magnificent and calm in the evening light. Over the next two days the conference continued relentlessly, with some Africans making very good speeches, but many others were (it seemed to me) long-winded, pointless or political. I met Tom Odhiambo, a Kenyan working for a PhD in zoology at Cambridge, who, according to my diary, came in for undeserved criticism. I met Les Robinette, a senior and respected north American wildlife worker, who asked if I was the son of the eminent Professor Laws who had worked on whales and seals! I also met Irven Buss, who had carried out research on elephant in Uganda and was coming out again to study forest elephants in Bunyoro. At the time I didn't think we would overlap much, because I expected to have my hands full with the hippos. Things were to turn out differently.

One morning ended with an announcement by Chief Fundikira that on the attainment of Independence, Tanganyika was going to raise the budget of the Game Department and others by 40 per cent, and rename the Minister of Lands and Survey, the Minister of Lands, Forests and Wildlife; wild applause ensued! This is what the organisers had been hoping for – a clear African commitment to conservation.

On Friday the 8th we left at 2 p.m. on the mid-conference field trip to Amboseli just over the border in Kenya. The drive was by way of Moshi, a town on the southern foot of Mount Kilimanjaro, and thence through lovely scenery and plantations on the slopes of the mountain up to the Marangu Hotel where we spent the night. Arising early, both Kilimanjaro's peaks – Kibo (19,000 ft) and Mawenzi (16,000 ft) – were free of cloud. The view was that much more spectacular because with Moshi little more than 1,000 ft above sea level, they towered above us in what is one of the world's tallest perspectives (other mountains may be higher, but they stand out of high ground).

After breakfast the tour went on around the flanks of the mountain to Oloitokitok, through banana and coffee *shambas* (farms); interplanting ensured that the banana trees shaded the coffee bushes. Irrigation channels with sparkling mountain water formed an extensive network. At one point there was a hairpin bend in the road, which required some 'backing and filling', and ominously a smashed bus which had left the road was lying in the valley below. (Later we learned that its driver had escaped, but half the passengers had been killed! However, he had been travelling too fast and we were really quite safe.)

As we progressed towards Kilimanjaro's northern flank and into its rain shadow the road dropped down towards the plains below and the lush vegetation changed. It became drier and dustier until we passed through the border hamlet of Oloitokitok and into Kenya, and from there to a luxurious tented camp in the Amboseli Game Reserve. That evening and next morning we were taken on game drives and saw elephant, black rhino, giraffe and a spectrum of plains game that was interesting, yet my overall impression was of fine, white dust inches deep that rose in choking clouds. Everywhere large herds of Masai cattle threw up the dust and there was virtually no grazing left. The trip's value was enhanced by a specially produced conference handbook written by Lee Talbot, which introduced me to the general ecology of the area and issues such as fire, overgrazing and bush encroachment that beset local conservationists. After lunch we drove back to Arusha. It had been an interesting, though depressing experience to see this seeming wasteland or battlefield, and I am sure it coloured my views in the years ahead.

After two further days of now rather dreary presentations and resolutions, the Uganda contingent set off by air for Entebbe via a three-hour stopover at Seronera in the Serengeti National Park and another to refuel at Musoma on the eastern shore of Lake Victoria. At Seronera a ranger with a Land Rover met us at the grass airstrip and drove us around the surrounding area. In the brief time available we saw lion, giraffe, zebra, wildebeest, kongoni (hartebeest), topi, Grant's and Thomson's (tommies) gazelles, etc., as well as mongooses, jackals, vervet monkeys and ostriches, including a nest. While the conspicuous male attracted attention, the drab female looked just like an anthill when it sat on the nest with its neck stretched out along the ground – and it was easy to see how the story originated of them burying their heads in the sand.

**Waller's gazelles, also known as giraffe-necked gazelles,
but also as gerenuk – their Somali name**

At Entebbe we refuelled again and headed to Murchison Falls National Park (MFNP). Roger Wheater was there to meet us; he had been in the army in West Africa, then in the Uganda police, and had been warden for only nine weeks when we first met. He drove us to Paraa, the Park HQ, which stood some miles from the airstrip, in a lovely setting on the Nile. The wardens' houses were of modern concrete-block construction and might well have been in an English suburb. They didn't have the character of the houses at Mweya though were no doubt more comfortable and easier to keep clean; though maybe not so cool. The next few days were a kaleidoscope of new experiences: boat trips upriver to Murchison Falls where the Nile forces itself in a welter of foam through a nineteen-foot-wide gap; seeing my first crocodiles – real monsters – that are surreal in a repulsive kind of way; unsuccessfully fishing for giant Nile perch; and both along the river and in drives by Land Rover seeing many different animals in absolutely great surroundings. Capping the visit was the hospitality and friendship and the overall air of camaraderie that pervaded us all.

Two insurance agents – Alec Ward and John Kelly – making a business trip to westernmost Uganda had stopped off at Paraa and joined our party. John was a keen mountaineer, so we struck an immediate rapport. Thus instead of going directly back to Entebbe, I opted to join them in their trip into West Nile District first to Pakwach and then further downstream to a place called Rhino Camp. We set off early on Monday 18 September in their low-slung Opel saloon. At Pakwach a sign pointed to Rhino Camp which we followed. The road was bad at first and became worse. At times we thought we wouldn't make it due to the car's very poor clearance. However we persevered through very attractive green rolling country with wooded hills. Eventually we arrived not at Rhino Camp but at Arua, the District Headquarters and Uganda's north-westernmost town hard against the Congo border. Nothing daunted, John and Alec were able to conduct their business at the West Nile Cooperative Union, instead of at Rhino Camp. From Arua we headed back via Pakwach across the Nile, through the northern part of MFNP northwards to Gulu, the headquarters of Uganda's Acholi District. From Gulu we drove back over the Nile at the Atura ferry and on to Kampala. While having nothing to do with NUTAE, this unscheduled side-trip with Alec and John allowed me to see yet more of Uganda.

Next morning I said my farewells and flew from Entebbe to Nairobi, changed planes and left for London. It had been an extraordinary experience to see so much of East Africa and its problems among experts in so short a time – less than four weeks – and everyone had been extremely kind and helpful. I had made many new friends and had no doubt that I wanted the job. The set-up in Queen Elizabeth was excellent as regards work and I was sure the family would be very happy there, but I still had to persuade Maureen!

14

NUTAE and the Queen Elizabeth National Park

I accepted the post of Senior Investigator (subsequently renamed Director) of NUTAE, resigned from NIO and in November 1961 returned to Uganda with Maureen, Richard and Christopher. We were met and seen through Customs by none other than Uganda's Deputy Governor (though I hasten to add not in that role, but as Chairman of the Uganda National Park Trustees). Ensconced in Makerere University College's guest house, we spent just over a week in Kampala equipping ourselves with the long-wheelbase Land Rover I had previously ordered and various household goods. The Land Rover had some refinements, such as a roof hatch for viewing game and also a front capstan winch for getting ourselves out of trouble. It would be useful for handling large animals, weighing them and pulling them around; also a spotlight for night work on hippo and other animals.

We left Kampala on a Saturday despite heavy rain and various gloomy predictions as to the state of the road we were to negotiate en route to the Queen Elizabeth Park 273 miles away. As it happened the roads were not too bad, though we wouldn't have made it without having four-wheel drive. The weather improved as we climbed the last hill to the top of the escarpment that looks over the Queen Elizabeth Park from the east. It was in sunshine, with the forest stretching away into the blue distance to the south-west and the open plains of the park below us. We stopped for a while so that Maureen and the boys could take it all in.

The Mountains of the Moon – Ruwenzori – were fairly clear in the background and the lakes were silver in the low sun.

Having taken in the magnificent view, we drove down the escarpment and entered the park, almost immediately seeing buffalo and waterbuck and Uganda kob, which thrilled the children of course. Then we passed through large herds of grazing elephant and more buffalo in the very tranquil evening light with the hills of the crater area forming a blue backdrop to the north. The road to the Mweya Peninsula, where we were to live, ran along the top of a narrow isthmus like an approach to some medieval castle. It was magnificent with the waters of the Kazinga Channel on one side and Lake Edward on the other. Crossing the Equator, marked by a white line over the road, we arrived as the sun was going down and experienced the first of many wonderful sunsets that were so outstanding a feature of Mweya. It was all rather magical as we passed through the park headquarters gates to the park warden's house – just eight hours after leaving Kampala.

Our arrival was something of a surprise as floods were occurring across East Africa putting many roads out of commission and cutting the railway line (our main communication with the capital) between Kampala and Kilembe, the copper mine not far north of Mweya.

I had of course already met the warden. Frank and Inge Poppleton would be our neighbours and were an interesting, friendly and attractive couple. Their son John (two), would be a friend for Richard (five) and Christopher (coming up three) to play with. Initially we occupied their guest house for a few nights before moving into our own house next door.

From our veranda there was a lovely view across Lake Edward to the mountains of the Congo – the Matumba range – to the south-west, while to the north-west stood the massif of the Ruwenzori. On clear days we could see snow on the Equator and the summit of Mount Margharita. On my first visit Frank and I had already planned to climb it in February 1962, some three months off. Far away to the south – about 100 miles – three volcanoes on the border between Uganda and Rwanda could be seen on a clear day. Behind us on the other side of the Peninsula lay the Kazinga Channel joining Lake Edward with the smaller, shallower Lake George to the north. There were always the most wonderful cloud effects across this vast expanse of sky.

The house was quite large and attractively built. Having no ceilings it was like a large barn, but partitioned into different rooms with log walls standing

In front of our Mweya home in Uganda with Maureen, Richard and Christopher

about eight feet high. The floors had to be swept twice a day and, apart from dust, surprises did drop down on us sometimes, such as lizards, geckos and snakes! We slept under mosquito nets and the windows had fly screens, mainly to keep out the tiny lake flies, but also many other flying insects, especially when the lights were shining at night. There were two bedrooms and a bathroom in the right half of the house (looking from the west); a long corridor led to the dining room and large living room, and there were two kitchens. One, the domain of our African cook, was used for cooking and was separate from the house. To get to it one passed a lovely flamboyant tree hung with weaver birds' nests.

Close by we had a small whitewashed guest house. Also built of palm logs, it contained two bedrooms, one on either side of a tiny bathroom, with a veranda in front. It, too, had a thatched roof and a water drum over a fire at the back to provide hot water.

The garden was attractive, but as buffaloes and elephants occasionally passed through, at times it got rather trampled. From the outset Maureen was keen to produce whatever fresh vegetables she could grow and keep a few chickens for eggs, and established a small enclosure for this purpose. However elephants were to step over the chicken run/vegetable garden fence and eat the vegetables – usually just as they were ready to pick. We tried hard to scare them off, making noise and shining flashlights at them. On one occasion Maureen woke up to a noise just outside the window. She got up and threw open the curtains and the wire mesh screen and had a glimpse of some enormous grey bodies right outside the window. Then there was a terrific bang and a flash went off against the backside of the last elephant, which sent them scuttling off as fast as they could. The Poppletons' gardener had thrown a thunder flash to frighten the elephants off, but it gave Maureen more of a shock than it gave the elephants, as no one had warned us that this might happen. Her vegetable project was never much of a success!

We were also to have hyena in the garden quite often, and sometimes they came onto the veranda and tried to chew the doormats and drag canvas sun chairs or anything leather – shoes, straps, etc. – away to eat. They made hideous, maniacal laughing noises. Scavenging throughout the park headquarters, they really were a serious nuisance and danger to the African staff and families. Unlike other predators such as lions and leopards who kept themselves to themselves and only occasionally wandered into where people lived, these spotted hyena treated the human encampment as a rewarding resource. Short of walling in the entire headquarters, which limited finances made impossible (and would have greatly detracted from the scenic beauty of the area), Frank shot some to make the others keep their distance. Going out with Frank looking for hyenas, using a spotlight, was an opportunity to see many of the park's smaller nocturnal animals: civets, genets, mongooses and even rabbits.

We had three 'boys', as servants were called without any pejorative sense in those colonial times: a head boy, Augustine, a second boy, John (both of them from the Congo) and a very good cook called Batuka (who was of the local Batoro tribe). In addition, the national parks provided a couple of garden boys to cut our grass, tidy up after elephant damage and generally keep the garden in shape. They were also responsible for providing the domestic hot water from a 40-gallon drum over a wood fire outside the bathroom. In addition a 'specialist' came every day to clean the toilet, though it was a flush one! This was a hangover from earlier times when bucket latrines needed emptying.

Electricity was provided in the evenings from 6:30 to 11:30 p.m. by a generator maintained by the Parks staff and, last but not least, we were provided (free) four large fish each day, caught by the fishermen in the Kazinga Channel. These were a species of tilapia – *Oreochromis niloticus* – and one of the most delicious fishes we had ever tasted; unusually for a freshwater fish it is remarkably like a sea fish, so that one can cook it in many different ways. As a result of the culling activities, we also had a supply of fresh meat! Maureen produced a very good hippo stew, and Uganda kob both as fried fillets or roast was excellent.

Naturally in those first few weeks we often drove out into the park where there was always something new of interest to see – a great variety of animals and a very large and varied bird fauna, which we slowly began to know. I usually did some office work before breakfast and then went out on field work, perhaps to observe or count animals, in which case Maureen was often the driver (and throughout our time in Uganda acted as my unpaid secretary), and the children came along too. Richard became skilled at spotting animals. From the outset being able to involve the family directly in my work was a huge bonus. That Maureen and the boys were so obviously entranced by living at Mweya and in the QENP was a great advantage and made me very happy to have accepted the leadership of NUTAE.

Crested cranes flying over the Mweya Peninsula

The great variety of birds never ceased to impress. Calling fish eagles was to be one of our favourite and most evocative memories of Uganda. They throw back their heads to make a wonderful, loud, seagull-like cry that echoes all around the lake, being answered from one bird to another. In flight, throwing back the head is synchronised with wing-beats. They are beautiful to look at too – white breast, chestnut back and black wings. In the garden there were many resident birds; brightly coloured sunbirds, gonoleks (a shrike), and weavers; as songsters little could beat our white-browed robin chats.

I took up painting again – impossible not to in the surroundings. Often after a morning working at the lab, I spent the midday hour at my easel and within our first six months painted two canvases – 'Crested cranes flying over Mweya Peninsula' (a large oil) and 'Elephant by a euphorbia tree' (a watercolour).

While there was no rigid colour bar in Uganda – unlike in Kenya – and despite the good relations between the Africans and Western expatriates, there was little socialising between them. The very different cultures and interests, our inability to speak the vernacular languages (which were all that many of their wives could speak) and not racism kept our two basically friendly communities apart by mutual choice. Our small white and somewhat isolated group comprised our neighbours on the Mweya Peninsula, Frank and Inge Poppleton, Bert and Ann Cottingham, the McLennans – the husband and wife team who managed the tourist Mweya Lodge and their two teenage daughters and a son who worked at the nearby Kilembe mine – and Litza and Theo Spyropoulos, who had two small children and ran the modest Kabatoro Hotel just outside the park for Mr Roussos our local entrepreneur and Mr Fixit. We all got on well and became firm friends.

Roussos provided QENP with a sailing boat and as I was the only sailor, it was moored in the small bay below us and sailing it became a much-enjoyed relaxation in the coming months. We sailed often and combined it with swimming well offshore in the open water (the boys in red inflatable life jackets), with little risk of catching the debilitating disease of bilharzia from its host snails which occur in the shallows. Coming back down the Kazinga Channel one evening, we sailed quietly up to an elephant feeding at the water's edge and gave him the shock of his life – the large sail suddenly materialising in front of his eyes! He gave a high-pitched squeal, reared up on his hind legs and nearly sat down. His trunk waved and his ears flapped and he continued to emit little screams as, stumbling, he hurried away up the slope of the bank, turning around once or twice on the way as if to make sure his eyes hadn't deceived him. It was terribly funny and I'm sure it didn't have any lasting effect on him. (In their fighting and threat displays large size is important – hence the ears are held out sideways to increase their apparent size – and the yacht, with its high mast and broad sails, was a very large threat.)

There was no school nearby that Richard could attend and, at an age when this was becoming necessary, Maureen started Richard off with simple kindergarten lessons. The only cloud over our idyllic family life at Mweya was family news. Maureen's father in Portugal had had two heart attacks and it was clear that her parents would never visit us in Uganda, as had once been hoped. On my side, my father was also not well, having been stricken with cancer.

Towards the end of 1961, Frank and I had started strenuous training walks to prepare for our planned climb in the Ruwenzori. We would be joined by John Blower, the Chief Game Warden, and the expedition would take place in the coming February. Family life in QENP was idyllic beyond our expectations.

* * * *

My small laboratory, known as the library, also constructed of palm logs and like the other Mweya buildings thatch-roofed, was about a hundred yards from the house. It was quite well appointed and there was a newly built (breeze block) photographic darkroom and plenty of storage space. Also a covered dissection area, with running water, which the Parks had assumed would be needed for our work – presumably its design based on the advice they had had from veterinarians. However, good as these were as a starting point, I foresaw that more extensive facilities would be needed as the research expanded. In the interim I used the library as an office until a new laboratory block was completed. So began NUTAE with the initial goal of concentrating on the biology of large mammals. My first six months, however, was as a new boy – learning the ropes generally. Only then would I be in a position to draw up scientific research schedules that while driven by good science, also fitted as far as possible with the park management needs.

We could buy our normal food supplies from the Kilembe Mines Store and sometimes went as far north as the town of Fort Portal which had greater choice. The mines also provided basic medical facilities. Yet Kampala was really our nearest source for anything other than routine needs. Rather than reinventing any wheels, we took our lead from the Poppletons. The Uganda National Parks had appointed Amannullah Din, a Pakistani businessman in Kampala, as their Purchasing Officer. Following this lead I appointed him Purchasing Officer for NUTAE. We would send him in our requirements and he would ship them out to us either by rail to Kilembe or truck to the park. It proved an excellent arrangement.

My Chief Assistant was Nathanial Oyet, a well-educated Sudanese Acholi (the Acholi are one of those unfortunate people split between the Sudan and Uganda when colonial boundaries were established) with a wife and child, and they had to live in rather primitive quarters in the African camp at Mweya, until I was able to build and offer him a more modern house in keeping with his status. In the Sudan he had owned a chain of several shops. However, when the Sudan became independent in 1956 and civil war broke out between the Muslim north and Christian south, he fled as a refugee to Uganda. He had a presence and was supported by the other African staff, also mainly Acholi, and some indeed from the Sudan like himself. Nathaniel became a key figure in the NUTAE set-up until he left several years later. He could take charge and was relied on to undertake quite complicated and demanding tasks. Lino Oboma, also an Acholi, was a park ranger seconded to NUTAE and became a valued member of my team.

From the very outset of our time in Uganda, NUTAE received a constant stream of visitors, and not many weeks went by without our guest house being in use. They naturally included members of the NUTAE Committee from Cambridge: Carl Pantin the Chairman, Alan Parkes, Bill Thorpe and Barton Worthington – all FRSs and eminent biologists. Others from outside included my friend Morton Boyd FRSE (Fellow of the Royal Society of Edinburgh), and Professors J. Z. Young FRS and David Assibiye from Ghana. From within Uganda the unit developed particularly strong connections with Makerere University College. Foremost was Professor Leonard (Len) Beadle of the Zoology Department who as a member of the NUTAE Committee had been very influential in establishing the unit at Mweya. Others from Makerere were Prof. David Allbrook of Anatomy, Dr John Locke of Pharmacology, Dr Henderson of Geology, Dr Jane Thurston of Zoology, Drs Kate Miller and Robert Milburn of Botany. From other research institutes were Dr Alec Haddow FRS and Sandy Harrow both from the Virus Research Institute at Entebbe. From within the local government departments there was Alan Brooks, the Game Department biologist whom I had first met on my introduction to Uganda, and game warden Dick Newton who was a pilot with his own aeroplane in which he flew aerial counts for us. From agriculture there was David Thornton who had already undertaken research transects of the vegetation on the Mweya Peninsula and John Harrop who was interested in conducting a soil survey there. On top of these colleagues in science there were a string of VIPs to show around – among them Sir Frederick Coutts when incoming

Governor of Uganda, and the *Omukama* (King) of Toro whose fiefdom lay to our north. The foregoing is but a small sample of our guests across our five years at NUTAE. In very marked contrast to my Antarctic years where I had had very limited contact with peers with whom I could discuss science, at Mweya the exact opposite was true!

All were understandably as keen to see as much as they could of the park, its animals and scenery as they were to discuss work. This meant that we spent a great deal of time as their in-house tour guides. This occasionally held up our programme, but overall the constant contact with people from many walks of life was stimulating and I did not begrudge the hours spent with our guests. The interest shown in what the unit was doing was not only instructive but was surely the hallmark of what a successful research institute should be all about.

I was not the first biologist to work in QENP. As earlier mentioned, in the mid-1950s four American biologists had come out to Uganda on Fulbright Scholarships. Of them I had already met Bill Longhurst and Hal Buechner at the Arusha Conference, but had yet to meet George Petrides and Wendell Swank, both respected for their work in the USA. Developing cordial ties with the Uganda authorities they had undertaken some basic research in QENP. They agreed with the national park trustees that it looked as though hippo were causing extensive erosion and through competition, restricting and reducing numbers of other large grazing animals. The Fulbrights endorsed a programme of hippo reduction which had been put into practice in 1957. This involved the park warden shooting a quota of hippo twice a month which were sold to local traders, who came into the park, cut up the carcasses and marketed the meat to the local population. The actual quota for any cull was determined by orders traders had put in on the day before and paid for in advance: the arrangement managed for the national parks by Roussos already mentioned.

The system in place was principally to shoot hippo at night. It involved driving through the *bundu* (bush) in a short-wheelbase Land Rover, the animals being picked out by spotlight and shot while they were grazing away from water. Next morning the previous night's tracks were followed and the widely dispersed carcasses re-located for the African buyers to cut up. Sometimes it was difficult to find all the victims. For as long as the hippo reduction was an end in itself, the system had worked well enough. However, if I was to conduct research in the depth that I wanted to and match what I had been able to do in South Georgia, these nocturnal hunts with widely spread carcasses were a nightmare. Instead of getting the biological material needed simultaneously from several carcasses, it called for tackling them one at a time and waiting until each had been opened up, making for a long and tiring day's work.

A party of veterinary scientists from Muguga in Kenya, led by Pat Guilbride, came up from Kampala to do some experimental hippo darting (the dawn of tranquilising wild animals in the field). At one point an irate hippo rushed out of a small wallow unexpectedly and whammed into the back of Frank's open Land Rover – the '*bundu* basher' – which he had driven into a cul-de-sac and stalled in dense bushes! There was no escape. The hippo took a large bite out of the Land Rover, then climbed part way into the back of it. The Africans sitting there frantically scrambled forward onto and over us and onto the flat windscreen with some almost sitting on our laps, including the hippo! Joking apart, it was really quite frightening, but no harm was done.

Collecting data after a hippo shoot

Towards the end of October I drove off to MFNP (Uganda's biggest park a day's drive to our north) for an East African Wildlife Society (EAWS) Scientific Committee meeting, for three or four days. Membership included some scientists of several disciplines from East Africa's tertiary educational institutes (Makerere was the only university college at the time), research institutes, national parks and game departments. The interlude expanded my widening circle of contacts and friends in the regional conservation field.

* * * *

Taking hippo when gathered in schools in the water would have made the culling work easier for all concerned. However, it called for a very high standard of shooting when the top of the animal's head was all that could be seen. The degree to which this marksmanship was critical only became apparent later when it was lacking. Shot in the brain, the victim died instantly and sank. Depending on stomach fill, the gases generated in digestion made the carcass float anywhere between twenty minutes to two hours post-mortem. Once floating, a rope could be attached to it and it was dragged ashore. I discussed this with Frank Poppleton who was doing all the shooting.

Many hippos spent daylight in wallows away from the Lake Edward shore or Kazinga Channel. These depressions filled with rain water during the wet seasons and most then dried. The larger of them might hold an acre or more of open water when full. However, whether large or small, hippo seek safety in water and are reluctant to emerge from it. Thus when a wallow contained more hippos than required for a day's take, retrieving the floating carcasses from among animals still living put those who waded or swam out to them at some risk. This problem was altogether less where they were taken in the lake or channel, as the survivors from a shoot could rapidly disperse away from the site.

December 8 1961 was the day of my first 'water' hippo shoot. We left at 7 o'clock for the Lion Bay area which is south of the Kazinga Channel on the shore of Lake Edward. With Frank leading the way in his vehicle, I took my Land Rover, with Martha Worthington (a visiting researcher – daughter of Barton), Lino Aboma, and a couple of park rangers.

Frank had prospected some wallows the previous day and we headed for one anticipated to contain about ten hippo, the number needed. Coming up to the wallow we found it now held some twenty to thirty hippo, far more than we needed. Retrieving ten from among up to twenty survivors was dangerous. However, fortuitously, there was a single hippo on land at the south side of the wallow which Frank shot. Leaving me to dissect it, he went to look for more suitable wallows with the right number of animals.

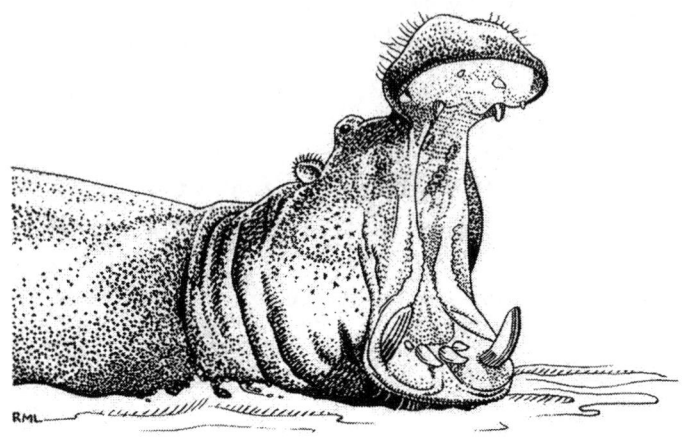

A hippo's prodigious gape and threat-yawn

We developed a post-mortem routine. First, a veterinary assistant cut off an ear, made a blood smear and examined it for anthrax. This fatal disease occasionally turned up in the local hippo and as it can be transmitted to people, this test was mandatory before he would give us the all-clear to proceed. We recorded sex, length, height and general condition. Given the go-ahead the meat buyers began their butchering, removing the limbs and breaking down the carcass with an assortment of large knives, pangas and, for cutting bone, rather primitive axes. While they did so we started collecting, nipping in and out to secure material for later study, tissue from the genitalia, ductless glands like thyroid, adrenals, pituitary, and a sample of stomach contents. Finally the lower jaw was collected for age determination from the teeth; to this we affixed a metal tag with the animal's serial number for future identification.

After a while Frank and his men returned. He had not found any wallow with the number of hippo for the day's requirements, so decided to take the remaining nine from among those where we were. Everything was complicated by the traders and their men being distributed all around the wallow, so that someone was always in Frank's line of fire. Eventually, when the rangers had herded them out of the way behind the rifleman, he shot his nine victims. Now arose the problem of getting them out of the water. The initial attempt was to mobilise the crowd of traders, their men and all others present at one side of the wallow to shout and throw clods of earth at the live hippos. In addition Frank had brought along a small dinghy and with two rangers on board he launched it into the water. Hopefully, the hullabaloo from the bank and his presence in the boat would drive the remaining hippo out of the water. A couple bolted for it, through where we were completing our work on the one shot earlier, causing us to scamper aside. These were exceptions and the rest simply stayed put.

Hippo and calf

There was nothing for it but to go into the wallow (which was only ten to fifteen yards wide) to get our victims from among the by now very agitated survivors. I joined Frank in the dinghy and while he covered me with the rifle, we paddled up to the carcasses one by one and attached a rope to them, so that the people on shore could haul them to the bank. As we came up to the last one, another hippo surfaced just beside us; it was a close shave – a little closer and we'd have been thrown out into the stinking water.

At the shore a chain made fast to a tractor was passed around the lower jaw, which by its shape fortuitously provided a secure attachment, and the huge, grotesque carcasses, some weighing over two tons, were hauled out. Having got them all out, we carried on with our examinations as the hippos were being cut up. It was a gory scene, but we were able to work on all the carcasses at the same time.

We finally finished about 2 o'clock and left the scene of carnage. Within a few moments we were driving along the track above the lakeshore with the water shining silver in the sun, and the blue mountains behind us. All were conscious that this beautiful environment was disfigured by our activities, however necessary they might be. By 3:30 p.m. we were home to a glass of cool beer, bath and lunch.

This was a fairly typical hippo shoot in the early years of NUTAE, although boating in a wallow was unusual. As time progressed, with my sealing and whaling experience of handling large animals, and as Frank came to appreciate the NUTAE needs, the system was refined to a relatively slick routine. For their part, once the butchers knew what we wanted, they also helped by calling our collectors to take whatever had been exposed by their dissections. When a number of hippos were being shot each was numbered as it was hauled out of the water, and that number displayed on a flag placed next to it. Around each flag we placed numbered glass collecting jars containing preservative, and into which tissues from each hippo went directly so that we didn't get the specimens from different animals mixed up.

The day after my first hippo water shoot we collected several of the abundant Uganda kob for Dr Mann from the East African Veterinary Research Organization (EAVRO). He was experimenting with both kob and hippo, salting and canning their flesh to see whether the product would be of any use commercially for sale to African communities. One of the Arusha Conference sentiments was that, in contrast to the era of British rule in which using wild animals as food was banned, there had been general agreement that this was counter-productive. Used cautiously and upon scientific principle, there was no reason why they should not be used as a valuable food resource. Mann's research was going down this track and was why Uganda Parks were prepared to help him.

Because hippo were so large, they had to be processed in the field where killed. Kob was small enough to take for processing to the hygienic, abattoir-like TUFMAC fish-factory on Lake George. It gave me an opportunity to see the tilapia catch being filleted, the fillets packed in cartons, weighed and frozen. Afterwards, again in contrast to the killing and butchery, we drove up through the beautiful crater hills on our way home. It was very lovely in spite of dull weather spoiling distant views.

The following recollections outline my work across my first six months with NUTAE. Frank and I went out several nights to try and catch baby hippo, elephant or buffalo to tag them for future recognition. We concluded it was too dangerous and gave it up. An enraged mother elephant chased us up the road and we failed to tag her calf, but we managed to tag a hippo and a buffalo, receiving many bruises in the process. As already indicated, drug immobilisation that was to become the primary means of catching large wild animals was still very experimental.

From 17–22 January, Dick Newton, of the Uganda Game Department, visited in his aircraft. This gave me a chance to see the park from the air. On the 18th we spent 5½ hours, counting hippo from the air – and again on the following two days. They were extremely useful experiences.

A team from the East African Veterinary Research Laboratories, Muguga, Kenya team, led by Dennis Rollinson, visited for a few days. Hippo shoots were arranged for them on 23 and 26 January, and a buffalo shoot on the 25th, turning up 'panzerherz' (armoured hearts) and myocardial infarction in hippo and massive tuberculosis infections in the buffalo.

On the day these vets left, a new fast, fibre-glass sheathed motor boat named *Askari* arrived. Fitted with a 50-h.p. outboard engine, a steering wheel and gear lever, its primary use was for chasing poachers, but we could also use it for hippo counts in the channel and along the lake shores.

On another day a party of us went in the *Askari* to the mouth of the Semliki River in the Parc National Albert in the Congo – on the western shore of Lake Edward, only about ten miles or so as the crow flies from Mweya. It is a most attractive place and we enjoyed the trip very much. Taking the shortest route across the lake we entered the mouth of the Semliki River, where it leaves Lake Edward. There it flows over a rock sill and, leaving the turbid waters of the lake, is miraculously transformed into a crystal-clear fast-flowing shallow river, its flow broken by sandbanks. On the south side of the river mouth there was a curving sandbank, with basking hippos and numerous water birds, mainly pelicans and cormorants.

We beached the boat at the base of some sandy cliffs and followed a zig-zag path to the top, about 40 ft up. The Congo was in chaos after the departure of the Belgians and there had been reports of Congolese rebels – *simbas* – in the region, so we didn't know what to expect and carried several guns. However, as we breasted the top we found the local ranger force drawn up on parade on the beaten level earth. They were well turned out, the corporal wearing a highly polished Sam Browne-type belt, and they were delighted to see us and showed us around their camp which was well found and tidy. There had been no trouble there for a long time they said, but the rangers had not received wages for six months. Deeply saddening, they were trying to keep a system going in what developed into the anarchy that has persisted ever since. This political turbulence then seemed to be contained within the Congo, and it was impossible to imagine it spreading into Uganda as it did with Obote and Idi Amin.

We wandered along the cliff tops above the river, taking in the scenery and the vegetation – very similar to Mweya. From the cliffs we had an excellent view of numerous hippos in the river. On leaving we gave the rangers a present of some Ugandan money and received effusive thanks. We had a swim to cool off and then took the boat down the river for about half a mile before heading for home. Our passage startled hippos clearly visible underwater, galloping fast enough along the bottom (20–25 mph) to create a surface bow wave.

On 8 March I wrote up the aerial counts made with Dick Newton and compared them with counts Frank had made in 1960. In Lake George and the Kazinga Channel where there had been 6,153, now in 1962 there were 3,071 a reduction of some 3,082. In the other areas there were 6,181 in 1960 and now, in 1962, 3,240, that is 2,941 fewer. These reductions were assumed to be the result of the cropping program. Unfortunately there was no way of comparing the counting 'ability' between the two observers.

I also analysed the air photos of topi photographed at Ishasha at the south end of the park. A large herd on the Ishasha Circuit contained 3,227 and the small herd 382, total 3,609. I also counted the Lion Bay hippos from the aerial photos which showed 294, compared with my direct count from the boat – 305 – quite a good agreement. I also analysed the numbers of hippo cropped.

In March we had Leonard and Sydney Beadle to stay for a meeting of the Parks Board of Trustees, including Ralph Dreschfield (Deputy Governor) who was retiring and Ian Hunter who was taking over from him as Chairman of Trustees.

The meeting was held in the NUTAE laboratory on 10 March. I gave my report on NUTAE and we discussed my proposed Lion Bay experiment. This would involve completely clearing the area of all hippo young and old, thus removing the hitherto dominant herbivore to see resulting changes over the next year. It would also provide a great deal of material for studying hippo age, growth and reproduction and population ecology. That afternoon I took the trustees to see the site and talk about the plans. They gave their approval to go ahead. It was during this visit that Len Beadle suggested NUTAE take on two of his zoology graduates, one called William Banage, the other Francis Katete. Neither came to NUTAE. William turned down the idea flat and in a move that surprised me at the time, Francis was very shortly appointed to succeed Bombo Trimmer as Director of Uganda National Parks.

Naturally given my success in being able to use growth rings to age seals and whales, I examined hippo teeth for growth layers hoping for similar success. Using rock-slicing machinery in the Makerere Geology Department I had some cut into thin sections, but found that resorption in older teeth complicated the process of age determination.

David Thornton, the agronomist, came and we discussed the design vegetation transects etc. for Lion Bay and others at Ishasha. A couple of days later Professors J. Z. Young FRS and David Allbrook (Anatomy Department, Makerere) arrived and while driving them round the park we had broad discussions on the unit's work. I seized the opportunity to bring to their attention hippos' astonishing wound-healing properties and the possible role of the animals' 'sweat' glands' secretion. Both seemed to have potential for human medical research.

I classified the collected lower hippo jaws into twenty age groups, I – XX, developing Bill Longhurst's very useful age class schema based on the eruption and wear of teeth. Taking it further I had illustrated the groups and allocated estimated ages to each of them, taking into account various evidence. (In 1968 I published a detailed scientific paper on 'Growth and Age of the Hippopotamus' which, though imperfect compared with my later elephant age criteria, is still used for studies of hippo populations.) I had also transferred data on vegetation patterns from aerial photos onto the 1:50,000 map series of the park for later use. The foregoing gives some outline of field work in my first six months at Mweya. In addition the research involved analysis and writing that kept me indoors (the results are described in later chapters), as did administering the unit and routine correspondence.

My immediate goal was to collate the results of my first six months into a report for presentation to the NUTAE Committee, outlining my preliminary findings and making detailed proposals for future research. Flying to the UK, I put them to the NUTAE Committee chaired by Carl Pantin. It centred initially on hippopotamus population because of the animal's 'keystone' role in the QENP. Further, while hippo management was already under way, we still needed a better understanding of their biology. It was an ideal entry point for studies of that tropical ecosystem. The programme was to be experimental, and in a series of study areas the local hippo numbers would be manipulated to produce a range of different densities. Their effects on the vegetation and on the densities of other grazing animals would be documented, by botanical transects and large animal counts.

My proposals were accepted, and only one member of the Committee was opposed, – George Salt FRS, who had taught me ecology as a student. He felt that the unit should be investigating tropical ecosystems on a broad front, not so narrowly focussed. George maintained his position, but agreed to accept the majority view. My proposed programme was thus endorsed by seven Cambridge professors and seven FRSs and it was to take off from there.

Chris Field, a graduate in zoology of King's, Cambridge whom I would supervise for a PhD on hippopotamus grazing behaviour, was appointed NUTAE's Deputy Director. So I returned to Mweya with my mandate, to develop the research programme as I wanted.

Chris Field and I were later joined by Gerald Clough who had started a Cambridge PhD on mice pheromones, but wished to change to hippo reproduction! Later Mike Lock and Jeremy Grimsdell, also Cambridge research students, came to work respectively on the vegetation and buffalo population ecology. Clive Spinage, a London University PhD student, came to study waterbuck population ecology. In addition to Chris, I had also agreed to supervise Gerald, Jeremy and Clive for their PhDs. At the same time I had accepted supervision of Murray Watson, another Cambridge research student doing a PhD on wildebeest population ecology in the Serengeti. He used to come to Uganda for supervisions in the Serengeti Research Unit's Piper Supercub aircraft, and in turn I visited the Serengeti. Later other students joined us, including Tom Kangwagye, a Ugandan working on biting flies, and Richard Neal, a Canadian working on small mammals.

* * * *

Monday 8 October 1962 was the start of celebrations of Uganda's Independence Day (from British rule) and John Poppleton's fifth birthday; we had tea at Inge's. The Independence of Uganda from colonial rule was to be celebrated throughout the night, so we men went off to shoot some buffalo in the park for the *ngoma* – celebrations. Frank and I were invited and went off at 10 o'clock to the African camp, where there was a large bonfire, drum-beating, dancing and talk. I made some tape recordings on my Butoba recorder, but they were very monotonous, mainly drums, with occasional snatches of conversation. Many of the African staff came up to us and said they hoped we would not be leaving now the country was independent. They were not looking forward to Independence and said they would be much worse off under their new *African* masters! How right they were! The 9th was the actual Uganda Independence Day and I slept late having returned at about 3 o'clock in the morning.

At the time, life continued very much the same both before and immediately after Uganda became independent. The politics of the country had not figured in our lives, and seemingly things would keep going as they were. Here and there, there were straws of impending change in the wind. An example was in the middle of March 1963 when there was a hippo shoot at the big wallow near TUFMAC. It was to be the first time Abondio (Frank's Deputy) was in charge. Poppleton was in Kampala as the national parks' Acting Director while Bombo Trimmer was on leave pending retirement. We arrived too early, at 6 o'clock, before dawn.

Abondio and Ranger Sgt Paulo did the shooting and it was atrocious. They took about 150 rounds for 28 hippo and we were still hauling them out twelve hours later at 6:30 p.m. as dusk approached. We made our comprehensive biological collections, but didn't get home until about 8 o'clock – in the dark. The appalling performance brought home the critical role of marksmanship in such work, as armies have found out worldwide. Training can improve shooting competence up to a point, but true marksmen seem to have an innate skill. Of soldiers perhaps only 1 per cent are real marksmen. Frank Poppleton was one such, but until he was replaced I had not appreciated just how good he was or how critical this skill was to successfully culling wild animals. It had not been apparent on Signy Island or South Georgia because seals allowed such close approach that this need for marksmanship was not apparent.

I quote this instance of Abondio's first hippo cull, not in criticism for overall he was a thoroughly good man whom I liked and with whom I got on well. I record it because I had come to accept that the wonderfully smooth manner in which NUTAE had evolved to date was the way things were in Uganda. It never entered my mind that it was the outcome of a propitious set of coincidences bringing together a unique collection of personalities in the NUTAE Committee, trustees and wardens of Uganda's national parks,.

For the rest of 1963 and well into 1964, NUTAE continued to surge forward. In November 1963 there had been a meeting of the Scientific and Technical Committee (of which I was now a member) at Mweya. Among the participants were two personalities who would figure in our lives for the rest of our time in East Africa: David Sheldrick, warden of Kenya's Tsavo East National Park, and Ian Parker, a warden in the Kenya Game Department who was shortly to establish a firm of wildlife research and management consultants. David was in the mould of Frank Poppleton; both were of Kenya settler stock, both had become soldiers barely out of their teens when the Second World War broke out, both had become officers in the King's African Rifles – Frank a captain and David a major. Perhaps even more than Frank, David was held up as an exemplar of what a national park warden should be. Ian was younger and had served in the Kenya Regiment and as a temporary District Officer during the Mau Mau rebellion, before joining the Kenya Game Department. In the colonial mould, Frank, David and Ian had no formal qualifications, but were self-made men with whom I identified.

In 1964 the Park Trustees drew my attention to the MFNP where there was a high density of hippo on both banks of the Nile between Karuma Falls and Lake Albert and sought my advice. There was similar erosion to that we knew from QENP, and in addition a more serious situation where elephants had converted large tracts of woodland and forest into open grassland. From 1965 onward MFNP was to draw more and more of my attention away from QENP. For convenience this allows me to divide my time in Uganda into two phases: 1961–1964 when my own research was focussed on hippo in QENP, and 1965–1966 when, while still based at Mweya and running NUTAE, my personal interest swung to elephants. The first phase was idyllic for both the family and myself.

Looking up the Bujuku Valley across Lake Bujuku

15

Over the Mountains of the Moon

We could see the snow on the peaks of the Mountains of the Moon from our veranda. Frank and I had already decided to climb it during my initial visit to Uganda, and had planned this for February 1962. John Blower – then Chief Game Warden of Uganda – would join us. For most of the year the mountains are shrouded in cloud. Only in the dry season of January and February do they shed their mantle for a few days. The snow and distant summit of Mount Margherita posed a challenge I simply could not resist.

The Ruwenzoris lie along the western border of Uganda, between lakes Edward and Albert, rising over 16,000 ft above sea level. About sixty miles long and thirty in width, the range was formed from a block that has tilted and been thrust upward as the western arm of the Rift Valley evolved – a process still going on. At the centre of the range are six peaks carrying permanent snow and glaciers: Stanley (whose highest peak is Margherita at 16,763 ft), Speke (16,042 ft), Baker (15,889 ft), Gessi (15,470 ft), Emin (15,720 ft) and Luigi di Savoia (15,179 ft). Although the mountains are not volcanic, numerous small craters that are occur as foothills around the northern and southern ends of the Ruwenzoris (some occurring in QENP).

The massif receives very high rainfall and dense, wet forests clothe the lower slopes and are a centre for endemism which includes the brilliant Ruwenzori turaco. Their fauna includes some elephants and buffalo in the lower valleys, with chimpanzees, blue monkeys, red forest duikers, hyrax and leopard common among the more widely spread large mammals. However they are not easily seen in the dense cover. Above 10,000 ft, the trees give way to Afro-alpine moorland where the main botanical attractions are the fantastic giant forms of lobelias, heathers and groundsels.

So on Sunday 11 February 1962, Frank, John and I left Mweya early. We arrived at the Uganda Mountain Club hut at Ibanda, at the entrance to one of the Ruwenzori access valleys, at about 9 o'clock and were met by crowds of cheerful and keen Bakonjo porters. The Bakonjo are a mountain tribe who originally lived by hunting in these valleys up to 10,000 feet, using the numerous rock shelters which are a feature of the area. With British rule they gravitated and settled along the lower edges of the forests. While still great hunters, they now only ventured into the upper valleys as porters to expeditions such as ours.

These Bakonjo were hardy – as we were to discover. The terms upon which we employed them were standard and negotiated with them by the Uganda Mountain Club. We engaged a headman (who carried no load) called Benezeri at eight shillings per diem and fourteen porters for four shillings a day. One – Bwambale – agreed to be our cook for an extra shilling daily. They each carried loads of 50 lbs up to 15,000 feet, often over snow, with bare feet and little clothing. We also had to provide each with a 'sweater' (more of a T-shirt) and a blanket – costing together eleven shillings and fifty cents.

Already at the base hut we had a good view of the Portal Peaks, framed by the valley walls. They were very steep and rugged and the skyline was reminiscent of Skye and the Cuillin hills, except for the vegetation. In addition to the fifteen porters there were Frank, John and myself, John's gun bearer and Dario, one of Frank's park rangers. I didn't have a bearer. We left at 9:30 a.m. and the track led first through tall elephant grass, then open woodland by the Mubuku River. There was a steep climb in open forest up over a ridge and then down to the Mahoma River, where we paused for a while and drank from the clear water and I first experienced the virulence of the local stinging nettles!

The next part of the climb in the hot sun was in a way the worst because the track went steeply up through bracken, then on and on and on, up to the ridge between the Mahoma and Mubuku Rivers. The Bakonjo had built a number of small shrines near the path to appease the *shaitani* (spirits). These were small structures of grass about 18 inches high, usually an inverted V with an offering of banana in the opening. On the ridge the track levelled out through *Podocarpus* forest. Then we came upon a rock shelter and a few yards further on at 2 o'clock, the Mountain Club hut of Nyabitaba. This was an aluminium alloy hut with six bunks and an alloy cooking shelter. The porters slept in the upper rock shelter – there is one on either side of the hut. They are very like some of the rock shelters we had visited in the Dordogne, and used by Bakonjo until the area was made forest reserve and banned to residence.

The view across the very deep Mubuku Valley to the Portal Peaks was magnificent. There were few signs of animals – some elephant tracks in the forest and a few birds near the hut, including a small flock of red-winged starlings. After a meal we spent a relaxed afternoon taking some photographs and enjoying the scenery. Next morning we rose at 7 o'clock and breakfasted on tea and porridge. The porters were loaded up and off by 8.30 a.m., and we sent one porter back as the loads were getting lighter. Our way led downhill at first, through bamboo forest, to a small suspension bridge over the Mubuku River – rather like some of the flimsy structures one sees in the Far East. Then came some climbing through varied forest, with occasional views of the valley. In places the tracks were steep. We plugged on, myself taking many photographs, and reached the Nyamileju Hut at about 12:00 noon. It was sited at a rock shelter that catered for the porters, but this hut had no view. After we drank a bowl of soup and the porters had a meal, we decided to go on to the next camp site called Bigo. We had a little trouble here as the Mountain Club arrangement equated one stage between huts as the equivalent to one day's porterage. I am not sure how the dispute was settled, but we left again at 1 o'clock for Bigo and a most interesting part of the climb began.

We entered the tree heather zone – a place of fantastic red, brown, yellow and orange mosses – the tree heather with spongy moss clumps on the trunks and branches and with wispy grey-green hanging *Usnea* lichens. The going was bad; boggy tangles of roots had to be negotiated and there was a lot of plunging into deep mud, which was tiring. Following the Bujuku River gave occasional views of very attractive-looking reaches of water. Here we saw for the first time the tree *Hypericum* – a relative of the English garden plant St. John's wort, giant groundsel and giant lobelias up to some twelve feet high. The latter were very attractive in their oddity, especially when in flower, but the young plants with large rosettes of leaves and no flower stalk are also beautiful. It really was an 'enchanted forest' and I hoped that my colour slides would do it justice. The colourings were rather sombre, but attractive combinations of the grey, brown, black of lichens and the orange, yellow, green and brown of the mosses. It was very damp, but on looking back just before we came out of the forest there was a large burnt area on the north side of the valley (the bare trees covered in soft grey lichen growths). So fire evidently plays its part in the succession, as elsewhere, presumably caused by lightning strikes. One wonders how it is ever dry enough to burn!

Eventually we came out of the forest and into a flat, boggy area with *Helichrysum* (everlasting flowers) and giant groundsel dominating the vegetation, and with tree heather up to 30 ft high bordering the bog, where the drier ground began to rise. This last part of the day was a matter of progressing by leaping from one tussock to the next and trying to avoid the deep, boot-sucking bog in between. Unsuccessful leaps usually meant sinking in to our knees. However, we made good time and reached Bigo Hut at about 3 o'clock in brilliant sunshine.

This hut stood near a rock shelter with a fine view of Mount Speke to the north and views down the Bujuku Valley to the Portal Peaks. We washed in the river, which was icy-cold – not surprisingly as we could see the glaciers above. The night was cold though we were warm enough in our sleeping bags. The canvas of John's bunk came undone during the night and he hit the floor with a crash that shook the foundations, but he managed to right it again. In the morning frost glittered and sparkled outside. Two more porters were sent back and we set off further up the Bujuku Valley for Bujuku Lake at 9 o'clock. This brought us to a hanging valley (Kibatsi) of *Helichrysum* swamp, with groundsel and lobelias. Then followed a steep stretch through heather and groundsel – again beside a stream and fairly boggy. Levelling off into a groundsel forest, we rounded a corner and came on Bujuku Lake, with superb views of the Stanley Plateau, and Mounts Margherita and Alexandra behind. After a swampy stretch along the lake shore we arrived at the steep rock buttresses of the Trident to 'Cooking Pot' shelter. The porters slept here and for their comfort the Mountain Club had walled it in with aluminium alloy sheeting. The Bujuku huts for mountaineers were a little further on in a groundsel forest with views of Mount Baker and the Stanley Plateau – or rather the hanging ice cliffs at its edge which we reached at 1:45 p.m.

At that camp we saw a red mountain duiker, much higher than we had expected to see such animals. I followed it up the hillside; it was fairly tame and I took several photographs with my 200 mm lens, which came out well. The vegetation was different again – groundsel, lobelia, giant parsley and sphagnum. The groundsels really are trees, some of them over twenty feet high in the forest! The two huts were very comfortable, provided with Tilley lamps, pressure cooker, primus stoves etc., and previous parties had left a certain amount of food. The Mountain Club was certainly to be congratulated.

On Wednesday 14 February we climbed Mount Speke's Vittorio Emanuele peak – 16,047 feet. Rising at 7 o'clock after a bad night, I had a headache, no doubt caused by the altitude (now 13,000 feet). We left at 8:30 a.m. having paid off another three porters and with them went John's gun bearer and Frank's park ranger; no doubt they would do the equivalent of 'dining out' on their stories for months. Our route lay over the Stuhlmann Pass, up a steep pull almost to the top of the pass, then an easy scramble up some mossy slabs, before a cairned track led off to the north after we sighted the Speke Glacier. At the foot of the snow the porters left us and we climbed up a gully onto the ridge, pausing about half way up to put on crampons.

Continuing on up the ridge and then traversing to the right to avoid some rocks covered with a layer of ice (verglas) on the normal route, we climbed a small gully to a snow basin. From there we traversed across to the ridge between Vittorio Emanuele and Johnston – across a steep snow slope above some large crevasses. We roped for this and reached the ridge above a large cornice, from whence it was an easy walk to the summit. We reached the top, which was heavily embellished with large bosses of rime ice, at 12:40 p.m. From there we had splendid views of the neighbouring mountains, Stanley, Baker, Gessi and Johnston, but the surrounding plains were obscured by smoke haze from the grass burning that is a feature of dry-season Uganda. Clouds moved in and cut off the views so we started down at 1:30 p.m. The descent was straight-forward and we removed our crampons near the bottom for an exhilarating glissade! We lunched at the first stream we came to – on biscuits and chocolate. I stopped to take some flower photographs on the way. We were back at the hut by 3.15 p.m. and in the afternoon we rested – bathed and shaved. That evening I read the hut book.

Next day was easy, up at 7:30, we lazed in the sun under the tree groundsel and left at 12:15 p.m. for Elena bivouac two and half hours away. The route included some rather muddy going, then up steep screes, below some vertical crags and views to the Elena Glacier, Coronation Glacier, and the peaks of Savoia, Great Tooth and Elena. Unfortunately the clouds came down so the views were not as good as they might have been. The porters in bare feet were feeling the cold but pressed on to the huts across a series of rough rock ridges and troughs full of snow. As there were no facilities for them to camp at the Elena Glacier, they returned to Cooking Pot to come back in the morning.

The two corrugated aluminium alloy huts were tent-shaped and very small. One slept on wooden floors, which were in contact with the ice, and there was room for three people in each, one more at a pinch. They were partly snowed up. In one of them I found a pair of skis and sticks and, although they didn't fit very well, tried them out. I went up onto the glacier several hundred feet to where it steepened again after a level stretch. I was out for about an hour and had an exhilarating run down – I had always wanted to ski on the Equator! Returning to the hut we had a protracted meal. None of us was anxious to go to bed early because it was obviously going to be a cold and uncomfortable night. Unfortunately, John had left his sunglasses at Bujuku and would have trouble, even snow-blindness, from the glare, so Frank and I would be on our own next day. We planned to climb Margherita and intended to leave at 6 o'clock so as to get the best of the weather.

I had a very bad night because my lilo deflated and the floor of the hut was not insulated. It was one of the coldest nights I had spent, even including Antarctic camping. I didn't sleep and was glad to get up at 5 o'clock. Frank and I then had a cup of tea and a few biscuits waiting for the dawn. It was a quiet starlit morning with few clouds and when we set off at 6:30 a.m. up the Elena Glacier, dawn was just breaking. There was a clear black line along the horizon where the smoke haze lay like a blanket; above that the dawn colours and some small black and brownish clouds scudding along in the strong wind. The surrounding mountains were silhouetted in varying tones of purple against the dawn. It looked like the beginning of a perfect day and we made good speed up the glacier – noting, however, some ominous clouds behind Speke. The surface was crisp and the going good.

Sadly, the cloud soon descended on us and visibility varied between 30 and 100 feet. We pressed on, but coming to some crevasses decided to wait a while to see whether the clouds would lift. We were then just on the edge of the Stanley Plateau where the gradient eased off, but I didn't like to take any risks in such weather. It was very cold in the wind at nearly 16,000 feet and the moisture in the air was depositing as rime on our hair, so that we looked grey-headed. We heard birds calling on the crags to our left but didn't see what they were. At times the sun appeared to be about to break through but didn't. We were treated to some amazing light effects – like a Turner painting – luminous hazy clouds with small shafts of light hitting the ice in places. By 8 o'clock it was clear to us that the weather was not going to improve and we turned back in white-out conditions – rather cold by now.

John was up and we consumed hot porridge and tea, then packed our gear and waited, freezing cold, for the porters. We had the primus going but it didn't seem to give out much heat at that altitude. We thought the porters might be along by 11 o'clock but when noon came we began to contemplate another night in the bivouac. However, just as we were thinking of a meal they appeared out of the mist on the rocks below, at 1 o'clock. They were a very good bunch – freezing cold, most of them with bare feet, but they hadn't let us down. So now we set off down the slopes to the Scott Elliot Pass. Through great lichen- and moss-covered boulders at first, with large snow patches between, Benezeri had no hesitation in guiding us through the mist, although there was no obvious trail. As we left Elena the mist cleared slightly and we had a last impression of the place as we had seen it. The tiny silver huts perched on black rocks below a steep, heavily crevassed glacier, with massive crags and hanging glaciers above disappearing into the clouds. Then the mist closed in again. In clear conditions it must be stunning indeed.

The Scott Elliot Pass was very forbidding – sheer rock walls either side rising thousands of feet – the pass itself boulder strewn and very steep on the Bujuku side. These boulders and scree slopes were reminiscent of the Cairngorms. We picked our way down beneath the vertical wall of Mount Baker on our left with the cloud base following us down. Soon the first of the two Kitandara lakes was sighted below us – a mysterious place – rather dark and gloomy as we saw it, like a loch or tarn. Benezeri informed us that *shaitani* (spirits) lived there.

However, this was a much less bleak valley than the Bujuku, the vegetation similar and yet essentially different. There were plenty of *Hypericum* trees with red-orange flowers. The lower Kitandara lake was more attractive: glass-clear water and surrounding it *Helichrysum*, groundsel, lobelia etc. It is one of the most beautiful places I have ever seen and the hut was in a perfect setting, beneath a crag at one end of the lake. To the south Mount Luigi di Savoia dominated the view with a rock tooth, known as McConnell's Prong, very conspicuous on the skyline. Behind was Mount Baker – or rather its buttresses which are all that could be seen from the hut.

We washed and shaved and had a meal of potatoes and tinned salmon. I took some photographs although the light was bad and then a terrific thunderstorm began and hailstones assaulted us, rattling on the tin roof. Lightning played around the peaks and the sounds of thunder reverberated loudly; it went on and on. The porters came for medical treatment, probably not because they felt unwell but because they wanted some pills and ointment – *dawa* (medicine). We gave them aspirin for headaches, caused by the snow, and Vick ointment to rub on their feet and chests for pains also allegedly caused by the snow. We then had a fairly early night in comfortable surroundings.

After a very good night's rest for a change – warm and comfortable – I was woken as Kwambale came in to make the fire up and prepare breakfast. The weather was still gloomy with a sprinkling of new snow low down and thick mist. We decided to push on to Kabamba Rock Shelter as with such weather there was little else that we could usefully do. This was unfortunate as I should have liked to see more of Kitandara, but clearly there was not much point in staying under those conditions. It must be a jewel of a place in the sunshine.

So we set off at 9:50 a.m., up the steep slopes behind the hut, through snow patches and lush vegetation – *Helichrysum*, groundsel and heather. It was a hard pull up to and then across the Freshfield Pass (14,050 ft). Unfortunately there were no views, but the mist imparted an eeriness to the place, the giant vegetation being so many grotesque looming shadows. There were occasional patches of sun lighting a crag or a hillside. We then turned down through some interesting country where on a clear day the views must be superb and came to Bujongole Rock Shelter about noon – making very good time. This was a huge overhanging rock cliff with a sleeping platform beneath, but we decided to carry on past Kabwamba Rock Shelter to Kichuchu Rock Shelter because we were making such good time. The porters asked for half a day's pay extra but when they realised there was nothing doing, they were not upset – it was a try-on!

Kabwamba itself was impressive – a similar very large overhanging cliff with sleeping platforms and a waterfall at the upper end, set in pleasant heather forest with the clear stream very close. We had a brew of canned soup there – asparagus – and then at 2 o'clock we set off again for Kichichu. First came a level stretch through the grassy glades by the river; then steep downhill through the forest – the usual tangle of roots and branches concealed by large growths of sphagnum. The gradient eased and we made a final very steep descent in bog, moss, roots, rock, etc., to one side of a large cliff, at the bottom of which lay our rock shelter, with a stream a few yards away. Frank found an old clay pot while clearing the site.

Mount Luigi di Savoia

The porters cut grass for our sleeping platform and we washed and sat talking for a while under the stars. The porters came for medicines again – only one or two that evening. They all sat around talking for a time and then Benezeri picked up a burning log from the fire and went off into the forest, followed by some of the others. They were going to find a bee colony. Soon we heard triumphant chants and smoke drifted slowly down the valley. Kwambale appeared with a honeycomb and gave us some to taste. It was delicious – real heather honey from the giant heather, so naturally superb! In that kind of environment one rather expected giant bees as well; fortunately, none appeared! The weather looked ominous, we heard thunder, and clouds were creeping down the hillside – but it cleared and we spent a pleasant evening drinking the medicinal brandy and watching swifts and martins which were nesting in the cliffs above us.

It was almost a full moon that night, a glorious night – the moon providing sharp but subtle light and shadow and the cliff, apparently of infinite height, hanging above us. I lay for a long time in my sleeping bag drinking it all in. Delicate traceries of plants and grass growing on the cliff were silhouetted against the light sky. Occasionally the fire would flare up and the flames would be reflected on the cliff. The smoke from the fires added to the mystery of the place. It was quite warm in my sleeping bag and I woke from time to time to see clouds rushing across the sky at one time, the next moment it was quite clear with the stars twinkling. It was one of those wonderful experiences, feeling so close to nature.

On 18 February we woke to a colourful dawn and the sound of Kwambale making up the fire for breakfast. This was our last day and we departed at 8:30 a.m. for Nyabitaba and Ibanda along a rough, muddy and slippery trail through bamboo forest. We took about two hours to Nyabitaba, with occasional glimpses of the hills from view points on the ridge. After a short rest there, we continued on down the steep ridge which had taken us so long to ascend a week ago, but it took only half an hour to descend to the Mahoma River where we drank the clear water. Then on through undulating forest, and finally through the elephant grass to Ibanda, reached at 1:20 p.m. – to find no transport there! We paid off the porters, who had been an exceptionally good lot. They immediately spent some of their hard-earned pay on *pombe* or rather *kwetta* – a banana beer. I tasted some and found it very like cider, though not so pure, with grubs and other unidentifiable inclusions.

Indefatigable Frank decided to walk to the power station to get transport. He had been gone about half an hour when the park Land Rover turned up; we loaded it and met Frank coming back along the lane in a borrowed vehicle. So off to Kasese at great speed, for a beer at Patel's *duka* (shop) and then home to Mweya. The trip had been unforgettable, never to be repeated because intertribal fighting broke out and the mountain was closed to visitors.

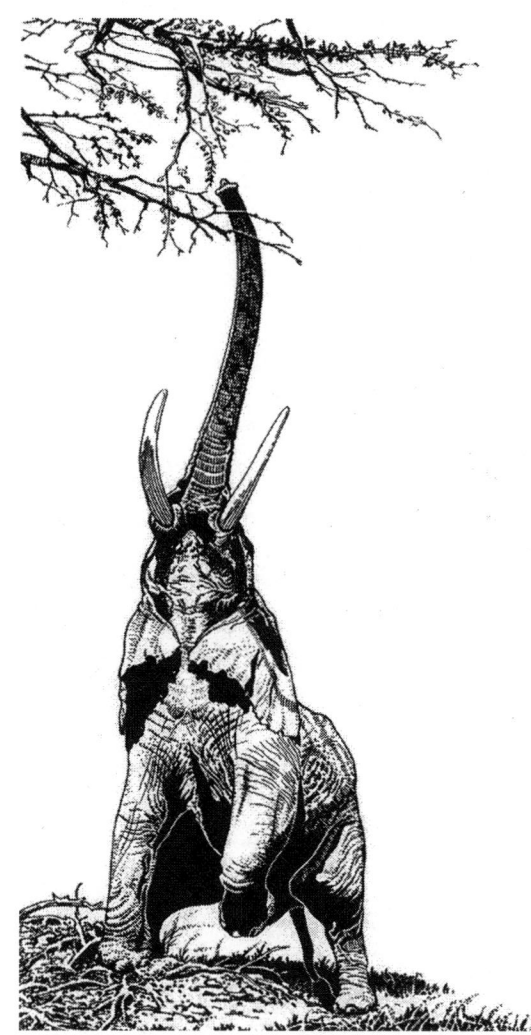

On its hind legs a bull elephant can reach up 16 metres

16

Expanding Horizons

As already explained I decided to build the NUTAE research programme around a core of research on hippo. From the outset the pace of progress constantly surprised and gratified me. Where distance and difficult communications in the Antarctic had always been an unavoidable brake on how fast I could proceed, in Uganda this was largely removed and the interest and help available was at times almost overwhelming.

Chris Field was a good man (Cambridge and a rugby player!) and an excellent deputy. With the others of our tight NUTAE team, Gerald Clough on hippo reproduction, Mike Lock on vegetation, Jeremy Grimsdell, on buffalo and Clive Spinage on waterbuck, research surged forward with everyone 'mucking in' and helping one another. By 1964 we were developing a satisfying grasp of some basics in the QENP ecology. True to Ralph Dreschfield's word when I first arrived, the national parks staff were helping and participating in our work across the board.

We had rapidly come to terms with the 'hippo problem' that had weighed heavily upon the Trustees when I first arrived. Our research had confirmed hippo in high densities did both decrease diversity, particularly of other large mammals, and modify vegetation. The changes had been measured and documented in a cascade of scientific papers published or in preparation. Perhaps most impressive had been the overall integration of science with park management. Jointly we had demonstrated that a large African herbivore could be managed to recover diversity within a national park. I stress, however, that it had been a tentative first step. Whether hippo culling might have to be a permanent feature of QENP management was moot. To answer that fully called for a far wider grasp of the overall ecology that would take decades, perhaps centuries, to acquire.

When NUTAE started, what was known of hippo biology was largely limited to the (good) behavioural studies by Belgian scientists in the very early 1950s working in the then Belgian Congo. By its fourth year the NUTAE work had made the species one of the best known, biologically, of Africa's fauna.

I have no doubt that I could have been fully occupied for the rest of my life describing ecology in QENP in ever greater depth. However, given our success in this park, the Uganda Park Trustees now wanted me turn attention to the same problem in the MFNP.

* * * *

First a little background to MFNP. In 1964 the Park Trustees sought my advice and NUTAE's involvement in the MFNP. Comprising some 3,480 km², it is bisected into two roughly equal portions by fifty miles of the Victoria Nile between Lake Albert and the Karuma Bridge (from here on I shall refer to the park north of the Nile as MFNPN and that south of the river as MFNPS). The Nile in this section was turbulent, fast flowing with many cataracts, and had been an effective barrier to not only humans, but also many animals and plants. Effectively, therefore, MFNP had two separate ecologies. The only species of large mammal to which the Nile had not been a barrier was the hippo. The Trustees were worried that hippo over-abundance existed creating a very similar situation to that with which I was familiar in QENP. In addition, elephants had eliminated forest, woodland and their associated fauna over very large areas on both banks of the river.

MFNP's historical background was similar to QENP's. The areas both north and south of the Nile were littered with pottery sherds that attested to the past presence of many humans in pre-colonial times. When white men first arrived, the river was the dividing line between Nilotic Acholi people to the north and Bantu-speaking Banyoro to the south.

A virulent outbreak of human sleeping sickness (*Trypanasomiasis*) was raging in the first decade of the 20th century. Once shown to be derived through tsetse flies (*Glossina palpalis*) whose distribution coincided with dense shade in proximity to water, in 1913 people were evacuated away from the Nile and its tributaries. The vacated land north of the Victoria Nile and east of the Albert Nile was designated the Gulu Game Reserve (the HQ of Acholi District being Gulu), and that south of the Victoria Nile the Bunyoro Game Reserve. As Game Reserves were barred to human residence, this conservation measure was used as a legal device to reinforce the sleeping sickness laws. MFNP was proclaimed in 1952 and derived from the southern quarter of the Gulu Game Reserve and most of the Bunyoro Game Reserve.

Directly and indirectly, the build-up of both hippo and elephant numbers in MFNP was attributed to the 1913 sleeping sickness evacuation of people. It was added to by the Game Department policy of eliminating elephants from agricultural areas. As people increased and farming expanded, they formed an ever tightening collar around what became MFNPS, displacing and pressing them into it. Since 1925 over 16,000 elephants had been shot in Bunyoro as this policy of 'elephant control' was implemented. It involved harrying and shooting elephants wherever they were unwanted, and involved an unrecorded number getting away from hunters, but later dying from their wounds making the total killed substantially greater. From evidence of control shooting around the Budongo Forest, I calculated this to be at least 20 per cent of the recorded deaths making a likely total nearer 20,000.

On the face of it, all the unwanted hallmarks of high hippo densities known from QENP were apparent along the banks of the Nile. The bare eroded areas and lack of grazers close to the river told the same story. My first task was learning how many hippo we were dealing with. As the Nile between the actual Murchison Falls and Karuma Falls is a fifty-mile series of turbulent cataracts, counting from a boat as we had in QENP was not possible, and there were no roads along the river banks from which counting could be done. The only practical option was counting from the air. At the time, neither the Uganda National Parks nor NUTAE had an aircraft. Consequently Ian Parker's Kenya-based company – Wildlife Services Ltd (WLS) – was contracted to make an initial survey of the first ten miles downstream from the Karuma Falls. Ian and one of his fellow directors, Alistair Graham (also ex-Kenya Game Department and a qualified biologist), did so in July 1964, and their result was far higher than had been estimated by the park's Scientific Warden, John Savidge a year earlier. Nevertheless, an experimental cull was agreed for this part of the river.

Unlike QENP, shooting hippo in the Nile's turbulent water was not feasible as, when carcasses became buoyant, they would have been swept downstream and impossible to recover. Again, as the Uganda Parks did not have sufficient of their own staff to do this work they contracted it out to WLS with the condition that they collect whatever data I wanted and were under my scientific supervision. Both parties needed to get the measure of one another, and WLS needed to see whether the QENP system of selling to local traders was possible.

Hippo culling on the uppermost section along the banks of the Nile commenced in October 1964 and was immediately successful. I had laid down what I needed from animals taken, and having seen our work in QENP, WLS had no trouble in complying. Traders would buy the carcasses. However, the remaining forty miles of the Nile downstream of the section already counted needed counting, and I wanted to get first-hand experience of the terrain, the animals and the overall ecology myself.

So, with Maureen and the boys, on the 19 of November 1964, we motored to the MFNP headquarters at Paraa (in the Acholi Lwo language *pa* means the place of and *raa* means hippo). Ian flew in from his camp at the east end of the park to collect me and for the next three days he and I counted hippo.

Hippo in Lake Edward

I immediately appreciated why Ian and Alistair's earlier counting had produced results that were so much higher than previously estimated. Typical of this iconoclastic couple's approach, they didn't just get in the air and start looking for hippos (or whatever else they were going to count), but first became familiar with the terrain and habitats where animals were to be counted. To this end they had obtained large-scale aerial photographs of the Nile from the Uganda government's Survey Department, from which they had drawn up maps of the river scaled 1:5,000. On these maps they had then marked in all islands, rapids, deep water and fast sections. One could immediately see those parts of the river where hippo would not be, and the places where they could lie up in the lee of islands or on sandbars out of strong currents, and where there was water less than three metres in depth.

This saved me, as the counter, from wasting time searching habitat unsuitable for hippo and knowing in advance where to look. With a sheaf of consecutive maps on a clipboard on my lap, we commenced moving from one likely spot to the next. As the observer with the map I indicated the successive possible sites, which Ian then flew to and circled. The water was clear and getting the light behind us, we could not only see hippos with their heads above water, but also all those completely submerged. This was unique in my experience as from a boat or in the more conventional methods of aerial counting, and in Africa's usually turbid rivers and lakes, one missed those completely underwater.

We circled each site repeatedly, wing tip down, steeply banked, circling and circling both looking and counting until I was satisfied. The height flown was chosen as that which best suited me, the counter. Satisfied, we then flew to the next potential site. It was a slow process. Again, the good fortune that saved me from seasickness in the Southern Ocean, served me well in the air. Most people would have quickly become dizzy and airsick and I could see why the technique would not be widely applied. The system was not only very tiring, but occasionally large flocks of Abdim's storks tried to join us, calling for evasive action. These migrants soar up and down sub-Saharan Africa moving from thermal to thermal along their route and our count coincided with their presence in Uganda. Like all such thermal soarers, they are constantly looking ahead for other soarers in the circling flight that marks a thermal. Seeing us circling endlessly, they and many vultures assumed we had found good lift and came to share it. At the end of a day's circling, Ian flew me back to Maureen and the boys at Paraa.

The principle WLS employed rested on having very good maps and knowing exactly where one was on them. It also called for robust stomachs! They were later to use it when counting elephants in MFNP where the ground was open rolling grassland and the national park's 1:250,000 maps had every watercourse and drainage line marked in. These permitted the whole area to be divided into small blocks, each readily recognisable from the air, which could be methodically and carefully searched until the searcher was satisfied all animals had been counted (often calling for the same herd to be counted several times) before moving to the next compartment.

The technique was not widely employed in East Africa because so many of the big wildlife areas were neither mapped on the scale nor with the detail available for MFNP. Without clear drainage lines and covered with featureless bush, it is difficult to keep accurately located. The mapping was hugely improved by familiarity with the terrain which is usually lacking. Finally and perhaps the greatest influence against its application was that it was much more expensive than flying routine sample transects that became the norm in African game counting. A further important factor was that most animal counts in East Africa were ends in themselves and not means to management action. Consequently while general orders of population size or establishing trends in numbers were all that was being sought, I wanted a far higher level of precision to apply to such management as I might advocate.

Several points emerged from my first intense working connection with the WLS team. Among them was their use of light aircraft. Treating them as aerial Land Rovers, take-off and landing was by no means restricted to airstrips: roads, tracks, sandbars and any area of relatively smooth ground sufficed. Again, their iconoclasm showed through. Aircraft were tools to be used! They set aside many of the regulations, and the resulting assertion by those who flew within the rules that they were 'cowboys' overlooked a high level of skill. I approved their approach.

After analysing the aerial hippo counts and confirming that the negative aspects of high hippo densities were just as apparent along the Nile as they had been in QENP, I recommended that the Trustees should reduce them by 4,000 out of the 14,000 present between the Murchison and Karuma Falls. Dividing the river into some twenty-five sections, I allocated an offtake based on numbers within each and which varied from zero as controls across a range of numbers so that the influence of removal could be monitored. The offtake should be completed within two years. While it was not within my purview to select whoever should do the work, I was nonetheless pleased when the Trustees contracted WLS to do it, as this was an organisation I felt comfortable working with. To that end, and given the scope of the contract, WLS formed a subsidiary Uganda company – Game Management (Uganda) Ltd – which became known to all as GMU. Satisfied that the local people around MFNP would buy the hippo carcasses, GMU agreed to pay the Parks a fee for each hippo taken.

Fortunately the easy relationship that I had found so attractive in QENP was also apparent under the park's Senior Warden, Roger Wheater, and his wife Jeannie. His easy-going manner made for a very smoothly run ship.

17

Murchison Falls National Park and Elephants

Having settled the hippo policy I now turned to the elephant problem. National parks in most of Anglophone Africa only started to appear on the continent's maps after the Second World War. There were exceptions; for example South Africa's Kruger National Park was first proclaimed as a game reserve at the end of the 19th century and the Belgians had created the Albert National Park in 1927. The majority, however, were scarcely into their second decade when NUTAE was formed. Yet within that short period, many managers became aware that elephant were causing a common problem by destroying trees and woodland. Indeed, it had been first reported in the 1930s in what became MFNP. It was unsettling for those with faith in there being a 'balance of nature'.

This ecological change had first been brought to wider notice in 1947 by Joe Eggeling, a forester (later to become Director, Scotland, of Nature Conservancy) in a classic ecological study of Uganda's Budongo Forest, contiguous with the south-western border of MFNP. He concluded that elephants, not fire, were the primary agent in reducing East African forests, flying in the face of contemporary forestry theory that, worldwide, fire was the greatest threat to forests.

By the early 1960s the widely shared elephant problem had become an issue of some urgency. In dry, arid Kenya's Tsavo East under David Sheldrick it was being given a lot of publicity. Yet the problem was patently far advanced in well-watered MFNP at the other end of the rainfall spectrum.

The Scientific and Technical Committee of the EAWS had taken it up and the issue was generating considerable interest outside East Africa. The solution set in motion by Uganda's hippo culling seemed the obvious approach and all agreed that reduction was called for. However, it was generally perceived that for an iconic, charismatic species such as the elephant, embedded in our culture for its sagacity and longevity (whereas hippo were seen as buffoons in comparison), reduction would be problematic. At the core of the claimed difficulties was the issue of disturbance. Whereas hippos were relatively easy to shoot when they were solitary and feeding at night without disturbing a population, elephant were social and it was widely held that shooting individuals out of herds would cause great disturbance and even put visitors to parks at risk from enraged survivors. They would have to be taken out as entire herds to minimise this prospect. The prevailing wisdom was that this would be well-nigh impossible.

In fact, with hindsight, this thinking was more than a little irrational. Forgotten was that hippo shooting at night in QENP had been abandoned in favour of taking them in the water where they lived in groups, without any obvious disturbance. Equally overlooked was that both Uganda and Tanzania shot several thousand elephants annually. They had done so, from at least as far back as the 1920s, without any untoward consequence for nearby humans. Nevertheless, a statement endorsing elephant reduction as essential was made by the Scientific and Technical Committee of the EAWS meeting at MFNP Park HQ, Paraa, and met with agreement by the official conservation authorities in all three East African countries. In this era immediately before and for several years after African Independence, this committee was treated as the public arbiter in regional conservation matters.

The Uganda National Parks Trustees bit the bullet and on my advice agreed to take a trial sample of 200 elephants in MFNPN. If this was successful, then a further sample of 200 should be taken in MFNPS on the reasoning that it was likely that we would be dealing with separate populations. Results from the two samples would determine the next appropriate action. Again, GMU was contracted to undertake the work under my scientific direction. A condition of the contract was that, as with hippo, the elephant carcasses had to be used; the idea of unused carcasses lying scattered about the park was unacceptable to everyone. The company had suggested two options: either the Trustees paid the company a fee for each elephant culled, or the company paid Parks a fee for each elephant taken and were then free to market the carcasses and by-products. The Trustees decided not to take the risks inherent in the first option, as such work had not been done before, and let GMU carry the commercial risks. They were contracted to collect all the scientific data I requested and had to take entire herds to minimise disturbance. Taking complete herds from the youngest to the oldest animals could produce a cross-section of the populations that would be an enormous scientific bonus for me. If GMU found taking whole herds routinely was not possible, we would have to reconsider the programme.

I first met Ian Parker when he came to Mweya in November 1963 to attend a meeting of the EAWS Scientific and Technical Committee of which he was also a member. When I mentioned that elephants had six molars in a lifetime, his healthy disrespect for scientists was immediately apparent when he demanded to know how I knew. I explained palaeontologists had established it through study of teeth of *Proboscidea*, of which present elephants were members. In truth I had taken the six molars as read, but Ian was unconvinced, and I was obliged to prove it, first for myself and then to him on the jaws we had collected from natural mortality in QENP.

There were 385 jaws in my sample and first I had to identify the teeth in wear. For the first two teeth this is easy enough, because they are relatively small; the third is bigger but has characteristically 'wavy' enamel; the sixth tooth is easily identified because it is much larger and not usually followed by a seventh. The fourth and fifth presented initial difficulties but I was able to show that when measurements of length and width were plotted they fell into six well defined groups on the graph. I then divided my 385 jaws into thirty recognisable groups to which, with the help of deaths in a few known-age captive animals, I allocated arbitrary ages up to a maximum of between 60 and 70 years. In due course this would be modified as more evidence from known-age animals accumulated. (Running far ahead of my narrative, the remarkable work of Kenya's Amboseli elephants by Cynthia Moss in which all elephants are known, and the exact birthday of all that died during the three-decade study was known, their collected jaws and teeth provided such exact comparative evidence. Gratifyingly and somewhat surprisingly, Cynthia's data confirmed that my original hypothesis was so close to the truth that my calculations based on age needed no modifications of my findings.)

In August 1965 I drove to Paraa in MFNP to age about 250 elephant jaws representing natural deaths that Roger Wheater had collected for me in order to get some insight into elephant survivorship in the park. I took the opportunity to go to Chobe in the east of the park where GMU had established their hippo culling base camp, to cull two elephants and show Ian Parker what biological samples I would want from them. While at Chobe I made the acquaintance of an Italian, Dominico Bardana, the contractor then building a lodge for Uganda Hotels at Chobe. He looked a brigand, beefy and with a big black beard, but was in fact a very agreeable fellow. I found that, just as the little community at QENP had involved not only NUTAE and park staff, but some of the local white community, so it was with MFNP with Bardana being very much part of it. The co-operation between its members was memorable. Bardana kept a wonderful Italian table and was a delightful host. Thus when he invited Ian and me to dinner with himself and his two attractive nieces, we not only consumed lots of spaghetti but far too much Chianti. Afterwards we played cards and only managed to extricate ourselves at about 3 o'clock in the morning. We'd been up at 5 o'clock the previous day and I had to drive back 320 miles over the dirt roads to QENP so I was quite tired by the time I got back to Mweya. It recalled the boisterous occasions with the Norwegians in South Georgia.

* * * *

Although elephants had fascinated people across recorded history and in Asia had been domesticated for millennia, in 1965 surprisingly little was known of their biology. It was almost as though they had been deliberately kept behind a curtain of mystique and speculation. The greatest stimulus to rend this veil was the problem they posed by their impact on the very places set aside for their conservation: Africa's national parks.

In modern times my work on elephants was preceded by that of John Perry, for whom I had the greatest admiration and who, fifteen years earlier, had almost single-handedly spent two years examining 150 elephants shot in Uganda. His work when I began represented almost the sum of knowledge on elephant reproduction. He was followed by the American Fulbright Scholar, Irven Buss, who had collected 167 elephants in North Bunyoro and whose sterling work certainly significantly added to the accumulating body of evidence. Starting before the work in MFNP and overlapping it for a while was the research of Sylvia Sykes who reached her conclusions on the basis of forty animals selected from varied areas in Kenya and Uganda. She, too, had amassed an impressive body of information.

These three scientists were the vanguard in African elephant research after the Second World War. Operating independently, they faced the vastness of dissecting elephant carcasses with untutored helpers that, perforce, limited what they could handle in a day to single animals. While exercising some selection on which animals to collect (e.g. mature males or mature females etc.), the exigencies of approaching an elephant herd, often in thick cover, restrained what they could collect. They had to hunt in the traditional manner: tracking the quarry, carefully approaching downwind, closing in and then waiting undetected for a suitable animal to present itself favourably to the hunter. Commonly the desired specimen was screened by unwanted members of the herd and waiting in close proximity the hunter was at the mercy of sudden changes in wind direction and not without risk. Such factors often meant collecting an elephant took hours and the outcome of each hunt was always unpredictable. In such circumstances the results of Perry, Buss and Sykes were all that much more admirable. One could understand the widely held apprehension over demands that elephant reduction in a national park such as MFPN should be carried out by the whole herd, as all envisaged magnifying this routine hunting procedure with a big team of riflemen trying to shoot all of a herd before it scattered after the first shot was fired.

Yet should it prove feasible, the opportunity for collecting scientific material would be incredible. No one before had been able to look at a random, instantaneously collected, cross-section of an elephant population (or any large mammal for that matter). GMU had credentials that were the ground for choosing them to make the attempt. Two of its Directors – Ian Parker and Tony Seth-Smith – had, as game wardens, set up and run Kenya's Galana Game Management Scheme between 1960 and 1963. It had given them experience in trying to take an annual quota of elephants and marketing their meat and hides. Established for Wata traditional elephant hunters, the programme was a novel departure into using elephants in a commercially viable 'farming' sense. In addition, other GMU Directors included Chris Parker, Ian's wife (who ran the administration of the Galana Scheme), Alistair Graham, already mentioned, as well as Tony Archer and Mike Rowbotham, both experienced hunters.

Contrary to apprehensions and expectations, a facet of elephant behaviour made taking the first 200 elephants in MFNPN remarkably straightforward.

It pivoted on the control that the biggest females exercise over family units. The Wata termed such females *dadnaba hadmina* which, in their Oromo language, translates roughly as 'the owner of this village'. In due course, using the ageing key that I had developed, and the composition of herds, we were able to substantiate that these biggest females were in fact both the oldest and the genetic matriarchs. It was pleasing to acknowledge through science what the Wata with their elephant-based culture had known for centuries before any Western scientists studied elephants!

Sketching elephants was always a pleasant diversion

Matriarchal control was the elephants' Achilles heel. A family unit's first response to alarm is to cluster around its matriarch. Approaching a herd from downwind so that they could not detect the hunters' through scent, all one had to do was create a little unease with an unusual noise and they would come together. Once bunched, and in the order of biggest first, all were brain-shot to produce instant collapse. Knocking out the matriarch literally paralysed the rest of the herd for the few seconds it took to take the rest out. I timed a GMU team of two men take fifteen animals in forty-two seconds. Mature males in male-only units did not exhibit the same bunching behaviour upon an alarm. However, as they seldom formed groups of more than about six, they were still easily taken in MFNP's open grasslands. Indeed, elephants must be among the easiest of all social mammals to kill in groups. Yet, as I learned from QENP hippo culling, it calls for marksmanship that, even among habitual hunters, is rare.

GMU quickly developed taking whole herds into an efficient routine. To ensure the offtake was as random as possible, a brief aerial reconnaissance located herds and the nearest to an access track with twenty or fewer members became the target for the day – the only restriction upon the sample being random was herd size. The largest taken was twenty-nine, though twenty was the arbitrary upper limit set by GMU's resources.

The culling team approached the selected herd in vehicles getting as close as possible without alarming it. The shooters then closed in on foot, if necessary bunching it, then shooting it. The rest of the crew then drove up, usually in two Land Rovers and one or two five-ton trucks. A research tent consisting of a tarpaulin erected for shade, with a table, chair, weighing scales, preservative fluids and containers etc. was laid out. At the same time each elephant was given a serial number and a data sheet, and measured. Where they lay on top of one another (such was the speed at which they were shot that this was usual), a truck pulled them apart so that all were accessible. Once numbered and measured, thirty Wata, imported by GMU from Kenya, divided themselves among the carcasses and commenced skinning (the hide was later tanned) and dissecting them. Every man had specific tasks. Dissected organs were taken to the research tent, weighed, tissue samples taken and preserved. With the routine established it was all the recorder could do to keep up with the flow of material coming in. Once the team had learned the ropes, which did not take long, elephant culling for the day was over and the team often back at base before midday. In the wake of the dissections and data collection, local traders descended on the carcasses and removed the meat, leaving only viscera and bones in the field.

Routinely, all lower jaws were collected. The information we recorded included various body measurements (the most important being shoulder height), body weight, tusk weights and dimensions, stomach fill and organ weights (including brain, kidneys, heart, lungs, spleen, thyroids, adrenals, mammary glands, ovaries, uterus, conceptus, embryo or foetus, testes, seminal vesicles, prostate, and bulbo-urethral glands – depending on sex). Placental scars were counted (giving unique insight into a female's reproductive history) and the distribution of the scars in the uteri were recorded in the field. Tissue collected for histological examination included reproductive and endocrine organs, eye lenses (another indicator of age), stomach content samples, whole blood, blood serum, milk, depot fat, urine, sperm smears and living sperm (examined for motility). Tusks were collected and their dimensions, weights and other characteristics recorded.

The research team was augmented by a post-graduate PhD veterinary student – Keith McCullagh. His work included observations on the pathology of elephant hearts and aortae, establishing instantaneous growth rates, and chemical analyses of stomach contents, blood and milk. Again, his study of arteriosclerosis in these giant vegetarians was ground-breaking and established very obvious genetic predispositions regarding the condition. This was only apparent because in taking complete herds we had samples of entire families.

The very slickness and almost factory-like precision of GMU's elephant culling and sheer volume of data collected was immensely impressive, but sinister in its efficiency. If I had found killing seals, whales and hippos repugnant, this distress was immeasurably greater where elephants were involved. To an impartial scientist there should be no difference between taking the life of a mouse and an elephant, but no one is that impartial! Somehow doing what we were with these fantastically interesting entities with all their analogies to humans, and in the very places set aside for them to be safe from people, generated strong emotions of distaste in all involved.

Then and in years afterwards, I was often asked 'how could you be party to such culling?' My answer was simple: it had to be done. Elephants had been compressed into ever smaller areas like MFNP. Their excessive presence locally had eliminated a diverse vegetational mosaic of closed forest formations, low forest, woodland, bushland, wooded grassland, bushed grassland, grassland and swamp. By 1965, the landscape was grassland of recent origin, comprised of three main types: medium-height *Hyparrhenia* grasses on the lower and drier ground to the west; tall *Hyparrhenia* grasses between 850 metres and 1,100 metres above sea level, and giant *Pennisetum purpureum* (elephant grass) above 1,100 metres. All were annually ravaged by fire – sometimes caused by lightning, but usually lit by humans outside the park. Hundreds of acres of dead trees (*Terminalia glaucesens*) testified to the rapidity with which change had taken place. The forest and woodland animals were gone. Some 40 per cent of the birds recorded in the park when it was first formed in the early 1950s were no longer being seen in it. The park's floral and faunal diversity had declined steeply in a mere fifteen years.

This was a situation of immediacy. The only product of 'further careful study before taking action' that has become something of a mantra among many conservationists today would have been further losses. So obviously were elephants causing the trends that reducing their numbers was not open to debate if MFNP was to meet its goal of preserving all the species of flora and fauna that had existed within it when it was proclaimed.

In the process of reduction, collection of scientific data from this first step would allow us to document the species' biology – as I had done with hippo in QENP and earlier with elephant seals in South Georgia. That advance in knowledge would not only provide ground for subsequent policy in MFNP, but enhance our understanding of the elephant problem that was emerging so widely elsewhere. It was the immediate fate of all the plants and animals that had gone or were disappearing that justified the unpleasant work of culling.

Taking the 200 elephants in MFNPN was so successful that the Trustees approved my second recommendation that a further 200 be taken in MFNPS. Serendipity no doubt, but perhaps resulting from the coming together of Roger Wheater as Park Warden with GMU directors who, perhaps unexpectedly in a commercial concern, were as interested in science as they were in turning a profit, and a team of Wata whose interest in and familiarity with elephants complemented my own experience of working with commercial sealers, whalers and very large carcasses. At the time it did not seem out of the ordinary, but with hindsight it was a rather remarkable combination of talents and interests melding harmoniously.

The high quality of biological material collected on a scale never contemplated was intellectually exciting. At the end of each day in the field we returned to camp with our scientific trophies and examined them, making many new discoveries. No period in my research career has been as satisfying as this first eighteen months working on elephant biology. In less than six months not only had I co-authored a paper with Ian Parker that confirmed that the Nile divided two different populations, but we had also derived age structures, growth curves, mean ages of sexual maturity, calving intervals and break-downs of all herds in which relationships between members could be imputed. The eminent British biologist Frank Fraser-Darling who had made a long-term study of red deer on the island of Rhum wrote: 'if we had produced for red deer on Rhum in twenty years, what you have produced for elephants in six months, we would have been well pleased.' He was not implying that the work on Rhum had been in any way deficient, for the contrary was true: it was exemplary. His comparison was simply one of amazement over what we had achieved in so short a time. I found this accolade from a scientist of his standing a real reward.

Elephants swim well, but though a few bulls cross the Nile below Murchison Falls where there are no rapids, the river is an effective barrier between two distinct populations on either bank

* * * *

Integral to coming to terms with the elephant problem was understanding what was happening to the local vegetation. Initially I was concerned with that in MFNP only, but as word of our advances in MFNP became known, the Uganda Forest Department asked us to include the Budongo Forest – contiguous to the park – in our research programme. Elephant within it had been in conflict with the department's management of timber production (then worth £7 million annually and £84 million in 2004). This gave us access to additional but less complete data from some 300 animals shot inside the Budongo Forest and its vicinity by forest guards, as well as to the department's own research results.

MFNP flora had been established in sufficient detail for the Survey Department to have mapped the diverse vegetational mosaic of eight types listed in the previous section. This is what we had to build on. Limited resources meant that we could only undertake four novel projects.

First, aerial photographic transects across the park, funded by the Royal Society, were made and analysed by my former student Murray Watson. These quantified the destruction of woody vegetation and established a base line from which the national parks could monitor future changes. Sixteen photographic transects, half north and half south of the Nile, totalled 456 linear kilometres (285 mi.) and sampled an area of 250 km^2 (98 mi.^{2}). Numbers of mature trees, small trees and bushes, dead trees and animal tracks were recorded. The picture emerging was that tree damage had progressed radially from within the park towards the periphery through the woodland, leaving behind grassland. It stopped abruptly at the edge of the elephant distribution established by the aerial counts. If fire had caused the tree loss, a reverse picture would have been the case. Disappearance of trees would have been greatest where fire frequency was highest – that is in the vicinity of people outside the park – and least where there were no people in the depths of the park.

This was confirmed on the ground re-examining radial transects of two tree counts; in the Wairingo area of MFNPS made by Hal Buechner, and by Richard Dawkins of the Uganda Forest Department in 1958. By 1967 all living trees (*Terminalia*) they had noted had disappeared or were dead. Further, despite burning, tree regeneration had only occurred where there were no elephant.

Second, two sets of experimental plots were set up by Roger Wheater, one in MFNPN and the other in MFNPS, both in open, treeless grassland. Each was surrounded by an elephant-proof moat and divided into three one-acre plots. Of them one was kept free of fire, one was burned early in the dry season – a so-called 'cool' burn – and one was burned late in the dry season as a 'hot' burn. Within two years of their establishment all had some saplings and shrubs showing out of the grass. Eight years after establishment, all three plots in both sets had closed tree canopies of between nine and fifteen metres' height. The unburned plots had the greatest diversity of trees, the cool burns had intermediate diversity, while the hot burns showed the least – yet all had grown trees despite fire. Incontrovertibly in the MFNP circumstances, without elephants, trees re-established themselves despite fire. An altogether different but fascinating question that was never answered was how had the tree seeds got there?

Third, in 1967 I looked into the history of elephant use of the Budongo by examining the stumps of felled forest giants – mahoganies – for dated indications of earlier elephant usage far back in time. These trees are strongly buttressed. Elephant occasionally eat their bark. However they can only tusk it loose on the buttresses' outer edges, and cannot get into the valleys between them. Almost immediately the tree lays down bark over the wound made by an elephant. As the tree continues to grow the bark that sealed the original wound is in turn covered over by new wood, but a patch of bark remains sealed into the body of wood. I aged the trees from their growth rings and the position of the bark wound covering in the ring pattern gives an approximate date of when the wound was inflicted. Seemingly, there had been a rise of elephant barking mahoganies in the Budongo between 1780 and 1820 and then again as the 20th century advanced. With the latter I can, with some confidence, attribute it to human increase compressing elephant into the forest as it had progressively confined them into the next-door park. However, we had no idea of what had caused the earlier surge in elephant debarking mahoganies. It never progressed beyond a tantalising glimpse into the past.

Fourth, I had access to studies carried out by Ron Johnstone – the forester responsible for managing the Budongo Forest – which measured elephant influence on forest regeneration. Budongo's management was based on the forest being divided into a set of cells, one of which was clear felled annually, which brought the forest canopy to the ground. Trees would regenerate over the next ninety years before timber was again extracted. By holding the canopy on the ground, elephant were extending the ninety-year cycle by ten years which, in the foresters' terms, was unacceptable. In addition, Ron found that elephant ate mahogany saplings preferentially, meaning that their place was being taken over by commercially uneconomic species.

Unexpectedly, however, the most dramatic demonstration was provided much later that in MFNP elephants and not fire were the primary cause of woodland and forest loss when Uganda fell into chaos under Idi Amin and all but fewer than 200 of MFNPS's elephant were killed. Within two decades, the open, rank grassland of the mid-1960s had been almost completely replaced by dense, regenerating forest – this despite no decline in the incidence of fire. Without elephants, forest and its flora had not only reappeared, but had become sufficiently dense and lush to exclude fire completely. In this area with a 1,200 mm annual rainfall, trees had overcome fire and re-established themselves.

* * * *

Our scientific evidence was again lodged in the scientific literature to which I added numerous papers and reports emanating from MFNP. It covered establishing the numbers, distribution and varying densities across the park and followed changes resulting from the culling. I had established growth, longevity, reproduction, nutrition, population and social structures in elephants in three areas – MFNPN, MFNPS and Budongo – and differences between them. The work has shown that elephant could be handled more easily 'by the herd' than had ever been expected and with no evidence of population disturbance. (This is in contrast to similar work which followed in South Africa and Zimbabwe, where larger herds were taken and/or herds were driven long distances in a protracted period of stress.) At the same time the vegetation and their influence upon it had been documented: all this being done in parallel with monitoring a large hippo reduction programme.

Ancillary to working in MFNP, and though it was not part of either NUTAE's or GMU's brief, the work in MFPN drew us so deeply into forward planning that recommendations on managing the park's fauna would only make sense with some understanding of the economics involved. Land use in the region was overwhelmingly agrarian and was expected to be so indefinitely into the future.

In terms of monetary returns per unit area, MFNP tourism at that time in the late 1960s was yielding £667 per km^2 annually. If the steep rise in tourism of the previous decade persisted (and there were no grounds to believe that it could not), then this figure was set to follow suit and increase.

Budongo Forest at that time yielded some £163 per km^2 gross from timber production. The area designated as forest reserve contained extensive grassland and the foresters' long-term plan was to convert this to trees. Income from timber production was thus also expected to expand, providing that elephant numbers were reduced or eliminated.

One of the positive aspects of elephant eliminating woodland and forest had been the removal of tsetse flies. If the grasslands persisted, cattle ranching had become a possibility, and an extensive project to develop the land around MFNP's northern border for cattle and game ranching had been proposed by Roger Wheater. On the basis of preliminary research, it was estimated it would yield £150 per km² annually.

Current peasant farming was producing about £28 km² annually. However, with human increase and the general growth of Uganda's economy, we believed this relatively modest figure must rise and in the long term would compete directly with the national park in monetary terms and for space. The return from sport hunting alone was negligible.

As cultivation occupied ever more land the conflict between agriculture and the park's wildlife would intensify. Already a few cultivators were at the park's western border, just south of the Nile. Crop destruction would increasingly prejudice local farmers against wildlife and poaching could be expected to increase. We believed that the National Park Trustees should anticipate these events and recommended constructing barriers (electric fencing), initially along the western boundary of the park, but to be extended later in phases, first south of the Nile, but later, if necessary, in the north too. We said if necessary, because if cattle and game ranching evolved around the northern half of the park, a porous border between the two compatible systems seemed acceptable. Erecting elephant-proof barriers as hard edges to the park would also involve eliminating those elephants currently still partially or wholly resident outside the park, and eliminate compression into what was initially the Bunyoro Game Reserve and now MFNP.

Such long-term economic and political planning had to match the equally long-term biological and conservation planning with which we were so directly involved. Unless there was some confidence in the marriage between economics, land-use and conservation plans, our proposals for further large reductions in elephant numbers would not be justified.

We advanced a case for reducing the populations to levels we believed would allow woodland recovery, and recommended removing 3,500 elephants south of the Nile over a four-year period in two phases. Here I must stress that this recommendation was made in the understanding that it was an experiment. We did not know how low elephant density had to be to permit woodland and forest recovery. Thus while we knew it happened where elephant were removed completely, our recommendations involved approaching the issue on a basis of trial and error and the flexibility to change quickly.

We recommended reducing hippo to an average grazing density of 7.7 per km². Detailed quotas for sections of the River Nile (and control areas in which no cropping was to be carried out) were defined. In this proposal for hippo we had the QENP results as a guide for what to expect.

We understood that, after the new population levels had been achieved by reduction cropping, sustained culling might well be needed to conserve the habitats and such sustained hunting would probably involve taking up to 5 per cent of the elephant population annually, and about 6 per cent of the hippos. Yet as with QENP, while what we had learned in eighteen months may have seemed a great deal, it was no more than having examined the very tip of a huge iceberg of MFNP's ecology – a first step on a very long road that had to encompass a host of other plant and animal species. Here I interject from half a century after we made these recommendations, that with modern advances in the anaesthesia of large wild animals, there may be means of collecting much of the biological data we could only get from dead animals through, for example, blood assays.

Looking back four decades it amazes me that we were so far ahead of our time. It was not long before culling whole herds was being applied in South Africa, Zimbabwe and Zambia. Far greater numbers were subsequently taken in the decades following our work – indeed in Zimbabwe some daily culls exceeded seventy elephants – but the scientific output never came close to that in our Uganda study. Though this was a pity, it is not written as a criticism. The objectives of these central and southern African programmes were principally reduction and less ambitious where pure science was involved.

Reiterating what I have already stated, no time in my research career was as satisfying as this first period working on elephant biology in Uganda. With hindsight it was like gloriously surfing down the face of a huge wave, conscious only of exhilaration and looking ahead, oblivious to the knowledge that this wave was the precursor of a violent storm.

18

Uganda's Darker Side

In late 1965 it was time to take a fortnight's leave and give the family a taste of other parts of East Africa, so Maureen and I decided to sample the attractions of the Kenya coast. We would travel there through northern Tanzania, enter Kenya beyond Moshi at the base of Kilimanjaro and visit friends on the way. Entry to Tanzania was by steamer from Port Bell near Kampala on the northern edge of Lake Victoria to Mwanza at the southern end. The return run would be more direct, for the most part up the main highway from Mombasa to Kampala.

We went off early on Monday as the lake steamer left at 9:00 a.m. from Port Bell. The Land Rover was hoisted on board at 8:00 a.m. and travelled as deck cargo. We had comfortable and clean adjoining cabins and the boat was well found, though the food wasn't thrilling. No rolling motion, so one hardly felt that one was on a boat at all. We sat in the sun and slept as there wasn't a lot to see – it's a large lake, an inland sea in fact! Next morning we arrived early at Mwanza. The Land Rover was offloaded and we headed east to the Serengeti National Park.

It was a lovely day as we drove through the parkland with the multitudes of animals, especially in what was known as 'The Corridor' – an arm of the park that almost reaches Lake Victoria. There were zebra, gazelles, impala, wildebeest, topi, plenty of giraffe and seven young lions who were very timid. We drove for about four hours – picnicking under the trees on the way – to get to Seronera, the park headquarters. There we dropped in on Myles Turner, the Warden, and his family. We already knew Myles, but met his attractive wife Kay for the first time, and his two children, just a little younger than ours. Then on to the research station at Banagi, nearby, where we were staying with Murray Watson, whose PhD work I was still supervising.

We had one full day in the Serengeti and Murray, the Turners and Sandy Field, the Chief Warden, took us to see the wildebeest migration. Thousands upon thousands of wildebeest and many hundreds of zebra were all around us for miles and miles, close-up and diminishing to black specks in the distance. It was an incredible spectacle. The next day on our way to the Ngorongoro Crater we drove through them again and the numbers were even more fantastic.

The Ngorongoro Lodge at over 8,000 feet above sea level was perched right on the edge of the enormous caldera. The crater is 100 square miles in extent; about 12 miles across and full of animals. We spent the next day in it before moving on to the Lake Manyara National Park. Our next stop was with the Poppletons at the Mweka College of African Wildlife Management on the slopes of Kilimanjaro, several miles above the town of Moshi. Frank, who had played so large a part in our lives when we first arrived in Uganda, had completed his service with the Uganda National Parks in late 1963 and was now nearing the end of a two-year contract as an instructor at Mweka. After a recent meeting with the NUTAE Trustees in England, I was able definitely to invite Frank back to Mweya as NUTAE's administrator. He was keen to accept.

Next stop was the Jardini Hotel on Diani Beach, some twenty miles south of Mombasa. We had a wonderful few days swimming in the sea and in large pools among the rocks at high tide, as well as goggling on the reef and collecting shells of all sizes and shapes from the sand, and relaxing in the shade of the palm trees fringing the sandy beach. We bought lobsters from the fishermen and had the restaurant cook them for us. After this idyllic interlude we started back towards Uganda.

First stop en route was with David and Daphne Sheldrick at Voi where David was the Warden in charge of Tsavo National Park East. We spent three days with them as David, given the scale of the elephant problem in his park, had been keenly following the elephant work in Murchison. We had been in contact since we met at Mweya in late 1963 and at my request he had been collecting elephant jaws (from natural mortality) which I aged in order to draw up survivorship curves for comparison with what we had in Uganda. While the Sheldricks took us on picnics and showed us Tsavo East so that the family enjoyed the visit, David and

I had deep discussions about the general ecology of the area and elephant biology, in particular the perceived overpopulation problem. While there we were joined in some of our discussions by Hugh Lamprey, Director of the Serengeti Research Unit, and two American biologists whom we had already met at Mweka.

Especially memorable were two visits to Mudanda Rock. On the first one hundred elephants came to drink and bathe in the big pool below the rock. On the second even more – about one hundred and fifty came in. As we talked elephants, they came in lines through the bush in their family units, from every direction. The soil around there is brick red and in the rays of the setting sun the animals really were pink elephants! Our three days in Tsavo were very profitable and David and I found we were in broad agreement on all aspects of the 'elephant problem'.

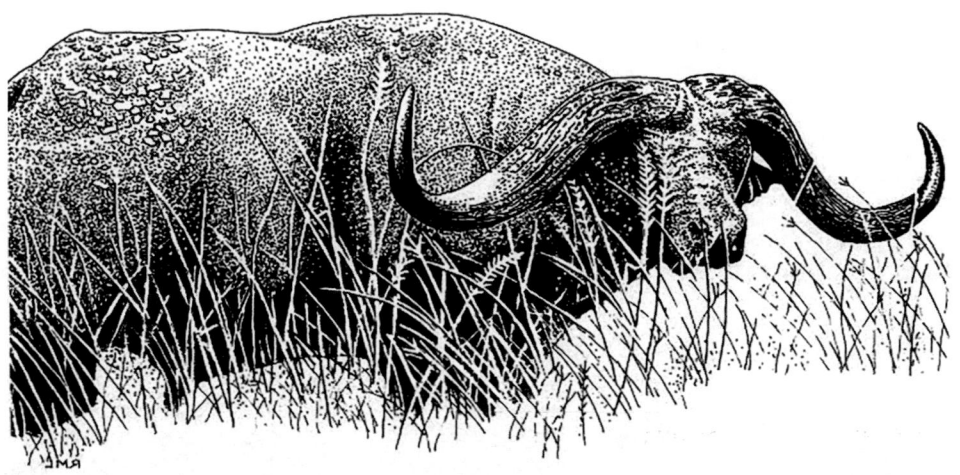

The African or Cape buffalo was abundant in all the parks we visited

After this enjoyable interlude, we drove on to Amboseli Game Reserve and a rather glamorous tented camp below Mount Kilimanjaro. This was scenery on the grand scale. The night was beautiful, with stars scintillating above the silhouetted mountain. Next morning was lovely too, awakening at sunrise and seeing the mountain through the door of the tent, the snows on top glistening pinkly. After an early-morning drive with a guide, we left for Nairobi, arriving there at 3:30 p.m.

I took the opportunity while in Nairobi to meet with the men running the Ford Foundation's East African office. While the Nuffield Foundation's funds had been adequate to establish NUTAE, they were for a ten-year period and, given our progress, were now inadequate to cover the ambitious expansion of our research that I had in mind. The American Ford Foundation was not only very wealthy, but philosophically deeply interested in advancing African progress. They invited me to address five of them and I spent an afternoon outlining NUTAE's progress and what was in relatively easy reach if funds were available. My ideas were well received and I returned from our holiday in an optimistic frame of mind.

Yet there were dark clouds on our horizon. One's life evolves like a rope made up of distinct and separate strands. From a distance the rope seems a single entity. Close-up its strands, while clear enough, take time to unravel enough to see each separately. Looking back now, the components that made up my life become easier to see for what they were.

Black rhino in Amboseli's then acacia environment.

* * * *

Administering NUTAE was severely crimping my personal biological research. Involvement with elephants in MFNP, and its widening impact on the elephant problem elsewhere in eastern and southern Africa, was calling for so much of my attention that it was clear that NUTAE needed an administrator. Chris Field, my deputy, like me would have had to compromise his scientific research if pulled into administration. Maureen had given unpaid help in a general way, and in particular as my secretary, but the situation now called for more than this. There was no one better suited to this role than Frank Poppleton who was approaching the end of his contract with the College of Wildlife Management at Mweka in Tanzania.

My own horizons had expanded with the elephant work and offers of collaboration from elsewhere in East and Central Africa created the possibility of a much bigger role for NUTAE. With Mweya as its base, it could get into tropical animal ecology beyond Uganda. My approach to the Ford Foundation in Nairobi had borne fruit to the tune of £100,000 (equivalent to £1.2 million in 2004) for work in QENP, MFNP and also Tsavo National Park in Kenya, under my direction. It would allow getting an aircraft for the unit and cover the costs of an administrator and three research Fellows, two zoological and one botanical. The prospects for an expanded NUTAE seemed to be on course.

Though I had already got the NUTAE Committee's agreement to employ Frank Poppleton as NUTAE administrator, this needed ratification from both the Trustees of the Uganda National Parks and those in Makerere University who had not been present in Cambridge. Instead of the enthusiasm I was expecting, there was outright opposition. When this became known in the UK, the Committee members there backed away from their earlier approval.

I had not appreciated the degree to which Africans assuming power after Independence truly wished to shed all vestiges of a subservient past. One feature of this was that when a British official was replaced by his African successor, there would be opposition for that individual returning to any other place in the country's infrastructure, even when there was no African available to fill it. In such cases the preference seemed to be for another expatriate, often not a Briton, who had no experience of the country. I am sure there are many explanations for this, but all that concerned me then was the fact it existed.

Had I been aware of it at the time, I might have appreciated the attitude of our new Director of National Parks. He was Francis Katete, the student who

Len Beadle had suggested came to NUTAE to work for a PhD shortly after my arrival in Uganda. Young, inexperienced, proud of his status and determined to live up to expectations of him, he was also a polite and gentle person, very much a product of his culture in which it was good manners to avoid confrontation. While this made it easy for him to agree, it also predisposed him against issuing a direct no, and to procrastination. This happened when I sought his approval to employ Frank as NUTAE administrator.

In this he would have the support of his fellow Africans in Makerere. The outcome was that the absolutely free hand I had been given by Uganda Parks had evaporated. Now I could no longer count on the Park Trustees or the Committee members in Cambridge being four square behind me.

On top of this, Makerere had a somewhat proprietorial attitude towards NUTAE. With some ground perhaps, those in the University felt that it was their 'child' and they were due a share in the kudos accorded to it. There was an element of professional jealousy that was in proportion in some degree to NUTAE's increasing recognition. It rose substantially with the Ford Foundation donating large funds to expand NUTAE. It rose yet further when the International Biological Program (IBP), whose UK component was administered by the Royal Society, made a considerable grant for botanical research. This, too, would be largely undertaken through and by NUTAE.

However, for etiquette and politics, the Ford Foundation made the actual grant of funds to Makerere College, on the unwritten understanding that as I had initiated it, this was a formality and that as the Director of NUTAE, the selection of candidates would be my prerogative. The Principal of Makerere, supported by his academic staff that included Len Beadle, did not accept this and took a hard line. The Ford grant had been made to Makerere, not to any individuals, and would be handled by the college. The Ford representative in Nairobi made both the NUTAE Committee in England and Makerere aware that his Foundation's grant had been made because of confidence in me, and regarded Makerere as the vehicle through which funds would be channelled.

A further issue of controversy lay in the Ford understanding that one of the three researchers to be under my direction would work on elephants in Kenya's Tsavo National Park. In the dialogue that developed, neither Ford's representatives nor I appreciated the interterritorial relationships between the three East African territories – Uganda, Kenya and Tanzania – in which Kenya had a very strong sense of being *prima inter pares* and the senior among them. Thus the authorities there made it clear that they would not accept research in their national parks being directed by a Uganda-based institute.

Frank Poppleton's prospect of returning to Mweya was an early casualty of the situation. With a family to support he was unable to sit around and accepted a contract with the Tanzanian National Parks. At this point the idea arose of sounding out David Sheldrick's possible interest in becoming NUTAE's administrator. It never really got further than an exploratory letter or two.

One way or another, my directorship of NUTAE was being challenged from several directions. Untangling the conflicting skeins of interest called for strong and decisive leadership from the Committee in Cambridge. It was not forthcoming and I was not getting the support that I needed. Sadly, Carl Pantin, who had been the driving force behind NUTAE's conception and establishment, was a sick man and dying. From far-off Cambridge the Committee was unable to keep up with developments in Uganda. I felt obliged to warn the Committee that without its support I would not renew my contract as Director when it came up for renewal in September 1966. Obviously someone from Cambridge needed to get out to Uganda and assert the Committee's authority. Pantin's declining health prevented him from doing so and in his stead Professor Alan Parkes FRS, a Committee member (and later Pantin's successor as Chairman) came out. While he found my attitude well grounded and sympathised with me, he did not give the decisive leadership needed. Instead he fell back on that civil service stand-by to all problems – form a committee – summing his findings thus in his autobiography:-

> The Unit is not and never has been an independent concern. It is dependent on the parks for electricity and water, for about half of the laboratory technicians, for the gardeners, for the regular servicing of its vehicles, for much help from the Wardens and on the agreement of the Parks Trustees for any other than purely observational work. Moreover, of the seven buildings now being used by NUTAE only one (Bachelors House) was paid for and is owned by NUTAE. In the days of Poppleton and Trimmer, this dependence on the Parks presented no great difficulty, but in spite of the helpfulness of the present Chief Warden, we have to recognise that those days are ended.

The introduction of the Ford and IBP elements is going to turn NUTAE into a four-legged affair, two based in England and two in Uganda. Even with a two-legged unit adequate control and support from Cambridge of the Nuffield element has proved to be impracticable, and in my opinion, a quadrupedal unit cannot be organised from Cambridge.

The first need is to improve liaison between the interested parties, and to this end I recommend that the Cambridge Committee should invite IBP, Makerere and the Parks Trustees to join it in the formation of a Co-ordinating Committee which should meet at least three times a year at Mweya. I envisage the work of this Committee as being to co-ordinate activities and smooth out difficulties on the site and in this form the proposal was warmly welcomed by all those with whom I talked. I hope that the Cambridge Committee will give serious attention to the proposal.

Crucial is Parkes' recognition that there had been a change from the days of Poppleton and Trimmer (he forgot to include Wheater). The relationships with Poppleton, Trimmer and Wheater had been critical in NUTAE's success and international recognition. Missing entirely from Alan's summary is the very clear understanding by all elements of the Cambridge NUTAE Committee – including the Trustees of the Uganda National Parks and the representatives of Makerere College – that I would have a free hand running the institute. For the first four years or so I had had this freedom. Yet as the unit's scientific output gained recognition, particularly as the elephant results started appearing, my free hand was being eroded and compromised.

Ironically, these rising disappointments and apprehensions were developing in counterpoint to the emerging successes in elephant research. In the midst of my rising frustrations, I learned that I had been awarded the Zoological Society of London's Scientific Medal, awarded annually to one or two scientists under the age of 40 for outstanding scientific work. It pleased me deeply.

* * * *

In my uncertain frame of mind, the contacts I had made in Kenya assumed rising importance. Ford had indicated its interest in developing a project in Tsavo.

While Kenya had been hostile to the idea of research in Tsavo being directed by me in Uganda, there was no such antagonism to me personally working in Kenya. Now, decades later, I cannot recall who made the suggestion that I make Kenya my base. Suffice it that David Sheldrick and Ian Parker, who were aware of my tribulations in Uganda, both felt I would have fewer problems if Tsavo became the centre for the elephant research I had in mind.

The most influential body in East African wildlife research between 1963 and 1966 was the EAWS's Scientific and Technical Committee (STC). However, its membership was overwhelmingly white and its influence only grudgingly accepted by the region's official conservation bodies now completely under African administrators. The influence of the STC was only sustained because the Society provided significant conservation donations that had to have the committee's approval. An early indication of replacing the STC influence on policies – particularly those about elephants – was the Kenya government's creation of its own 'Elephant Committee'. At the outset, it not only contained a sprinkling of senior officials, but also a few STC members. The Elephant Committee's policy appeared to be a seamless adoption of the STC position.

In March 1966, Kenya's Elephant Committee sent a delegation that included the Chairman of Kenya National Parks Trustees, David Wasawo, the Director of Parks, Perez Olindo and David Sheldrick to witness for themselves how NUTAE was run at Mweya, then on to see elephant culling being done in MFNP. They also wanted to discuss the prospect of my going to work for them in Tsavo as Director of the Tsavo Research Project, funded with the Ford Foundation money I had initiated for work there, but now greatly increased to cover the development of a completely new and self-contained unit. They were enthusiastic to head-hunt me away from Uganda.

The delegation flew back to Nairobi on a Sunday, met with the Kenya National Park Trustees on Monday and on Tuesday I got a telegram confirming my appointment as Director of Tsavo Research Project for a three-year contract with effect from early 1967, by which time accommodation would be ready for us. The Kenya delegation's visit resulted in a request for a demonstration cull of 300 elephant in the Koito area of Tsavo under my personal supervision to be carried out by Ian's Kenya-based WLS.

After I telegrammed my acceptance, the family and I drove off up into the QENP crater hills as it was a lovely day with the mountains nearly clear and with great views and colour everywhere. It was sad though to think we had to leave all this behind us, but it is always good to look to the future.

I notified the NUTAE Committee that I would not be renewing my contract as the unit's Director. As I was due several months' leave on full pay, we left Uganda in July 1966. However the Kenya National Parks Trustees were keen to waste no time with the sample of 300 elephants in Tsavo and signed a contract with WLS to do the job, stipulating that WLS should fly me to and from the UK and meet all my costs. I was agreeable, even though it would cut into my NUTAE leave. The cull was successfully completed in eighteen days in August 1966. It differed in one important aspect from the work in Uganda.

Ian's earlier experience trying to secure a quota of elephant in the Galana Scheme involved doing so in woodland where visibility from the ground was usually less than 100 metres. He feared that the similar vegetation in Koito might obscure some members of an elephant herd, even if bunched. To avoid this possibility, WLS hired a helicopter, not as a shooting platform, but as a 'sheepdog' to close up and move herds to where they were wanted. While expensive, it was better than the system adopted in MFNP's open grassland.

In August 1966 GMU still had a year to go on their contract in MFNP and were about half way through their quota of 2,000 elephants. Although I ceased to be Director of NUTAE as from October 1966, and thus in a legal sense GMU might come under the scientific direction of my successor as NUTAE's Director, both the company and Roger Wheater – now Director of Uganda National Parks following the untimely death of Francis Katete in a car accident – chose to interpret the commitment as to me personally.

By now Ian and his teams were well able to arrange data collection and recording without my presence, so the flow of elephant data and material followed me wherever I was in the UK or in Tsavo. This unique collaboration was sustained by both Ian and Roger and continued until 1970 with aerial count results that continued even after the GMU elephant and hippo culling ended in August 1967.

* * * *

While we were involved in research and the affairs of NUTAE, greater events were taking place in Uganda. Milton Obote, the country's Nilotic Langi Prime Minister, methodically destroyed the country's Constitution. Seeking total power, his first priority was to be rid of the President – the Muganda Kabaka (King) of the Baganda, and leader of the southern Bantu people. In this he had the support of the nation's mainly Nilotic army, over which he and many officers started to lose control. While it didn't affect us immediately, we were nevertheless aware of rising tensions.

There was some trouble at this time with Congolese coming over the Uganda border and causing disturbances. The respective presidents – then Obote and Tshombe – blamed one another! A contingent from the Uganda Rifles was sitting down at the Ishasha Park gates – about ten miles from the frontier – but all they seemed to do was bother defenceless tourists and demand passes which no one had because such passes were unnecessary in Uganda, and bribes from anyone who wanted to go anywhere. They had even stopped planes flying to western Uganda, so our mail had to come and go by train.

It was all a bit of a nuisance as it hindered travelling around. I was to go to the Semliki Game Reserve at the southern end of Lake Albert with Hal Buechner, who was studying Uganda kob there, a photographer, Bill Cowan, and veterinarian Roger Short (now Professor Short FRS). On arrival we were forbidden entry by a unit of the Uganda Rifles – no reason except their pleasure in being bloody-minded. It was all a sign of things to come and the rising level of unpleasantness played a prominent part in my resignation from NUTAE and accepting the position in Kenya.

So on Sunday 29 May 1966, we left Mweya for the last time at 8:30 a.m. amid rumours of the army having run amuck. It coincided with relations between the Prime Minister and President breaking down completely. It was a sad parting. We ate en route and made no stops until we reached Mbarara where I called in at the police station to check on the situation. They told us that a convoy of vehicles had just left for Kampala under police protection, and if we hurried we would be able to catch up with it. Indeed, just outside Mbarara some cars had stopped by the roadside and a police captain was there. I asked if it was the convoy and the captain, who was very pleasant, said it was but he was leaving it there and we would be on our own!

We had little choice but to continue as our flight was booked and I hoped it would not be too risky. A little further on we were stopped at a police road block. They asked me if I had any weapons and, facetiously (and foolishly), I drew out my trusty Swiss Army penknife and said, 'No, only this.' The sergeant grabbed it, but I protested and asked to see the officer in charge; I managed to persuade the officer to return it, but was warned that if the army stopped us and found it he couldn't be responsible for the consequences. The police also wanted to search our Land Rover, but as it was piled high with luggage I protested and they didn't do so. Had they done so we'd have been there for hours *and* they would have found a couple of pangas (machetes) at the bottom of our load (about which I had completely forgotten)!

We saw several unpleasant situations where a car or lorry was stopped and the African or Asian driver was being beaten up by troops, but we drove on – there was really nothing else to do in our circumstances. Later we ran into a police patrol (both army and police warned us against one another!) and they told us to join some other cars in a line on the road, to be escorted to Kampala where we were to report to the police station there. I decided that we were safer without the police escort, drove past the line of cars and arrived in Kampala on our own, reporting to the police station as requested. Several Land Rovers containing police or soldiers had passed us on the road, with rifles pointing out the windows which could easily have gone off and shot someone. In fact one saloon car overtook us, driven by a terrified Asian driver. He drove alongside us for a while and the soldier in the passenger seat had his gun pointing out of the window at me – at point blank range, with his finger on the trigger and a sinister smile on his face. He was wearing large round wire-rimmed spectacles above his brilliant white teeth. Whenever they saw a lingering African near the side of the road, they took a pot shot at him for fun.

We had a police escort to go from Kampala to Entebbe too, where we were to stay a few nights before catching our plane late Tuesday night for the UK. But after a long wait in the police station forecourt, the escorting police Land Rover suddenly without warning pulled out of the courtyard and across some traffic lights; these changed to red before we could cross, so the convoy was unprotected. We next saw our escort on the steps of the police station at Entebbe and they waved cheerfully to us! Fortunately we had had no trouble – what a relief.

Others were not so lucky. An acquaintance of ours, Dr Woolf of the Tsetse Control Department, was beaten up and left for dead in a ditch. He was in a Land Rover with an African assistant when it was stopped at an army road block. Rashly he objected and was obstreperous, whereupon they set on him, beat him up, cut off both his hands with pangas and threw him in a ditch. Our informant didn't know what happened to his African assistant. Late that night another African on a bicycle pedalled along the road, heard moaning from the ditch, discovered Woolf and got help to take him into hospital, where fortunately, his life was saved, but not his hands.

I had to go to Kampala for tax clearance, tickets, advance luggage arrangements and so on. Before I went, there was a statement on the radio from the Kabaka telling Obote and the government that if they were not out of Kampala and HIS country by evening, then he and his people were going to attack them. However, all was quiet and I managed to do everything necessary before returning to Entebbe. In due course Obote turned the army onto the Kabaka who fled to Britain, and dictatorship commenced. Fortunately we were gone by then.

The breakdown of law was general and inevitably extended into the national parks. Within a couple of months of our departure, the hippo culling programme in Mweya was stopped. The methodical plan of different offtakes in different areas for comparative purposes gave way to only taking hippo where it was easiest. From the outset of the programme a couple of hippo had always been retained for staff consumption. This increased until the park's employees were putatively consuming 18,000 kg of boned red meat a week. 'For staff use' was the cover for selling for 'the warden's benefit.' Thus the work of the previous decade and more started to unravel.

NUTAE continued under my successor, Dr Keith Eltringham, but in progressively more difficult political circumstances. As Alan Parkes had observed, the original relationship between Park Trustees, wardens and researchers had changed. At the end of its planned ten-year life granted by the Nuffield Foundation, NUTAE morphed into the Uganda Institute of Ecology.

Along with the rest of Uganda, work more or less stopped when the head of the army, Idi Amin, turned upon Obote and installed himself as dictator in 1971. Among other things, elephant and hippo were killed at will by the army. The negatives and prints of our unique photographic transects of MFNP's vegetation were destroyed by fire when the park offices at Paraa were burned to the ground. The only cohesive records of all the work done in Uganda were the personal copies which I and Ian Parker took with us. What was so shocking was the speed at which law and order broke down. Within a decade after Independence, Uganda had become a shambles.

* * * *

Once I was established in my next post in Kenya, the Trustees of both the Uganda and the Kenya National Parks were keen that I should tie up loose research ends in MFNP before Ian completed his contract there. In those days one could move between the three East African countries – Kenya, Uganda and Tanzania – without having to undergo Customs and Immigration formalities. So I was flown by Ian with Maureen and Christopher to GMU's well-sited camp on the Nile. A troop of black-and-white long-haired colobus monkeys were in residence and very tame. The trees were full of lovely birds and the fish eagles' iconic calls filled us with nostalgia for QENP and our early happiness there.

Then came a most interesting interlude. Daily, Ian flew us to a short airstrip on the edge of the Budongo Forest – Maureen, Ian's wife, Chris, and two children, Christopher and Suzie Parker. A Forestry Department Toyota at the strip was available and took us to where lumberjacks were felling mahoganies. This is where we measured the position of bark patches along the radii of fresh-cut stumps referred to in the last chapter. They had to be fresh as more than a day old they would be covered with a thick exudate of sap that made reading the rings difficult. The inappropriate alternative was to wait several months until the sap was dried out and washed away by rain. Connecting dendrochronology to elephant presence is clearly a field with great promise.

I took a tape recorder along to record the myriad sounds: bird calls, insects stridulating, the voices of forest workers far and near and the incredible sound of a centuries-old forest giant falling to earth. If felling an elephant was dreadful, which it was, it was nothing compared to the death of one of these magnificent, huge forms of life. The lumberjacks first removed a big wedge of wood from the bole on the side where they wanted it to fall, then at the same level on the opposite side they commenced sawing with long two-man saws and banging big iron wedges into the extending cut with sledge-hammers. It might take a couple of days before the tree started to lean. To the experienced woodsmen, the first indications were soft, widely spaced cracking sounds forecasting the imminent fall. Warning shouts cleared the area of people, for there was apparently a surprisingly high casualty rate of those caught unawares. While the sawmen were pretty accurate in predicting where the tree would fall, last minute gusts of wind could tip it in an unwanted and unexpected direction. Those who wanted to be close to the action, as did Ian and I, were advised to be prepared for agile and speedy getaways. Gradually the soft sounds got closer together and louder until the tree started to go, faster and faster. Now the tearing uncut section of the bole was sundering apart with a rising crescendo of awful groans rising to a roar as it moved into the final fall, branches breaking on and from neighbouring trees to slam into earth with a thump whose shock wave literally bounced anyone within fifty metres into the air. As the fall started, the tree's residents abandoned ship: anomalures (a kind of flying squirrel), bats and birds in all directions as they scattered. The huge crash was followed by minutes of silence – the only movement a declining rain of falling leaves – as though all life was appalled. The death of these vast trees whose canopies covered nearly an acre was totally awesome and awful. The tree, its own life centuries old, was also a complete city of other life, plants, vertebrates and invertebrates. Its demise was deeply moving, and ineffably sad.

On returning from our last day in Budongo a sudden storm fell on the camp and blew the roof off our sleeping *banda*. It was the last night that we ever spent in Uganda at the end of a memorable visit.

19

Kenya and Tsavo

We left our house in Coton, Cambridgeshire, on Tuesday 7 February 1967, for Kenya. On our arrival we were met by a senior secretary from the Ministry of Tourism and Wildlife, and also by an old friend from St Catharine's College, Gordon Lowther, whom I had not seen for a very long time.

The first couple of days were spent meeting the officials within the departments and organisations with whom I would be working, and all the formalities that went with taking up my post. In this we were taken around by Perez Olindo, Director of the Kenya National Parks. Leaving our two boys with the Nelsons – Courtney Nelson was the Ford Foundation Representative in East Africa – with whom we were now good friends, Maureen and I flew down to Tsavo. There we stayed for a few days with David and Daphne Sheldrick to acquaint ourselves with our new home.

Back in Nairobi we met the Longhursts, whom we knew from Uganda days, and Aloys Achieng and his wife whom we had also met in Uganda, when Aloys was a fishery officer at Kichwamba just east of QENP. Aloys, of Kenya's Luo tribe, was now the Permanent Secretary of the Ministry of Tourism and Wildlife, under whose ambit the national parks fell. Aloys was, next to the Minister, the most powerful person in the Ministry. Indeed, given his professional training and responsibility for its day-to-day running, and given that the Minister over him was a transient politician, he was the most influential man in it. This was of consequence to me as, resulting from my Uganda experience, I never again wanted to be vulnerable to vacillating committees – as had been the case in Uganda where the multiple interests of those in Cambridge, the Trustees, academics in Makerere and an unsure director had made decisions so hard to get. Consequently I had insisted in my contract with the Kenya National Parks that I be answerable only to the Permanent Secretary. In the euphoria surrounding the establishment of the Tsavo Research Project this had been agreed without demur.

Nine days later we eventually moved into our house, and the next few weeks were busy settling in and establishing a garden. As in Uganda we were inundated with visitors from the outset, both friends and professional colleagues. Throughout this period the Sheldricks were unstinting in their help and friendship. So too did we become close to Peter Jenkins and his wife Sarah. Peter was David's deputy and also Daphne's brother, which made his boss his brother-in-law.

The boys settled well into their new surroundings. They enjoyed Daphne's menagerie of orphaned wild animals that included a lesser kudu fawn, a young buffalo and a young rhino – all of which needed bottle feeding – as well as two well-grown young elephants. Early on when Daphne had been away and there was no one else to undertake the bottle feeding, Maureen had stepped in to help. Richard was shortly to go to a boarding school – St Andrews at Turi, west of the Rift Valley in the highlands – as he had reached a stage where the demands of modern education could only be met by professional teaching.

One way and another, the new Tsavo Research Project team had come together smoothly within a couple of months, and with the same pervading sense of goodwill and team spirit that characterised the early days in NUTAE.

* * * *

The Tsavo National Park had been proclaimed as a single unit in 1948 as a swathe of Kenya's semi-arid coastal *nyika* (a Kiswahili term meaning variously open bare, treeless wilderness, open forest with high grass, or a barren desolate region) hinterlands some 20,000 km^2 in extent. At the time it was covered by a blanket of *Commiphora* and acacia woodland, much of which was very dense, and *nyika* in the sense of a desolate region seemed apt. Rainfall over much of the area was around only 250 mm (10 inches) annually, though the north and east were generally drier than the west and south. The fauna included species that were able to survive for long periods without access to free water – larger mammals among them being oryx, gerenuk, Peter's gazelle and dikdik. Yet it also contained other water-dependent forms like elephant, black rhino, giraffe, buffalo, zebra, waterbuck and eland.

Kenya and the location of the Tsavo National Park

The Tsavo National Park was not a discrete ecological unit. It was surrounded by similar country on all sides. There were nomadic Orma pastoralists (a.k.a. Wagalla in the north and north-east, Masai in the south and west) and (illegal) African hunters. Settled cultivators only existed in very small numbers of Mijikenda near the eastern border, and by somewhat larger numbers of Akamba near the park's north-western border. In effect, the park constituted the core of a far larger ecological system whose borders had been decided arbitrarily because, in the words of the founding director, Mervyn Cowie, no one else wanted it.

Clearly elephants were the proximate cause of the change from widespread and dense woodland when the park was proclaimed in 1948 to the meagre spreading grasslands in 1967. However, the change needed placing in the context of past situations. East African lake levels and sediments indicated relatively substantial climatic fluctuations over previous centuries which were reflected in vegetation. Fluctuating circumstances had some support in local folklore as well as archaeological evidence. In modern times in Tsavo's low rainfall, where thickets were dense enough the tsetse (*Glossina longipenis*) thrived and prevented the presence of cattle. Orma graves imply that in past times such areas must have been sufficiently open for such cattle people and their stock to have been living there. Early in the 20th century this supposition had been borne out east of Tsavo when, for administrative reasons, Orma had to withdraw, and bush with tsetse rapidly invaded the grassland they vacated. Because of the tsetse these places had then become unusable by cattle.

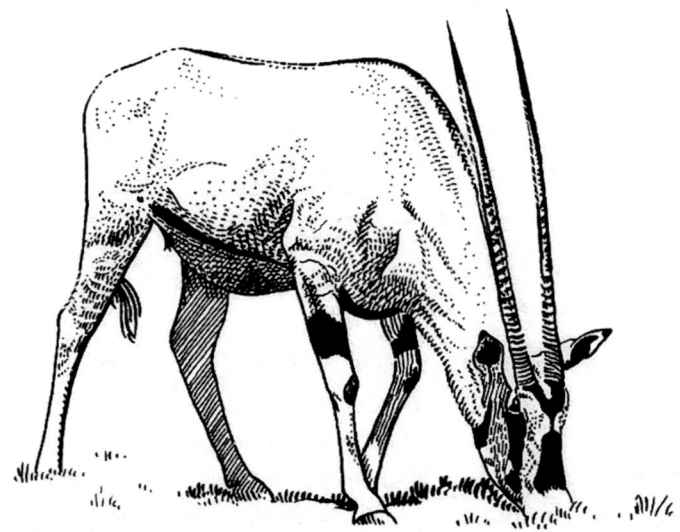

Oryx, quintessential large antelope of the semi-arid Tsavo National Park

Written records from the onset of the colonial era (late 19th century) exist in brief excerpts in the early explorers' records. Krapf 1849–50; New 1871, Jackson 1885, Gregory 1893, Thomson 1893, Lugard 1890, MacDonald 1892, Johnston 1894, Patterson 1897 (the dates here referring to when they went through the area, not their date of publication) are all descriptions along their routes. In the First World War soldiers based in Tsavo West to counter German incursions from German East Africa (Tanganyika) against the railway between Mombasa and Nairobi described the environment. A game warden – G. C. MacArthur, ex-policeman – had traversed it during the 1920s and 1930s, and arrested over 4,000 Africans for illicit hunting. Thus more than a decade before the park was formed, the one obvious fact about it was that Africans hunted elephants and rhino there on a substantial scale.

These sources of information are poor. For the most part, the early travellers were moving through the area and did not reside in it. They certainly do not provide sufficient information to decide whether what we were to refer to as the Tsavo ecosystem was more open in the 19th century than it was when the park was proclaimed in 1948. Even at its most dense, a seemingly homogeneous landscape of woodland would have been quite varied with grass *mbugas* (glades), usually edaphically determined and often along drainage lines.

Another hint of past vegetation lay in African place names (Mbuyuni – from *mbuyu*, Swahili for baobab; Mkongeni from *mkonge*, Swahili for sansevieria; Serengeti derived from *maa siringit* for endless open grassland). I decided that by selecting one's sources, one could postulate that at times it had been more open as easily as the case that, at others, it had been denser vegetation. I concluded that such records of the past were too thin other than to believe that such changes had happened.

Tsavo's first warden was Ron Stevens, a chemist, and under him he had two greenhorn assistant wardens, Billy Woodley and Peter Jenkins. Woodley, patrolling in the east between the Sabaki and Tiva rivers, reported elephant hunting by Wata (Waliungulu) and Kamba, hunting openly and on a large scale. It caused concern and was a major element in Tsavo's division into two administrative units: Tsavo East north of the railway line between Mombasa and Nairobi, and Tsavo West south, effectively making two separate parks.

In 1949 David Sheldrick was appointed warden of Tsavo East with Billy Woodley as one of his assistants. Peter Jenkins stayed in Tsavo West. Sheldrick confirmed the uninhibited hunting Woodley had noted and its suppression became his top priority. At the time the woodland over large tracts of Tsavo East was so dense, the *Commiphora* and acacia undersown by such thick sansevieria plants, that there was little grass and visibility was restricted to not more than fifty metres. Animals were difficult to see and in order to open it up and improve game viewing for visitors, David and another of his assistant wardens, John Lawrence, tried to burn the vegetation. They failed. Grass, the only flammable material, was too sparse to carry fire. This was in one place south of Sala Hill, and while it may not have been applicable everywhere, I considered it ecologically important.

At the time no one knew how many elephants there were in Kenya, let alone Tsavo, and the most optimistic speculators opined possibly 12,000. Thus when Hal Buechner came down from Uganda in 1953, and made an aerial flight over a small portion of Tsavo East between the Voi River and the railway and counted 3,000 elephants, it caused amazement – not least to David Sheldrick – who assumed that all the park's elephants must have concentrated there. It was a seminal figure. At the time both Woodley and Sheldrick had estimated that the Wata and Kamba poachers were taking more than 300 elephants a year – that is more than 10 per cent of Buechner's finding – which underpinned the claim that elephants in Tsavo would soon be exterminated by poachers.

A massive anti-poaching campaign was launched under Sheldrick's command that ran in 1956 and 1957. Most Wata males and an even greater number of Kamba hunters were jailed and until 1971, illegal hunting in Tsavo all but ceased and was greatly reduced in the surrounding lands. An extended patrol between Dakadima Hill and the Sabaki River scoured the land, most of which was rarely visited by humans, found 1,280 elephant carcasses or skeletons in $c.50$ km^2, 10 per cent of which were immature. The assumption drawn was that these must have been poachers' victims. No thought was given to natural mortality, or that such mortality, in itself, suggested there might be rather more elephants than 3,000.

An outgrowth of the anti-poaching campaign was the Galana Game Management Scheme, on 7,700 km^2 between Tsavo and the inhabited parts of the coast. Planned to give the Wata a legal means of benefitting from elephants that had been the basis of their culture, it was devised by Ian Parker collaborating with Sheldrick, and then implemented and run by Ian between 1960 and 1964.

In 1957 David Sheldrick noted extensive damage to woodland, first in the vicinity of the Aruba dam, built to provide permanent water where there had been none within 30 km when the park was founded. It planted the seed in his mind that, contrary to their imminent extinction, elephant numbers might need controlling and was at least one element in David backing the Galana Scheme. Based on taking annual quotas of elephants for meat and ivory, hopefully when

Tsavo elephants crossed the line into Galana, they could be culled there and avoid such action within the park.

By 1959 damage to woodland was so widespread that it was clearly not local to around Aruba, but general across Tsavo East. In 1961 drought struck the park and much of Kenya, but not the Galana area. Tsavo appeared a wasteland of bare earth and shattered timber. Black rhino died in large numbers: 300 were found dead of starvation along a 65 mile stretch of the Sabaki River. The woodland damage was greatest within elephant walking distance of water and the solution was deemed to be increasing water sources so as to more widely distribute elephants and other water-dependent species.

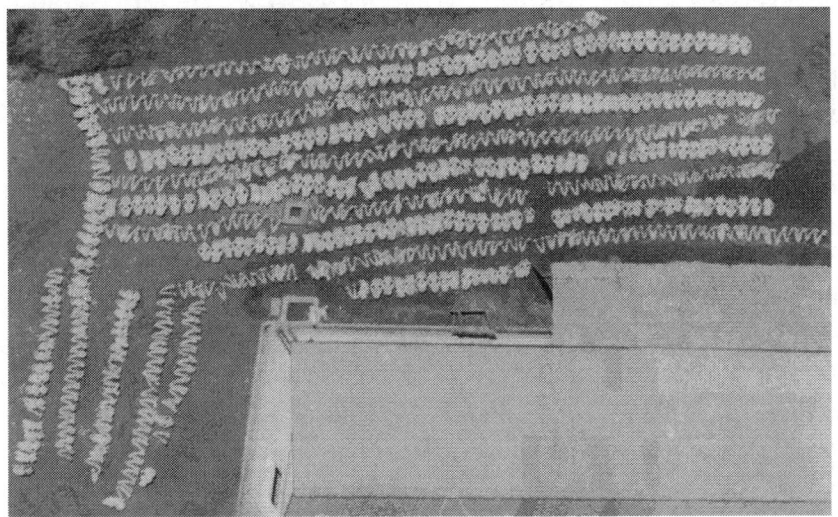

Black rhinos were early casualties of elephant influence on Tsavo's vegetation: some of the lower jaws and skulls collected by David Sheldrick at my request prior to my arrival in Tsavo

Overlooked at the time was that few park elephant crossed into Galana where good rain had fallen and where forage was still plentiful, despite its lack within the park. A massive campaign to raise money for new water sources was launched and a pumping plant built on the banks of the Sabaki River some way above Lugard's Falls, to send water 80 km north-east into the far reaches of the park's driest area.

In late September 1961 exceptionally heavy rain fell over the coastal hinterlands including Tsavo. In Galana the elephants on which the scheme depended vanished into the now soaked land. Critically, Ian needed to know where they had gone and hired an aircraft to undertake a three-day reconnaissance of both Tsavo and all its surrounding lands including the Galana area and the Mkomasi Game Reserve adjacent to Tsavo in Tanzania. With Peter Jenkins they flew a meandering course all over this vast area, counting such elephant as they saw. Their total was between six and seven thousand elephants. As this was not an attempt to estimate total numbers in the region, it nevertheless proved what woodland damage had been suggesting: that there were more than Buechner's 3,000 elephants, that they were scattered widely over the land, and that total numbers were most likely to exceed this recce flight's results.

David Sheldrick quickly organised further aerial counting to establish total numbers. It produced >10,275. This was soon followed by another count that resulted in 15,603 and eventually 20,300 in 1965. In the wake of the heavy September rain, the heaviest rains yet recorded in Kenya then fell in October and November; lush grass carpeted the land where trees had formerly stood, but where they still stood, the elephant continued to destroy them. When eventually the dry season arrived, this grass dried and fire swept the park south of the Sabaki River introducing the debate that had prevailed in Uganda – fire or elephants? The Director of Parks – then still Mervyn Cowie – convened a small Elephant Committee (the first of a succession of elephant committees) chaired by a Trustee, Sir Charles Markham, with Sheldrick and Parker among its very few members. It concluded that there were obviously too many elephants and that they would have to be reduced, but wondered how this might be done.

By now public interest was aroused. The government's Chief Zoologist, Dr Phil Glover, was called in for an opinion. This was followed in 1964 when the Director of the East African Agriculture and Forestry Research Organization convened the Aruba Research Conference on Elephant Behaviour and Control. It was attended by twenty-five delegates representing a variety of biological disciplines (though not myself; I was not at that time working on elephants) including representatives of Kenya's national parks, and the EAWS. David Sheldrick, reported that:

> The grassland which is replacing the bush at present, although at first it seems in good condition, is largely composed of pioneer annual grasses such as *Aristida* and is very similar in appearance to land over-grazed by cattle. The perennial grass cover will gradually increase as long

as favourable wet years continue, but if drought years should return before the perennial grass cover is established there will be severe erosion to contend with.

It was at this meeting that he also introduced the plausible idea that the changing environment might have some cyclic relationship to fluxes in climate and not be entirely due to animal pressure. It was conceded that an issue of public relations existed, not so much with the media and Western public as with local African communities. For years poachers had been punished for taking elephant in the park and would doubtless be cynical about any mass killing of elephant because there were too many. It was accepted, however, that explaining its necessity would just have to be faced and was no ground for not culling.

The conference agreed with the national parks' own Elephant Committee that elephant reduction was necessary. Shortly thereafter Sir Julian Huxley was in Kenya, his opinion was sought and he too thought it obvious numbers should be reduced, opining that this should be by at least a third. This would have meant killing >5,000 elephants of the 16,000 then believed to be present. While no longer clear who first quoted the actual figure of reduction by 5,000, it was for some time thereafter loosely quoted in discussion about what was perceived as a looming necessity. The Director of National Parks accepted the principle and it was endorsed by the Council of the EAWS in a letter to President Kenyatta.

At the Second World Conference on National Parks it was agreed there was a need for planned management of national parks and following a paper by Hugh Lamprey, the dilemma of 'letting nature take its course' as against 'active management' was given a thorough airing. Inevitably the Tsavo elephant problem was the pivot for this discussion and, according to the session rapporteur: 'the speakers generally supported Dr Lamprey's contention that elephant should not be allowed to drastically modify an ecosystem.' Two world conferences on national parks, the International Union for the Conservation of Nature and the prestigious Leopold Committee on Wildlife Management in the [United States] National Parks, all subsequently endorsed the need for management.

Uganda culling had broken the ice of caution that surrounded the concept of culling whole herds and proved it possible. The trial sample of 300 taken at Koito in August 1966 proved it was feasible within Tsavo. This, then, was the background to my arrival in Tsavo East and the challenges that the Research Project had been set up to resolve.

Obvious now in hindsight, there was a world of difference between the down-to-earth, matter-of-fact approach of the Uganda National Park Trustees and their counterparts in Kenya.

* * * *

At the outset the Tsavo Research Project was staffed by myself as Director, Dr Murray Watson as biologist/pilot (he had been the Cambridge post graduate student I had supervised for his PhD when he was working on wildebeest in the Serengeti) and Canadian John Goddard, who arrived with his wife Shelley and a small daughter. He was financed by Canadian sources and had previously worked on black rhino in Tanzania. The unit's administrator was a Mkamba – John Mutinda – from Kenya's Kitui District.

All of us were allocated houses, purpose built for the project. The facilities included three laboratories, each 24 x 14 ft, equipped with gas, electricity, running water and Formica-topped workbenches. I had a central office for administrative work. There was a darkroom which we equipped to handle all the project's photographic requirements, including the processing of large-format aerial film. I soon employed a technician – Mohammed Sher – experienced in mechanical engineering and building, to build additional facilities. These included a photo-interpretation room, designed by Murray, which was fitted with a movable mirror system worked by pulleys, to use sunlight for examining aerial photographic negatives. A chemical store was built and a general storage block (80 x 20 ft) with sliding doors was erected by a local contractor under Mohammed's supervision.

For transport we had three vehicles and adequate safari equipment for the field work. The EAWS had loaned the project a Piper Supercub aircraft equipped with an ex-RAF F24 aerial camera, which Murray acquired second hand (unbeknown to me at the time). I was also unaware that ownership of this camera was disputed by the Serengeti Research Institute.

The terms of reference which I drafted for the project in April 1967 were:

> To carry out research and to advise on the conservation and management of the Tsavo Ecological Unit, as defined by the movements and distribution of the elephant populations using the Tsavo National Park,

so as to develop a balanced diversity of its habitats and ecosystems, so far as this may be possible. Current and probable future land-use policy for the surrounding areas should be based on an integrated land-use system with the objective of optimising economic, cultural, and conservation values.

I wanted to develop the programme as an interdisciplinary effort, aimed at better understanding an area of some 43,520 km² of which Tsavo comprised the central block. The first priority, however, was to come to terms with the elephants that were pivotal to everything. Their numbers and distributions would be established by regular aerial observation, during which other animals would be recorded, but as a lower priority. The exceptions to this would be black rhino whose numbers and locations John Goddard would estimate through his own separate flying programme. The second arm of the aerial work was to set up fixed photographic transects, analysis of which would allow description of the vegetation, and monitor changes as they occurred.

Analysing aerial photography was a technical and very time-consuming skill, then absent in Kenya, and Murray arranged for two experienced English girls to come and do this for him.

John Goddard would make a detailed study of Tsavo's black rhino population but without the cull data that had underpinned the work on hippo and elephant. At the time it was assumed that there were too few black rhino for this to be practical on the population scales applied to hippo and elephants where, in both cases, reduction in numbers was a goal. Dentition provided ageing criteria and collecting lower jaws would allow construction of survivorship curves for the population as a whole and any sub-units within it. However, for the greater part, he would be getting his information from visual observation.

Fire would be studied and experimented with to come to terms with its use in management and to separate its influence from that of elephants. Particular emphasis would be given to describing past land use; the area's historical occupation was to be studied through environmental archaeology; past climatic and vegetational history would be established using dating methods, such as pollen analysis, carbon-14 and dendrochronology. After three years, partial or complete findings would be analysed, and management proposals drawn up for the foreseeable future.

It was ambitious and obviously beyond the resources of the project at the outset. However, given the considerable international interest that had arisen from my work in Uganda, I foresaw no great difficulties raising funds from grant-giving bodies and engaging the participation of other qualified workers. Already my old friend Gordon Lowther, an archaeologist/anthropologist, and with a post at the University in Nairobi, was keen to excavate some of the Orma graves in Tsavo. He felt he could raise the necessary funds for this and hoped it would take us back several centuries into the area's past.

After an initial two-months' flying to familiarise ourselves with the area, in June 1967 Murray and I began a monthly programme of survey flying. We flew for 4–6 days each month. Flight patterns were not systematic over a pre-calculated course, but made as a general reconnaissance of the whole area and, when concentrations of elephant were found, flying a close pattern over that locality to define their limits.

A random sub-sample of the elephants seen, usually amounting to 60–70 per cent of the total count (depending on their distance from the aircraft flight-line), was classified as single bulls or cows, bull herds or family units. It recorded calves estimated to be less than a year old (those that could walk under their mother!). Within Tsavo we estimated a population of about 23,000 elephant in 1967. A further 17,000 were estimated outside the park borders bringing our total estimate to around 40,000 elephants for the total 43,520 km^2.

It quickly became apparent that the elephant distribution was discontinuous with conspicuous clumping into large aggregations (each numbering thousands), and each occupying a relatively small area (some 770–1,000 km^2) at any one time. As the data accumulated we realised that these groups were remarkably stable and localised.

When we found that they apparently had different biological parameters, it dawned on us that they could be treated for practical purposes as separate 'populations'. This meant that although there were more elephants than had been thought, their management should be more tractable. Differences between these 'units' were in ratios of bull herds to family units, in the proportion that were calves, in their age structures after 1945 and in mean group-size frequencies.

Our observations implied that there were ten 'separate' populations, ranging in size from about 2,000 to 4,000 elephants, separated from other groups by areas of low elephant densities, with ranges that overlapped little or not at all at any one time. For example, after heavy rainfall in August and September, individual populations moved en masse some 10–20 miles and clumped together more closely, effectively increasing their separation. The received wisdom was that they clumped in dry weather and scattered widely when it was wet, whereas the reverse was true. So we concluded that social and foraging behaviour, allied to the availability of water, restricted their distribution in the dry season; but, when rainfall removed the restriction and vegetation was 'flushing', they were freed to adopt an optimal social and foraging configuration in relation to resources. The dry season and wet season distributions were distinctly different. There was some indication of clumps within the larger groups, strengthening my earlier ideas during the Uganda studies about a possible 'clan' system within populations. There was little, if any, indication of large-scale migrations or movements out of these areas on a seasonal basis.

These findings increased the complexity of the research because, instead of one homogeneous population there were ten or so to be described and investigated. But, if this separation could be confirmed by further work, it would greatly simplify the management problems and allow different treatments for each group. It created the possibility of an experiment rather on the lines of the hippo management which I had set up in QENP: by distributing separate but simultaneous cropping regimes ranging between zero and heavy culls, the different responses of both flora and fauna would be known. We now had the necessary knowledge and experience to implement a similar programme for elephants across the whole Tsavo Unit.

As an aside, the 1966 cull of 300 elephant in Koito had already sampled one of the ten populations. Two more of them were based in the Mkomasi Reserve in northern Tanzania which, though treated by us as part of the Tsavo ecosystem, came under the jurisdiction of the Tanzanian Game Division. Independently, the Tanzanians wanted to establish the status of two Mkomasi populations by taking samples of 300 each – following that which we had already done in Tsavo and which they had followed closely. In parallel they had a financial goal to make as much money as possible from such offtakes in an area that had at that time no other sources of revenue.

The dual objectives were compatible and the Tanzanian warden responsible – David Anstey – contracted WLS to take the samples, on the same basis that had applied in Uganda and Tsavo of paying a fee per elephant and then marketing the produce on their own behalf. Anstey wanted the data from the two Mkomasi culls analysed by me as part of the Tsavo Research Program. I agreed. WLS agreed and now had the experience to gather the data without supervision. Thus, at no cost to the Tsavo Project, we acquired a large body of scientific information from three separate Uganda populations and three of the Tsavo groups – Koito, Mkomasi East and Mkomasi West.

The samples showed the three Kenya groups had faster growth rates compared with the Murchison Park elephants. In order of fastest growth, the Mkomasi elephants showed the greatest acceleration, so that at 30 years old the average Mkomasi female weighed 400–500 kg more than the Koito females, who in turn were faster than MFNPN, with MFPNS the slowest. It was of course possible that there might be genetic differences between Kenya and Uganda elephants. The heaviest elephant sampled also came from Mkomasi – a male weighing 6,260 kg, but only 41 years old. Similar disparities following the same order were apparent in all reproductive parameters.

Differences in the age structures, growth rates and reproductive parameters of the Koito, Mkomasi East and Mkomasi West confirmed what we had deduced from aerial records: they were indeed separate entities.

A new measurement had been introduced in the later elephant culls: in addition to the shoulder height taken routinely, back length in a straight line from the base of ear to base of tail was recorded and related to age. The result was pleasingly close to the tight correlation between height and age. It meant that we could collect this important information from the living animal from vertical aerial photographs more easily than trying to get shoulder heights from living animals in the field.

By 1968 I had age data on some 5,500 elephants in nine different population units, half directly aged from jaws and half from aerial photography. I concluded that in all populations there had been declining recruitment from the 1940s, probably due to increasing human numbers and activities – though climate cannot be entirely ruled out. (In synchrony, Ian Parker's later research into ivory exports, which are an index of elephant mortality, showed that they were increasing exponentially both before and after this period 1945–1967.) Notably, in Koito there had been much enhanced recruitment from the late 1950s, which it is tempting to associate with the anti-poaching campaigns in 1956/7.

* * * *

The aerial counts continued to yield high-quality data on elephant social organisation. For 1,313 bull groups counted in August to November 1966 the mean size was 2.4, and for 2,411 mixed herds the mean size was 11.3. In August 1,031 groups were classified into 427 single bulls and bull herds, and 604 family groups and single females. Of bulls 50 per cent were single animals. Just over 1 per cent of other 'groups' were single females. No bull herd had more than 14 animals, whereas nearly 40 per cent of mixed herds were larger than 30 and the largest was 128 animals. The mixed herds had a modal size of 6 animals and seemingly a polymodal distribution with further peaks at 12, 18 and possibly 24 and 30. This suggested the basic family unit averaged 6 animals and that larger groups were aggregations of several such units, and bull herds. These data were all apparent in the culling records.

In September–November 2,593 groups were analysed. In September the modal mixed herd size was 5 and the second peak at 10; in October and November, the modal group size was 7 and the maximum group size was 700. The largest all-bull herd seen numbered 35, but Ian Parker told us he had seen one of 144 bulls in the Galana Scheme area (north-east). The proportion of single bulls increased slightly between August and November (August 50 per cent, September 38 per cent, October 62 per cent and November 60 per cent). The period August–November is dry and lies between two mating (rainy) seasons and peak conceptions occur in May and December. Our incomplete data suggested there might be a decline in the mean family-unit size from the previous mating season and a build-up towards the next breeding season, towards a peak in December.

We also noted that there were high proportions of bulls in the three north-western populations (15.3 per cent, 15.5 per cent and 15.7 per cent) and far lower in the three most easterly (4.4 per cent, 4.8 per cent and 5.9 per cent). We could not explain this apparent discrepancy. It may have been connected with past differential poaching pressures, but we have to note that such disparities had been observed but not explained elsewhere. For example the elephant population around Marsabit Mountain in northern Kenya is reportedly heavily weighted towards bulls and has very few family units. The claim is supported by the district's ivory recoveries.

These findings changed ideas about elephant social organisation and, broadly speaking, our pioneer work on this synoptic scale was confirmed by the long-term, more detailed behavioural studies undertaken from the late 1960s onwards by others.

John Goddard established the extent, density and trend of the population(s) in Tsavo and set out to determine whether the observed habitat changes in the area were adversely affecting the species, as had been claimed. His results were added to by what we saw on our flights. The two sets of data, both combined and treated independently, told the same story: there were possibly as many as 8,000, or 1 per 2.6 km^2, black rhino within the Tsavo National Park. Yet, while this was far more than had been anticipated, they were nevertheless declining in numbers.

During the course of the systematic aerial counts, John classified rhinos by relative age and, whenever possible, by sex; cow/calf ratios were calculated from these data and preliminary information collected on recruitment. Ground studies of certain populations provided more detailed information and using the methods I pioneered on elephant and hippopotamus, some 450 skulls from natural deaths that David Sheldrick and his staff had collected were ascribed to twenty relative-age classes. Chronological ages were allocated to these classes, partly from known-age material. A survival curve, both sexes combined, was then constructed.

In addition 120 rhinos were individually identified and catalogued on the ground from distinctive features: the characteristics used included sex, age, horns and ears, and position of prominent body scars; the wrinkle pattern on the head was used in some cases. The locations of sightings and re-sightings were recorded, also group structure, behaviour and other information was collected. If the animal was feeding it was watched for a period of one hour and a note made of the plants which it selected and rejected.

* * * *

Major vegetation types were recorded on 1:250,000 maps by Murray Watson and detailed studies made of the key tree and bush species. The project installed a network of ten storage rain gauges, as well as three agro-meteorological stations (financed by the EAWS) adding to the two already in existence.

Five transects, each about 20 km long, were photographed periodically from which a wealth of botanical information was extracted. This work was made possible by a generous grant (£7,000) to me from the Royal Society, London.

These data were intended to provide long-term comparisons through repeated photography. They would be followed up with more detailed sampling from ground studies by the plant ecologist when appointed. Areas of recent tree damage were related to elephant concentrations.

In this chapter and at the risk of boredom, I have indicated in some depth how the project was producing large volumes of data from the outset. To a substantial degree it was a roll-on from my programmes in Uganda: while I may have changed location, the breadth of ambition was still the same.

20

A House of Cards?

I was well pleased with our start. The data collected was substantial and most of all, it had produced an overview of Tsavo's elephant problem. That this was obtained within ten months was in keeping with the high standards set in Uganda and that I was able to integrate it with the ongoing work which continued there after I had left was an enormous bonus.

Yet a massive spanner was thrown into the works when the Director of Parks – Perez Olindo – summarily dismissed Murray Watson in November 1967. Murray had applied to me as his boss to take local leave, which I had granted. As a formality, this approval should also have been sought from Perez Olindo. It wasn't, so Murray was sacked. I was as 'guilty' as he for this breach of protocol.

With hindsight perhaps I should have noticed earlier warning signs that all might not be well. Ian Parker had picked up a hint that David Sheldrick was not altogether happy with the way the research was developing. Having been very influential in bringing David and myself together and a close friend to both, he had flown to Voi on 6 April 1967 to dispel this disquiet. It seemed a storm in a teacup. David, or more to the point his wife, Daphne, felt that I would bring about large-scale elephant culling and suspected that the underlying motive was for commercial gain and not conservation. Ian had scotched this suspicion and David had accepted that it was ill-founded.

Nevertheless, looking back it is apparent that the terms of reference that I had drawn up for the programme in April had not been responded to; neither had ideas I submitted in July on the prospect of further culls for deeper investigation into at least some of the different groups that were emerging from our aerial work. At this time I was also expressing my conviction that given the state of the vegetation and the rapidity with which it had come about, we were on the brink of an elephant population crash. I was able to show, in 1967, we had just passed the peak in a rainfall cycle, and could expect increasingly dry years ahead. A drought would elevate the elephant problem from chronic to acute crisis which would happen in the early 1970s. It was to prove accurate!

David had not reacted to my terms of reference, which gave me responsibility for drawing up a research programme, or to my tentative proposals, both of which I had submitted to him for comment. Of course I should have followed this up this silence, and can only suggest that I read agreement into his silence. I was still infected with the euphoria of getting the programme up and running and that the relationship with David was a continuum of that which I had enjoyed with Frank Poppleton and Roger Wheater. Yet, looking back, David's failure to comment on terms of reference and further culling possibilities marked the onset of cooling relations between us. It was also the point to which I time his *volte face* from being the most prominent advocate of reducing elephant numbers to an outright opponent. I can only speculate on what may have brought this about.

Without question, Daphne was very influential. Passionate and emotional, in the years since then, she has stridently opposed killing wild animals for any reason. David, once a professional hunter, then advocate of culling, had obviously not been opposed to rational killing. However, when he witnessed the culling at Kioto in 1966, he had told Ian that it tore him in two: on the one hand admiring the cold efficiency with which the undertaking was carried out, on the other horror at killing whole herds of elephants in the very park set aside to protect them from humans. He found it truly awful. Yet for most of the next year he had suppressed these honest feelings with reason.

Murray Watson irritated David from the outset. Sheldrick was a martinet, ran a disciplined and very tight ship in keeping with his military background (he had been the youngest major in the King's African Rifles during the Second World War). He liked to know who was doing what and where in his park at all times. In particular, he demanded that all flying in the area covered by the study be logged beforehand in a register kept at the Park HQ airfield. His request was both logical and reasonable. If an aircraft had the mishap of a forced landing in the vast, mostly trackless wilderness, he needed to know roughly where to look for it. Murray was self-willed, disliking authority or rules of any kind. Coupled to this he didn't like David and went out of his way to needle him. Thus he repeatedly failed to sign the airfield register, and also avoided telling anyone (including me) where he was going on the ground. On one occasion it narrowly missed causing a tragedy: he had motored with a guest – colleague Richard Bell from the Serengeti Research Institute – without water into the furthest corner of Tsavo East where his vehicle broke down. Murray walked fifty miles back to the Sabaki River and then on to headquarters, leaving Bell to await rescue.

Murray's photo-interpreter girls were his unpaid guests, and in Kenya on tourist and not work visas. This was another source of contention. They were abusing the latitude that surrounded the programme; again an understandable sentiment. Technically Murray and all working with the unit were under my control and I should have stepped in and rectified things. Matters should have been resolved by talking face to face – which never happened. Consequently the irritations festered until David could take it no more and persuaded the Director to summarily dismiss Murray, which he did in November on a very petty issue. This was not only discourteous, but sacking one of my subordinates without reference to me effectively stopped a large part of our research in its tracks.

This was clearly intentional as next to come under attack were my plans to fund and bring established scientists to look into botany, soils and archaeology, etc. In July 1967 I was informed that any expansion of the research would have to be tackled by scientists recruited locally as permanent staff of the Kenya National Parks. This contradicted the assurance that I would have the free hand that I was given as part of the inducement to accept the Tsavo Research Project's directorship. My previous experience in Uganda had alerted me to the passionate wish to replace expatriate scientists with African researchers. It was for that reason that I had insisted on freedom to recruit the most suitable people for the tasks I had in mind. There was nothing racial in this and if competent Kenyan scientists were available I would have willingly taken them.

The fact was, however, that experienced African scientists in the biological fields were non-existent. If the Kenya National Parks were now insisting on young local graduates it would not only involve all the bureaucracy such civil service recruiting procedures entail, it would load me with on-the-job training which was not my forte, virtually removing me from the field. At the same time they told me that if any culling were done it would be by Africans recruited by the Parks to be trained by me. This specialised work was not my field at all and hardly the duty of a Director of Research. Effectively it would castrate the scope, speed and thoroughness of data collection and analysis that had characterised the work on elephants and hippos. They knew that there were no such people available then, and in some of the disciplines I have mentioned there were then few scientists even in the international field. The hostility towards recruiting staff went further. Gordon Lowther, who had been so actively encouraged by David Sheldrick to undertake research on Orma graves that he had started planning the work, was told that if he entered Tsavo to do so, he would be prosecuted.

Here it is difficult not to dissociate Sheldrick's ego from what was happening. He considered Tsavo as his creation, which in many senses it was. He had clearly not foreseen that so large an effort as I had planned would be possible or necessary, nor had he expected us to make such rapid progress: advances that would inevitably erode his control of what, until then, had been his absolute fiefdom. And this is of course true. Possibly I added fuel to an already combustible situation by pointing out that Kenya National Parks had no basic policies, not even the simple policy under which Uganda National Parks operated. As the long trail of meetings to talk about the elephant problem illustrated, Kenya National Parks lacked the clear foresight of their Uganda peers and functioned very much on an ad hoc basis.

David was well aware that suggesting all further scientists working under the aegis of the Tsavo Research Program should be permanent members of the Kenya National Park staff was politically attractive to the government as Africanisation – the term describing the policy – was being applied across the board. While in sympathy with the philosophy, I had been brought in to solve a pressing biological problem as quickly as possible. For this reason not only had I insisted on a free hand to engage staff and raise funds to finance them, but everyone on the Kenya side with whom I had made this case had agreed that there would be no problem. If scientists now had to go through the bureaucratic process of selection by the National Parks employment system, not only would few established in careers elsewhere apply, but it was impossible for me to engage scientists quickly, on merit and for specific purposes. With the idea lodged, David now set about getting his superiors to reverse their approval for all culling.

Public distaste for culling was not new. However, where Uganda was concerned and the authorities were clear in their rationale, there had been no outcry and the media treated it almost as a non-event. The case for having to cull elephants in Tsavo was first mentioned in public before it was expressed in Uganda. While everyone was dismayed by the prospect, it was accepted as necessary and the figure of 5,000 had been repeatedly mentioned. The only concern had not been the number, but whether it would be possible.

However, once the word went out that there was uncertainty over the very principle of culling in a national park, the opponents who had until now been held in check by reason, became very vocal. The media sensationalised it, with the tabloids being ever more critical of the very idea. The Director of Parks, Olindo, Aloys Achieng, the Permanent Secretary, the Minister, Sam Ayodo and the government in general were impressed by and wary of the press, and sought to put as much distance as possible between themselves and support for the idea. Nothing confirmed their attitudes more than David Sheldrick's *volte face*.

Initially he publicly pooh-poohed my prediction of an imminent population crash, but then in a manner that was becoming expected of him, accepted that it was indeed likely, but now argued in favour of letting the next drought take care of the situation as 'nature's way'.

When asked about my needs regarding further culling, I had answered tentatively that, *if* there were ten populations, and if they were to be sampled at the same level of 300 as the trial at Koito in 1966, it would amount to such a sample from every group: a total of 3,000 elephants. However, this was said in a discursive, hypothetical overview. I never said that I wanted such sampling. My formal request in my July 1967 proposal was for 300 elephants from one 'population' in the south-east of the park. Of particular note, I also pointed out in that proposal that it might not be necessary to sample the remaining populations. I have no doubt whatever that David Sheldrick knew I had never requested more than one further sample of 300. Indeed, now with a firm grasp of elephant biology on which to relate observations, I had stated that observation in the field could largely replace much of the need to cull.

Independently of my research proposals, I held the view that major reductions in at least some of the separate groups was the only way in which the destruction of woodland could be stopped and a population crash averted. With the Mweya hippo work as an illustration, an arbitrary approach through a range of reductions seemed rational. Proof of what reduction was necessary for Tsavo's woodland to regenerate would only be apparent when elephants reached that level. This could be produced by intervention – which I advocated – or by simply standing by and letting it happen with all the accompanying losses of other species. As apparent in MFNPS, this might take decades. Yet, while I believed it irresponsible not to intervene, I could not get David or his superiors to even discuss the subject.

While David saw two separate issues were involved between the sample I had requested and the need for large-scale reduction, I am not so certain that his Director, Perez Olindo, or those above him, like Aloys Achieng and the Chairman of Trustees, did. That will be forever moot. Yet at all levels from David upward, the word went out that Laws was asking for thousands of elephants to be killed.

Matters were not helped by the Ministry's failure to reappoint a Board of Trustees for the National Parks after their current term expired in 1967. For four months there was no board to whom I could appeal for a fair hearing. When it was appointed, new members were unaware of the previous history, or the oral assurances that had led me to take up the work. By that stage it was my word against those of Sheldrick, Olindo and Achieng before a bemused panel – most of whom were completely alien to biology and conservation.

This very unhappy situation was made intolerable when it was alleged that my advocacy of culling was for financial gain and that this explained the collusion between myself and Ian Parker. When evidence was called for to substantiate this by a member of the press, Olindo said they had indisputable proof that WLS had paid me to be present for the 300 elephant culled at Koito in 1966. That is true: it was a condition in the contract made with WLS at the Trustees' insistence that the company would pay my air fare and expenses. It showed how far he would go to discredit both Ian and myself.

I tried to discuss matters with Aloys Achieng and the Chairman of the Trustees, David Wasawo. Appointments were made, I drove the 320 km to keep them, but every meeting was cancelled when I arrived. Finally I said they would receive my notice of resignation effective from 1 March if there were no positive developments. A meeting was promised for a week's time at Voi, at which all would be resolved. It wasn't kept and my resignation became effective. Even then I had no further communication until 9 April when a press release from the Trustees announced my resignation and I left the park at the end of May.

There was a rash of newspaper headlines – one of them: 'Gun Law Doctor Moves Out'. These were followed by a blizzard of articles promoting direct and oblique attacks on me and my scientific integrity. One paper – the *Reporter* – did not accept my figure of 40,000 elephants in the Tsavo region, opining that some years before, the national parks had spent several weeks on a project to count the elephants in and around Tsavo, using four aircraft and helicopters:

> In all they counted 20,000 elephants between the Tana River and the Tanzania border. Being modest men they suggested they may have erred a little, and that if they had done so it was on the conservative side. But at no time did these skilled and experienced observers suggest that they may have made a 100 per cent error.

Yet he forbore to mention that in 1953 the skilled observers had doubted that there could be 3,000 elephants; in 1962 this was increased to over 6,000 by Parker and Jenkins on a reconnaissance, then raised to 10,000, then 15,000 and finally over 20,000 by Sheldrick. This steady progression from 3,000 to more than 20,000 in a decade (666 per cent) was hardly evidence of any great skill! To the contrary, it illustrated the failure to come to terms with counting that sample counting was eventually adopted to correct. As an aside, after I had left Kenya, Dr Walter Leuthold undertook an aerial sample count within Tsavo 'which agrees with Laws and Watson'. Journalists too lazy to do their homework cause a great deal of grief!

In October 1968 the East African *Reporter* carried an article ('Reprieve for the Tsavo Elephants') saying that David Sheldrick had reported that nature had been taking a hand to save the elephants, and that 'a new ecology' was developing. He claimed a lot of lush and highly nutritious grass had sprung up over vast areas – contradicting what he had said at the Aruba conference in 1964. As elephants eat mainly grass anyway, said the article, they were eating away at it merrily, and looking very well on it. In fact some experts' (not named) reports now suggest that the Tsavo scientific research team is now concentrating, not so much on ascertaining how many elephants must be killed, but rather how many more the park will support.

Of course it is easy to condense events through hindsight. In fact it had taken me many months to grasp that research on the scale envisaged and planned for had generated considerable hostility. While I had been finding David progressively more difficult to get on with (perhaps our personalities were incompatible which I do not believe), this surely wouldn't account for him reversing his principles?

Looking back past the anger and hurt, I recognise that it was often difficult 'to see the wood for the trees'. Yet it was an intensely distressing situation for me and my wife. The latter part of my time in Tsavo was undoubtedly the most unpleasant period of my life.

* * * *

In 1971 a severe drought produced the crash I had predicted. Sheldrick acknowledged that 10,000 elephants had died of starvation. Data from ivory entering the trade internationally suggested the total was more than 15,000. When the next counts took place, there were only about 8,000 elephants left in Tsavo, down from 23,000 within the park borders – a loss of 65 per cent. Some of this loss was undeniably also due to poaching which followed the die-off.

The drought that killed the elephants also afflicted the Tsavo Park's neighbours. Their crops failed and destitute, they quickly learned of the dead elephants leaving tusks in their hundreds available for collection. Under the duress of the drought, they started to venture over the boundaries that they had feared to do since the anti-poaching campaigns of the 1950s. They went in such numbers that Sheldrick's forces were unable to apprehend more than a small fraction. Kamba ivory gatherers came in ever-increasing numbers. Word of their bonanza attracted Somalis. When the sources of ivory from starvation started to dry up, having found out how easy it was to trespass, they switched to poaching the living elephants. Initially it was mainly the Akamba doing this, but in due course the Somalis armed with firearms displaced them and exercised a monopoly over first Tsavo's and then the whole region's ivory.

While events in Kenya never matched those where Uganda's people were concerned, it was little different for the country's elephants. Corruption within government was spreading throughout the system. Game wardens were at the forefront of this. The President ordered certain favoured individuals be granted permission to collect ivory and sell it. His daughter, Margaret, became a major ivory exporter. So corrupt was the system that when Sheldrick managed to get men into court for poaching, they were let off with ludicrously light sentences.

In due course David Sheldrick became the victim of his own efficiency. The better to get at what remained of Tsavo's elephants, John Mutinda (onc my storeman but now his boss), moved David out of his beloved Tsavo and

292

stationed him in Nairobi to plan parks. He died prematurely of a heart attack aged 56 in 1976.

At the outset of my East African experiences, managing populations within national parks was not incompatible with their objectives. However, an emotionally driven ill-informed public did not like this. The underlying sentiment was inflamed by the media – particularly through television – so much so that many biologists now won't even consider the possibilities. Always in need of funds for research that the public provides, recommending culling invites career suicide.

At least in part, if not mainly, my experiences in Kenya and Uganda have to be attributed to the collapse of civil services and loss of government probity. Even if my ambitious plans for research in Tsavo had not met opposition from within, I doubt whether they could have gone far in the face of internal politics and the declines in standards of governance.

21

African Epilogue

On leaving Kenya I decided to give Maureen a break – she had found Tsavo particularly stressful. Leaving both boys to complete their current term at St Andrews, we flew from Nairobi to Greece, where we took a three-day cruise in the *Stella Solaris* going around the Greek islands. The following afternoon, 18 June, we flew to Dubrovnik, Yugoslavia. On 27 June, we flew to Munich via Zagreb where we had to change planes. We picked up our new BMW 2000 from the factory, then took a leisurely drive through Austria, Italy, France and Spain, before ending with Maureen's parents in Portugal.

The culture, ancient history, scenery, graciousness, the beauty and the enormous contrast with crude Africa was marvellous and wonderfully relaxing. We considered that we had really earned and deserved it and both felt so much better and more civilised! We enjoyed Gordon Lowther's company for part of the trip. He had flown over from Kenya to join us and was glad to be out of the emotional maelstrom which anything to do with conservation had become there.

Richard and Christopher flew to Lisbon from Kenya where we met up and we spent a month in Portugal with Maureen's parents and sister and her family. On Friday 23 August, leaving the two boys with their grandparents to fly back to London at the end of the month, Maureen and I left Estoril to drive back to England where it felt good to be home again after a superb holiday in Europe. It had really cast off the gloom that we had felt towards the end in Kenya.

However, extricating ourselves from Africa had been expensive, and at forty-two I was unemployed for the first time in my adult life.

Reviewing our time in Africa, and to be immodest, I am still amazed that we achieved so much in so short a time. My field research on hippo and elephant ran from 1961 to 1966, overlapping with elephant research that lasted only from August 1965 to March 1968. Back in England I obtained two Fellowships (from the Leverhulme Foundation and from Cambridge University) which supported the writing-up of results in 1968–69 until I took up a senior post with the British Antarctic Survey.

Yet by 1975 I had over twenty significant papers on elephant biology and management published in scientific journals, alone or in collaboration. A substantial scientific book, *Elephants and Their Habitats*, with Ian Parker and Ron Johnstone was published by Oxford University Press in 1975 (the text and illustrations completed in 1970 took five years to publish). By then my energies had long been diverted to Antarctic matters – science, logistics and politics.

The field research on elephant was the most rewarding period in my research career, although it lasted – part-time – less than three years. From the perspective of a new century our findings over a period of less than ten years were far reaching, putting research on elephant population biology on a sound scientific footing for the first time. In the subsequent forty years our basic findings have been largely confirmed. While elephant biology has attracted many to study them and cost a great deal of money, I consider very little of this work really ground breaking. Foremost of that which has been is the outstanding behavioural study of Kenya's Amboseli elephants by Cynthia Moss. Though she had close collaborators – notably Joyce Poole – Cynthia put elephant behaviour on the map definitively. Iain Douglas-Hamilton may have started the behavioural ball rolling, but was subsequently dwarfed by the decades of results from Cynthia and her collaborators.

Another notable behavioural study has been that of Anna Whitehouse in the Addo Park of South Africa. A major aspect of elephant behaviour and physiology that we did not pick up from our elephant work was the phenomenon of musth in the male. This was recognised simultaneously and independently by Joyce Poole in Amboseli and Anthony Hall-Martin in Kruger. As soon as I read the clinical symptoms of a male in musth – the strong smell, the dribbling penis and green staining – I recognised them. We had collected a few such males in musth during the culling, but had not appreciated the significance of the signs. All that we could add to the knowledge of this condition is that the temporal glands were swollen and the seminal vesicles contained litres of fluid as opposed to one litre or less in non-musth males.

Another landmark was Katy Payne's discovery of elephant communication by infra-sound. Not diminishing her finding in any way, it again came as no surprise if only because the Wata had always maintained that elephant could communicate over long distances. They said that they did so by 'dreams' – in the sense of telepathy. Ian reported that on many occasions he found a spooked elephant herd had somehow communicated its alarm to others over long distances. Other hunters were also aware of this.

Then there have been new advances arising from radio and satellite tracking technology. The most impressive such study of which I know was that by Rowan Martin in Zimbabwe where every herd in the Sengwa population had a transmitter with it and they were followed for over two decades. Sadly, he has never published the results which would have complemented Cynthia Moss's findings of how herds associate with one another at many levels over time, but in a bigger population.

Impressive information on the overall relationship between elephants and humans came out of Ian Parker's study of the ivory trade. His 'discovery' of Customs records of tusks imported and exported internationally for centuries was strangely overlooked by conservationists and, for all that they were hard facts, when they indicated tusks from tens of thousands of elephants had been leaving Africa annually for decades, they were initially rejected as false. Even less acceptable was that the exports were incontrovertible proof that elephant must have numbered in millions. Such high numbers surprised me. At one time I had guessed that there might be 300,000 in all of Africa, but the trade statistics could not be denied. Nothing brought home how incredibly successful these huge mammals had been and still were.

When the work I have outlined above is combined, the African elephant has advanced from a subject more of myth than fact a mere forty years ago to one of the world's better-known animals today.

As it does over Africa itself, an aura of apprehension hangs over the African elephant's future. This is not new. As Ian pointed out, Pliny said it in Roman times, then Petherick in 1869, Holder in 1886, Bryden in 1903, Kunz in 1916,

Moore in 1931 and now a crescendo of voices repeated the chant in such numbers as to be beyond identity. One stark fact stands out across the litany: how wrong all have been about elephant abundance and resilience. The Tsavo saga illustrated it. If it wasn't wicked poachers threatening them with extinction, it would be equally wicked scientists culling them!

If one looks at the shrinkage elephant range has undergone over the past century, there are very few places indeed where in this process they have not been replaced by people. The records of the Uganda and Tanzanian Game Departments and the ivory auction rooms in Mombasa and Dar-es-Salaam, and international Customs statistics all tell the same indisputable story of decline that if it is sustained must culminate in extinction. Yet there is still time to review what science has accumulated about elephants and to plan a rational strategy for conservation based upon it.

In reality, while it is difficult to see any number surviving the current trend in human increase, there are still sufficient elephants extant to warrant many experimental management strategies as we grope towards conclusions. However, doing nothing and letting nature take its course is not one of them.

Compare this photo taken in 1974 with the one on the next page taken in 1968. Through the dust haze the waterhole in the mid-foreground, its green fringe and the odd clumps of green prove it was taken in the wake of good rain. While predicting catastrophe, I had never envisaged anything on this scale. There was nothing left for any animals to eat and small wonder over 15,000 elephants starved. That it went unreported in the media, or that it took place in a national park is astonishing. Yet what neither I nor the opponents of culling predicted was that two decades later and with far smaller elephant numbers, this devastated scene has reverted to open woodland.

A Tsavo scene after rains in early 1968: the trees had been replaced by grasses

PART III

Antarctica
and
Academe

Our home in Coton, Cambridge

22

Head, BAS Life Sciences Division

From 1961 to 1968 I had worked on tropical animal ecology, until 1967 as Director of the NUTAE in Uganda, and from 1967–68 as Director of the Tsavo Research Project in Kenya. That research had been mainly on hippopotamus and elephant biology, in all quite a change from the Antarctic and the Southern Ocean! In July 1969 when Ray Adie, an old Antarctic friend (I had been best man at his wedding), telephoned to ask if I would consider a new post at the BAS. I expressed interest and was short-listed, interviewed and appointed.

Professors Alan Parkes and Bill Thorpe, both FRS, who were familiar with my African work, provided good references. In his, Alan had written:

> …because of his dedication to scientific work he tended to be impatient and sometimes intolerant of what he regarded as obstruction or lack of support, but this undoubtedly contributed to his capacity for getting things done!

He might have added that I expected scientists to deliver and publish good results quickly. In this way I returned to my earlier Antarctic and marine mammal interests, and took up my new job at the Nature Conservancy's Monks Wood Research Station. In the years since working for FIDS there had been much development. The following list of snippets in rough chronological order gives some idea of changes that had taken place.

1950 (i) Bunny Fuchs was appointed Head of FIDS office in London, and Principal Scientific Officer managing the FIDS Scientific Bureau directly responsible to the Colonial Secretary. Logistics and running the Rear Base for supplies and recruitment was still the remit of the Crown Agents, also in London.

1952 (i) The Royal Society formed a British National Committee for Antarctic Research.

1953 (i) With extended funding for three years, the British National Committee for Antarctic Research became part of FIDS.

1955 i) The Scientific and Management Bureau amalgamated with and took over Rear Base Logistics, until then run by the Crown Agents but both now under Fuchs.

(ii) Fuchs took leave of absence to set up and lead Trans-Antarctic Expedition. Over the next three years the TAE collected much scientific data on geophysics, geology, glaciology, meteorology; seismic shots every thirty miles and gravity readings every fifteen miles.

(iii) Sir Raymond Priestley took over as FIDS Acting Director.

(iv) FIDS Aerial Survey Expedition based on Deception Island under contract to Dept. of Colonial Surveys. Aircraft now in the Antarctic.

1956 (i) Priestley, a high-powered academic administrator, started a complete reorganisation of FIDS administration.

(ii) Royal Society established a scientific station at Halley Bay.

(iii) FIDS got a new ship, the RV *John Biscoe*.

(iv) The Scientific Committee was reconstituted with greater representation of government scientific institutions.

(v) Priestley outlined a five-year plan.

(vi) Priestley set about establishing research units, each dealing with a specific scientific discipline and attached to a UK university or research institute.

(vii) The first such was geology under Ray Adie in Prof. R. W. Shotton's department in Birmingham University.

(viii) Investigations into Very Low Frequency (VLF) whistler phenomena set up under supervision of Sheffield University's Space Physics Unit.

(ix) Oxford's Edward Grey Institute became the FIDS Ornithological work centre.

1957 (i) International Geophysical Year (IGY) established an Antarctic programme under the Royal Society. Ran for 2 years.

(ii) There were fifty-four scientists now working for FIDS – mainly geologists, surveyors and meteorologists.

1958 (i) The multinational Scientific Committee for Antarctic Research (SCAR) was formed under the aegis of the International Council of Scientific Unions (ICSU).

(ii) The Royal Society's IGY responsibility transferred to FIDS.

(iii) Fuchs returned and Priestley left, but Fuchs continued to implement Priestley's plan. FIDS now had the following programmes running and attached to:-

(a) Geophysics team led by Prof Griffiths – the Scotia Project at Birmingham University.

(b) A geophysics observatory team under Joe Farmer at Edinburgh University.

(c) A biology programme under Martin Holdgate at Queen Mary College, London University.

(d) A topographical survey programme under the Director of Colonial Surveys.

(e) Medicine and physiology programme under Otto Edholm at the Medical Research Council.

1960 Signy Island became the permanent site for FIDS principal Antarctic biological station.

1961 (i)   The Antarctic Treaty came into Force with UK a signatory.

(ii)   FIDS became the British Antarctic Survey (BAS).

1965   National Environment Research Council (NERC) came into existence. It would be best described as a conventional Civil Service Department.

1967 (i)   1 April, BAS came under NERC.

(ii)   Until then BAS had no permanent and pensionable posts in science or administration.

(iii) The BAS Biological Unit was renamed the Zoological Section and moved to Monks Wood near Huntingdon.

1969 (i)   A Botanical Section was created based in Birmingham University.

(ii)   A Turbo Beaver aircraft was added to Antarctic aviation unit to support the Twin Otter already there.

(iii) BAS took over administering South Georgia, assuming duties formerly held by the Magistrate for which the Falklands government paid £25,000 p.a., later raised to £30,000.

(iv)   The Zoology and Botanical sections of BAS became sections of the Life Sciences Division, of which I was appointed head.

* * * *

During Bunny Fuchs' fourteen years as Director, the Survey underwent a transformation. The greatest difficulties were experienced in the first half of this period, when the future of the Survey was in doubt. The second part was in the nature of a 'honeymoon' with NERC, when each partner was learning about the other. With skill and vision he had guided BAS from its political origins and emphasis on geographical exploration to become a front-rank Antarctic research organisation. When he retired the Survey was one of the larger bodies in NERC; its organisation, its efficiency and its cost-effectiveness in an expensive field of endeavour, were the envy of most other countries engaged in such work.

But it was still far from as efficient and productive of science as it would become. On his retirement from BAS in 1973 the total staff under Fuchs was some 350 and the annual budget about £1.5 million (about £11 million in 2004). At times the survival of the Survey had been in doubt, but he successfully led the organisation through the transition from the aftermath of the 'heroic age' of polar research, through the change from static observatory science and essentially geographical exploration, towards the modern era of global science, when the Antarctic is increasingly seen as a key component in understanding global environmental problems. All this had come about through Bunny's energy and determination, helped by the fame he had achieved as a result of the TAE. After the peak of achievement in 1958 he made no more lengthy field expeditions himself, but undertook regular Antarctic field visits, of a couple of months, every two to three years.

BAS joined NERC in 1967 and twenty-six years later, Bunny had reminisced: 'At the beginning NERC was just forming and didn't know anything about the Antarctic – so they really left it to me to direct matters. They never interfered with me.' Charles Swithinbank asked him: 'Was it a wrench to retire in 1973 or were you just glad to escape the inane questioning of NERC Committees?' Fuchs replied: 'No, because the NERC Committees did what I told them!' I have always felt that they didn't wish to tangle with him both in view of his eminence and also because BAS was exceptional in the diversity of its activities, scientific, logistical and political, combining within one organisation a unique spread of expertise – and unique problems.

Yet Bunny's comments in retirement were somewhat rose tinted. He had certainly handled matters with great diplomatic skill, but right at the beginning NERC set up a committee to review BAS, without consulting Fuchs and without letting him see a copy of its report. Seeking advice from those without Antarctic experience and skill to advise on the only body in Britain that had such qualities was sadly typical of the Civil Service. Fuchs objected strongly, demanded to see the report, then picked its errors and misunderstandings apart in detail after which NERC left him alone for a while.

The De Havilland Turbo Beaver purchased in 1969 was replaced by a second De Havilland Twin Otter in 1973. In February 1973, the two aircraft flew across to Halley from Adelaide, greatly extending the range of field operations. It enabled a party of surveyors to be flown from Halley to work in the Shackleton Range. Yet when I joined BAS, field parties still mainly travelled by dog team.

* * * *

I noted earlier that NERC was a conventional Civil Service organisation in that its officers tended to secrecy and to seek power (to which Bunny's need-to-know approach in administering BAS could well have been a response). His forceful reaction to NERC's first review committee frightened off its members. In due course, it was replaced by a supportive NERC Antarctic Committee, chaired by Rear-Admiral R. L. G. Irving (formerly hydrographer to the navy). This body also replaced the Royal Society's British National Committee on Antarctic Research which hitherto had been the most influential scientific advisory body to both NERC and BAS.

However, in 1970, NERC appointed separate advisory committees for each institute. As part of the same reorganisation a system of Preparatory Groups (PGs) advising NERC on specific research areas was set up and BAS came under Preparatory Group D (Antarctic Research). This was disbanded in 1972 because BAS science was simply too diverse for it to handle. Instead BAS was required to report to five disciplinary PGs: Earth Sciences, Terrestrial Life Sciences, Oceans Physical, Oceans Biological, Inland Waters – their names and remits changing from time to time.

A new ship, RRS *Bransfield*, was launched at Leith on 4 Sept 1970 by Lady Fuchs, as the promised replacement for both RRS *Shackleton* and ships previously chartered annually for the Antarctic summer.

NERC next embarked on the saga of the RV *Jane*. Until now FIDS and then BAS research had all been conducted from the shore. However we wished to focus on the biology of the Antarctic krill, *Euphausia superba*, and expand offshore into the marine field. This meant giving the scientists involved a sea-going capacity. My predecessor Ted Smith and his staff had put forward this case. Consequently, when I rejoined BAS, a decision had already been taken to purchase a small vessel for work on krill and fish around South Georgia. Admiral Irving and Bunny had homed in on a small fishing boat design and an order had been placed. However, it was soon clear that this tiny stern trawler, a day boat, would not provide a suitable platform for South Georgia; it did not have the range, accommodation or lab facilities needed. So NERC set up a committee to redesign it.

Despite my objections and those of the BAS biologists (who were expected to work from it) and the BAS captains with long experience of southern waters, an already unsuitable design was modified by NERC and constructed. It was a disaster; the boat looked more like a house boat than a sea-going vessel, and it was under-powered. There were serious potential dangers; for example if it were blown out to sea by the ferocious catabatic winds of South Georgia, it would not have the endurance to get back. The unheated and uninsulated hull would severely limit its use in the South Georgia climate, but, worse, there were serious reservations about its stability, even in calm waters. The saying 'a camel is a horse designed by a committee' comes to mind.

Against all protests the vessel was forced upon us and named RV *Jane*, after James Weddell's small cutter, and launched at Middlesbrough docks by being lifted by crane off the back of a lorry. She was christened by Anne Todd as she lay alongside the quayside. Next the Board of Trade (confirming my own reservations) refused to allow it to go to South Georgia under its own power and so it would have to go as cargo to South America and then in convoy with another vessel to South Georgia, in case the fears about it proved well grounded. Fortunately, on its way from Middlesbrough to Southampton its engine seized up and it had to be rescued.

Reluctantly NERC accepted that the *Jane* was totally unsuitable for Antarctic work. At last good sense prevailed and it was given to the NERC Institute of Marine Environmental Research at Plymouth. It did a few day trips in the Bristol Channel, but these operations merely confirmed the concerns we had had and it was sold off.

* * * *

My first year back at BAS was spent getting to know the people and the structure of the Survey, and the way things were done. I visited HQ in Gayfère Street, London and met the HQ staff there, and they also visited Monks Wood for discussions. Thus I learned who was influential in BAS when it came to achieving my aims. Apart from the Director there was his PA, Eleanor Honnywill, who protected her boss from all comers (a job she excelled in even after his retirement). One had to be on good terms with this very influential lady to have any ease of access to Bunny.

Then there were those who controlled resources – manpower, logistics and money – who equally had to be one's allies. Bill Sloman was Head of the Office, and Eric Salmon Personnel Officer, a necessary ally in making cases for obtaining agreement on new posts. Together Bill and Eric were responsible for recruiting and did an annual 'milk round' of the UK universities, where they had many useful contacts with academics. Derek Gipps was in charge of logistics, which meant that he had strong influence on anything to do with the ships – sea time, annual refits – aircraft and bases; he often made decisions about scientific equipment as well. John Bawden was Finance Officer and properly asked critical questions on all matters involving expenditure, preparing the annual estimates and 'Forward Looks'. These officers were a strong team, 'politically' skilful, dedicated to the Survey, who saw Bunny daily. By virtue of this power they could exert 'patronage' and strongly influenced what science could be done. Early on I realised where resistance to or acceptance of my ideas for rationalising planning, manpower and spending in the Life Sciences Division would come from.

As already mentioned, at that time BAS seemed to operate on the principle of 'need to know' and information was restricted and compartmentalised. This emphasised and exaggerated the geographical separation of the Survey's various parts. The head of a Section, even of a Division – like myself – knew little of what was taking place in other Divisions or Sections. Information passed on tended to be what the Director or Executive Officers needed to know in Head Office. The Director rarely met his senior officers. He didn't make opportunities to visit the dispersed Sections and I don't suppose he visited Monks Wood more than two or three times a year. He held infrequent 'staff meetings' of HQ staff and senior scientists. He tended to give instructions or discuss problems face to face in private meetings, rarely with all, or the majority, of his senior officers present. But he was usually available to anyone who wanted to see him and who managed to get past Eleanor Honnywill.

I often discussed the political background to BAS and science plans with Brian Roberts, Head of the Foreign Office Polar Regions Section, and his assistant Ena Thomas. Brian was a tremendous enthusiast and a fount of information on all matters polar – notably the Antarctic Treaty, international relations and diplomacy, international law, Antarctic science and, in particular, polar literature. Indeed I saw more of Brian than of the Director and HQ staff and other BAS scientists (other than those at Monks Wood) because Brian, a chubby, energetic bachelor in his late fifties, worked a five-day week in London and two days a week in Cambridge, based at the Scott Polar Research Institute (SPRI). I used to see him at the institute many Saturday mornings for an hour or two, when we explored a wide range of topics. He was broadly influential, providing good advice and support, had his feet firmly 'on the ground' and was a sounding board for ideas. Through these meetings I also realised early on the peculiar interplay between science and politics in Antarctic affairs. (It was Brian, of course, who had recruited me to FIDS in 1947.)

* * * *

Our temporary base at Monks Wood near Huntingdon was congenial. Kenneth Mellanby was the Director of the station and a senior ecologist, with broad experience of academia, biological research and conservation politics. He had been President of the Institute of Biology, and was always very helpful to the BAS section. Well-known ecologists there included Norman Moore and Eric Duffey. The BAS biologists, by their adventurous nature, field experience and attitude to life, were a breath of fresh air in this relatively conservative Civil Service outpost. For example, Eric Twelves, a BAS fish biologist, kept two ferrets and could be seen coming back from the Nature Conservancy Reserve during lunchtime with rabbits for the pot, which stretched tolerance. It was apparent that there was little scope for the unit's expansion.

So, for all that Monks Wood was congenial, I was soon having discussions with Professor James Beament, then Head of the Department of Applied Biology at Cambridge, which had a research site for Applied Biology on the Huntingdon Road near Girton. Jimmie was a member of NERC Council and later, as Sir James, he became NERC's Chairman (1977–80). I had known him for some years, most recently during my time in Africa (1961–68) as a member of the NUTAE Committee and Chairman of the Department of Zoology. In negotiations with Jimmie, I explored the possibility of obtaining a sufficient parcel of land for development of BAS Biological Laboratories off the Huntingdon Road, on the university farm, near his field station. This project was moving along well in discussions within BAS and NERC when, at a BAS staff meeting, I proposed that if biology was to move to Cambridge, why not bring the whole of BAS, science, administration and logistics together. This was agreed within BAS and in 1971 NERC decided to support the amalgamation of the disparate parts of BAS in the UK by providing a purpose-built complex to house all the UK activities of the Survey. This would of course require a larger site than I had been informally offered on the university farm.

First we had to explore all possibilities, as several other universities were interested in having BAS on their campuses, and had offered possible sites. Apart from Cambridge, locations considered were (in alphabetical order) Aberdeen, Aberystwyth, Birmingham, Bristol, Lancaster and Norwich. I spent some time going over their respective advantages and even visited some to see what they had to offer. In my mind, although much taken with the idea of Lancaster because of its proximity to my beloved Lake District, it came down to a choice between Cambridge and Aberdeen. Several BAS scientists had taken higher degrees at Aberdeen and Professor V. C. Wynne-Edwards, Regius Professor of Zoology and Chairman of NERC (1968–71) was very supportive. There was a strong lobby at Birmingham, which already had two BAS Sections, geology/geophysics and botany, as well as co-operative work with Professor Griffiths in Antarctic marine geophysics.

Surprisingly there was opposition within Cambridge from the last quarter I would have expected, the SPRI, where the Director, Dr Gordon Robin, a glaciologist, was a former Fid. I had first met him at Signy Island in 1948, and we were friends, but he was unhappy about having a large, well-funded government organisation competing on his turf in his backyard! By 1973 the permanent UK staff of BAS totalled 54, a number that was augmented to about 140 each summer by the influx of contract staff being trained prior to Antarctic service, others writing up results and additional secretarial staff. Sadly, although BAS provided much support to SPRI – scientific, logistical and financial – over the years, since the decision to base BAS in Cambridge, relations between the two organisations have never been warm, even when a later Director of SPRI, Dr David Drewry, succeeded me as Director of BAS.

SPRI's opposition notwithstanding, by 1972 NERC had agreed to fund the move to Cambridge. This was the only stimulus I needed to involve myself deeply in trying to bring it about. A 4.5 acre site on the university's West Cambridge land on the Madingley Road, which had been suggested informally with Dr Ian Nicol, the Secretary General of the Faculties in the university, was chosen. Perhaps it helped that Dr Nicol's son Colin was a Fid so he knew the ethos and other strengths of the Survey! Also I have to declare a personal interest: the land offered was less than a mile from the home Maureen and I had bought some years earlier in the village of Coton, which proved very convenient.

Meanwhile, involving staff at all levels in BAS, we had looked closely at the needs to be met by the buildings in terms of space and facilities. To guide the architect, when appointed, we drew up a tight brief for a two-storey building, with offices, laboratories and other facilities tailored to the users' needs. NERC appointed an architect to design the BAS HQ complex and a contract was signed with a builder, all, once again, without consulting BAS. I believe that the architect's remit had included the need to keep the costs down, and a shoebox would be cheaper than what we actually needed.

At this stage we 'users-to-be' in BAS saw the outline plans. Clearly the architect could never have seen the expressed BAS needs and what we wanted. Instead he submitted a totally unsuitable design both for the university's approval and planning permission. It was a proverbial shoebox-like structure, an oblong in shape, with three floors, and a central core unlit by natural light that would need forced ventilation. It neither addressed our needs nor had any redeeming features. In 1973 Cambridge City granted outline planning permission. This was the good ship RV *Jane* all over again.

Yet while these political and administrative issues took up much time, there was the science to attend to. I agreed with my predecessor's belief that BAS research, particularly in zoology, should expand into the enormous Southern Ocean, especially the biology of the krill that seemed such a cornerstone of Antarctic ecology. Yet until now, in first FIDS, then BAS and the Research Council, there had been resistance to moving offshore, and we would have to demonstrate that BAS biologists could tackle significant shipboard science, even if necessary from a cargo ship like the *John Biscoe*! So I set about implementing this change of emphasis in my Division's research. Ship-based benthic surveys would be necessary – deploying grabs and beam trawls which called for conversions to facilitate such research.

Yet discussion was productive enough in Britain, I knew there was nothing like getting back into the field among the scientists that I now led. I had to renew my acquaintance with the Antarctic, and modern conditions for work (quite a change from life on the Equator!). I took up my post too late to usefully plan an Antarctic visit for the 1969–70 austral summer, but I began planning a trip in 1970–71 – which is the subject of the following chapter.

23

Return to the Antarctic

Setting off to meet my team in the Antarctic, unlike my first trip south over twenty years ago by sea, I flew from Heathrow via Paris to Montevideo, where I was met by the BAS agent Roberto Ward. Next morning I moved onto the *John Biscoe* which was in port and we sailed for Port Stanley on 20 November 1970. There was a beautiful display of bioluminescence that night – a green neon glow and sudden springs of green fire as the bows cleaved the waves. All breaking waves as far as the horizon were sparkling green and reflected in the sky. It was a remarkable spectacle as the ship began to pitch and roll in a familiar way.

On 25 November we drew alongside the jetty at Port Stanley at 4 a.m. There I met Ted Clapp, head of the local BAS Office, and Ray Clements joined us aboard. Later I discussed the biology programmes and sealing with the Governor before heading for South Georgia.

On 1 December we arrived at King Edward Point, the government station, and met by Ricky Chinn the Base Leader, were shown around. The main changes since I was last here in 1952 were the additional buildings, Shackleton House, Coleman's (the new Magistrate's) house and two more bungalows, as well as some extra storage capacity. Three-storied Shackleton House was palatial, built on laminated pillars to flex in the wind – at the gable ends by as much as 38 cm (15 inches). It was extremely well fitted out with a large kitchen, dining room, lounge with bar, billiard table and oil-fired central heating. Coleman's House was on concrete pillars in pebble-dashed prefab construction. It was roomy and also well fitted out: kitchen with refrigerator, washing machine, drier, set of copper-bottomed pans etc., carpeted throughout with 'award-winning' material, velvet curtains, tiled bathrooms, conservatory, study, morning room, dining room, large lounge with comfortable chairs and a superb view up the fjord. All would have been unimaginable luxury in 1950.

The old Discovery House was still going strong, as were the post office, Met office, radio shack, engine room and workshop – all much as I remembered them. The workshop held two large cold stores and two smaller ones were in Shackleton House. A tractor path had been constructed around the shore to the whaling station; Grytviken had closed in 1965 and now looked derelict, with grass growing on the plan and rust eating away metal structures. Thorson, the caretaker, had been doing a good job of patching it up but it had been a losing battle. The church, however, still looked trim, freshly painted and neat. There were three old sealers at the jetty: *Albatros*, *Petrel* and *Diaz*, all of which I had sailed on in the past. Of the three the *Albatros* seemed to be in the best condition.

On 3 December we headed south for Signy Island. Once out of the bay the weather closed in and there was nothing to see. However at 5 o'clock several Russian ships came up on the radar screen. There had been nothing like nine large stern trawler/factory ships such as these in 1950. We passed close to five of them: *Khrustal, Koltsov, Voldemar Azin, Electrenai* and *Novokuybyshevsk.* Large (3–4,000 tons), all except one were trawling, probably midwater trawls from the angle of the wires. One was stopped, the hawser vertical (hauling in); another was just bringing the net aboard and it seemed to be very full. There were many birds in their wakes, some wandering albatrosses so full that they couldn't fly. These nine ships represented a considerable capital investment. We thought there was another coming up on the screen, but this turned out to be our first iceberg and soon we saw another. I felt I was home.

On 5 December I phoned Maureen. All was well and our house full, including the two grandmothers. What a change from the 1950s! In Africa Maureen and the boys had accompanied me into the field, which had been a tremendous bonus from the family's point of view. Now a matron with a family and education to contend with, and my research thousands of miles away from home, Maureen was obviously unable to travel with me.

Signy Island slowly emerged from the fog as we approached. We anchored at about 11 p.m. and a boat came out to collect their mail. We sat in the wardroom talking shop until about 2 o'clock in the morning. It was exciting being so close to my old home. The *John Biscoe* departed leaving me and I stayed on the island until 1 February 1971, working with all the scientists now based there, talking with them about their work, going with them into the field and familiarising myself as deeply as possible with their research.

Certain aspects were novel, particularly the underwater marine research that involved scuba-diving. To gain first-hand experience I also scuba-dived which I had never done before. My instructors were Ray Townley-Malyon (Diving Officer), Peter Hardy and Mike Richardson (the marine biologists carrying out the research). Wet suits were remarkable and I didn't feel at all cold. In my first aqualung dive the weather was clear and sunny with good visibility and we went down about 18 ft without trouble. It was beautifully clear and really enjoyable swimming effortlessly over the rocks, observing anemones, ascidians, feather worms, starfish, small fish and lovely seaweeds. A leopard seal came to within 30 ft of us and I felt rather vulnerable. Though there were no reports of these big predators harming humans, they had a sinister aura about them and were obviously physically capable of taking a human (they easily kill other seals).

Peter and Mike were studying the biology of the bivalve lamellibranch *Yoldia*, and using the 'green zotter' – a bizarrely named vacuum tube device – to collect them. The zotter was a long metal tube connected to a compressed air cylinder and the air flow cleared the substrate from around the molluscs. Being able to dive allowed me to see the method at first hand, but it also gave me new perspectives of Antarctica's beauty.

Naturally I retraced all my old steps from 1949–1950, visited all my old research sites and managed to undertake seal and bird counts, get in some skiing and rekindle many happy memories from those long-gone days. One of my strongest impressions was that almost everywhere, there was less ice: the edges of all the glaciers I knew had retreated considerably from where I first knew them. It was easy to immerse myself back into Antarctic life, the routines, and with the hard physical work, the great team spirit and parties so characteristic of Fids, I was back in my element. While life was now somewhat easier than when I first lived on Signy, ability to live and work there still involved hardship and called for strong characters.

Monday 1 February *John Biscoe* appeared through Normanna Strait and for the next fortnight or so I was on board in the vicinity of the South Orkneys. This was historic as it was the first offshore shipboard work conducted by BAS – we called this project the South Orkneys Benthic Survey (SOBS). It turned out to be the precursor of a later Offshore Biological Programme (OBP). In turn, OBP led to the international programme on Biological Investigations of Marine Antarctic Systems and Stocks (BIOMASS). However, this first work focussed on collecting benthic samples by means of a grab and trawling at various places around the South Orkneys. We also took advantage of the opportunity to send terrestrial teams onto the unexplored islands to record seals, birds and plants.

The Baird grab worked well, bringing up samples of the clayey ooze and the animals living in it. The grab was used on a 350 m nylon rope, fed over a block attached to the end of a small boom run outboard from the forward well-deck. It was triggered on reaching the bottom, closed and was hauled in on the drum of the main cargo winch. The samples were put in polythene basins and washed through two sieves of progressively smaller mesh, using a seawater hose. The residues, mainly worms and molluscs, were bottled in preservative. We shot the trawl net at variable depths between 100 and 130 fathoms (180–234 m). The ship's drift rate of around half a knot, in wind of about 10–15 knots, was adequate and we needed relatively little use of the engine.

Catches were variable, for example a good haul contained several species of fishes; pearly clusters of brachiopods, urchins, starfish, brittle stars, holothurians, two species of small octopus, lovely cup corals (red and creamy yellow), amphipods, worms, a fascinating jar-like spiky sponge (a volcano sponge), the many-armed sun starfishes, polyzoa, hydroids, anemones, polynoid worms, nemertines, several gastropod molluscs, lamellibranchs, other sponges and more. Such a haul took four hours to sort and preserve.

I went ashore with the terrestrials as and when I could. On one such occasion we landed on the promontory which forms the north-east end of Monroe Island. There we counted 389 fur seals (some at least 300 ft above sea level) including 21 sucking pups, 1,207 elephants, 248 Weddells and 31 leopards. Back on board the *John Biscoe* I was feeling tired, but after a shower wrote up the day's notes. My overall impression of that day had been of a sea bursting with life: penguins erupting from the water around us as we motored along, birds filling the air and masses of seals, including leopards feeding and the mysterious, sweet-smelling fur seals. Their recovery from near extirpation early in the century was marvellous: truly one of the best days in my life. To round it off I made a phone call to

Cambridge and spoke to Maureen and Richard. It was wonderful to hear their voices and know that all was well. What a contrast to the tumultuous and rough experiences of the day and the circumstances of my first years in the Antarctic.

BAS ships *John Biscoe* (left) and the *Bransfield*

At the end of our SOBS cruise, I was taken back to Signy and *John Biscoe* left to service the other BAS stations on her schedule. After dinner on aboard everyone went ashore where we threw a party for the ship's men. They all left at about 11:30 p.m., the launch disappearing into the blackness, with a motley ribald singing crew.

Two days later the *Bransfield* arrived with Bunny Fuchs and Derek Gipps. Next day they came ashore and were shown round the base. Then we discussed various problems and went on board for lunch; I moved my gear to the ship, but for the next two days I was able to hold discussions both ashore and on board with both my superiors and my subordinates. Hopefully both sides saw that the new head of BAS Life Sciences Division was meeting expectations!

Time had passed all too quickly. Immersing myself back into Antarctic life had been easy and very enjoyable. By joining in all the research activity as well as collecting new seal data on my own account, I gained hands-on experience of what was going on. Equally important, I got to know the individuals at work and play, which, in the Antarctic traditions of FIDS and now BAS, was robust, enthusiastic and a good measure of morale. Further, I had had the time to talk through each individual's research programme.

* * * *

Hugely refreshed by my trip south, I came back to Cambridge brimming with renewed self-confidence, knowing my team in the field were excellent people – all producing good science. Particularly pleasing was our demonstration that good, offshore research was possible from *John Biscoe*. I had also started to pick up the threads of my personal research into seal biology.

However, my post carried other responsibilities that projected me into, for me, the new international world of scientific politics as opposed to the politics of science with which I had some experience. For example in 1972 I attended an International Conference on the Biology of Whales at Skyland, Shenandoah National Park, Virginia, USA, with about ten colleagues from Europe, making my first flight in a Jumbo jet. It was my reintroduction to international research on whales. I shared a room with Sidney Holt, whose work on the dynamics of fish populations had given me insights that I applied later to mammals – seals, hippo and elephants.

Also in 1972 I had participated in the International Conference on Antarctic Seals held in London, 3–11 February, and was appointed chairman of the ad hoc scientific committee. Afterwards the UK delegation was invited to lunch at the Russian Embassy, Kensington Palace Gardens – or at least four of us were. We had allied ourselves with the Russian delegation in opposing the wishes of a particularly arrogant, boorish and bullying American 'roving ambassador', Donald L. McKernan. As a result the Americans found themselves in a minority of one, out of the twelve countries represented.

It was memorable from the moment I walked up to ring the bell at the side of the massive oak door, was let into a large panelled hall and eyed appraisingly by several heavy 'bouncers' – large men wearing ill-fitting suits and heavy shoes. Passing their scrutiny I was led upstairs alongside a number of 'heroic' soviet paintings of workers and one of Lenin. It was all a bit 'James Bond' in flavour. Four of our Russian counterparts were waiting to greet us in an attractively furnished room. First we had aperitifs and then moved to a groaning table, covered with fine linen, attractive china, silver, and flowers.

The long menu started with three kinds of caviar in unlimited quantities – red, white and black – then went on to fish, a large meat course, dessert and cheese. The several wines, white and red – from the Crimea – were excellent, and we were offered superb Georgian brandy and cigars. A delightful touch was the several attractive waitresses, dressed in colourful Georgian national costumes. Toasts were exchanged repeatedly: '*Za vashe zdarovye*' (to your health), '*Za Angliyu*' (to England), '*Za CCCP*' (to the USSR) and '*Za vashu Karolevu*' (to your Queen). The meal went on for hours; the conversation was interesting and there was no need of translators. Eventually we staggered off in our various directions.

This conference was a considerable coup for the Russian and British delegations, for it was the first rapprochement since Sir Alec Douglas Hume had expelled 105 Soviet intelligence personnel from Britain (Operation Foot), and the lunch marked that achievement as much as the alliance against the Americans (who were just being silly). It was a good example of the value of the Antarctic political connections breaking a log-jam caused by more serious events. This was also to happen later in connection with other Antarctic Treaty parties, notably Argentina.

24

Director of BAS

The BAS Coat of Arms

Bunny Fuchs retired in 1973, aged 65. Apart from a break for his Trans-Antarctic Expedition, in an epic career he had largely directed the Survey since we returned from the Antarctic together in 1950. His shoes would be hard to fill. At the time I was not really interested in trying to do so, because I wanted to follow my heart and keep up my field research which, even as Head of Division, I was having difficulty finding time for. However, I was invited to apply for the position and was successful. Why did I change my thinking?

Having seen a short list and realising that I might find myself working under someone whom I did not respect, reluctantly, and still undecided whether or not I would accept the job if offered it, I put in a late application. Well into my career, I was still very ambitious. I foresaw a huge future for BAS and the idea that it might be directed by someone with lesser aspirations was intolerable.

I was interviewed by a committee chaired by Ray Beverton, and included Admiral 'Egg' Irving (Chairman of the NERC Antarctic Committee), Brian Roberts, Professor Tony Fogg FRS, Professor John Sutton FRS as well as a representative from the Civil Service Commission. I was pretty relaxed about it and enjoyed the interview. When Ray Beverton telephoned in July to offer me the job I accepted, but decided to delay assuming the position for about six weeks until after the annual BAS Conference for the new people going south in early September. I did put in some time in the London HQ to begin to familiarise myself with unknown elements of the job, like the politics. I also had access for the first time to personal correspondence between colleagues and the Director, some of which changed my opinion of them! None more so than in respect of Stanley Green's correspondence that had by-passed me (his superior in the Life Sciences Division) to build his botanical empire! I had been unaware of his endeavours behind my back until I was Director-designate!

When I succeeded Bunny, we set up a fund by subscription to institute an annual award for people who had made outstanding contributions to the Survey – the Fuchs Medal. He was the first recipient and I made the presentation, following a short speech.

* * * *

On becoming Director the first thing I did was to get NERC's plan for our new Headquarters in Cambridge reversed and our original design reinstated and accepted both by the university and by the city's Planning Committee. This was complicated by the city planners having already approved the three-storey shoebox. A loophole was that the university had not changed its earlier approval for a two-storey building. Going to see the university's Secretary General, Dr Ian Nichol, I explained my dilemma. Ian asked what I wanted to hear, to which I replied: a quick decision in favour of the BAS design and rejection of NERC's plan. Being a Cambridge man had its advantages! He had replied that if they could see a detailed two-storey design, a quick decision and the city planners' approval could be forthcoming. However, I had only three weeks in which to produce the plan before the relevant committee met.

We approached the building contractor already chosen and by using its architect, produced our plan within the three weeks! Much midnight oil was burnt and the deadline was met, the committee approved and we went on from there. Eventually the NERC-appointed architect was given responsibility for the interior decoration, for which minor task he received about £45,000! Eventually, after all these 'alarms and excursions' we got what we wanted and the building has served the Survey well. NERC had been played at its own game of acting independently.

HRH Prince Phillip dedicating the new BAS building

This might have strained my relationship with that institution had NERC's Chairman, Sir Hermann Bondi, not been a staunch supporter. He wrote in August 1974:

> Although much pressed for time before going on leave, I must write to you to convey the warmth of feeling and appreciation for your work which was so widely expressed at Council and which I wholly share. Your leadership of BAS, your always co-operative attitude, your successful stimulation of first rate science in BAS, are very much admired and have won you many friends.

In the circumstances this was very welcome.

The entrance to the new BAS building

* * * *

As Director (1973–87), the administration, logistics, management and politics of this large government institute (including involvement in the Falklands War) took far more of my time away from field research than I wished to surrender. Nevertheless I did manage to sustain some of the seal research that I had resumed when visiting the Antarctic in the 1970–71 season, concentrating mainly on the world's most abundant species, the crabeater. Again the key was producing a reliable method of ageing as a base from which to develop understanding its population ecology. I was able to make comparative studies of the seven Antarctic seal species, published in a lengthy chapter in the two-volume book I edited (*Antarctic Ecology*, 1984).

A new finding from this work was the proof that there were major fluctuations in year-class strengths, which appeared related to environmental fluctuations.

I speculated that the El Niño–Southern Oscillation might be involved, but did not formally publish the idea. I had also been aware of such fluctuations with elephants and hippos which, given the vagaries of climate from year to year, should be expected generally in all ecosystems. I also became interested in the ecological interactions within the 'great waters' of the vast Southern Ocean, publishing several review articles in this area.

Though a biologist, I had always been interested in science generally. My new post now demanded I acquire more than a casual grasp of the other BAS fields, geology, meteorology and surveying, that had for so long been the backbone of British Antarctic interests. This broadened in 1971 when a new BAS Glaciological Section was established at SPRI under Charles Swithinbank.

New fields for me were international politics and diplomacy. I had never had to negotiate with a research council, nor control expenditure in a large budget or handle more than forty staff. In practical terms, my three years in the Antarctic as a young man with FIDS in 1947–52 and my few years in Life Sciences had given me considerable field experience. However, running the whole gamut of BAS operations placed me on a steep learning curve where a great deal was new. More than ever I was fortunate in the early years of my directorship to still be able to call on Brian Roberts, Foreign and Commonwealth Office (FCO), for comment and advice, both on the science in general, but also on the political angles. We continued our meetings in Cambridge on Saturday mornings when Brian came up for the weekends.

A particular area of concern was BAS connections with the Royal Navy. The historical co-operation between BAS and its forerunners with the Royal Navy went back to our foundations. Though it had different responsibilities and was constrained by limited resources, through HMS *Endurance* it was the only other organisation routinely representing Britain in the Antarctic. Good terms with the hydrographer and his successors and with the captains of HMS *Endurance* were part of our heritage and our cordial relations in the southern hemisphere were important and contributed to our mutual welfare. Consequently I hoped that the close relationship in the field would be reciprocated by NERC and the higher echelons of government in far off London. Regrettably, relations between the two were more distant than they might have been.

* * * *

Firmly believing in knowing all my staff – in as far as this was possible – and being able to judge and advise on the quality of their research, the need to get among them and join them was always a high priority for me. However, the breadth of my multiple remits was such that I was never again able to spend the sort of time in the field I had been able to in 1970–71 when Head of Life Sciences. While throughout my tenure as Director of BAS I tried to get down to the Antarctic as frequently as possible, my contact with field staff was unavoidably more distant than I would have liked. Yet one complaint that I rectified was that of field men not knowing what was going on generally in BAS. I made a particular point, whenever and wherever I could, of getting all together and briefing them on BAS's policies and fortunes. Where Bunny Fuchs had managed on a 'need-to-know' basis, I adopted the opposite: that, within what was practical, 'all should know'. Despite assuming office at a time of international financial chaos due to the enormous increase in the price of petroleum products, and thus a period of financial stringency when cutting costs was the order of the day and I was often the bearer of more bad news than good, I think this policy was appreciated. Of particular importance to me was sustaining and strengthening the feeling that all should feel members of the BAS team and have pride in being Fids.

* * * *

While I spent much of my first year visiting the various scientific units still dispersed around Britain, of greater importance was getting back to the Antarctic and inspecting all our bases. On New Year's Day 1974 I set off with Paul Whitman (then BAS Head of Logistics), flying via Zurich, Geneva, Dakar, Rio, Sao Paulo and Santiago in Chile. This reflected the changing international political situation and rising tension between Britain and Argentina.

Our first port of call was Port Stanley where we arrived on 5 January. The tension over Argentina's claims on the Falklands made it necessary for me as Director of BAS, to be up to date with developments. This involved meetings with the Governor and the UK Ambassador to Argentina (Sir Donald Hopson), who was in the Falklands at the time. My inspection of our base in Stanley was satisfactory and we left for the South Orkneys three days later, arriving at Signy Island on 10 January.

Next morning I went ashore with Dave Fletcher, Base Commander (BC – a term replacing leader) and Paul to formally inspect the base. Dave was the first of a new breed of professional BCs – men whose strengths were not necessarily in science, but who qualified through leadership and administrative ability. This replaced the former ad hoc selection of BCs from among the researchers, which had worked well, but as the number of people on BAS bases increased (there were now thirty-one on Signy), 'man management' was becoming more important.

After our physical inspection Paul and I sat for an hour or two with Dave Fletcher going over the base activities, personnel, needs etc. They had obviously had a good winter with no serious problems and appointing a 'professional' BC had evidently paid off. I was pleased with what I found on Signy; morale was good and though over-crowded (twenty-five was the foreseen complement), planned developments had taken place and the base was in good order. I naturally met the researchers – many of whom I already knew from Monks Wood – transformed from youngsters into mature, if scruffy individuals with beards, who were obviously enjoying themselves.

After discussions and forward planning with the BC, I then talked with the researchers themselves – either on shore or on board the *Bransfield*. Each in turn spoke about his project, and was given the opportunity to put forward ideas for future work or discuss problems. I also gave them up-to-date information about BAS and its economic situation and how this would affect them individually and BAS collectively.

Naturally, when the opportunities arose to engage with them in the field I took them, but my schedule was constrained by the *Bransfield*'s programme of delivering supplies and equipment to stations, getting new men to their allocated posts and picking up those who had completed their stints. The foregoing brief description gives an idea of what most of my trips to the Antarctic involved during my tenure as Director. Basically, they all followed similar routines: inspecting bases, speaking with the BCs, interviewing scientists, aircraft pilots, mechanics and ships' crew, and, overall, checking the welfare and morale of what was becoming a big organisation. I demanded high standards, but wherever possible I believed in giving my men their head within the fields of their remits and placing great importance on the FIDS–BAS ethos. This revolved about producing good science, mucking in and helping one another regardless of one's personal research, acting as teams that both worked and played hard and exhibited a spirit of adventure.

Occasionally there were individuals who did not deliver what was expected of them or who, for some reason, did not fit into the very tough way of life. They were few and I quickly moved them out of BAS. Later in my directorship when the number of people had expanded and the quotient of technicians equalled scientists, there were occasional complaints about having to undertake work that was perceived as outside an individual's field (e.g. a scientist objecting to manual labour handling cargo etc.). However, it never became disruptive and I made a point, whenever possible, of personally carrying cement etc. and undertaking the menial necessities of life I expected of everyone else.

The Director inspecting bases in Antarctica

The absence of women was a hardship of Antarctic service that men had had to bear. With expanding numbers and longer-term research developing, the question of allowing wives and families to join their spouses was several times raised, but rejected. Nevertheless, with demands for sexual equality and the women's liberation movement growing, it was inevitable that keeping the BAS bases the preserves of men only in and peripheral to Antarctica had to change. My tentative policy was to allow some wives into Grytviken for the summer and for the ships' masters' wives to accompany them. It called for caution for just as our selection of men for Antarctic service involved vetting for character and ability to withstand hardship and isolation, the same criteria would apply to women. Just being a wife, on its own, would have been inadequate.

It was all complicated by the advent of Antarctic tourism that for the first time introduced ladies to southern polar regions. Then there were private ventures where a scattering of intrepid sailors, both male and female, in their yachts visited the Antarctic. The Americans were allowing female scientists to work at their bases. The desire for women to become more professionally involved in the Antarctic was both understandable and natural. A few Norwegian wives had lived on South Georgia far back during the whaling industry. In 1981 Cindy Buxton and Annie Price had breached the men-only barrier and were on South Georgia making films for Survival Anglia Ltd, the British wildlife film makers.

Eventually BAS started to put women in the field in the 1986–87 season when two were assigned to our Faraday Base (formerly Argentine Islands). Even then John Buckingham (Ionospherics) expressed the view of about half the station, that the introduction of women had changed base life and was a bad idea. (Debbie and Sandra had only been there for ten days and to me seemed to be fitting in well.) However, on the issue of sending women south and into the rigours of Antarctica, I decline to comment further as it only commenced towards the end of my tenure as Director and I have had no personal experience of how it has worked out since. Suffice it that such reservations as I might have had were all of a practical nature. In principle I had nothing against deploying women, and as the tide of Western opinion in general was strongly in favour of advancing equality between the sexes in all walks of life, logically it made sense to 'go with the flow' and make it work, rather than oppose it.

When I took over as Director of BAS from Bunny Fuchs, we owned 160 sledge dogs. In the early years they had been the principal means of travel. However, mechanisation was catching up and we were already extensively using 'skidoos' as well as our aircraft for longer-distance movement. It was hardly surprising that two schools of thought had developed: one pro retaining dogs, the other anti, advocating giving them up and becoming fully mechanised.

The disadvantage of dogs was that they were slow and had to be fed and looked after. Indeed we had a Veterinary Officer (Bob Bostelmann) as a member of our polar establishment. Each dog required 1.4 kg of seal meat daily, equal to

81.8 tons annually for our pack of 160. I calculated that one seal would feed one dog for 40 days, and we would thus need about 9 seals a year which for 160 dogs meant killing 1,440 seals annually. While this took time away from research to assemble, it could be done as and when suited, because the environment was a vast refrigerator. Scientifically it produced a large amount of research material on seal biology, but it was unlikely that such need would continue into the long term. The advantage was that this 'fuel' for the dogs was available locally and set against the great cost of bringing in fuel for machines by boat.

However safety was the main area of doubt, particularly where crossing crevasses in the ice sheets was concerned. These were a great hazard to all who traversed the ice. The arguments went thus:-

(a)   With dogs, if the leaders fell in, their harnesses held them suspended by the weight of the sledges, and they could then be easily extracted. However, on occasion, a dog team had crossed a bridge that held their weight, but collapsed under the heavier-loaded Nansen sledge behind them. Also dogs are slow and must be fed all the time; skidoos are faster, can make detours if country is dangerous, and can be switched off when not in use.

(b)   Although skidoo track-loading psi (pounds per square inch) is less than a man on skis, it is the total weight in the middle of a crevasse bridge that is important. Yet this applied even more to loaded Nansen sledges – and on the Trans-Antarctic Expedition heavy vehicles were forced to cross bad crevasses when detouring was not possible, and did survive.

(c)   When faced with bad, not easily circumvented crevasses, a party in summer operations could now call on an airlift over that area.

(d)   In any case, if for any reason they found themselves in a badly crevassed area, they should take the usual precautions – a roped man probing ahead.

(e)   Was it possible to design a remote driving system, by cords or wires to the handlebars and throttle? Then, if the skidoo breaks through, the driver is safe.

(f)   Dog operations require a wintering party.

In general and while sad to see the dog teams made obsolete, I thought that whatever its attendant risks, mechanisation with such as skidoos and air support (aircraft with skis) was the way to go, given summer-only operations. Thus another chapter in our Antarctic record was slowly closing. I did insist, however, that in the interests of economy we should standardise on whatever models of machines (like skidoos) were chosen.

On my 1975 visit to the Antarctic I noted in my diary:

> ... the Alpine 640 skidoos were considered to be a great success, even by the 'doggy-men'! ... They pulled well, did up to 50 miles a day, and left time for scientific work in the same day which was impossible with dog travel, because the men were knackered after a day's dog-sledging. They are considered safe, working in teams of 2 men with 2 skidoos pulling 2 sledges. A sledge is linked to the skidoo by a 50 ft trace and the man on the skidoo in front is linked to the sledge by a safety line. So if the skidoo goes into a hole, it and the driver are prevented from falling far by the weight of the sledge ... part of the bridge had fallen in to reveal from the air an enormous chasm going down into hundreds of feet of deepening ice-blue. Here we found Brian Sheldon and Les another geophysics team. They also had ... praise for the skidoos and confidence in the new system ... On the question of safety in the field they were quite happy and said that they had taken the skidoos through country that they would not have entered with dogs ... However, the skidoos give a bumpy ride – and cause back and knee trouble. The remedy – drive slower in *sastrugi* (parallel wave-like ridges caused by winds on the surface of hard snow) and fit better sprung seats?

I was delighted at this first-hand vindication of my new field-travel policy.

* * * *

I have had a lifelong compulsion to draw and paint. While as a scientist I can explain my fascination with biology, there is another half – perhaps even more – of me that is enraptured by beauty that is so much greater than my ability to convey in words. I try to capture some of this aesthetic world on canvas or paper, realising that whatever I do is so much less than its immensity in my head. Just as I love music in a broad spectrum from the classical to jazz, other than to confirm it exists, I shall not try to explain why.

In writing this autobiography I have relied on diaries written at the time. Day after day, in passage after passage, my notes are interspersed with visual impressions of beauty, especially in the Antarctic. The following five random extracts are examples:-

The colours were breathtaking: bergs to the west of us had pale reckitt's-blue cliffs, purple-pink tops, and lemon yellow sides where facing the sun. All were made mysterious by the mirage-refraction effects. The colouring of the sky was graduated through pink at the horizon to yellow-green-blue on high, with alto-cumulus clouds a pale beige.

It was very still in the evening light and the water between the floes was a burnished copper colour – due to reflections from the ice cliffs.

On 20 January we woke to thick fog through which the *Bransfield* was slowly moving into Stewart Strait. The sea around us abounded with life: fur seals porpoising, penguins bounding away, superb albatrosses gliding around, shoemakers, giant petrels, prions and others. …

Dave reduced height until we were flying at only 50 ft or so above the fantastic shapes of the ice chasms and blocks of the 'Hinge Zone'. It was out of this world – an agonised lunar landscape and in the light of the low sun the pastel shades of the ice masses were extraordinary in their variety. Horizontal surfaces were pink-mauve, shadows deep purple and the vertical cliffs facing the sun bright creamy yellow. Flying so low one can appreciate the vastness of the scale; these are no ordinary glaciers … There was a bay, filled with a fleet of icebergs at anchor behind it. …

On the evening of 11 January were passing through open pack ice, with the searchlight casting a bright shaft and illuminating the ice ahead; it was most beautiful, theatrical and dramatic. One hoped to see a ballerina leap into the limelight. The calm sea was an absolute black, contrasting with the blindingly white floes.

Perhaps these recollections are an indulgence in a scientist's autobiography, but I give these disconnected glimpses of visual impressions during my first voyage south as Director of BAS. They may at least partly convey the endless pleasure and scenic beauty and the life around one in the Antarctic, without which my connection to it would be incomplete.

25

Plans Awry and Rising Tension

We again set off for the Antarctic via Chile, flying to Santiago and on to Punta Arenas, arriving at 3:30 p.m. on New Year's Day 1976. During a walk around the town the main interest for me was the monument to Chilean Antarctica, with citations of discovery dating from 1555 or so. Clearly national versions of history differed! I also took time off to visit the reconstructed fort at Fuerte Bulnes. It had been almost completely rebuilt – log cabins, stockade, turf-walled huts and some exhibits including an Ohna Indian dugout canoe. The fort was built (by the Spanish) in 1584 to deny the straits to English and French ships, with cannons on the shore as deterrents. There was a chapel, prison, various workshops and other facilities. On the way back we paid a short visit to the fort of King Felipe II; only the ruins of its foundations were left. I mention these facets of history as the political situation regarding British and South American rights and activities was progressively to intrude deeper into BAS activities throughout my tenure as Director of BAS.

On 4 January we cast off at 7 o'clock, heading for the Falkland Islands. It was a bright, clear day and we had a good flat passage to the Narrows and saw the gas installations along the shore – methane, butane and propane production. They had piers and special ships with refrigerated containers to carry the liquid gas. The industrialisation of Chile's far south had progressed greatly since I first visited twenty-five years earlier.

Arriving on the 5th we found HMS *Endurance* and our own RRS *Bransfield* in Stanley Harbour. Our arrival coincided with Lord Shackleton and a group collecting evidence for his economic report on the Falklands for the British government. That afternoon I visited the new airfield: it would be 1,250 metres long, about 70 metres wide, dug down to clay or bedrock, with three layers of stone and then a tarmac surface; it was 34 cm thick in all.

On the 6th we attended a meeting at Government House for discussions with Lord Shackleton's group. French, the Governor, was very talkative – not a listener – so we didn't say much. Relations between the Falklands and Argentina were tense and he had been under considerable strain. The Argentines wanted to talk about sovereignty and weren't interested in a slow handover. The outcome looked uncertain.

On 8 January the sirens woke me as *John Biscoe* left; we followed her out in *Bransfield* and passed the Russian ship *Akademik Knipovich* coming in. Under weigh, Luiz Ferraz (Brazilian Air Force Observer), who was on board, presented his orders – fortunately translated into English. We talked for an hour or two. He was a likeable man and mucked in throughout his time with us.

A few days later we were approaching Halley to unload the substantial cargo necessary to keep the base operating through the coming winter. Normally we could do so very near the base, but due to the ice conditions the nearest low ice shelf suitable for discharging was some fifty miles to the north. This meant that in addition to getting all the material onto the ice, it then had to be ferried the intervening distance by tractor and snowcat with all hands turning to the task. The weather was awful and we were beset with problems. The shelf edge was very cracked and twice while alongside large chunks weighing tons fell onto the ship blocking the main deck companionway and bending the bulwarks. At times the ship had had 15 ft of snow on the decks. It made unloading and stacking the cargo very difficult.

The route between the discharge site and Halley was marked by a line of black drums, yet even with these to guide the vehicles there were periods when the blizzard and snow were so strong that they had to stop and wait for the weather to calm down. I made the trip in a snowcat with three Fids – at 8 mph. The big IH tractor only made 2 mph. At times white-out conditions made it difficult to see where we were going. Through optical illusion we sensed we were travelling downhill most of the way; not so, for the shelf ice was floating and so the surface was flat with slight undulations.

At last Halley Bay base came in sight. We drove along by the airstrip to the stores area and left the snowcat to be unloaded by the Fids. It was good to be back and climb 20 ft down the ladders to the warm lighted accommodation below – under the ice. Despite bad weather, breakdowns and soft snow, the spirit was tremendous and everyone was pulling their weight. One of the IH drivers – Ken Lax – said progress had been so slow (33 hours) that he had read two books while driving. However, at Halley I was at least able to carry out my annual inspection.

On the 10th I received a message from *Bransfield*, still struggling with the Halley relief, indicating that she had been forced to vacate her berth again that morning by a large berg bearing down on her. I spent the morning up top, unloading cargo and stacking it on the dumps. The temperature was just about freezing and conditions deteriorated as we worked. Essentially, it was a matter of towing the loaded sledges to the dumps with snowcat or IH and unloading boxes marked 1401 etc. onto the '1400' dump, 1301 etc. to the '1300' dump and so on. In due course, with all the heaviest items discharged, *Bransfield* was able to work her way much closer to Halley, though even then there were endless delays. As Director with duties mounting elsewhere I could not afford to be isolated and left Halley by air to meet up with the *John Biscoe* – an eight-hour flight across a great chunk of Antarctica.

John Biscoe would drop me off at Port Stanley from whence I would catch a plane to Comodoro Rivadavia and thence another on to Buenos Aires and home. However on the 12th I had a crop of disturbing telegrams. An Argentine destroyer had fired across the bows of the RRS *Shackleton* and instructed its master to stand to. He refused and proceeded to Stanley. This had triggered a flurry of diplomatic action in which, among other things, BAS was directed to use Chile instead of Argentina. In view of the captain of RRS *Shackleton*'s calling the Argentine bluff, it all passed without too much fuss. However, it did reveal some disorder in our British responses: a warning of things to come.

In the end I arrived back in Britain without further disruptions but it had been an interesting and informative 'tour'. The relief operation at Halley had been an eye-opener on just how unexpectedly plans can go astray. The initial mistake was not to have done a closer reconnaissance of the coast in advance and identified all the alternative landing sites. It would not be made again! The diplomatic incident towards the end introduced me to international problem solving of another kind.

* * * *

This and the preceding chapter give some idea of my work in the Antarctic as Director and what would, to a degree, become routine (even though the term routine is not really applicable to anything in the Antarctic).

A welcome disruption of the pattern arose in 1977 when my friend and colleague Don Sinnif invited me to join him on an American project. Don was Professor in the College of Biological Sciences, University of Minnesota, and the foremost US scientist on Antarctic seals. Under the aegis of the US National Science Foundation, Division of Polar Programs, he was leading an international group to undertake research on crabeater seals – the species I had made my speciality since returning from Africa. It would take place in the pack ice off the Antarctic Peninsula, from a small wooden vessel, the RV *Hero*. From it I would keep up to date and participate in BAS decisions by radio, but I left day-to-day administration to our HQ in Cambridge and the BCs. Thus while not entirely free of my BAS responsibilities, my cruise on the *Hero* enabled me, for the last time, to undertake extensive hands-on field research.

I boarded the *Hero* at Ushuaia – the most southerly city in the world – on 22 October and met all the others in our group. The line-up was Don Sinnif, Ian Stirling, Torger Öritsland, Doug DeMaster and John Bengtson (two of Don's graduate students from University of Minnesota), Nick Wolkman and Wayne Trivelpiece (graduate students of Dietrich Muller-Schwarze from Columbia University).

Our vessel was named after a 30-foot American sailing sloop, captained by Nathaniel B Palmer, an American sealing skipper who in 1820 was one of the first to view the Antarctic mainland. The modern *Hero* was serving as a platform for American Antarctic research. She was strongly built of wood on the lines of a New England trawler, powered by two Caterpillar tractor diesel engines, but also equipped with red sails. Her specially strengthened oak hull was sheathed in tough American greenheart to protect against abrasion by pack ice. Normally she carried a crew of ten, and ten scientists. She was small: 125 ft overall, beam 30 ft, 14 ft draft and 300 gross tons, range 6,000 nautical miles, 760 shaft horsepower, cruising speed 10 knots. Captain Peter Lenie was a real character – a small Belgian who fought in World War I and lived in England for a while, he was now an American citizen. Over-qualified for the *Hero* command he presumably stayed because he liked the life and work.

Torger and I were sharing the best cabin, in deference to our ages, but even so it was so small that we had to pack and stow our gear in turn. On 25 October, lying in my bunk, separated from the elements by about four inches of oak planking and with my head at about the waterline, I could hear the brash ice going by close to my head, and there was an occasional loud crash and judder when we hit a floe.

Our work began at 11:30 a.m. on 25 October, when a family group of crabeaters (male, female and pup) was sighted near the ship, and a party went onto the ice down a ladder over the ship's side. The two adults were drugged with 'Sernylan' (injected using a syringe on the end of a pole) and literally 'bagged' by having a canvas bag guided by four ropes drawn over their head and neck, and down over their fore flippers. The drug dose administered was just sufficient to slow them down and make handling possible. All three were marked with numbered plastic tags, their length and girth measured, samples of blood taken, and the pup was weighed. The operation took 100 minutes, the first hour herding them to an appropriate site and 40 minutes from drugging to the end. In the course of the next few weeks we repeated this performance many times and became very proficient.

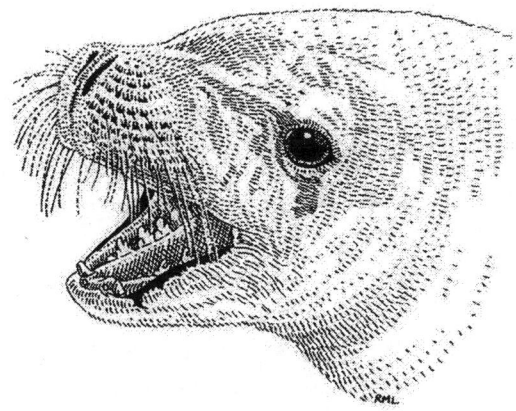

Crabeater seal head

This was the first time that researchers had stayed in the ice with the crabeaters to not only collect physiological data but to observe their behaviour. As a species that does not normally come ashore on land, or have to select sites suitable for giving birth and mating, crabeaters distribute themselves over the vast fields of pack ice. Instead, in their breeding season when a female hauls out onto the ice to give birth, she is accompanied by or soon joined by a male who tries to monopolise her and keep other males away. The female comes into oestrus and mating takes place some time after giving birth. Courtship is rough, with the female biting her partner about head and neck, while he tries to subdue her, also biting her, and holding her down with a flipper over her back or using the whole weight of his head and neck. Courting couples are obvious from the wounds they inflict on one another. However, such scarring is light compared to the wounds from fights between males. We established that males are frequently displaced by one or several other males in succession.

We bagged and tagged adults and fitted a radio transmitter around females' 'ankles'; the transmitter was the size of a small flat torch battery and had a short antenna. This was an early and very welcome introduction not only to the application of drugs for handling seals, but also application of radio transmitters that permitted researchers to follow the animals' movements for protracted periods. This allowed us to establish that males do compete for females by fighting in true seal fashion and that individual males often do not hold their monopoly of a female very long before being displaced. In two days watching, three, possibly four, males had been attracted to the same female.

It was now very clear from our observations that the crabeaters – at least the mated pairs and family groups – chose floes with some relief on the surface. They would have a ridge or hummock and were often bowl-shaped which may hide them from leopard seals, of which, though not visible, there were a lot around. An experiment was planned, to translocate crabeater triads to the shoreward extent of the fast ice, and keeping them under observation to establish whether wandering males would be attracted.

We immobilised the adults of a chosen group; the pup was a large one, but only just beginning to moult. They were weighed: the male was 545 lbs, the female 445 lbs and the pup 260 lbs. By now in bright sunshine, though it was still windy, we went back to Ezcurra Inlet and offloaded the three of them, still in their nets, onto the fast ice. Then we sledged the female and pup across the ice to a point about a mile in from the edge, attached radio transmitters to them, then came back and did the same with the male. In the relatively short time it took us to return for the male, another younger male had hauled out from the tidecrack and was lying with his head on the female's back! I am not sure how he located her!

From scarring on many crabeater adults, leopard seals appeared to be their major predators. We saw leopards eating young crabeaters and on one occasion a yearling crabeater was at the edge of a floe, submerging its head and looking all around under water. Then it slipped into the water, only to emerge almost at once pursued by a leopard which chased it with great energy.

Three times the crabeater exploded out of the water onto a floe, hotly pursued by the leopard. We landed on the floe the third time and this scared the leopard away. As far as I know this was the first time that leopard seal predation on young crabeater seals had been observed directly and in detail by biologists. In fact about 83 per cent of adult crabeaters bear healed scars on their bodies; for a long time these were thought to have been inflicted by killer whales. It was now clear that they were evidence of unsuccessful leopard seal attacks.

A group of crabeater seals

Ian Stirling was investigating seal communications underwater and occasionally a harsh, pulsed creaking could be heard, which Ian assured me was a crabeater. Seal vocalisation underwater was a vast new field to be researched.

The time allotted for our field work was now at an end so we tidied up, packed specimens, finished writing up notes and headed for Ushuaia. It had been a very successful voyage and one of the most interesting months I have known.

* * * *

In the Antarctic we had long pursued a policy of collaboration between the various nationalities and bases – it was part of the Antarctic ethos. Even the long-standing hostility between Britain and Argentina was put aside in the field, with each helping the other whenever need arose. The region was dangerous and both visits to and residence in the Antarctic called for careful planning, as ensuring adequate supplies was difficult and expensive. With the world becoming more aware of the region, and cruise ships starting to visit regularly, it was inevitable that private adventurers would appear. I had no objection to this, providing that they were completely self-contained and able to extricate themselves from difficulties.

Regrettably, this was not always the case. Coming south with publicity, too often they ended needing BAS help. Such was the case with the American Hoover Expedition which had given us a lot of trouble at the planning stage, because they expected a great deal of help – dogs, depots etc. Once, as we were leaving Paradise Harbour in the *Bransfield*, two inflatables holding four people chased us. We stopped and found they were from this Hoover expedition – three men and a girl. Thinking we were the last ship out they were hoping to get a lift! It was refused: I told them there were two more Argentine ships due. The Fids passed down a crate of beer and some oranges and everyone thought I was being very unkind!

Our policy was not to help private adventurers because if they got into trouble, which was quite likely, the BAS programmes would suffer. One such adventurer with whom my staff became fed up was Ranulph Fiennes and his Transglobe Expedition. Fiennes promoted himself as an explorer in the heroic tradition of Amundsen and Scott, and expected BAS people to help further his ambitions as though his fame bequeathed them some benison.

In the 78–79 season I had to demand the expulsion of one Jimmy Byrd. This was a pet budgerigar on one of our bases and while unlikely to upset Antarctic ecology, he was there in contravention of the Antarctic Treaty that forbade introducing alien animals to the region. I did not want BAS, the international Antarctic model, to contravene the law, no matter how harmless it might seem.

In our Antarctic jargon a 'husky' was an emergency message and I was at Rothera when Jerry Bergen (third officer) had run over from *Bransfield* with the news that had come in for me from Halley. There had been a serious accident. While making a low pass prior to landing, an aircraft had hit and instantly killed Miles Moseley (BC) and injured Colin Morrell. They had been on top of the caboose at the skiway taking photographs. I spoke with the men and asked Jack Scotcher to take over as BC. The medical officer reported that Colin had fractured a vertebra, which should heal in two to three weeks, so evacuation might not be necessary. After due consideration I decided that there was no point in *Bransfield* going back to Halley and that after a day or so the aircraft should resume scientific flying. With all respect to Miles it would not be good to shut down the programme and that would not have been Miles' wish anyway.

I drafted messages to the bases etc. and to the Coroner at Stanley. I managed to get through to Ray Adie in the UK on the telephone to explain the situation and asked him to contact Miles' mother. An important question was what about the body – I felt we must bury him at Halley and hoped she would agree. I also asked Ray to phone Beverton (Secretary of NERC) and Jimmie Beament (Chairman, NERC). It threw a blight over our little community.

Mid-morning, I had a phone call to Harold Bennett (Coroner) and the Acting Governor at Stanley and also spoke with Baker (Chief Secretary and Acting High Commissioner for British Antarctic Territory (BAT)). They were very sympathetic and helpful. They told me that burial could occur and an inquest be conducted by report and telephone questioning of those involved.

We all accepted that life in the Antarctic was dangerous and during my tenure as Director we had several fatalities. Another example was when John Anderson and Robert Atkinson had been together on one skidoo and fallen into a vast hidden crevasse, their bodies unrecoverable. We erected a cairn and cross in their memory at Rothera, sited on the point, with a magnificent view of the Peninsula mountains. Although I am not religious, the Christian funeral rituals of our culture do provide a widely acceptable form of closure and I felt it incumbent upon me as the community's head to bring this about. The vicar, Harry Bagley in Stanley, gave me a form of service and lent me twenty hymn books, so that when next at Rothera I had conducted a service for John and Robert at their memorial. It seemed it was the least I could do and I think it was appreciated.

Somewhat overlooked so far in this narrative have been our relationships with other nations' polar research bases. Early in my 1982 visit south we set off for Hope Bay/Esperanza, but it proved too rough to land and make our courtesy calls. We looked through binoculars at this Argentine establishment: rows of red huts, like a small housing estate – or a 'gulag'? I counted twenty-five huts in all. There were about eight families living there, including some children, evidence of the Argentine claim to have colonised the territory! Unable to land, *Bransfield* went out into Bransfield Strait and turned left.

Next we visited our American colleagues at Palmer Station where we stayed until the weather improved. Arriving about noon we went ashore at 2 o'clock where we had tea with the Station Manager, Garth Brown, and two krill biologists, Langdon Quetin and Robin Ross, a married couple. There were two other girls – one working on krill, the other a carpenter/handywoman. They showed us around the station: well-built, plenty of space but ill-used by BAS standards. Krill were being kept in primitive tanks with no difficulty, using an open circulation system. A large krill research programme had begun in conjunction with the *Hero*. There were twenty-two people on the station of whom eight would winter including two atmospheric physicists. One was working in a very well-equipped clean-air laboratory, the other on a VLF experiment. We returned to *Bransfield* at 5 o'clock, showed our guests around the ship and entertained them to dinner in the wardroom.

It was early morning on 19 March 1982 as we approached Faraday along the Penola Strait and so foggy that we could see nothing much, when suddenly *Hero* loomed out of the fog, looking very mysterious, sinister and flying a pirate's 'Jolly Roger' and the Union Jack – but no US flag. In the mist and ice we could initially see only her masthead lights. They lowered an inflatable and several came aboard *Bransfield*, including Captain Peter Lenie – one of the world's real characters. Wearing a Confederate Air Force Colonel's uniform and managing to look quite villainous, he professed the bridge of the *Bransfield* much too spick and span, and our officers' uniforms too smart, ribbing Stuart our captain about it. He told us he had just been into Paradise Harbour and had sailed past Almirante Brown Station, close in, with both the Jolly Roger and Union Flag displayed, so we will no doubt receive comments on the intrusion by a British ship! Lenie's irrepressible humour was a breath of fresh air!

Next on our visiting list was Marsh (the Chilean 'airport' on King George Island). The commandant was still in bed at 10:30 a.m. (9:30 their time) and while we looked around he eventually turned up: 'We had a hell of a party last night,' he said in explanation.

That day, 20 March, was Chilean Air Force Day and they were holding a ceremony, to which we were invited. I saw around the meteorological office and a very modern communications centre, put in by Racal (a British company). Apart from this and the airfield, with a C130 aircraft and a Bell 212 helicopter, the base was rather old and uncomfortable.

The Chilean flag was raised to martial music from a band, officers and junior grades were drawn up on parade. Then we went inside for a party – *pisco* sours and snacks. Several nationalities were present: Chilean, Polish, Russian, Brazilian, American, Irish and British. Things had come a long way since I first arrived in the Antarctic in 1947!

26

South Georgia and the
Falklands War

For many years Argentina had laid claim to the Falkland Islands and its dependencies, South Georgia and the South Sandwich Islands. As long ago as 1952, when I was working on and around South Georgia, an Argentine warship had opened fire on one of our parties at the FIDS Hope Bay base. Later I learned, when visiting the Argentine naval base of Ushuaia in 1977 on my way home from the *Hero* voyage, that their navy was preparing to grab the Falklands. I passed this on to our Ambassador in Buenos Aires but wasn't taken seriously (though to be fair it was unconfirmed). However it later became clear that at the time the British government wanted to resolve the long-running Falkland Islands problem through a de facto hand over of the islands.

The old whaling stations on South Georgia were potentially a large source of scrap metal. Thus when Constantino Davidoff of Buenos Aires secured a contract with the company Christian Salvesen to recover this scrap it had seemed a perfectly logical commercial enterprise. That he was based in Buenos Aires rang no alarm bells as many of the old whaling operations were Argentina based. Davidoff was very much an '*hombre de negocios*' and had been involved in several large salvage operations – some said to be rather dubious and irregular. He was described as an Argentine Onassis with connections in Argentina, the USA, the UK and elsewhere. At the time we were unaware that the South Georgia scrap metal project was in a 50 per cent partnership with men highly placed in the Argentine government or of financial involvement by the Banca Juncal. It appeared that Davidoff had estimated the costs involved in the salvage operation as: salvage rights £500,000; effect salvage £2 million; value of salvage £7 million; profit £4.5 million; total turnover £9.5 million.

On 15 December 1981 Davidoff informed the British Embassy in Buenos Aires of his intention to visit South Georgia to follow up his 'scrap metal' contract. He was reminded of his obligations under the contract's terms and in accordance with international law, to report to the Magistrate at King Edward Point upon arrival.

On 20 December he visited Leith Harbour aboard the Argentine naval icebreaker *Almirante Irizar* and made a brief inspection. Neither he nor the ship's master, Captain Trombetta, made contact with the Magistrate at Grytviken, and the landing was therefore illegal under contractual, local and international laws. The then Magistrate, Peter Witty, BAS BC at Grytviken, reported the visit to Governor Hunt in Port Stanley on 23 December and on 31 December Hunt recommended to the FCO that a protest be made to the Argentine government and that Davidoff be prosecuted. A few days later the FCO instructed Ambassador Sir Anthony Williams to deliver a strong protest but told Hunt not to initiate legal proceedings against Davidoff.

On 6 January Williams met with officials of the Argentine Ministry of Foreign Affairs who denied any knowledge of the *Almirante Irizar* visit notwithstanding that it was one of their navy's ships. However, the formal protest about the landing was not delivered until 9 February and it was rejected by the Argentine government on 18 February. From what we now know, the Argentine junta had in early February already decided to seize the Falkland Islands and the process was, in fact, already underway.

On 13 February 1982 two members of that season's British Joint Services Expedition to South Georgia were visiting Leith Harbour to film the island's old whaling stations. There they found three yachts: two, *Isatis* and *Kim*, were French. The former was there lawfully, but *Kim* was not. The third yacht was *Caiman* and was also there illegally. This was reported to the Magistrate (Peter Witty) at King Edward Point by radio. Witty travelled by launch to Carlita Bay, thence overland to Husvik where joining up with a BAS field party he continued to Leith Harbour arriving on the 16th.

Despite previous warnings and knowing that it was illegal, the master of the yacht *Isatis* had killed two reindeer and prepared the meat and skins. The yacht *Kim* was ordered to leave which she did on the 17th. The crew of *Caiman* inspected the Leith whaling station, walked overland to inspect the Stromness whaling station, and stole several food boxes, tins, cutlery, a primus stove and items from the BAS accommodation. *Caiman* had three radio sets and was in regular communication with Buenos Aires.

Her master was Adrion Marchessi; born in Buenos Aires, he was also an officer of the Banco Juncal in Buenos Aires. He claimed he was associated with the Davidoff salvage contract and had come to independently assess and inspect the project and to take back samples of the salvageable materials to Argentina. All three yachts had come to South Georgia from Argentina. *Caiman*'s master confirmed that Davidoff and some others were aboard the Argentine ship *Almirante Irizar* when she illegally entered and departed our territorial waters on 20 December 1981 and incidentally revealed that two earlier 'irregular' Argentine visits in 1971 and 1977 had been made about which we had been ignorant.

All this information was passed to the Governor of the Falkland Islands and after discussion with Peter Witty it was agreed that the situation be normalised with retrospective issue of the necessary permissions for the yachts' presence; the firearms they held were licensed, and the thefts of BAS property and contraventions of the Flora and Fauna Conservation legislation overlooked.

In a nutshell the yachts and the unlawful activities of their crews were swept under the carpet. Yet, with hindsight, they had clearly been reconnoitring the situation in South Georgia for the Argentines. On 21 February a broadcast was intercepted when Marchessi was heard communicating with Buenos Aires. *Inter alia* he described the BAS base and its administration.

On 9 March Davidoff had informed the British Embassy that he was ready to start work at South Georgia and would transport his workforce and equipment on board the naval auxiliary *Bahia Buen Suceso*. He was reminded of the requirement to observe normal Customs and Immigration procedures upon arrival. On 11 March a C-130 Hercules of the Argentine air force was observed flying along the north-east coast of South Georgia by BAS men and the joint Services Expedition and reported to Hunt in Port Stanley, who informed the FCO.

On 16 March Christian Salvesen informed the FCO that Davidoff's contract had been extended and the Governor urged the FCO to find some way of preventing Davidoff's return to the island.

On 19 March I was on board RRS *Bransfield*, on my way home, when informed by radio by Steve Martin (now the winter BC, Grytviken, replacing Peter Witty) that a BAS field party had just reported that an Argentine ship, the *Bahia Buen Suceso*, a naval vessel, was in Leith Harbour and had put a military party ashore. An Argentine flag was flying and a notice stating the property was British had been defaced, 'Argentine' being substituted for 'British'. About fifty men were in the vicinity, some wearing civilian clothes and others in paramilitary Alpine-type white uniforms. They had been shooting reindeer (carcasses were seen) and loading cargo containers. The field party learned that the Argentines expected to be there for sixteen weeks and delivered a note instructing them to proceed to Grytviken for clearance. Some shooting continued on shore. Our field party returned to Grytviken. Governor Hunt was informed and recommended to the FCO that the Argentines be told to leave immediately. HMS E*ndurance* was informed and Steve Martin, a BAS man, was asked to keep the Argentines under observation. I concurred with what was proposed. The observers, Robert (Bob) Headland and Peter Stark, were stationed strategically with binoculars and appropriate radios. Headland, who was fluent in Spanish, monitored the Argentines' ship-to-shore VHF radio.

On 22 March the *Bahia Buen Suceso* departed from Leith Harbour, leaving behind a party of forty-eight scrap metal workers and next day the FCO told the Argentine government that the Davidoff party would be evicted because it had not complied with legal requirements. It was decided to double (temporarily) the number of Royal Marines stationed at Port Stanley.

RRS *Bransfield* delivered me to Punta Arenas at 1.30 p.m. on 25 March and I took the afternoon flight to Santiago. On 26 March I had a meeting at INACH (Chilean Antarctic Institute) with Pedro Romero (Director), Morchio and José Valencia to discuss some problems Rothera was experiencing, which were resolved satisfactorily, and the Chileans seemed keen on co-operation. I took a flight to London that evening, worried by the rapidly deteriorating situation with Argentina. It was to be only a week before they invaded South Georgia and captured thirteen of my people!

On 24 March Ambassador Williams and Colonel Love, Military Attaché, had warned the MOD (Ministry of Defence) and FCO of the risks inherent in a direct confrontation with the Argentine navy under the current circumstances and the FCO lost its nerve and decided not to evict the Davidoff party!

HMS *Endurance* arrived in Cumberland East Bay and her Royal Marines took over from the BAS the task of watching Leith Harbour. The following day the *Bahia Paraiso* arrived at Leith Harbour from Southern Thule and illegally landed a party of Argentine marines with six months' stores for the scrap metal workforce. She left three days later and proceeded to a 'loitering' position approximately fifteen miles off the mouth of the Cumberland Bays. The situation was getting warmer.

On Friday 26 March Captain Mitchell, Naval Attaché at our Buenos Aires Embassy sent a long and urgent signal to London announcing that Argentina's naval bases were now almost empty of ships and that at least one battalion of marines had been reported embarking with armoured vehicles. The FCO advised the Ambassador in Buenos Aires to prepare for a worsening in the situation. The first of three SSNs (nuclear powered submarines) to be deployed, HMS *Spartan,* was ordered to load stores and war-scale arms at Gibraltar and to proceed to the South Atlantic with all despatch.

Tuesday 30 March dawned as *Bahia Paraiso* continued its patrol off the Cumberland Bays, shadowed by the HMS *Endurance.* At least two Argentine frigates, a tanker and possibly a submarine were reported to be at sea somewhere between South Georgia and the Falkland Islands.

On Wednesday 31st HMS *Endurance* was ordered back to Port Stanley but disembarked her reinforced detachment of twenty-two Royal Marines at King Edward Point before departing under cover of night. HMS *Spartan* left Gibraltar.

The first alert issued by the MOD to UK-based troops was to the Marines Special Boat Service (SBS) at Poole. The majority of other armed forces units prepared for Easter leave. The Joint Intelligence Committee (JIC) – having now made its first assessment of the South Atlantic situation since July of the previous year – decided that imminent invasion of the Falkland Islands was a strong possibility. In the evening, Mrs Thatcher, the Prime Minister, having seen the new JIC assessment, consulted with senior political advisors and the First Sea Lord, Admiral Lewin. The decision was made, in principle, to mount a major Task Force, if that should prove to be necessary.

In Stanley, there was a dinner party at Government House and the Governor was unaware of developments in London; consequently he didn't alert the Royal Marines at Port Stanley, nor the BAS and Royal Marines personnel at South Georgia. In Buenos Aires, Colonel Love, also uninformed by London of the latest JIC assessments, entertained General Mario Menendez to dinner (who soon after emerged as the new Argentine Governor of the Falkland Islands!). Disgracefully, and to my fury, BAS HQ in Cambridge had been left *completely* in the dark about most of the developments and assessments of the past week, although I was responsible for twenty-eight people at South Georgia, by then known in London to be at risk.

On Thursday 1 April the Argentine invasion force was steering towards the eastern extremity of East Falkland. Off South Georgia, the *Bahia Paraiso* awaited the arrival of at least one frigate. Two other warships en route were delayed by bad weather and mechanical problems aboard their supporting tanker. By then *Endurance* was approximately halfway between South Georgia and the Falkland Islands, hoping to arrive at Port Stanley on Saturday.

In Britain, however, the captain of the aircraft carrier HMS *Hercules* departed for Gibraltar on leave. Lacking any advice or orders to the contrary, thousands of other servicemen similarly departed for home or holiday. The Royal Marine Commandos were an exception – some were recalled. At Poole, 2 SBS and 6 SBS were ordered to mobilise for service in the South Atlantic. HMS *Splendid* departed Faslane. At 16:00 (London time), on his own initiative, the First Sea Lord brought the carriers HMS *Hermes* and HMS *Invincible* to forty-seven hours' notice to sail. At 16:30 the FCO telephoned New York and instructed our Ambassador, Anthony Parsons, to request an emergency debate in the UN Security Council. The FCO sent a cable to Stanley advising the Governor that the town could be invaded by dawn the next day. In the evening, the Prime Minister met again with John Nott, William Whitelaw and the First Sea Lord, and authorised the mounting of a large-scale Task Force. During the evening, in New York, the UN Security Council called upon both sides to exercise restraint.

On Friday 2 April at approximately 04:00 (local time), Argentine special forces landed at Mullet Creek, south of Port Stanley, and advanced inland in two groups. At 05.55 the western group attacked the empty Royal Marines barracks at Moody Brook. At 06:00, the eastern group set about attacking Government House.

That same day HMS *Hermes* and HMS *Invincible* were brought to four hours' notice to sail. The captain of HMS H*ercules* returned to Portsmouth from Gibraltar. Britain was starting to plan 'Operation Corporate'. The Fleet Air Arm began to mobilise. A Commando Forward Observation Battery RA (Royal Artillery) was recalled from leave. Port Stanley fell. At 11:00 (London time), the proceedings of the House of Commons were interrupted by an announcement from the Lord Privy Seal, Humphrey Atkins: 'There is now a real expectation that an Argentine attack against the Falkland Islands will take place very soon. It has become increasingly evident over the past few days [sic] that the Argentines had assembled a fleet which was operating in the vicinity of the Falkland Islands [sic].' The invasion was confirmed by the Leader of the House, Francis Pym, at 14:35 hours.

* * * *

On the afternoon of Friday, 2 April, Steve Martin, BC at our King Edward Point base at Grytviken, received a message by radio from the *Bahia Paraiso* that Port Stanley had surrendered unconditionally and that Martin was to do the same on South Georgia to avoid any unnecessary violent action. Because he had conflicting instructions from the Governor to surrender and the UK government to resist, Steve asked the *Bahia Paraiso* to give him time to clarify the situation.

On Saturday 3 April Steve told the Argentine Commander on *Bahia Paraiso* that he had been told by the British government to resist the Argentines. The response was that a helicopter carrying Argentine marines was on its way to seize Grytviken and King Edward Point and that Steve should have all his men in one place where they could be seen. However, he had already evacuated the base of all BAS personnel to the church at the whaling station and he was the only civilian left on the base. He told *Bahia Paraiso* that British troops on the base would oppose any landing. Until the Argentines landed, he was the senior civilian in charge. After the helicopter landed the matter was a military one and so out of his hands. As they spoke the Argentine corvette *Guerrico* had arrived and trained her gun at the BAS station.

At that point, having briefed our four field parties, Steve Martin wished them 'good luck' and left to join his men at the church. Before he got there firing broke out and he went to ground in the tussock grass.

Lt Mills and his Marines detachment shot down a helicopter, badly damaged the corvette with an anti-tank gun and killed an estimated five and wounded seventeen of the enemy before surrendering. Steve lay until the shooting had stopped and the Marines had surrendered. He then joined his men from the church and went to the base where all became captives. No one was harmed.

Previously he had told the field parties that if they came into contact with the Argentines they were not to resist; they were to state they were civilians and ask to be given the same conditions of the Truce as the Falkland Islands. After his capture he told the Argentines about our four parties still in the field, and showed on a map where they were located (four men at Lyall Glacier; three men and two women at St Andrew's Bay; two men at Schlieper Bay; four men at Bird Island), but was refused permission to speak with them.

In captivity on the *Bahia Paraiso*, Steve Martin also asked to see someone from the Swiss or American Embassy or the Red Cross and to have the non-combatant status of the BAS party confirmed. He added that they had been treated well by the Argentines and that his party, the BAS members, regretted that there were Argentine casualties in the brief fighting.

Meanwhile our ship RRS *Bransfield* retreated first to the American base Palmer Station. Subsequently she left Palmer for Faraday and then Signy where I ordered her to wait until further notice. Initially, most aboard preferred to stay in the Antarctic Treaty Area until the enemy had been kicked out of the Falklands and South Georgia.

Radio-linked through HMS *Endurance* and Signy Island base we could communicate with our four field parties in South Georgia from Cambridge. The Lyall Glacier party had climbed over the mountains to look down on Grytviken. They could see little damage but quite a number of army personnel. Originally intending surrender, they changed their minds, as we had received no news about what had happened to the Royal Marines or BAS personnel who surrendered at Grytviken (in fact they were well treated). On 6 April I instructed them to stay where they were.

Stuart Lawrence, *Bransfield*'s captain, gave all aboard a daily situation report. HMS *Endurance*, Britain's sole military presence in the area, had apparently sailed for Britain on 6 April. Stuart felt strongly that *Endurance* should at least have made an attempt to get our BAS field parties off South Georgia instead of leaving them totally in the lurch. Consequently, he felt his own responsibility for them even more keenly. I admired Stuart immensely in this as his attitude mirrored my own. I wanted to be with them on the ground. To Stuart's disgust on 17 April I ordered the *Bransfield* to proceed north to Ascension Island, in a decision made in conjunction with the Foreign Office, the MOD, as well as NERC. Stuart saw it as shameful, and would have tried to force us to let him stay in the Southern

Ocean if he had 100 per cent backing from all aboard. By now this initial backing had waned and the majority on board favoured running for home. However, given the overall strategic situation, and despite great sympathy for Stuart's attitude, had *Bransfield* been captured, the situation would have become even worse than it was. What he did not know was that there were already plans afoot to retake South Georgia by force and *Endurance* had not been running for home.

By 7 April a secret decision had been made to mount 'Operation Paraquat' and Captain Young in HMS *Antrim*, HMS *Plymouth* and HMS *Tidespring* were to detach from Admiral Woodward's Falklands invasion force, rendezvous in the South Atlantic with HMS *Endurance* and steer for South Georgia.

Our BAS teams were providing us with intelligence about the Argentine activities on South Georgia. Back in Cambridge we were visited by teams from the navy, SBS, SAS and Marines by road and helicopter for briefing about the conditions on South Georgia and for advice on planning its recapture. They were a tough bunch, but quite ignorant of conditions at South Georgia and some of them overly optimistic about what was possible.

On 19 April HMS *Conqueror* – a nuclear submarine – was in South Georgian waters; on the 20th RAF Victor reconnaissance aircraft were flying a maritime watch over the northern approaches to the island and the Paraquat force was 100 miles off its northern tip. Our BAS teams had the Argentines under observation, sending back regular intelligence.

I had great pleasure on the 20th to welcome back all those taken captive by the Argentines at Grytviken on the 3rd of the month. They had been moved to Montevideo and flown from there to RAF Brize Norton, where Eric Salmon and I were on hand to meet them. Steve Martin and the other BAS personnel now added up-to-date information for the military actions now commencing.

As things turned out, and tough though our troops may have been, they were totally unprepared for the realities of South Georgia as the southern winter approached. One team proposed to land on the west coast of South Georgia, and to retrace Shackleton's (1916) journey across the island from King Haakon Bay to Stromness! An adventure indeed, but if not impossible carrying heavy weapons, quite pointless as BAS reports indicated that the Argentines had not left the confines of Grytviken. Stromness was as yet unoccupied, with glaciers and Cumberland West Bay to be crossed. We managed to dissuade them. Nevertheless, HMS *Antrim* took the SAS Mountain Troop into Stromness Bay during the night of 23 April, landing them on Grass Island, where the ship's helicopter had to rescue three SAS soldiers drifting in an inflatable dinghy.

Others planned to land at Hound Bay, cross the Barff Peninsula carrying inflatables and then boat across Cumberland East Bay. We pointed out that in brash ice, likely to be met, progress would be impossible across the fjord but they clung to the idea and on 21 April an SBS reconnaissance party was inserted at Hound Bay, where they met two BAS men who bore out our predictions. This party had to be evacuated by the *Endurance*'s Wasp helicopter.

There were other impracticable plans, the one with the worst consequences being to land troops by helicopter on the Fortuna Glacier, separated from Grytviken by miles of rugged country, glaciers and/or water. We pointed out again that there were nearer landing places to Grytviken and that the Fortuna Glacier was exposed to violent catabatic winds that could damage or destroy helicopters attempting to land. They ignored our advice, inserted an SAS reconnaissance party on the Fortuna, also on 21 April, and in the process crashed two (Lynx) helicopters on the glacier, fortunately without casualties, and were lucky to extricate the men with a third helicopter on 22 April.

On 23 April three Argentine C-130 Hercules made reconnaissance flights along the north-east coast of the island and detected the British ships. On the 24th one of their military Boeing 707s made a reconnaissance flight to Hound Bay and identified HMS *Endurance*. In Buenos Aires news agencies broadcast their sighting reports. On the night of the 25th the Argentine submarine *Santa Fe* disembarked passengers at King Edward Point. The *Antrim, Plymouth* and *Brilliant* raced in towards the coast. Helicopters were launched; the *Santa Fe* was found, attacked and driven back to King Edward Point. A scratch military force was landed by helicopter at Hestesletten and the Argentine garrison at King Edward Point surrendered in the face of intimidatory naval gunfire.

The small Argentine garrison at Leith Harbour, together with the scrap workers (some of whom were in fact marines out of uniform) who were one of the original causes of the conflict, surrendered to Captain David Pentreath of *HMS Plymouth*. There was a similar formal surrender to Captain Young of *HMS Antrim* by the King Edward Point garrison. Operation Paraquat was over.

Throughout I thought our British military approach regarding South Georgia had been overly cautious. Their units were tough and efficient no doubt, but equalled in these respects by the BAS people who had the added advantage of experience. I felt the soldiers were professionally arrogant in their disregard for our advice and learned this the hard way. To give them their due, however, this was not lost on them as after the Falklands War the SAS made several training visits to South Georgia. For my own part, I was extremely proud of the manner in which the BAS people had conducted themselves, and of the military role of providing intelligence by my 'civilians'.

The recapture of the Falkland Islands themselves has been described so widely in the literature that there is no need for me to further detail it here. Suffice it that, at least to a substantial degree, the timing of the war was brought about by a vacillating policy from Whitehall. The Argentines had for years been testing British resolve with pinprick irritations and eventually convinced themselves that Britain would never offer more than a token defence in the face of an attack on the islands.

27

After the War, BAS Expansion

The Falklands War re-established Britain's political interests, not just in the South Atlantic, but in Antarctica where the Argentines also claim all that is claimed by Britain. BAS was the obvious illustration of British commitment to the southern polar region and its pre-eminent international stature scientifically in this realm. Not least among its attributes had been BAS's advisory role to the military in the South Georgia conflict and what had been a military intelligence role in all but name.

After the Falklands War the government announced an increase in the BAS budget of £5 million, earmarked for an expanded programme of research. Undoubtedly this had a substantial political element to it. While this was gratifying it led to a very difficult relationship with NERC and the Department of Education and Science (DES) under which NERC was established. The root of this is encapsulated in a single word: jealousy! It is an unfortunate but not immutable characteristic of government institutions and civil services that those who administer them are deeply committed to formality, seniority, status and proscribed procedure whereby all their activities are governed. Thus, as BAS came under NERC, and NERC in turn was under the DES, the proper procedure for any policy concerning BAS had to filter down to it through established channels. The logic in this system is at least in large part that they are staffed by men and women who are competent in their fields and, further, that the more senior they are, the greater that competence. Thus those overseeing a scientific institution like BAS should have both high scientific qualifications and matching administrative abilities.

Regrettably, this is usually not the case. I have recounted NERC's early endeavour to review the newly formed BAS under Fuchs, without consulting him, and then having to back off when the review eventually arrived on his desk and he tore it to shreds. In similar but lesser illustrations were the design of the RV *Jane* and then NERC's plan of BAS HQ in Cambridge. I had been lucky in my first NERC Director – Sir Hermann Bondi – who was a friend with whom I could communicate directly and who appreciated that the experience to run both the science and logistics in the Antarctic lay within the staff of the organisation specifically charged with carrying them out, and not in a cadre of administrators lacking that experience. Consequently he let me have my head.

The Falklands War brought the latent conflict between BAS and NERC into the open. The exigencies of the war demanded decisiveness and quick action ill-suited to bureaucratic procedure. There was thus direct communication between BAS and both the military and FCO, by-passing both the DES and NERC. It exposed BAS's shortage of funds and led to the immediate increase of its budget by £5 million. Although I, with the help of my staff and John Heap at the Foreign Office, drew up the proposals, through NERC it was known as 'the Bondi Programme'! This did not trouble me unduly, but it showed up that body's thinking.

Of all controls exercised by civil services, those controlling finances are the most closely guarded. My involvement outside their proper channels infuriated NERC. Just as this started to become apparent Bondi retired and was succeeded by Hugh Fish: no leader, with few achievements as a scientist or a manager. He was prompted by John Bowman, a man similarly lacking in qualities, and both epitomised the 'proper channels' approach. As explained earlier, I became Director of BAS from fear that I might find myself working under someone whom I did not respect. This nightmare had now come to pass and Fish did his best to frustrate my efforts. Fish and Bowman complicated the management of BAS, causing us great difficulties. For the last four years of my directorship a great deal of my time was spent fighting to keep the money without which we would have been on a declining budget in real terms and unable to carry out the expanded programme.

NERC's financial rules were changed as Fish and Bowman fought to gain control of the increased BAS funds. They claimed our baseline budget (then about £7 million annually) was not 'ring-fenced', that is they could reallocate money destined for us into other NERC agencies. Up till then extra capital needs – e.g. for building UK laboratories and offices, rebuilding a base, replacing a ship or aircraft – had always been provided outside the baseline budget, by NERC (under Bondi) making a special case for extra funds. Now I was told that we would have to make provision for such needs from within the overall budget. It was clear to me that NERC saw the extra funds as being there to help them with their overall financial problems – robbing Peter to pay Paul.

It soon became obvious that BAS would not be able to implement the new programme agreed at Cabinet level unless these NERC decisions, changing the ground rules, could be reversed. Failing to persuade Fish and Bowman, I was not going to see BAS progress blocked in this way and chose to go outside the system in order to protect my organisation and implement government policy as required. I drew moral support from the Foreign Office, but little more, and so decided that I must lobby at the highest level. My contacts put the Prime Minister, Mrs Thatcher, 'in the picture'. She was disturbed – I saw some of the correspondence – and a Cabinet Office Committee was set up under the Chairmanship of Christopher Malaby, later the UK Ambassador to France. It became a battleground between the Foreign Office and the DES.

I was involved in the first meeting and made my position clear; I did not support the NERC case and NERC did not invite me to join their delegation for the later meetings! However, it was enough and eventually, a month or so before I retired, the size of the whole BAS budget (baseline and extra) was set and ring-fenced at £12.3 million. Also it was agreed that the former rules for funding capital projects would be reinstated, that is from outside our recurrent budget. So when I retired I was able to do so knowing that I had left BAS in a strong position, with an expanded and ring-fenced budget. It was a position that it was to maintain for the next decade.

If I had not successfully protected BAS science, the world might still be in blissful ignorance of a major global problem. BAS had discovered the ozone hole during my directorship. Identifying the problem led to the first global treaty to reduce pollution, held under the auspices of the United Nations in Montreal in September 1987: the Montreal Protocol. It was only one among many of BAS's scientific achievements that led Kenneth Baker, the Cabinet Minister for Education and Science, to have reportedly said that BAS was 'a jewel in the crown of British Science'.

* * * *

Between 1983 and April 1987 BAS had initiated a number of major capital projects. A large addition to the Cambridge laboratories and other facilities was almost complete; a fourth Twin Otter aircraft had been ordered; the case for a larger aircraft had been made; a hard airstrip and hangar at Rothera Point had been designed and the work carried out by a Canadian company. A radical new design for replacing the Halley Station was in its final stages, with a German company as consultants (in the form of large platforms kept above the ice surface by hydraulic jacks). Designing a ship to replace the RRS *John Biscoe* had reached an advanced stage, employing a Finnish company as consultants. BAS staff had increased as planned, by about 100 to 425.

When he retired in 1977, Bunny Fuchs had established BAS as one of Britain's most prestigious institutions. In an autobiography one has licence to blow one's own trumpet a little. I think that when I retired on 30 April 1987, and using the momentum inherited from Bunny, I had elevated BAS far along the trajectory he had set to unique pre-eminence in Antarctic affairs.

I had had an outstanding record in Antarctic research and management for an aggregate of twenty-four years and as Director of BAS for fourteen years had played an important role in national and international policy making. Also, as chairman of the respective scientific committees, I was instrumental in the achievement of two important international conventions (the Convention for the Conservation of Antarctic Seals and the Convention for the Conservation of Antarctic Marine Living Resources); this in addition to my contribution in Africa.

On my retirement from BAS a sum of money was collected to establish a prize to be awarded annually in my name. The Laws Prize is awarded to outstanding young scientists of BAS in recognition of their achievements, while fulfilling the primary purpose of the BAS. The first prize was awarded in 1989.

Just before I retired there was a visiting group from NERC to BAS (a 'top-level inspection') which reported in 1986. The group was 'impressed with what it saw of the overall organisation of BAS for which the Director, with his unique combination of scientific, management and personal qualities, must take great credit'. The report said that the group had been 'impressed by the commitment and enthusiasm of the BAS staff, the quality of the science, and the effectiveness of the logistic support operation. BAS has attained a justifiably high international reputation both for its science and its expertise in Antarctic operations and was second to none in giving value for money.'

Had NERC at last conceded to the public's and government's perceptions of BAS? On the face of it this was so. Yet there was a small sting in their tail. A normal valedictory farewell to the directors of institutes presided over by NERC is the award of a knighthood. Exceptions are rare, yet I was one. BAS was one of the three largest institutes in NERC, the most varied and complex in its science and management problems, and had in my tenure as Director been 'second to none in giving value for money'. In both BAS's and the national interests, I had clashed and become very unpopular with both NERC and DES. As they formed the channel along which recommendations for knighthoods passed, they simply avoided the normal procedure where I was concerned.

Naturally I was disappointed. However, I was angry over the slur implied upon the people of BAS. These valedictory knighthoods are as much awards for the progress and successes of the institutions they have led, as they are personal awards. My team had done magnificently and deserved the due recognition and it was utterly petty to have withheld it.

28

Scientist among Diplomats

My professional career has been, apart from seven years in Africa, science in the Antarctic. When I started, the emphasis in Antarctic work was still largely on geographical discovery. In 1948, I experienced my first of three winters in the Antarctic: man-hauling and camping at -40°C in the South Orkney Islands, with totally inadequate equipment. I was 21 years old and newly graduated, the Base Leader of a team of three men – the smallest wintering party since 1922 – and none of us with previous polar experience. We lived in a hut about 8 m x 4 m and initially had to build a laboratory from local material – the remains of an old whaling station. Our way of life had much in common with the experiences of Amundsen, Scott and Shackleton during the heroic era, decades earlier. My field research broke new ground but over the first two years was conducted in almost complete isolation and there was no other national component, let alone an international element.

Nearly forty years later, I had the good fortune to reach the apogee of my scientific career as the Director of BAS for fourteen years. It had been a great privilege to be appointed to this position, but an even greater privilege by far was being part of a team of marvellous people whose enthusiasm and dedication to science carried me forward. Yet while leading BAS was my crowning achievement, there were other sources of satisfaction in my professional life and none more so than my connections with SCAR.

* * * *

The ICSU was formed in 1931 to promote international activity in the different branches of science and their applications for the benefit of humanity. ICSU is a non-governmental organisation with two categories of membership: national non-government scientific academies or research councils which are national, multidisciplinary bodies, and scientific unions for specific disciplines (for example, the British Ornithologists' Union specifically concerned with the biological discipline of ornithology). It can set up programmes. The Second World War interrupted progress, but among its early post-war programmes was one entitled the International Geophysical Year (IGY) with a focus on Antarctica. For this ICSU set up a special committee to coordinate research of the twelve nations active in Antarctica at this time. The French ran it as the Comité Special de l'Année Geophysique Internationale (CSAGI). By 1954 more than twenty nations had agreed to participate.

Scientific, it would be non-political; thinking would not be financially restricted – scientists should develop ideas and worry about the cost later. Fields to be covered were in geophysics and geography, including weather, atmospheric/ocean dynamics, aurora, ionosphere, geology, biology and medicine. Thirty-five Antarctic stations would be involved. Planning took several years building up to 1957–58 when the programme was implemented.

As planning for the IGY proceeded, interest in the scientific potential of Antarctica grew so much that in December 1956 the US National Committee was proposing to CSAGI that the IGY be extended by a year to realise the full scientific benefit from the large investment in stations and equipment made by the participating nations. This view was widely endorsed but went further than extending IGY for a year, resulting in the 1957 recommendations to form a standing ICSU committee to be known as the Scientific Committee on Antarctic Research or SCAR. Permanent delegates nominated were scientists from the nations involved in Antarctic research – Argentina, Australia, Belgium, Chile, France, Japan, New Zealand, Norway, South Africa, UK, USA and the USSR. Representatives of the International Unions of Geography (IGU), Geodesy and Geophysics (IUGG), Biological Sciences (IUBS) and Scientific Radio (URSI) were also nominated.

While none nominated were government appointees, by virtue of their seniority and reputations, all had sufficient 'political clout' in their respective countries to be able to call on national funds and influence national attitudes without surrendering their scientific independence to political direction.

Science in the Antarctic covers diverse topics but it is customary to talk of Antarctic science in the singular rather than the plural. A remarkable feature of Antarctic science, and a theme throughout the life of SCAR, has been the political influence it exerts – in contrast with the situation for science in general.

SCAR first met in the Administrative Office of ICSU, Palais Noordeinde, on 3–5 February 1958. Plans were made for further scientific exploration of Antarctica in the years following IGY, by three working groups who met on 4 February: one dealing with meteorology and upper air studies; the second with geology, glaciology and cartography; the third (consisting of only one member, Bullen) with seismology and related matters. The three groups reported that afternoon and a comprehensive scheme was drawn up for future research in the Antarctic.

A feature of SCAR's *modus operandi* has been that while it can create working groups to initiate and oversee research in a particular field, these are closed down once their objective has been reached. They do not become permanent aspects of the institution.

SCAR has grown. At the IVth Annual Meeting in Cambridge, England, in 1960 there were sixty-four participants for a full five-day meeting. At the XXVth there were more than 300 participants in Concepcion, Chile. Naturally SCAR's membership has expanded: for example in 1978 the Federal Republic of Germany and Poland became members; in 1980 the German Democratic Republic (GDR – East Germany) was admitted. In 1984 Brazil and India became members. Annual meetings have given way to biennial meetings, though working groups can meet more frequently.

The creation and management of SCAR deserves a book for itself and I shall forebear to expand on this much further other than to say that since its formation this committee has been both effective and very influential across both the science and political realms of Antarctica.

My first SCAR meeting was in Paris in 1962 (the first SCAR Biology Symposium) and since 1972 I attended every delegates' meeting and many other SCAR meetings as either a UK delegate, member or chairman of three working groups, member or convenor of two groups of specialists, of the BIOMASS Executive and of that programme's various subgroups. Finally I was President of SCAR from 1990–94 and a member of its Executive until 1998, and now in 2004 am one of five Honorary Members. Even when I was based in Africa, I took time off for SCAR affairs.

For some forty years SCAR has also provided scientific advice to the Antarctic Treaty System and made numerous recommendations on a variety of matters, most of which have been incorporated into Antarctic Treaty instruments. Foremost among these have been the advice given for the many international agreements which provide protection for the ecosystems and environment of Antarctica. However, it behoves me to describe the Antarctic Treaty to see how SCAR fits into the scheme of things

* * * *

By the late 1940s the USA was so concerned by the developing East–West Cold War and how the disputes over the Antarctic Peninsula between Britain, Argentina and Chile in the Antarctic might play out in this, that it initiated steps to control the situation. In 1948 it proposed that Antarctica be ruled by an eight-power condominium or through a United Nations Trusteeship. Neither idea was taken up and it was another ten years before there was progress.

It took the success of the IGY in bringing an unprecedented number of scientists to the Antarctic and the scientific co-operation that arose from it to re-focus international interest on this southernmost continent. The need to expand IGY's programmes led to a general wish to create a firm foundation for its continuation and development. High among international concerns was that the region should not become, in the words of the Treaty, 'the scene or object of international discord'.

The US government took the initiative in May 1958 by proposing to the eleven other nations then active in Antarctica that a treaty should be drawn up to set the continent aside for scientific use only. After sixty secret meetings a conference was held in Washington in October 1959 which lasted six weeks; the Antarctic Treaty was signed on 1 December 1959 and after ratification by the twelve original signatory states, entered into force on 23 June 1961. The first consultative meeting was held in Australia in July 1961 and meetings have been held at two-year intervals ever since.

As we have seen Antarctica is unique as the only continent without a native population (though both Argentina and Chile have taken steps to create native Antarcticians by having a few women give birth there), free of war and entirely lacking in agriculture or manufacturing industries. It has no national government and its inhabitants are currently all temporary and concerned with investigating or supporting some aspect of science, or – a recent development – with tourism.

The rules governing Antarctica's transient international population, scattered over 14 million km^2 in isolated research stations, result from this unique international Treaty. The Treaty includes all land and ice shelves in latitudes greater than 60° S. The open waters of the high seas in these high latitudes were already covered under international law. The Treaty stipulates that Antarctica should 'forever … be used exclusively for peaceful purposes' and 'not become the scene or object of international discord'.

Nuclear explosions and disposal of radioactive wastes are prohibited (as an aside, this was the first international nuclear test-ban agreement), as are 'measures of a military nature'. There are provisions for exchanging information and personnel, and for inspecting stations, installations and equipment by Treaty-state observers.

'The Treaty does not recognise, dispute or establish territorial claims' and 'no new claims shall be asserted while the Treaty is in force'. Living resources – the Treaty does not mention mineral resources – are to be conserved. There is provision for peacefully settling disputes, ultimately by the International Court of Justice. Any United Nations member state can accede to the Treaty but can only achieve consultative status (participation in decision making) after demonstrating its involvement in Antarctica 'by conducting substantial scientific research activity there'.

Operating rules are set by the aforementioned consultative meetings held in alternate years and so far 164 resolutions have been passed. There are now twenty states with consultative status and a further eighteen have acceded; these governments represent 80 per cent of the world's population, developed and developing countries, East and West, North and South, giving the lie to allegations that it is an exclusive club.

SCAR was in existence when the Antarctic Treaty came into force in 1961, and conservation measures were already among its most important concerns. In 1964 the Treaty states adopted SCAR's Agreed Measures for the Conservation of Antarctic Flora and Fauna. These prohibit killing, wounding, capturing or molesting any native mammal or bird except under a specific permit – to provide indispensable food for men or dogs, to provide specimens for scientific study or scientific information, or to provide specimens for educational or cultural institutions or uses.

They cater for specially protected species of animals and birds, designated Special Protection Areas (SPAs), Sites of Special Scientific Interest (SSSIs) and they have management plans. Harmful interference is defined and steps to alleviate pollution were established. The introduction of non-indigenous species, parasites and diseases is prohibited and certain precautions were specified. There is provision for an annual exchange of information between governments, including records of permits issued and the numbers of each species killed or captured annually. The Agreed Measures are generally working, and over time have been added to – for example, all developments such as siting new bases or putting in airstrips are subject to environmental impact assessment requirements.

The Antarctic Treaty could not give protection to seals in the sea or on floating ice, since, as already indicated, the rights of states on the high seas are covered by other law. So separate agreement was needed and in 1972 a Convention for the Conservation of Antarctic Seals (CCAS) was concluded, entering into force in 1978. SCAR had a role in its drafting and – uniquely for a non-governmental organisation in respect of an international treaty – a specific continuing responsibility as an independent international source of advice.

An annex to CCAS specifies measures for conservation, scientific study and rational and humane use of seal resources and these measures may be amended. Permissible annual catches are specified in the annex, deliberately set at low levels. Ross seals, elephant seals and fur seals are specially protected and there are closed seasons for all species. Several seal reserves are designated where killing or capture is forbidden and of six defined circumpolar sealing areas one is closed to sealing each year in rotation. There is provision for an annual exchange of information and for actions to be taken if an industry starts. SCAR was given a pivotal role in assessing information received, encouraging exchange of data, recommending research programmes and the data to be collected, suggesting amendments to the annex and reporting on all consequences of sealing.

Fishing in Antarctic waters faced the same legal issue as seals and following the example of CCAS a Convention for the Conservation of Antarctic Marine Living Resources (CCAMLR) was concluded in 1980 and came into force in 1982. Again SCAR was a leading influence in bringing about this treaty. Its objective is the conservation (including rational use) of all Antarctic marine life and it applies to waters south of the Antarctic Convergence (Antarctic Polar Front). CCAMLR is managed by a secretariat set up in Hobart, Tasmania.

Like CCAS, CCAMLR is unusual in addressing conservation needs before commercial activities have had a significant effect – except in the case of demersal fish around South Georgia, where an industry had already depleted the stocks before the Convention was established.

Finally, there was the knotty question of mineral resources. Again, as SCAR's remit covers all research in the Antarctic, and even though my science – biology – doesn't cover minerals, my involvements in SCAR and the influence that the commercial exploitation of minerals can have on ecology generally made me take a particular interest in this area. The Antarctic Treaty makes no references to minerals because at the time it was drawn up it was believed that agreement would be impossible. Also, the mineral resource potential of Antarctica remains unknown although speculative estimates have been made. It is not possible to predict if or when commercial interest will arise, but there is general hope that exploitation, if it occurs at all, will be deferred for decades, while more economically viable deposits elsewhere are worked out.

My strong preference was that a mechanism should be in place to control such activities before they occur. Permission to exploit Antarctic minerals should be subject to meeting rigorous environmental criteria. While it is relatively easy to get agreement on environmental matters, it will be far harder to find common ground in the realm of 'big' economics. Any agreement should in democratic theory have to be acceptable across the international political spectrum, to developed and developing countries, to states claiming sovereignty in Antarctica and to non-claimant states. It should accommodate the interests of the international community as a whole and maintain Antarctica as an area set aside for peaceful purposes. It was clear in SCAR that negotiations would be more successful if carried ahead of serious commercial interests developing.

Interest in the minerals issue began in the late 1970s; formal talks between governments began in 1982 in Wellington, New Zealand, and after ten further sessions to January 1988, the final meeting was held in Wellington in June 1988. All twenty Antarctic Treaty consultative parties were involved and the seventeen other parties to the Treaty attended as observers. The resulting Convention on the Regulation of Antarctic Mineral Resource Activities (CRAMRA), was adopted on 2 June 1988. It was never ratified, but was replaced in 1998 by the Protocol on

Environmental Protection to the Antarctic Treaty which, under Article 7, prohibits any activity relating to mineral resources other than scientific research.

This then is the Antarctic Treaty System as it was in 2004, which now applies to a tenth of the Earth's surface. Uniquely among international treaties and agreements, it stands out for the prevailing common sense and lack of acrimony. SCAR has had a powerful influence on this prevailing situation and the privilege to play a role in it has not only been a source of personal satisfaction, but is where I have made my greatest contributions to conservation.

Looking to the future, the Antarctic Treaty, which is of unlimited duration and is open for signature by all states, seems to be serving the interests of the contracting parties. None have contracted out of it and indeed they are investing more political capital in it. Yet despite its undoubted achievements the Treaty has come under attack in recent years from some non-signatory governments and from non-governmental environmental organisations.

It is criticised for being exclusive, because it is based on the principle that only those countries making a significant (and costly) contribution to scientific research in the region are entitled to take part in decision making. Non-governmental organisations have criticised the present arrangements as inadequate to protect the Antarctic environment and natural systems. All these carry with them seeds of discord, notwithstanding that the avoidance of conflict remains the Antarctic Treaty's primary purpose. Indeed science had become almost secondary as the means to that end until BAS's discovery of the ozone hole elevated its importance as an early-warning activity for the planet.

The organisational consequences of increased membership and consensus decision making could lead to future stagnation. The United Nations Organisation illustrates what I mean. In it, striving for consensus slows progress and I can but note that general agreement is usually determined by the lowest common denominator.

Perhaps the number of consultative parties to the Treaty should be limited by more rigorous entry qualifications? There may be a case for helping poorer but genuinely interested newcomers. Yet if the quality of science that they can provide rests on how much money they are given, I do not think that participation in Antarctic affairs via 'aid' makes a persuasive case. Where, elsewhere in international affairs, does aid-dependent science match the quality of nationally self-funded science? If national pride is the stimulus for seeking entry into the

Antarctic, then surely this flies in the face of a system that has put such weight on diminishing nationalism. Possibly those seeking involvement but are unable to afford it could through bilateral arrangement with one of the existing members have their nationals work within those members' teams.

It is uncertain whether the question of sovereignty is receding. Certainly, in successive Antarctic Treaty System agreements sovereignty has become less relevant, but it is said that the Treaty has been built out of agreement on 'soft' issues and has still to show that it can cope with 'hard' issues such as jurisdiction and the expected pressures if mineral exploitation becomes a reality.

Jurisdictional issues can be expected to become important where tourism and increasing numbers of visitors to the Antarctic are not under direct government control. Given its potential to be an adverse environmental influence, the need for policing tourism may well arise. Suffice it that jurisdiction and sovereignty usually run hand in hand.

The scientific influence over the Treaty built up over the years since its inception by SCAR and ICSU is being overshadowed by the political agendas of vociferous, well-financed environmentalist groups. Purporting to speak for the interests of Antarctica, such self-appointed and self-interested groups manipulate the media and are a challenge to the Treaty System that has worked so well. Because they have funds and claim to speak for the public at large, politicians listen to them. Trying to replace science with political agendas, the Antarctic Treaty states were persuaded to embark on a series of meetings to reach agreement on 'Comprehensive Measures for the Protection of the Antarctic Environment', without consulting the scientists working there. This uninformed interference seems to me to be the most immediate threat to what has so far been achieved there.

To illustrate my point take the concept of ecological 'fragility', a term often applied to Antarctic life forms and ecosystems. Demonstrably, Antarctic ecology has proved very robust. The remarkable recovery from sealing and the ongoing recovery from whaling show what I mean. So, too, does the unexpectedly quick disappearance of environmental damage associated with the shore-based stations that processed whales and seals. They received (and spilt) fuel oil for up to sixty years and by modern standards produced massive pollution. They were followed by active scientific stations and though on an altogether lesser scale, they too polluted the local areas around them. Yet measured hydrocarbon levels fell off rapidly (to open ocean levels) outside these local sites and environmental impact is not detectable outside them. While this is no way reduces the need to ensure strict environmental protection now and in the future, failing to appreciate this ecological robustness is unscientific and anything but impartial. The reason for it is obvious enough: to raise funds the environmentalists and their associated media need sensation. To donate, the public needs to be 'alarmed' and alerted to imminent 'catastrophe'. Ecological fragility raises money, whereas robustness does not.

If the funds the environmentalist groups raised were spent on Antarctic research, and if raising funds in the way they do was necessary, I would be more sympathetic towards them. Yet the funds they raise seem to be spent more on themselves and their associated self-publicity than benefitting the Antarctic. The solid records of ICSU and SCAR speak for themselves and while both could always do better with greater funding, what they have achieved was done without public sensation or inaccurate dramatics.

Presently solid scientific research and its support is almost the only regulated activity in the Antarctic, and logically in this 'Land of Science' future development should be from this established system. There must be provision for scientific advice independent of politics. My concern is that the international, interdisciplinary scientific organisations like ICSU and SCAR that are the main sources of what we know about the region will be left out of whatever new arrangements are implemented for the protection of Antarctica's environment. Left to themselves the politicians will do just that with their manifest weakness of listening to the loudest voices who, by design, are those of environmentalism.

An insidious suggestion is that Antarctica be declared a 'World Park'. Such a step could establish a parallel system to the Antarctic Treaty. Other than introducing yet another bureaucracy, what would it do that the existing Treaty System does not or cannot already do? The only major power the Treaty does not currently possess is prevention of unauthorised ingress – principally by tourists – which could be secured without creating a new bureaucracy. I strongly favour developing step by step what we already have working.

* * * *

Through much of my life I have been a member of the Zoological Society of London (ZSL) and indeed attended many of its meetings and seminars down the years. Founded in 1826 the ZSL was a prestigious institution that played an important role in bringing zoology to public attention, principally through its London Zoo in Regent's Park and later the open air zoo at Whipsnade. Later still it set up a research wing as the Institute of Zoology to bring scientific attention to conservation. It holds regular scientific meetings and produces two journals, the *Journal of Zoology* and the *Transactions of the ZSL*, a series of Proceedings of Symposia and now other journals.

In 1982 I was elected to the Council of the Zoological Society and became a vice-president. Two years later the President, Lord ('Solly') Zuckerman, invited me to lunch at the Athenaeum and pressed me to stand for the Secretary of the Zoo. Under the Society's constitution the Secretary is the statutory responsible officer (de facto its Chief Executive) for the learned Society, accountable for the library (a major historical archive and modern collection); the extensive zoological collections at Regent's Park, London, and Whipsnade Park in Bedfordshire; and the Institute of Zoology, a centre of excellence in research on animal behaviour, physiology, reproduction, health and animal conservation. I held this position from May 1984 to 1988.

In addition to the Council, the duties included membership of a number of committees, including Zoo Management, Animal Welfare and Conservation, the Institute of Zoology Management, Publications, Awards, Gardens and Parks, and the Zoo Pension Trustees. In 1985 I was instrumental in setting up a link between the Society and the British University Zoology Departments, known as the Zoology Liaison Group.

Apart from research grants to the Institute of Zoology, the zoo had been unique, compared with other national (and international) collections, in being privately self-financing through gate receipts and private donations. Other large collections or museums – Kew Gardens, the Natural History Museum, and art collections – receive large government grants. However, with competition from television and films, visits to the London Zoo were declining and the 1980s were a period of financial difficulty.

Much effort was put into retrieving the situation. My own view expressed earlier at Council was that we should reduce costs by cutting the size of the collections where labour and animal foodstuffs were major outgoings. Solly Zuckerman understandably refused to countenance this, given his success and fund-raising skills in building up the zoo to what it had become. However, before the crisis was resolved, Sir William ('Gregor') Henderson FRS took over as President, with Lord Peyton (a former Labour minister) as Treasurer. Our Finance Officer, John Boyer had been a senior director of the Hong Kong and Shanghai Bank. Facing catastrophe, even closure, we set up a fund-raising Development Trust to secure an immediate injection of capital without which our zoos would close.

Talks with government pursued by John Peyton led to the appointment of management consultants, Peat Marwick, to advise on a solution. Eventually, and largely because of its status as one of London's more famous institutions, Peyton persuaded – blackmailed would not be too strong a term – the government to give the Society a 'one-off' £10 million grant to sort out the problems. Additionally, and to spread the Society's load, the Institute of Zoology was formally attached to London University (NERC having reviewed it with a high rating for scientific competence).

The maximum term permitted for the ZSL Secretary to serve was seven years. My two predecessors in this post had each served two years. I had served four when I retired at the Annual General Meeting of the Zoo on 29 September 1988. Then approached to stand for President, I declined. As it was, I was burning the candle at both ends with my many concurrent commitments to St Edmund's (next chapter), Cambridge University and SCAR. On retiring as Secretary the Society presented me with a Garrard carriage clock, which stands on my mantelpiece, a time-honoured tradition. My time at the zoo was enjoyable and a welcome ancillary to my professional focus on the Antarctic.

31

Master of St Edmund's College

While my connections with Cambridge University had been slight since my graduate student days in the 1950s and my African experiences, I have always been intensely proud of being a 'Cambridge Man' and that my Alma Mater was one of the world's great universities. My college, St Catharine's, made me an Honorary Fellow in 1982, but this entailed no more than attending a few dinners a year. Closer contacts started to develop with the university through the negotiations which led to moving BAS Headquarters to Cambridge and building the institute on university land.

However, despite these fringe interactions, in January 1985 I was elected to be Master of St Edmund's House, a small graduate college within the University of Cambridge. I spearheaded an approach to the University Registry to change its name to St Edmund's 'College' in 1986, shortly after my appointment, and I will refer to it here by this name. St Edmund's College is one of five Graduate Colleges of the University of Cambridge. It was founded in 1896 by the fifteenth Duke of Norfolk and Baron Anatole von Hugel. The college is dedicated to St Edmund of Abingdon (Archbishop of Canterbury 1233–40) and was until 1986 known as 'St Edmund's House'. It is the only Oxbridge college with a Roman Catholic chapel.

Some explanation is needed of how I, as an agnostic scientist, came to be Master of what until then had been widely regarded as a Catholic college (though this had not been the founders' intention). It arose from acquaintance with

Simon Mitton, a Fellow of St Edmund's, whose wife Jacqueline had worked for me at BAS, as scientific editor and later information officer. I knew little about the college, but Maureen and I had attended two college guest nights as Simon's guests and enjoyed both occasions.

Simon wrote to me in May 1984 to ask if they could consider me in their search for a new Master. In his words:

> Although all previous Masters have been clergymen, our new constitution allows us to appoint the best person for the job, and we have therefore decided to break tradition.
>
> The Fellows have assumed that our new Master will view this challenging opportunity as a part-time appointment. The essential requirements are to guide the strategic thinking; to represent our interests in Cambridge, as well as nationally and internationally; and to chair meetings of the Council and the major committees. Beyond that the duties are very much the choice of the individual.

I had expressed a guarded interest, but said that I would not be available in view of my commitments at BAS of which I was still Director. They pressed me to let my name stand on the understanding that if elected I would be obliged to obtain the consent of NERC before I could accept, and that it would not be more than a part-time undertaking.

The Dean of the college, Michael Winter, asked me for views on the general matter of religion. I responded frankly and he thanked me. He was to be one of those who opposed my appointment – not because he had anything against me personally, but because he felt it a matter of principle that the appointee should be Catholic. In November Simon wrote again about progress and to tell me that they now had new articles placing the absolute control of the college in the hands of the Master and Fellows alone. In November the Vice-Master invited me formally to stand for election to the office of Master and meet the Fellows of the college, individually and in groups of up to three. I met twelve Fellows on 4 December and it was clear having a non-Catholic Master was unacceptable to three of the Fellows who said they would resign if I was appointed.

In January 1985 I was selected Master with the necessary two-thirds majority. I wrote to John Bowman at NERC, explaining the situation, saying that the extent of the commitment was less than I had thought. Basically in a year there are eleven meetings of the College Council and eleven meetings of the Finance and General Purposes Committee. They are held between 5:30 p.m. and dinner. There are a few evening functions to attend, mostly social. They would like me to be a presence in the college for up to half a day a week in term time and say twice in each vacation. John replied proposing a compromise, in view of developments within BAS, by deferring my starting date with the college until 1 April 1986, to which I and the college agreed. Thus I was elected the eleventh Master on 1 July 1985, until the end of the academical year in which I reached the age of 67. However the Association that ran the college granted me a leave of absence until 31 March 1986, until when the Vice-Master took over my duties.

**As Master of St Edmund's my portrait was painted
for the College by Anthony Oakshott.
Reproduced by kind permission of St Edmund's College.**

* * * *

I accepted Mastership of a small college for several reasons. Of them the small stipend that went with the post was not one. My retirement from BAS was approaching; I did not want to become a nuisance to my successor by hanging around looking over his shoulder. I was unlikely to make further major contributions to biology as I had been too long away from personal research and my days in the harsh environments I had so enjoyed were over as my health was declining. Yet I knew I was a good administrator and committee chairman, assets that would be of use to the college, and it would be a challenge to bring the college out of a backwater and into the mainstream of the university.

As a Head of House I would have access at a high level to the centre of the university which I looked forward to. Several things in particular attracted me to a graduate college and to St Edmund's in particular: its international flavour, the relative maturity of its students, the friendly social life and the personalities of the Fellows in general. The challenge of developing it from a relatively low baseline to become a force to be reckoned with in the university was very attractive. It could only go up!

Also, when our youngest son, Andrew (born after our return from Africa), was graduating from Oxford about the same time as my retirement from BAS and would take up a job, Maureen and I would be 'rattling around' in our home and the additional social life of a college, with dinners and other events, would not come amiss, particularly for her. St Edmund's is one of the few Cambridge Colleges where 'spouses' or 'partners' are encouraged to participate in college life. Even in St Catharine's, another very friendly college and where I was an Honorary Fellow, spouses are not able to take part. I felt that all in all this would give me a satisfying part-time retirement job that would be sufficiently undemanding to allow plenty of time to pursue other interests.

* * * *

Now a word or two about St Edmund's. As St Edmund's House it became one of the new graduate colleges of the university in 1965. After having the status of an 'Approved Society' for ten years it achieved the more secure status of an 'Approved Foundation' in the university in 1975. The Master and Fellows looked after its day-to-day running but ultimate responsibility lay with an Association which, in law, was a limited company under the Companies Acts. Its board of directors had among its members some of the St Edmund's Fellows and several Catholic bishops. I shall refer to this, for reasons that will become apparent, as the Old Association.

In 1983, the relationship with the Catholic hierarchy underwent a significant change, when the ownership and running of St Edmund's was handed over completely to the Master and Fellows, who then constituted a New Association. As, *de jure*, a limited company, the New Association's board of directors was thus wholly internal under the Master's chairmanship. The only member of the college who was required to be a Catholic was the Dean, who had to be a priest because of his responsibilities for the chapel services. To avoid any impasse that the board of directors could not resolve, and as in all Cambridge Colleges, there was a right of appeal outside the college to 'the Visitor'. In St Edmund's case (stipulated in its Articles) this was the Catholic Archbishop of Westminster, who, in my Mastership, was Cardinal Basil Hume OSB.

The foregoing changes came about because the then Master, Father John Coventry SJ, and the more forward-looking Fellows wished to change the emphasis in the college towards academic excellence, while maintaining the Catholic tradition. They intended to seek full collegiate status in the foreseeable future, preferably at the time of St Edmund's centenary, 1996, which would involve the granting of a Royal Charter.

Most of the Fellows are university officers, teaching and conducting research in their departments as lecturers, readers and professors. At the time of my election St Edmund's had twenty-five Fellows, including one Professorial Fellow. The Fellows are elected to the Fellowship by the governing body (board of directors) and some hold posts within the college for which they are paid a small stipend or honorarium in addition to their university salary; these are the college officers and the tutors.

However, at the time of the transfer of responsibility from the Old Association to the New Association where the Master and Fellows were the authority that ran the college, doubts had been expressed about the maintenance of the Catholic tradition.

* * * *

I suppose I should have anticipated some reaction on religious grounds but was a little surprised by headlines in the *Catholic Herald*: 'Election of "atheist" Master rocks Catholic graduate college', and 'Storm rages around Antarctic appointee'. John Coventry SJ, the retiring Master of St Edmund's, wrote to the *Catholic Herald* supporting my election, pointing out that I was not an atheist, objecting to the term 'Catholic college' used in the piece, and saying that the college was 'not the least bit rocked' – but the editor declined to publish it.

I was inaugurated by the Vice-Master, Dr Geoffrey Cook, as the eleventh Master of the college on 10 October 1985. I made a formal declaration as required by the Articles, and in my inaugural speech, among other points, recognised that a minority of the Fellows had reservations about my election and regretted that I had been the cause of a much-publicised resignation. I hoped that I would be able to dispel most of the residual concerns as St Edmund's was a small, close-knit, friendly community – a special part of which was the Roman Catholic tradition. I did not wish by my actions to diminish this tradition and concurred in the Fellowship's decision to make provision for maintaining it.

One of my first functions as Master had been to chair the committee that recommended the appointment of a new Bursar. By May 1987 I had retired from BAS and was able to give more attention to matters at St Edmund's. The performance of the Bursar was causing considerable concern and I was under pressure from all sides – Fellows, students and staff – to do something about it. I chaired the committee that recommended his dismissal, which led to much correspondence with lawyers, unpleasant for all concerned. The bottom line was that either he went, or I went. I stood my ground and stayed. As for the rest of my tenure, the college's governance ran smoothly and I think we made considerable progress on a wide front.

* * * *

I now had around me the strongest team of officers that the college had ever had – a launching pad for future progress. One of the first changes I made with the agreement of the governing body (October 1986) was to change the name from St Edmund's House to St Edmund's College. We felt that students were more likely to apply for a place at a college rather than a 'house'. Along with this went the wish to have our own coat of arms, which was made possible by a generous benefaction from Mr Norman Young QC of Ontario, Canada. Until now St Edmund's had been using those of the Norfolk family who for centuries have been prominent Catholics. It took a little time to get the agreement from the university, and for the new arms to be designed by the College of Arms. The Duke of Edinburgh, the Garter King of Arms and the Rouge Croix Poursuivant presented the new arms at an impressive ceremony in the chapel in October 1987.

It is a magnificent calligraphed document, on parchment with three seals – one each of the Kings of Arms Garter (Principal King of Arms), Clarenceux and Norroy and Ulster – colourfully bearing the Royal arms, the arms of the College of Arms and the new armorial bearings of St Edmund's College. The new arms are based on the Norfolk arms, differenced with a canton and a border Argent – the canton being a square division less than a quarter on the upper corner of the shield with a device ascribed to St Edmund of Abingdon. This was placed over the Flodden augmentation, a battle honour personal to the Dukes of Norfolk. I was told it was usual to have a decorative border, with vegetation and animals. So I suggested the Virginia creeper and, indulging a personal vanity, an elephant seal, a king penguin, an African elephant and a mouse (trade mark of Mousey Thompson the Craftsman of Kilburn, whose firm produced the furniture in the College Hall). This makes it unique among armorial bearings!

I realised that acquiring full collegiate status within the University of Cambridge, St Edmund's would need to expand substantially and demonstrate a wide range of scholarship, a larger membership, and buildings and fabric suitable to a college within the university. St Edmund's was fortunate in having plenty of land for building new accommodation. Early in my tenure we established a College Development Committee under the chairmanship of the Vice-Master to bring plans for expansion to fruition.

New kitchens were added to the north end of an extended hall, with eighteen new sets of rooms above them. The old kitchens were converted into a new Senior Combination Room and a new small dining room (the Huddleston Room), and additional office space was created. I had also managed to negotiate an academic exchange agreement with the Teikyo Foundation of Japan, which resulted in a benefaction that built a striking, neo-Elizabethan, six-storey new College Tower. This includes the highest seminar room in Cambridge, with a wonderful panoramic view across the city, together with additional student and guest accommodation and a new Master's study over the main entrance at the base of the tower.

Starting in 1985 a substantial building and refurbishment programme was completed in three stages, and substantial repairs made to the structure of the older buildings. Finances and administration were put on a sound footing and invested capital – the endowment – increased sixfold from 1985 to 1996.

The college has seven acres of land. Adjacent to it is Bene't House on 1.1 acres of land which belongs to St John's College. It was leased by St John's to the Benedictine order and in 1989 I negotiated with the Abbot of Downside a transfer of the remainder of the lease to St Edmund's. Then, in 1994, we successfully negotiated with St John's College for a ten-year option to purchase the leasehold on the property for 99 years. A sum was agreed, but the college had still to raise the funds and take up the option, which would be an invaluable addition to the college estate for future development. We received planning permission for the next phase of development on our existing site, in the form of a masterplan (excuse the pun!), which provided for all the foreseeable future needs of a college with up to 400 students.

The new St Edmund's College tower

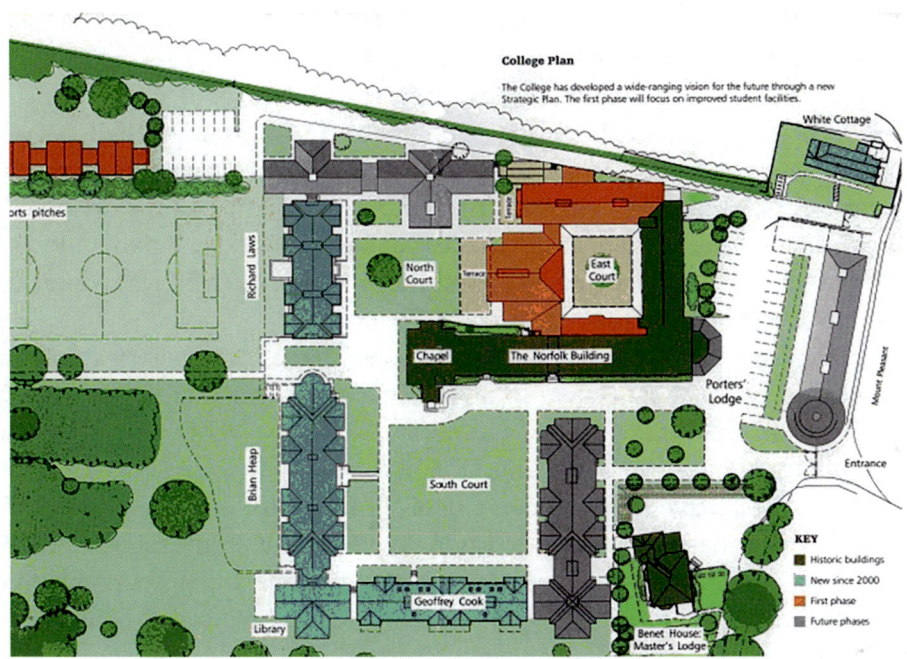

College Plan

The College has developed a wide-ranging vision for the future through a new Strategic Plan. The first phase will focus on improved student facilities.

White Cottage

sports pitches

Richard Laws

North Court

Terrace

East Court

Chapel

The Norfolk Building

Porters' Lodge

Brian Heap

South Court

Mount Pleasant

Entrance

KEY
- ■ Historic buildings
- ■ New since 2000
- ■ First phase
- ■ Future phases

Library

Geoffrey Cook

Benet House: Master's Lodge

The grounds of St Edmund's College after my tenure as Master

St Edmund's began its life with four students, rising to an average of ten in the early part of the 20th century and then up to forty by the mid-1960s. When I had been a student, it had had so low a profile in the university that I probably didn't know it existed! Until St Edmund's became a college of the university in 1965, students reading for Cambridge degrees had to be admitted by other colleges. Since 1965 St Edmund's has been able to admit its own postgraduate students and, since 1973, undergraduates in two categories – mature, namely over 25 (reduced now to 21) years of age, and affiliated students who are graduates of other universities permitted to read for the Cambridge BA degree in two rather than three years. Since 1969 the college has admitted women as well as men. Like all Cambridge Colleges St Edmund's admits students of all faiths or none.

When I started in 1985 the college was more narrowly academic with emphasis on theology and there were only sixty students. When I retired in 1996 there were 230 students from some 40 countries, of whom a third were women, and entrance applications were increasing.

About half of them read for the PhD degree, a quarter pursued one-year graduate courses, mainly MPhil; the first MBA students had graduated; the remainder were mature and affiliated students reading for the BA degree and the spectrum of subjects studied was now very broad. Two-thirds of the Fellows were in science and the remainder in the arts and humanities; more than two-thirds were university officers and almost a fifth were women. The Fellowship included two university professors (in earth sciences and astronomy) and two Fellows of the Royal Society. It had become a forward-looking society of scholars pursuing academic excellence with past conflicts forgotten.

Recalling my own student days my strong interest in sport was revived and I gave every encouragement to St Edmund's' participation in this field. To my considerable pleasure, the college became strongly identified with rowing and rugby, providing two Presidents of Cambridge University Boat Club and in some years as many as four rowing blues in the victorious Cambridge eight. It had also provided the university rugby captains and many rugby blues for several years running, as well as twice winning the rugby cuppers competition among the colleges. It had achieved large numbers of blues and half blues in other sports.

New Statutes and Ordinances were drafted to supersede the Articles and Ordinances of St Edmund's House, which had been *too* ambiguous. They stated that on approaching the retiring age of 67, a Master could be re-elected for another three years. On 9 March 1992 a resolution was passed unanimously by the board that I be re-appointed from 1 October 1993 to the end of the academical year in which I reached seventy. This would allow me to still be the Master for the college's centennial in 1996. It was a very emotional vindication of my stand during the earlier rough spot!

One of my last involvements was chairing the Charter Committee drawing up the new Statutes and Ordinances in anticipation of St Edmund's being given leave to apply for a Royal Charter for full college status. It produced an unexpectedly large volume of paperwork and, in the end, while we were honoured by Prince Philip, Duke of Edinburgh, an Honorary Fellow of St Edmund's, being present at our Centennial Celebration Dinner on 25 June 1996, we did not get our Royal Charter until two years later in 1998, by which time I had completed my extended term of office. Nevertheless it was a gratifying experience to have been part of the team that brought this about. So, too, was it a supreme moment when the college's new student accommodation was opened by HRH Prince Philip and named the Richard Laws Building.

Leaving St Edmund's after the Duke of Edinburgh dedicated the new Richard Laws Building for student accommodation

In improving the profile of St Edmund's, I served on a number of the Cambridge University committees. It was an honour to be involved in the management of one of the world's top research and teaching universities, at a time of major changes and many problems. Also I enjoyed the traditions, pleasures and customs of academic life as a Cambridge don.

In 1988 I was appointed a member of the university's financial board, on which I served for four years, as well as many other committees, among them the Science Building Committee (as chairman), Minor Works Committee, Investment Committee, etc. In 1989 I was elected a member of the Council of the Senate (the 'cabinet' of the university) for four years.

I was appointed Chairman of the University of Cambridge Local Examinations Syndicate (UCLES) and served four years. This was a worldwide business with a turnover of about £35 million a year and large reserves of around £100 million; it set school examinations and also examinations in English as a foreign language. In 1993 it received a Queen's Award for Industry.

All this was at a time of change, when the Wass Committee Report on constitutional change for the university was being debated and new Statutes and Ordinances were being drawn up. Towards the end of my time as a member of the Council of the Senate, as one of the two senior members of the Council I chaired the discussions leading to the election of Sir David Williams as the first Vice-Chancellor to serve under the new Statutes. For a dyed-in-the-wool Cambridge Man all of my adult life, I cannot describe the depths of my emotions and the satisfaction it gave me to contribute to my Alma Mater's governance as my career headed towards its close.

When Simon Mitton approached me about being Master he said it would be a part-time appointment. It turned out to be anything but part-time, and was a source immense satisfaction, but also a sense of humility over the opportunities it had opened up. This was topped on my retirement at the end of September 1996 when, in the Centenary Year, I was elected an Honorary Fellow

30

The Antarctic in Retirement

In 1999 Chris Rapley, Director of BAS, wrote inviting me to go to the Antarctic as the guest of the Survey. I wasn't able to take this up because of the short notice and other commitments, but he renewed the offer the following year and I accepted. I was given three options: to visit Rothera, Halley or Signy together with South Georgia and, hardly surprisingly, chose the latter – my first Antarctic station in 1948. The trip was between 16 October and 17 November 2000, and meant flying to the Falkland Islands and joining RRS *James Clark Ross* for a cruise to Bird Island, Grytviken, King Edward Point and Signy, then back to Stanley. BAS would cover all the costs of my trip. Accommodation on the *JCR* would be the chief scientist's cabin.

On the flight out I sat next to Amanda Lynnes – a penguin biologist working on penguin foraging biology (feeding and diving telemetry) at Signy. This was her fifth season with BAS, now working for a PhD. We had a deep conversation and I enjoyed her company and youthful enthusiasm.

Landing at Port Stanley on the 19th (we had been delayed en route) we were met at the *James Clark Ross* gangway by Hamish, the chief steward, and I was installed in the chief scientist's cabin on the bridge deck. Our captain was Jerry Bergan who I had appointed as a junior officer some years before. At anchor for the next two days, I met the Governor and several old friends.

On the 21st we left our moorings and anchored off Sparrow Point where all on board were put through a security drill: first a talk by the chief officer; an alarm sounded and we went to our muster stations in the lounge, another alarm and we donned life jackets (for the real thing we had also been issued with survival suits) and went to lifeboat stations. All climbed into the very modern, covered, motor lifeboats, each of which could take eighty people – even so it was very crowded and cramped inside. We were lowered into the water and drove around before re-attaching to the ship.

RRS *James Clark Ross*

We also looked around the ship including its gym and sauna – rowing machine, bicycle and step machines. The ship now had a crane of 20-ton capacity and 30-metre reach. On board was an impressive motorised 'scow' weighing 14.5 tons. This was picked up and launched by crane. After a test run around the ship it was picked up and stowed back on board again. Though the RRV *James Clark Ross* had been designed and ordered back when I was Director, this magnificent ship with its ultra-modern lifeboats and facilities was impressive, but I could not help but recall what had been available to us in 1948. And while I had played a prominent part in the modernising developments that I now looked upon, I wondered if the output of work per scientist had increased in proportion to what it currently cost in funds and ancillary services to put each researcher into the field.

At around 4 p.m. the anchor was weighed and we set sail for South Georgia. Initially calm and in sunshine, that night it became rough with the wind rising to Force 9. Satellite sea ice maps showed our Signy Station in the South Orkneys surrounded by 4–6 tenths pack ice, Rothera Station on Adelaide Island by 9–10 tenths pack. Again, the advances in science told us of the conditions ahead, whereas in the 'good old days' we had no such warnings.

Not that I complained. Now with the ability to email, the family was within almost instant reach. Our three sons – Richard, Christopher and Andrew – were now independent adults and had left our nest with family connections of their own. Indeed Maureen and I were grandparents as Andrew and his wife Martelle in Australia had presented us with Madeleine and Reuben (and would soon increase the number to three). Thanks to email, and even in this most remote part of our planet, we kept in contact.

As I stood on the bridge the masthead searchlight (maximum range about two miles) was turned down to hit the sea surface about 200 m ahead, picking out the foam on wave crests as brilliant white, contrasting with a beautiful luminous blue where the beam shone into a wave. Snow blizzards drove across the beam. Earlier I had watched the water drops back-lit on the bridge windows. They were dense like stars, of different sizes, occasionally coalescing and running down the glass – like shooting stars with a tail.

We called in at Bird Island where I had a good look around the base and met Maggie the BC. She seemed very pleasant, maybe in her thirties, slight, athletic, pleasant smile, and 'in control'. Not only were girls now integrated as Fids, but here was one as BC! With Maggie were Dafydd Roberts, a large, quiet Welshman, and Nick, a rapid interesting talker with blond dreadlocks, who were the birds and seals assistants. Jon Arnould was an Australian seal biologist. We entered the base and looked around, had a cup of coffee, all very impressive. The main base hut was open plan, with plenty of character, and had comfortable office chairs.

At 6:30 a.m. on 24 October we came alongside the King Edward Point jetty. I stood on the bridge as the vessel was mooring – a lengthy process with two lines, bow and stern, to shore, two lines amidships to the jetty. After breakfast I kitted up and went ashore. It was cold with a bitter wind, but clear. Walking through the 'settlement' past the post office, (former) radio office, Discovery House, Quigley's, the gaol etc. to Shackleton House and on to Shackleton's cross among the tussocks. On the way I stopped to watch the elephant seals, noting many black pups about 7–10 days old. A large dominant male and several subordinate males put on a display. I took in the well-remembered behaviour, smells and sounds. Sheathbills and Dominican gulls, one or two blue-eyed shags, terns and skuas were about. It was a nostalgic trip down memory lane.

Back in Larsen House for a cup of coffee at the bar of 'Arkright's Pub'. An RAF C-130 from Stanley flew over for the regular mail drop. We watched the parachute falling, preceded by two speedboats racing out to the dropping zone. How things had changed! Back on board, Jerry had invited guests from ashore for dinner – Tim and Pauline Carr who ran the museum, Pat and Sarah Lurcock, Capt. Brown (CO army detachment now based here) and the army doctor, a woman. It was a convivial evening.

Laws Glacier, Coronation Island in the South Orkney Islands

On the 25th I visited the museum and was very favourably impressed. It really was excellent and a tribute to Nigel (Bonner)'s efforts in setting it up and developing it, and to the Carrs, husband and wife, who ran it. Photos and artefacts covered all aspects of the island and its history. Some of the old photos took me back to 1951, particularly of the sealers and sealing. A very lifelike stuffed wandering albatross flew beneath the ceiling. There was a reconstruction of a two-man whaler's bunkroom, the products of the industry, scrimshaw and skulls, birds, vegetation, expeditions and so on. A small museum shop stocked clothes, jewellery, postcards, books etc. If anything testified to the growth in Antarctic tourism, this did.

I visited the church, whose interior was more austere than I remembered. Pine pews and bare wooden floors, a simple altar with curved communion rail, an organ and a gallery at the back reached by stairs, it was now well maintained.

Returning to our ship we had to don immersion suits and life jackets, which was an awkward struggle. Rules and regulations were intruding even here and, recalling the lives we had led without them, I wondered to myself whether they really represented progress. My walks ashore through deep snow had made me very tired and my knee, which had been operated on, was painful. I was lent a battery-operated device that delivered pulsed electric shocks that gradually increased. It seemed to help, though for a person who had led a hard life in the field, it was a reminder that time was passing!

The next day was perfect. Ashore at Pat Lurcock's house we talked and consumed coffee and cake, while the elephant seals roared outside. He then showed me around Discovery House where I lived and worked in 1951 as BC. It was now rather sad, very untidy, filled with rubbish, planks, with broken windows and stripped of furnishings. I identified my bedroom, office and wetlab, also the kitchen and lounge of the FIDS base but it was difficult to visualise it all as it used to be, because walls had been pulled down or moved, so the layout was not as I remembered it. There were now several large rooms where before there were many small ones, etc. It was to be converted – probably into a visitor centre.

On the 27th we headed out past West Cumberland Bay and tantalising glimpses of the Three Brothers. We were all rather red from yesterday's sun and UV exposure due to the ozone hole – despite liberal application of sun screen, protection factor 30. I couldn't remember anything remotely like this in the past – but of course I hadn't been south so early for many years and the ozone thinning occurs in October/November.

At night on the 29th we watched the collection of data on CTD (sea chemistry and temperature at different depths). I saw the control system in operation – with video observation and co-ordination from the bridge. It was dark, with the after-deck lit up and plenty of colourful monitors informing on activities. I reflected on the beginning of it all on my voyage in 1971 when we undertook the SOBS and

South Georgia Benthic Survey (SGBS) from the *John Biscoe*. That was the start of BAS oceanographic research, and it had come a very long way since then, but it had needed a strong initial push to get it going. Although I had been around the *JCR* while being built in dock, I hadn't had the opportunity to see her committed at sea until now. It was great! I was really enjoying the experience of seeing how the ideas sketched out with Chris Elliot in 1986 had come to fruition.

Next day seemed a better prospect. At 1 o'clock we went ashore on Signy Island in the cargo tender, through the biting wind wearing life jackets. The cargo was unloaded and taken by the Fids up to the base – 100 yards or so. I decided not to get involved in the unloading or in pushing wheeled trolleys up a wooden walkway to the base. There were plenty of strong young people about!

The dinner that night was rather special. I was photographed with the Signy Fids and we had an excellent meal – smoked salmon and salad, pepper steak, croquet potatoes and beans, cheese and biscuits and plenty of wine. To my surprise Martin Davey made a speech, which initially I thought was to thank the captain and the ship, but in fact was to thank me for all my support for Signy (I had never concealed that through the years it was my favourite base).

Later I looked around inside the new huts. Walls of the living hut had photos of the base over the years of its life including 1947, but sadly not 1948. There was a portrait of Signy Sörlle and I was pleased to see the flag from my time with the dedication:

SIGNY ISLAND FLAG'

WINTER 1948

Presented by the widow of D. H. Maling

A very tattered and torn Union Jack! There was also a brass porthole from the wreck of the *Tioga* (a vessel that was wrecked early in the days when Signy had a land-based whaling station, and whose remains were visible when I went to the island in 1947). There were four bunkrooms each with two bunks, a shower, flush toilets, large living room with comfortable chairs and a library in glass-fronted bookshelves, and a large kitchen – well fitted out. There was a BC's office, other facilities, and several laboratories, well equipped, and a computer room.

On one of the trips ashore I had been on a sledge towed by Amanda Lynnes in a skidoo. Making too sharp a turn, the sledge tipped over and I landed on my back onto hard ice. It was not only quite violent but painful too, and I had to retire. After a very hot shower, two paracetamol/codeine tablets and a small whisky I felt better! As I was dressing, Pippa, the ship's doctor, came in. She agreed I was taking the correct treatment and told me she, too, had put her back out lifting boxes.

I visited the Orwell Glacier, much receded since my last visit in 1987. From the height of the peripheral moraine it must have lost 20 ft in elevation and had undergone a substantial recession of the front.

We climbed the moraine and I pointed out garnets in the rocks, and took in the surrounding features. We climbed to Point 111, where Sevvy was standing proprietarily next to his time-lapse camera for recording ice in the bay, ready to demonstrate it. It recorded the ice cover on film four times a day, and was powered by solar panels that recharged two large batteries. It ran for a year without attention, and had been running for five years now without any problems. Then up to Point 121 and Point 93. We had lovely views of Paal Harbour and out to sea, returning via the snow chute near Factory Bluffs. I was quite tired because the snow was very deep in places and my knees/legs were failing, but enjoyed it all, glissading in places. Age was certainly making itself felt!

We departed, weather still lovely, heading towards Burdwood Bank and the squid fishing 'box' we were to sample. November 11 was a bright but overcast morning with moderate sea; the work was successful and we actually caught some squid larvae! Some twenty-three hauls in all were planned over the Burdwood Bank and we would end up near Beauchene Islands, south of the Falklands. All too soon the squid netting had been completed and at 8 o'clock Beauchene Island lay abeam, just a grey silhouette five miles away. In the evening a party developed, with free drinks at the bar from 6 o'clock and the dinner that followed was very good. Jerry stood up and made a speech about all I had done for BAS and how everyone had enjoyed my company on board. Then he presented me with a teakwood plaque which had a brass cut-out of the Antarctic, on which was engraved:

To Dick Laws:

Best wishes from all on board James Clark Ross

Voyage 10 – 2000

It had been made by 'Rags', the third engineer. I was hugely pleased. The convivial evening continued until midnight. I was among **my** people: the Fids, as diverse a group of men and women whose love of the Antarctic, its hardships and overwhelming beauty, who formed a tremendous team. It had been my privilege to have started at the bottom and eventually led it. Yet nothing touched me quite so deeply as their great kindness – from the Director to the most junior – and this gift on a most enjoyable and eventful trip. Thirteen years after laying down my BAS baton, and now somewhat frail, I had still been treated as one of their own. As nothing else, this ending to my Antarctic career was beyond thanks.

Publications

(Scientific publications and books are asterisked; others are popular
articles, grey literature, reports, reviews, obituaries.)

1*. Laws, R. M., 1952a. 'Seal marking methods'. *Polar Record* 6: 359–61

2*. Laws, R. M., 1952b. 'A new method of age determination for mammals'.
     Nature 169: 972

3*. Laws, R. M., 1953a. 'The elephant seal industry at South Georgia'. *Polar
     Record* 6: 746–54

4*. Laws, R. M., 1953b. 'A new method of age determination for mammals
     with special reference to the elephant seal, *Mirounga leonina* Linn.'
     Sci. Rep. Falkland Is. Dep. Surv., no. 2: 1–11

5*. Laws, R. M., 1953c. 'The elephant seal (*Mirounga leonina* Linn.) I: Growth
     and age'. *Sci. Rep. Falkland Is. Dep. Surv.*, no. 8: 1–62

6*. Laws, R. M., 1953d. 'The seals of the Falklands Islands and Dependencies'.
     Oryx 2 (2): 87–97

7*. Laws, R. M., 1953e. 'The reproduction of the southern elephant seal,
     Mirounga leonina Linn.' Ph.D. thesis, University of Cambridge,
     pp. xviii–191

8*. Laws, R. M., 1954. 'Giant ovaries of a blue whale'. *Nature* 173: 1003

9.   Laws, R. M., 1955. 'Natural history of the larger whales'. *Zoo Life* 10: 34–40

10* Laws, R. M., 1956a. 'The elephant seal (*Mirounga leonina* Linn.)
     II: General, social and reproductive behaviour'. *Sci. Rep. Falkland Is. Dep.
     Surv.*, no. 13: 1–88

11*. Laws, R. M., 1956b. 'The elephant seal (*Mirounga leonina* Linn.) III: The physiology of reproduction'. *Sci. Rep. Falkland Is. Dep. Surv.*, no. 15: 1–66

12*. Laws, R. M., 1956c. 'Growth and sexual maturity in aquatic mammals'. *Nature* 178: 193–4

13*. Laws, R. M., and Purves, P. E., 1956d. 'The ear plug of the Mysticeti as an indication of age, with special reference to the North Atlantic fin whale (*Balaenoptera physalus* Linn.)'. *Norsk Hvalfangsttid* 45 (8): 413–25

14*. Laws, R. M., 1956e. 'Determination of the age of the larger whales (Mysticeti)'. *Polar Record* 8: 175

15*. Laws, R. M., 1957a. 'On the growth rates of the leopard seal, *Hydrurga leptonyx* (de Blainville, 1820)'. *Saugetierk, Mitt.* 5 (2): 49–55

16*. Laws, R. M., 1957b. 'Polarity of whale ovaries'. *Nature* 179: 1011–12

17*. Laws, R. M. and Taylor, R. J., 1957c. 'A mass dying of crabeater seals, *Lobodon carcinophagus* (Gray)'. *Proc. Zool. Soc. Lond.* 129 (3): 315–24

18*. Laws, R. M., 1958a. 'Growth rates and ages of crabeater seals, *Lobodon carcinophagus*, Jacquinot and Pucheran'. *Proc. Zool. Soc. Lond.* 130: 275–88

19*. Laws, R. M., 1958b. 'Recent investigations on fin whale ovaries'. *Norsk Hvalfangsttid* 47 (5): 225–54

20*. Laws, R. M., 1959a. 'Age determination of whales by means of the corpora albicantia'. *XVth Internat. Congr. Zool. Proceedings*: 303–5

21*. Laws, R. M., 1959b. 'The foetal growth rates of whales, with special reference to the Fin whale, *Balaenoptera physalus* Linn'. *Discovery Rep.* 29: 281–308

22*. Laws, R. M., 1959c. 'On the breeding season of southern hemisphere Fin whales, *Balaenoptera physalus* Linn'. *Norsk Hvalfangsttid* 48 (7): 329–51

23*. Laws, R. M., 1959d. 'Accelerated growth in seals with special reference to the Phocidae'. *Norsk Hvalfangsttid* 48 (9): 425–52

24*. Laws, R. M., 1960a. 'Researches on the period of conception, duration of gestation and growth of the foetus in the Fin whale, based on data from International Whaling Statistics'. *Norsk Hvalfangsttid* 49 (5): 216–20

25*.   Laws, R. M., 1960b. 'Laminated structure of bones from some marine mammals'. *Nature* 187: 338–9

26*.   Laws, R. M., 1960c. 'Problems of whale conservation'. *Trans. N. Am. Wildl. conf* 25: 304–19

27*.   Laws, R. M., 1960d. 'The southern elephant seal (*Mirounga leonina* Linn.) at South Georgia'. *Norsk Hvalfangsttid* 49 (10): 466–76; (11): 520–42

28*.   Laws, R. M., 1961. 'Reproduction, growth and age of southern fin whales'. *Discovery Rep.* 31: 327–486

29.   Laws, R. M., 19--. Film review of: *Sanctuary in the South*. Margin for Life. Filmed by C. D. B. Thomas. 16mm Eastman Colour. 24 minutes, Pacific Films. *Geographical Magazine* 44, no.12: 883

30*.   Laws, R. M., 1962a. 'Some effects of whaling on the southern stocks of baleen whales'. In: *The Exploitation of Natural Animal Populations*, eds. E. D. Le Cren, and M. W. Holdgate. Oxford: Blackwell. *Brit. Ecol. Soc., Symposium* no. 2, Durham, 1960: 137–58

31*.   Laws, R. M., 1962b. 'Age determination of pinnipeds with special reference to growth layers in the teeth'. *Z. Saugetierk* 27 (3):29–46

32*.   Boyd, J. M. and Laws, R. M., 1962c. 'Observations on the grey seal (*Halichoerus grypus*) at North Rona in 1960'. *Proc. Zool. Soc. Lond.* 139 (2): 249–60

33.   Laws, R. M., 1963. 'Conservation of sea mammals and fish'. *Encyclopaedia Britannica.*

34*.   Laws, R. M., 1964a. 'Comparative biology of Antarctic seals'. In *Biologie Antarctique*, eds. R. Carrick and M. W. Holdgate. Paris: Hermann, pp. 445–54

35*.   Laws, R. M., 1964b. 'The true seals (Phocidae)'. In *Antarctic Research*, eds. R. E. Priestley, R. J. Adie and G. de Q. Robin. London: Butterworth and Co., ch.10, pp. 177–90

36*.   Laws, R. M., 1964c. 'The Nuffield Unit of Tropical Animal Ecology. Progress Report – June 1962–May 1963'. In *Report of the Uganda National Parks for the year ended June 1963*, pp. 23–30

37*.   Plowright W., Laws, R. M. and Rampton, C. S., 1964d. 'Serological evidence for the susceptibility of the hippopotamus (*Hippopotamus amphibius* Linnaeus) to natural infection with rinderpest virus'. *J. Hyg., Camb.* 62: 329–36

38*.   Thurston, J. P. and Laws, R. M., 1965a. '*Oculotrema hippopotami* (*Tremadota, Monogenea*) in Uganda. *Nature* 205: 1127

39*.   Laws, R. M. and Field, C. R., 1965b. 'The Nuffield Unit of Tropical Animal Ecology. Second Annual Report – June 1963–June 1964'. *Report of the Uganda National Parks for the year ended June 1964*, pp. 28–41

40*.   Laws, R. M. and Clough, G., 1965c. 'Observations on reproduction in the hippopotamus, *Hippopotamus amphibious*'. *J. Reprod. Fert.* 9: 369–70

41*.   Laws, R. M. and Clough, G., 1965d. 'Observations on reproduction in the hippopotamus, *Hippopotamus amphibius*'. In: *Comparative Biology of Reproduction in Mammals*, ed. I. W. Rowlands. *Symp. Zool. Soc. Lond.* 15: 117–40

42*.   Laws, R. M., 1965e. 'Seals as a natural resource: Future prospects'. In: *A Seals Symposium*, ed. E. A. Smith. The Nature Conservancy, Edinburgh, pp. 3–6

43*.   Thurlbeck, W. M., Butas, C. A., Mankewicz, E. M. and Laws, R. M., 1966a. 'Chronic pulmonary disease in wild buffalo (*Syncerus caffer*) in Uganda'. *Amer. Rev. Resp. Dis.* 92 (5): 801–5

44*.   Laws, R. M., 1966b. 'Age criteria for the African elephant (*Loxodonta a. africana*)'. *E. Afr. Wildl. J.* 4: 1–37

45*.   Laws, R. M., 1966c. The Nuffield Unit of Tropical Animal Ecology. Third Annual Report – July 1964–June 1965. *Report of the Uganda National Parks for the year ended June 1965*, pp. 17–27

46.   Laws, R. M., 1966d. 'The Tsavo Research Project; the Research Programme '(typescript), p. 7 (November 1966)

47*.   Laws, R. M., 1967a. 'Occurrence of placental scars in the uterus of the African elephant (*Loxodonta africana*)'. *J. Reprod. Fert.* 14: 445–9

48*.   Laws, R. M., 1967b. 'Eye lens weight and age in African elephants'. *E. Afr. Wildl. J.* 5: 46–52

49*. Laws, R. M., Parker, I. S. C and Archer, A. L., 1967c. 'Estimating live weights of elephants from hind leg weights'. *E. Afr. Wildl. J.* 5: 106–11

50*. Cowan, D. F., Thurlbeck, W. M. and Laws, R. M., 1967d. 'Some diseases of hippopotamus in Uganda'. *Path. Vet.* 4: 553–67

51. Laws, R. M., 1967e. 'Cropping of elephant in the Tsavo National Park and surrounding areas for research purposes'. Unpublished typescript, p.15 (22 July 1967)

52. Laws, R. M., 1967f. 'The Tsavo Research Project – First Progress report, July 1967'. Unpublished typescript, p.9 (26 July 1967)

53. Laws, R. M., 1967g. 'The Tsavo Research Project – Current problems and future needs'. Unpublished typescript, p.15 (22 October 1967)

54*. Laws, R. M., 1967h. 'The Unit of Tropical Animal Ecology. Third Annual Report – July 1965–June 1966'. *Report of the Uganda National Parks for the year ended June 1966*

55*. Laws, R. M., 1968a. Wildlife management in practice'. *Sylva* 48: 21–5

56*. Laws, R. M., 1968b. 'Interactions between elephant and hippopotamus populations and their environments'. *E. Afr. Agric. For. J.* 33: 140–7

57*. Laws, R. M., 1968c. 'Dentition and ageing of the hippopotamus'. *E. Afr. Wildl. J.* 6: 19–52

58*. Laws, R. M. and Parker, I. S. C., 1968d. 'Recent studies on elephant populations in East Africa'. In *Comparative nutrition of wild animals*, ed. M. A. Crawford. *Symp. Zool. Soc. Lond.* 21: 319–59

59*. Laws, R. M., 1969a. 'Aspects of reproduction in the African elephant, *Loxodonta africana*'. *J. Reprod. Fert.*, Suppl. 6: 193–217

60*. Laws, R. M., 1969b. 'The Tsavo Research Project'. *J. Reprod. Fert.*, Suppl. 6: 495–531

61*. Laws, R. M., 1970a. 'Biology of African Elephants'. *Science Progr.* 58: 251–62

62*. Laws, R. M., 1970b. 'Elephants as agents of habitat and landscape change in East Africa'. *Oikos* 21: 1–15

63*. Field C. R. and Laws, R. M., 1970c. 'The distribution of the larger herbivores in the Queen Elizabeth National Park, Uganda'. *J. appl. Ecol.* 7: 273–94

64*. Laws, R. M., Parker, I. S. C. and Johnstone, R. C. B., 1970d. 'Elephants and habitats in North Bunyoro, Uganda'. *E. Afr. Wildl. J.* 8: 163–80

65. Laws, R. M., 1970e. Review of *Antarctic Ecology*, ed. M. W. Holdgate, Two volumes. London and New York: Academic Press, 1970. *Polar Record* 15 (96): 435–47

66*. Laws, R. M., 1970f. 'The Tsavo Research Project'. *Oryx* 10, no.6: 335–61

67*. Laws, R. M., 1970g. 'Elephants and men in East Africa'. *University of Saskatchewan, University Lectures*, no. 22: 1–19

68. Laws, R. M., 1971a. 'The Tsavo Elephants'. *Oryx* 11, no. 1: 32–4

69. Laws, R. M., 1971 b. Review of *Antarctic Ecology*, ed. M. W. Holdgate. Two volumes. London and New York: Academic Press, 1970. *Oryx* 11 (2–3): 197–9

70. Laws, R. M., 1971c. Review of *Antarctic Ecology*, ed. M. W. Holdgate. Two volumes. London and New York: Academic Press, 1970, 2 vols. *New Scientist*, London 52:

71*. Graham, A. D. and Laws, R. M., 1971d. 'The collection of found ivory in Murchison Falls National Park, Uganda'. *E. Afr. Wildl. J.* 9: 57–65

72*. Laws, R. M., 1971e. 'Patterns of reproductive and somatic ageing in large mammals'. In *Ageing in relation to development and reproduction*, ed. G. A. Sacher, Argonne National Laboratory, Argonne Universities Association, Annual Symposium 6: 16–19

73*. Laws, R. M., 1972a. 'Seals and birds killed and captured in the Antarctic Treaty Area, 1964–69'. *Polar Record* 16, no. 101: 343–64

74. Laws, R. M., 1972b. 'Elephant'. In *Encyclopedia of the animal world*. London: Elsevier, pp. 653–8

75. Laws, R. M., 1972c. 'Hippopotamus'. In *Encyclopedia of the animal world*. London: Elsevier, pp. 948–51

76.   Laws, R. M., 1972d. 'Proboscidea'. In *Encyclopedia of the animal world*. London: Elsevier, pp. 1474–5

77*. Laws, R. M., 1973a. 'The current status of seals in the southern hemisphere'. In *Threatened and depleted seals of the world*, ed. H. F. Elliott, *IUCN Resources Publ. New Ser. Suppl. Paper* 39: 144–61

78*. Laws, R. M., 1973b. 'Effects of human activities on reproduction in the wild'. In *Comparative biology of reproduction in mammals and birds*, eds. J. S. Perry and I. W. Rowlands, *J. Reprod. Fert. Suppl.* 19: 523–32

79.   Laws, R. M., 1973c. 'Seals and birds killed or captured in the Antarctic Treaty Area, 1969–70'. *Polar Record* 16, no. 105: 901–2

80.   Laws, R. M., 1973d. 'Sea Mammals'. Review of *Functional Anatomy of Marine Mammals*, ed. R. J. Harrison. New York and London: Academic, 1972. *Nature, Lond.* 245, no.5425: 394

81*. Laws, R. M., 1974a. 'Behaviour, dynamics and management of elephant populations'. In *The behaviour of ungulates and its relation to management*, ed. V. Geist. IUCN paper 26: 513–29

82*. Laws, R. M., 1974b. 'Population increase of fur seals at South Georgia'. *Polar Record* 16, no. 105: 856–8

83.   Laws, R. M., 1974c. 'Presentation of the first Fuchs Medal.' *Polar Record* 17, no. 106: 49–52

84.   Laws, R. M., 1974d. 'Fauna'. In *The Antarctic Pilot*. Fourth Edition. *Hydrographer of the Navy*, pp. 27–47, 49

85.   Laws, R. M., 1974e. Review of: McKay, G. M., 1973, 'Behaviour and Ecology of the Asiatic Elephant in Southeastern Ceylon'. *Smithsonian Contributions to Zoology* 125: 113. In *Quarterly Review of Biology* 50 (4): 492

86*. Laws, R. M., Parker, I. S. C. and Johnstone, R. C. B. 1975. *Elephants and their habitats: the ecology of elephants in North Bunyoro, Uganda*. Oxford University Press, pp. 388

87.   Laws, R. M., 1976a. 'SCAR Group of Specialists on Seals'. *Polar Record* 18, no. 114: 317–18

88. Laws, R. M., 1976b. Review of: Douglas-Hamilton, I. and O. *Among the Elephants*. London: Collins & Harvill Press, 1975. *Quarterly Review of Biology*, 1976

89. Laws, R. M. and Christie, E. C., 1976c. 'Seals and birds killed or captured in the Antarctic Treaty area 1970–73'. *Polar Record* 18, no. 114: 318–320

90. Laws, R. M., 1976d. 'British research in the Antarctic'. *J. Roy. Soc. Arts*, no. 5243, vol. 124: 630–45

91*. Laws, R. M., 1976e. 'Antarctic ecosystem: Area case study', p. 15. Document submitted to FAO, ACMMR Working Party No.3

92*. Fuchs, V. E. and Laws, R. M., 1977a. 'Scientific research in Antarctica: a Discussion Meeting', eds. V. E. Fuchs and R. M. Laws. *Phil. Trans. Roy. Soc.*, B 279: 81–96

93*. Laws, R. M., 1977b. 'Seals and whales of the Southern Ocean'. In *Scientific research in Antarctica: a Discussion Meeting*, eds. V. E. Fuchs and R. M. Laws. *Phil. Trans. Roy. Soc.*, B 279: 81–96

94*. Laws, R. M., 1977c. 'The significance of vertebrates in the Antarctic marine ecosystem'. In *Adaptations within Antarctic Ecosystems*, ed. G. A. Llano. Houston, Texas: Gulf Publishing Company, pp. 411–38

95. Laws, R. M., 1977d. 'BAS expenditure not "excessive"'. *Fish News* 16, no. 9: 79–80

96. Laws, R. M., 1977e. (Chairman) Report of the Advisory Committee on Marine Resources Research Working Party on Marine Mammals. *FAO Fish. Rep.*, no. 194: 43

97. Laws, R. M., 1977f. Natural Environment Research Council, British Antarctic Survey: Annual report, 1976–77. Cambridge: British Antarctic Survey, p. 63

98*. Laws, R. M., 1978a. (Chairman). Proceedings of the scientific consultation on the conservation and management of marine mammals and their environment. (In: *Mammals in the seas*. Volume I. Report of the FAO Advisory Committee on Marine Resources Research Working Party on Marine Mammals, ed. J Gordon Clark. *FAO Fish.Ser.*, no. 5, vol. I: 45–185 (1978); vol. II: 1–151 (1979); vol. III: 1–504 (1981); vol. IV: 1–530 (1982)

99.   Laws, R. M., 1978b. Introductory statement by Chairman. In: *Mammals in the Seas*. Volume I. Report of the FAO Advisory Committee on Marine Resources Research Working Party on Marine Mammals, ed. J. Gordon Clark. *FAO Fish. Ser*. no. 5, vol. I: 47–49

100*. Laws, R. M., 1978c. 'Ecological studies at South Georgia'. *S. Afr. J. Antarct. Res*. 8: 3–13

101. Laws, R. M., 1978d. Natural Environment Research Council, British Antarctic Survey: Annual report, 1977–78. Cambridge: British Antarctic Survey, pp. 71

102*. D. B. Sinnif, et. al., 1978e. 'Biota of the Antarctic pack ice: R/V *Hero* cruise 77–5'. *Antarct. Jl., U.S*. 13: 161–2

103. Laws, R. M., 1979a. Obituary – B. B. Roberts. *Nature Lond.* 277, no. 5697: 585

104*. Laws, R. M., 1979b. 'Monitoring whale and seal populations'. In: *Monitoring the Marine Environment*, ed. D. Nichols. *Symp. Inst. of Biol*., no. 24: 115–40

105*. May, R. M., et. al., 1979c. 'Management of multispecies fisheries'. *Science* 205: 267–77

106*. Laws, R. M., 1979d. 'Southern elephant seal'. In: *Mammals in the Seas*. Volume II. Report of the FAO Advisory Committee on Marine Resources Research Working Party on Marine Mammals. Pinniped species summaries and report on sirenians. *FAO Fish. Ser*., no. 5, vol. 2: 106–9

107*. Laws, R. M., 1979e. 'Crabeater seal'. In: *Mammals in the Seas*. Volume II. Report of the FAO Advisory Committee on Marine Resources Research Working Party on Marine Mammals. Pinniped species summaries and report on sirenians. *FAO Fish. Ser*., no. 5, vol. 2: 115–19

108*. Laws, R. M. and Hofman, R.J., 1979f. 'Ross seal'. In: *Mammals in the seas*. Volume II. Report of the FAO Advisory Committee on Marine Resources Research Working Party on Marine Mammals. Pinniped species summaries and report on sirenians. *FAO Fish. Ser*., no. 5, vol. 2: 120–4

109. Laws, R. M., 1979g. Natural Environment Research Council, British Antarctic Survey: Annual report, 1969–70. Cambridge: British Antarctic Survey, p. 23

110. Laws, R. M., 1979h. Natural Environment Research Council, British Antarctic Survey: Annual report, 1970–71. Cambridge: British Antarctic Survey, p. 26

111. Laws, R. M., 1979i. Natural Environment Research Council, British Antarctic Survey: Annual report, 1971–72. Cambridge: British Antarctic Survey, p. 30

112. Laws, R. M., and Christie, E. C., 1980a. 'Seals and birds killed or captured in the Antarctic Treaty area, 1973–75'. *Polar Record* 20, no.125: 195–8

113*. Laws, R. M., 1980b (ed.). 'Estimation of population sizes of seals'. *BIOMASS Handbook*, no. 2: 21

114. Campbell, R.N. and Laws, R. M., 1980c. 'Eyesore on North Rona?' *The Times*, 16 July 1980. (Letter)

115. Laws, R. M., 1980d. Natural Environment Research Council, British Antarctic Survey: Annual report, 1972–75. Cambridge: British Antarctic Survey, p. 65

116. Laws, R. M., 1980e. Natural Environment Research Council, British Antarctic Survey: Annual report, 1975–76. Cambridge: British Antarctic Survey, p. 39

117. Laws, R. M., 1980f. Natural Environment Research Council, British Antarctic Survey: Annual report, 1978–79. Cambridge: British Antarctic Survey, p. 75

118. Laws, R. M., 1980g. Natural Environment Research Council, British Antarctic Survey: Annual report, 1979–80. Cambridge: British Antarctic Survey, p. 79

119*. Laws, R. M., 1981a. 'Biology of Antarctic seals'. *Science Progress*, *Oxford* 67, no. 267: 377–97

120*. Laws, R. M., 1981b. 'Experiences in the study of large mammals'. In: *Dynamics of large mammal populations*, eds. C. W. Fowler and T. D. Smith. New York: John Wiley & Sons, pp. 19–45

121*. Laws, R. M., 1981c. 'Large mammal feeding strategies and related overabundance problems'. In: *Problems in the management of locally abundant wild mammals*, eds. P. A. Jewell and S. J. Holt. London: Academic Press, pp. 217–32

123. Laws, R. M., 1981d. 'Protecting the Antarctic Wilderness'. *The Times*, 5 November. (Letter)

124*. Laws, R. M., 1981e. 'Seal surveys, South Orkney Islands, 1971 and 1974'. *British Antarctic Survey Bulletin*, no. 54: 136–9

125*. R. M. Laws and Nieuwenhuijs, G. K.1981f. 'A new sighting of southern right whale dolphins, *Lissodelphus peronii*, in the South-west Atlantic'. *British Antarctic Survey Bulletin* no. 54, 135–36

126. Laws, R. M., 1981g. Natural Environment Research Council, British Antarctic Survey: Annual report, 1980–81. Cambridge: British Antarctic Survey, p. 69

127. Laws, R. M., 1982a. 'Antarctica: the untouchable wilderness'. Review of *Antarctica, Wilderness at Risk*. B. Brewster. Orbis Publishing. *Geogr. Mag.* Nov. 1982, pp. 654–5

128. Laws, R. M., 1982b. 'Links with the Falklands and South Georgia'. *St. Catharine's College Society Magazine* 1982, p. 55

129. Laws, R. M., 1982c. Natural Environment Research Council, British Antarctic Survey: Annual report, 1981–82. Cambridge: British Antarctic Survey, p. 69

130. Laws, R. M., 1983a. '*Endurance* and the British Antarctic Survey'. In *H.M.S. Endurance, 1981–82 Deployment: A season of conflict*, eds. A. Lockett, N. Munro, D. Wells. Helston, Cornwall: A. J. Lockett, pp. 66–67

131. Laws, R. M., 1983b. 'Polar animals'. Review of *Antarctic Wildlife*. E. Hosking and B. Sage. *Natural World*, Spring 1983: 37–8

132. Laws, R. M., 1983c. 'Antarctica: a convergence of life'. *New Scientist*, 99, no. 1373: 608–16

133*. Laws, R. M., 1983d. 'Minke whale'. *New Scientist* 100 (1378): 48

134. Laws, R. M., 1983e. 'Ecological dynamics of Antarctic seals and whales'. In: *Proceedings of the BIOMASS Colloquium in 1982*, eds. T. Nemoto, and T. Matsuda. *Memoirs of National Institute of Polar Research Special Issue*, no. 27: 247 (abstract)

135. Laws, R. M., 1983f. Natural Environment Research Council, British Antarctic Survey: Annual report, 1982–83. Cambridge: British Antarctic Survey, p. 63

136*. Laws, R. M., 1984a (ed.). 'Biological research in the Antarctic'. *Polar Record* 22 (137): 221–6

137*. Laws, R. M., 1984b (ed.). *Antarctic Ecology*. Two volumes. London: Academic Press, pp. xvii, 850

138*. Laws, R. M., 1984c (ed.). 'Seals'. *Antarctic Ecology*, vol.2. London: Academic Press, pp. 621–715

139. Laws, R. M., 1984d. SCAR Group of Specialists on Seals. Report of a meeting held in Pretoria, South Africa, 7–8 September 1983. *SCAR Bulletin* no. 22, May 1984; *Polar Record* 22: 242–5

140. Laws, R. M., 1984e. 'The krill-eating crabeater'. In: *The Encyclopaedia of Mammals*, ed. D. MacDonald. London: George Allen & Unwin, pp.280–281

141. Laws, R. M., 1984f. 'Hippopotamuses'. In: *The Encyclopaedia of Mammals*, ed. D. MacDonald. George London: Allen & Unwin, pp. 506–11

142. Laws, R. M., 1984g. 'Introduction to the Colloquium'. In: *A decade of research on Antarctic and sub-Antarctic seals*. See *S. Afr. J. Sci.* 80: 25–35

143. Laws, R. M., 1984h. 'Explorers and bureaucrats'. Review of *Antarctic Odyssey*, P. Law. Heinemann. *New Scientist*, no. 144: 25–6

144. Laws, R. M., 1984i. 'Antarctic adventures of a past age'. Review of *Antarctic Days with Mawson*. H. Fletcher. London: Angus and Robertson. *New Scientist*, Dec. 1984, p. 69

145. Laws, R. M., 1984j. Review of the Year. *Zoological Society of London*, *Ann. Rep.* 1984: 5–19

146. Laws, R. M., 1984k. Natural Environment Research Council, British Antarctic Survey: Annual Report, 1983–84. Cambridge: British Antarctic Survey, p. 103

147*. Laws, R. M., 1985a. 'Ecology of the Southern Ocean'. *American Scientist* 73: 26–40

148. Laws, R. M., 1985b. 'International stewardship of the Antarctic: problems, successes and future options'. *Marine Pollution Bulletin* 16 (2): 49–55

149. Laws, R. M., 1985c. Review of *The Island of South Georgia*. R. Headland. Cambridge: Cambridge University Press. *British Antarctic Survey Bulletin*, no. 67: 83–6

150*. Siegfried, W. R., Condy, P. and Laws, R. M. (eds.), 1985d. *Antarctic nutrient cycles and food webs: the proceedings of the Fourth SCAR Symposium on Antarctic Biology*. Berlin: Springer-Verlag, pp. xiv, 700

151. Laws, R. M., 1985e. Introduction: 'Antarctic Biology, 1974–83'. In: *Antarctic nutrient cycles and food webs: the proceedings of the Fourth SCAR Symposium on Antarctic Biology*, eds. W. R. Siegfried, P. Condy and R. M. Laws. Berlin: Springer-Verlag, pp. 1–3

152*. Bengtson, J. L. and Laws, R. M., 1985f. 'Trends in age of maturity of crabeater seals: an insight into Antarctic marine interactions'. In: *Antarctic nutrient cycles and food webs: the proceedings of the Fourth SCAR Symposium on Antarctic Biology*, eds. W. R. Siegfried, P. Condy and R. M. Laws. Berlin: Springer-Verlag, pp. 669–75

153. R. M. Laws 1985g. 'Summary and conclusions'. In: *Antarctic nutrient cycles and food webs: Proceedings of the Fourth SCAR Symposium on Antarctic Biology*, eds. W. R. Siegfried, P. Condy and R. M. Laws. Berlin: Springer-Verlag, pp. 676–82

154. Laws, R. M., 1985h. (Chairman) Report of Working Group on Biology. Eighteenth meeting of SCAR, Bremerhaven, FRG. *Polar Record* 22, no.140: 577–594

155. Laws, R. M., 1985i. Natural Environment Research Council, British Antarctic Survey: Annual report, 1984–85. *Report for the period 1 July 1984–30 June 1985*. Cambridge: British Antarctic Survey, p. 114

156*. Laws, R. M., 1985j. 'Organisation of Antarctic biological research'. *Biologist, London* 32: 125–32

157. Laws, R. M., 1985k. Review of *Reproduction in whales, dolphins and porpoises*, eds. W. F. Perrin, et. al. *Rep. International Whaling Commission, Special Issue*, 6: xii, 495; *Marine Mammal Science* 1 (4): 344–6

158. Chaloner, W.G. et.al. 1985l. 'Ecological London'. *The Times*, 19 December 1985

159*. Bonner, W.N. and Laws, R. M. 1985m. 'Marine mammals'. In *FAO Species identification sheets for fishery purposes*, eds. W. Fischer and J. C. Hureau. *Southern Ocean*, vol. II: 401–56

160* Laws, R. M., 1985n. 'Scientific Opportunities in the Antarctic'. In: *Whither Antarctica? The Regulation of Activities in the Region*. Pp. 38–71. A Two-day Conference. The British Institute of International and Comparative Law, London, p. 206

161*. Laws, R. M., 1986a. 'Animal Conservation in the Antarctic'. In: *Advances in Animal Conservation*, eds. J. P. Hearn and J. K. Hodges. *Symp. Zool. Soc. London*, no. 54: 3–23

162. Laws, R. M., 1986b. 'Whales of the Southern Ocean'. *Whalewatcher, American Cetacean Society*,19 (4): 19–21

163. Laws, R. M., 1986c. 'Endangered species'. *The Times*, 4 June, 1986 (Letter)

164. Laws, R. M., 1986d. Meeting of the BIOMASS Executive, Hamburg and Bremerhaven, Federal Republic of Germany, 24–25 February 1986. *BIOMASS Report Series*, no.46: 1–13

165. Laws, R. M., 1986e. Correspondence [Antarctic Mapping]. *Geographical Journal* 152 (1): 148–9

166. Laws, R. M., 1986f. Natural Environment Research Council, British Antarctic Survey: Annual Report, 1984–85. *Report for the period 1 July 1985–30 June 1986*. Cambridge: British Antarctic Survey, p. 108

167. Laws, R. M., 1986g. Review of *Wildlife Resources and Economic Development*, S. K. Eltringham. New York: John Wiley & Sons, Ltd., 1984, pp. xii, 324. *J. Appl. Ecol.* 23 (1): 347–8

168. Laws, R. M., 1986h. Review of the Period. *Zoological Society of London, Ann. Rep.* 1985–86: 5–19

169*. Laws, R. M., 1987a. 'Science, the Treaty and the Future'. In: *Antarctic Science*, ed. D. W. H. Walton. Cambridge University Press. Chapter 18, pp. 250–65

170. R. M. Laws 1987b. 'Introduction: a historical perspective'. In: *Reproductive energetics in mammals*, eds. A. S. Loudon and P. S. Racey. *Symp. Zool .Soc. Lond.* 57: 1–6

171*. Laws, R. M., 1987c. 'Scientific opportunities in the Antarctic'. In: *The Antarctic Treaty Regime: Law, Environment and Resources*, ed. G. D. Triggs. Cambridge University Press, pp. 28–48

172. Laws, R. M., 1987d. SCAR Group of Specialists on Seals. Report of a meeting held in San Diego, California, USA, 11–13 June 1986. *BIOMASS Report Series*, no. 50: 1–32

173. Laws, R. M., 1987e. Review of the Year. *Zoological Society of London, Ann. Rep.* 1986–87, 5–19

174. Laws, R. M. and Harris, R. M., 1987f. 'Seals and birds killed and captured in the Antarctic 1975–85'. *Polar Record* 146: 622–7

175. Laws, R. M., 1987g. Review of: *Antarctic Treaty System: an Assessment. Proceedings of a workshop held at Beardmore South Field Camp Antarctica. January 7–13, 1985.* Polar Research Board (1986). Washington, D.C., National Academy Press, pp. xv, 345

176. Laws, R. M., 1987h. Meeting of the BIOMASS Executive. Paris, France, 1 June 1987. *BIOMASS Report Series*, no. 53: 1–11

177*. Laws, R. M., 1987i. 'Science'. In: *Antarctica: the next decade*. Report of a Study Group chaired by Sir Anthony Parsons. Cambridge University Press, pp. 47–63

178. Laws, R. M., 1987j. Letter from the Master. *St Edmund's Record*, no.2: 7–9

179. Laws, R. M., 1988a. Introduction. In: *Reproduction and disease in captive and wild animals*, ed. G. R. Smith and J. P. Hearn. *Symp. Zool. Soc. London*, no. 60: 1–5

180. Norman, J. N. and Laws, R. M., 1988b. 'Remote health care for Antarctica: the BAS medical unit'. *Polar Record* 24 (151): 317–20

181. Laws, R. M., 1988c. Review of *The natural history of whales and dolphins*, ed. P. G. H. Evans. London: Christopher Helm, 1988, pp. xv, 343. In: *Animal Behaviour* 36 (6): 1865–6

182. Laws, R. M., 1988d. Review of *Status, Biology and Ecology of Fur Seals – Proceedings of an International Symposium and Workshop, Cambridge, England, 23–27 April, 1984*, eds. J. P. Croxall and R. L. Gentry. NOAA Tech, Rep. NMFS 51, US Department of Commerce, 1987, pp. v, 212. *British Antarctic Survey Bulletin*, no. 80: 143–5

183. Laws, R. M., 1988e. Preface. In: *An assessment of environmental impacts arising from scientific research and its logistic support at Bird Island, South Georgia*, W. N. Bonner and J. P. Croxall, 1988. Cambridge: British Antarctic Survey, p. v

184. Laws, R. M., 1988f. 'A perspective on Antarctic cookery'. In: *But the Crackling is Superb*, ed. N. Kurti and G. Kurti. Bristol: Adam Hilger, pp. 157–61

185. Laws, R. M., 1988g. 'A barbecue on a large scale'. In: *But the Crackling is Superb*, ed. N. Kurti and G. Kurti. Bristol: Adam Hilger, p. 179

186. Laws, R. M., 1988h. Review of the Year. *Zoological Society of London, Ann. Rep.* 1987–88: 5–19

187. Laws, R. M., 1989a. 'Life at Low Temperatures', Royal Society, London, 1–2 June 1989. (Report of a meeting.) *Antarctic Science* 1 (3): 295

188. Laws, R. M., 1989b. SCAR Group of Specialists on Seals. Report of a meeting held at Hobart, Tasmania, 23–25 August 1988. *BIOMASS Report Series*, no. 59: 1–61

189*. Laws, R. M., 1989c. *Antarctica: The Last Frontier*. London: Boxtree, pp. 208

190. Laws, R. M., 1989d. Report of the Meeting of the BIOMASS Executive held in Barcelona, Spain, July, 1989. *BIOMASS Report Series*, no. 60: 1–15

191. Laws, R. M., 1989e. 'A dangerous crack in the ice pact'. *The Times*, 13 September 1989

192*. Laws, R. M., 1989f. 'Development of research on large mammals in East Africa'. In: *Biology of large African mammals in their environment*, eds. G. Maloiy and P. Jewell. *Symp. Zool. Soc.* London, no. 61: 267–98

193*. Franks, F. and Laws, R. M., 1990a (eds.). 'Life at Low Temperatures'. Report of a Royal Society Discussion Meeting, 1–2 June 1989. *Phil. Trans. Roy. Soc.*, B 326: 515–697

194. Laws, R. M., 1990b. Report of the meeting of the BIOMASS Executive held in Paris, 17–18 January 1990. *BIOMASS Report Series*, no. 61: 1–27

195*. Laws, R. M., 1990c. 'Science as an Antarctic Resource'. In: *The future of Antarctica: exploitation versus preservation*, ed. G. Cook. Manchester University Press, pp. 8–24

196. Laws, R. M., 1990d. *Antarktis: die letzte grenze*. Bergische Gladbach: Gustav Lubbe Verlag GMBH, p. 287. [German edition of *Antarctica: the last frontier*]

197. Laws, R. M., 1990e. Report of the meeting of the BIOMASS Executive held in Sao Paulo Brazil, 21 July 1990. *BIOMASS Report Series*, no. 64: 1–16

198. Laws, R. M., 1991a. Letter from the Master. *St Edmund's Record*, no.3: 1–4

199. Laws, R. M., 1991b. Foreword. In: *Assessment and Testing*, Robert Wood. Cambridge University Press, p. ix

200*. Laws, R. M., 1991c. Opening Statement by the President of the Scientific Committee on Antarctic Research (SCAR), XIth Antarctic Treaty Special Consultative Meeting. *SCAR Report*, no. 6: 3–4

201*. Laws, R. M., 1991d. Presentation by the President of the Scientific Committee on Antarctic Research (SCAR), XIth Antarctic Treaty Special Consultative Meeting. *SCAR Report*, no. 6: 5–11

202*. Laws, R. M., 1991e. 'Unacceptable threats to Antarctic science'. *New Scientist*, vol. 129, no. 1762: 4

203. Laws, R. M., 1991f. 'Conflicting interests in Antarctica'. *Biologist* 38: 37

204*. Testa, J. W., et. al., 1991g. 'Temporal variability in Antarctic marine ecosystems: periodic fluctuations in the phocid seals'. *Canadian J. Fisheries & Aquatic Sci.* 48: 631–9

205. Laws, R. M., 1991h. Letter from the Master. *St Edmund's Record*, no. 4: 204

206. Laws, R. M., 1991i. Letter from the Master. *St Edmund's Record*, no. 5, 1–3

207. Laws, R. M., 1991j. 'Antarctic politics and science are coming into conflict'. Guest editorial, *Antarctic Science* 3, no.3: 231

208. Laws, R. M., 1991k. Report of the meeting of the BIOMASS Executive held in Bremerhaven, Germany, 21 September, 1991. *BIOMASS Report Series*, no. 6: 1–12

209. Laws, R. M., 1991 l. Foreword. In: *An annotated bibliography of Antarctic invertebrates (terrestrial and freshwater)*, W. Block. Cambridge: British Antarctic Survey, p. i

210. Laws, R. M., 1991m. Biomass Farewell Dinner. Address to BIOMASS Colloquium Dinner. *BIOMASS Newsletter, SCAR* 13 (2):18–19

211. Laws, R. M., 1991n. Review of Headland, R.K. 1989. *Chronological list of Antarctic expeditions and related historical events*. Cambridge: Cambridge University Press. *Geological Journal* 26 (4): 351–2

212. Laws, R. M., 1992a. Review of *Biology and exploitation of the minke whale*, J. Horwood, 1990. Florida: CRC Press, Inc., p.238. *Marine Mammal Science* 8 (1):95–8

213. Laws, R. M., 1992b. 'A time to paint'. *BAS Club Newsletter* no.28: 32–3

214. Laws, R. M., 1992c. Foreword. In: *Elephants*, ed. J. Shoshani. Sydney, Australia: Weldon Owen Pty Ltd., pp.10–11

215*. Drewry, D. J., Laws, R. M. and Pyle, J. A. (eds.), 1992d. 'Antarctica and Environmental change'. *Phil. Trans. Roy. Soc.* Ser. B, vol. 338, no. 1285: 199–334

216. Laws, R. M., 1992e. Closing Remarks. In: *Antarctica and Environmental Change*, eds. D. J. Drewry, R. M. Laws and J. A. Pyle. *Phil. Trans. Roy. Soc. Lond.* Ser. B, vol. 338, no. 1285: 329–34

217. Laws, R. M., 1993a. The Master's Proof of Evidence. *Cambridge Local Plan, St Edmund's College*, p. 23. St. Edmund's College, Cambridge, (typescript)

218*. Laws, R. M., 1993b (ed.). *Antarctic Seals: Research Methods and Techniques*. Cambridge: Cambridge University Press, pp. xxii, 399

219*. Laws, R. M., 1993c. Introduction. In: *Antarctic Seals: Research Methods and Techniques*, ed. R. M. Laws. Cambridge: Cambridge University Press, pp. xiii–xxii

220*. Laws, R. M., 1993d. 'Identification of species'. In: *Antarctic Seals: Research Methods and Techniques*, ed. R. M. Laws. Cambridge: Cambridge University Press, pp. 1–28

221*. Erickson, A. W., Bester, M. N. and Laws, R. M., 1993e. 'Marking techniques'. In: *Antarctic Seals: Research Methods and Techniques*, ed. R. M. Laws. Cambridge: Cambridge University Press, pp. 89–118

222*. Bonner, W. N. and Laws, R. M. 1993f. 'Morphometrics, specimen collection and preservation'. In: *Antarctic Seals: Research Methods and Techniques*, ed. R. M. Laws. Cambridge: Cambridge University Press, pp. 161–93

223*. Laws, R. M. and Sinha, A. A., 1993g. 'Reproduction'. In: *Antarctic Seals: Research Methods and Techniques*, ed. R. M. Laws. Cambridge: Cambridge University Press, pp. 228–67

224*. Laws, R. M., 1993h. 'Development of technology and research needs'. In: *Antarctic Seals: Research Methods and Techniques*, ed. R. M. Laws. Cambridge: Cambridge University Press, pp. 316–35

225. Laws, R. M., 1993i. Letter from the Master. *St Edmund's Record*, no. 6, 1989–92: 1–5

226*. Drewry, D. J., Laws, R. M. and Pyle, J. A., 1993j (eds.). *Antarctica and Environmental Change*. Oxford: Clarendon Press, pp. vii, 137. (Book version of publication no.187 above)

227. Drewry, D. J., Laws, R. M. and Pyle, J. A., 1993k. Preface. In: *Antarctica and Environmental Change*, eds. D. J. Drewry, R. M. Laws, R. M. and J. A. Pyle. Oxford, Clarendon Press, pp. vii–viii

228. Laws, R. M., 1993l. 'Antarctica and environmental change: closing remarks'. In: *Antarctica and Environmental Change*, eds. D. J. Drewry, R. M. Laws and J. A. Pyle. Oxford: Clarendon Press, pp. 329–34

229. Weller, G. E. and Laws, R. M., 1993m. Preface. In: *The Role of the Antarctic in Global Change: An International Plan for a Regional Research Programme*. Scientific Committee on Antarctic Research, Cambridge, pp. 54

230*. Laws, R. M., 1994a. 'The Future of International Research in the Antarctic: Scientific and Political Background'. In: *Recherches Polaires: une stratégie. pour l'an 2000.* Paris: Académie des Sciences, pp. 17–27

231. Laws, R. M., 1994b. Review of: *The Structure and Dynamics of Antarctic Population*, J. C. M. Beltramino. New York: Vantage Press, pp. xxvii, 105. In *Polar Record* 30 (173): 144

232*. Le Boeuf, B. J. and Laws, R. M. (eds.), 1994c. *Elephant Seals: Population Ecology, Behaviour and Physiology.* Los Angeles; London: University of California Press, Berkeley, pp. xvii, 414

233. Le Boeuf, B. J. and Laws, R. M., 1994d. Preface. In: *Elephant Seals: Population Ecology, Behaviour and Physiology*, eds. B. J. Le Boeuf and R. M. Laws. Los Angeles; London: University of California Press, Berkeley, pp. xi–xiv

234*. Le Boeuf, B. J. and Laws, R. M., 1994e. 'Elephant Seals: An Introduction to the Genus'. In: *Elephant Seals: Population Ecology, Behaviour and Physiology*, eds. B. J. Le Boeuf and R. M. Laws. Los Angeles; London: University of California Press, Berkeley, pp. 1–26

235*. Laws, R. M., 1994f. 'History and present status of southern elephant seal populations'. In: *Elephant Seals: Population Ecology, Behaviour and Physiology*, eds. B. J. Le Boeuf and R. M. Laws. Los Angeles; London: University of California Press, Berkeley. pp. 49–65

236. Laws, R. M., and Strømberg, J. O., 1994g. Preface. In: *BIOMASS Colloquium Proceedings*, ed. S.Z. El-Sayed. Berlin: Springer-Verlag, pp. xiii–xiv

237*. Laws, R. M., 1994h. Discussant's Report: Antarctic Marine Systems. In: *BIOMASS Colloquium Proceedings*, ed. S.Z. El-Sayed. Berlin: Springer-Verlag, pp. 323–7

238. Laws, R. M., 1994i. Preface: SCAR and the Antarctic Treaty. In: *Antarctic Science – Global Concerns*, ed. G. Hempel. Berlin: Springer-Verlag

239. Laws, R. M., 1994j. Review of: *Elephant Life: fifteen years of high population density*, I. O. Buss, 1990. Ames: Iowa State University Press, pp. xxvi, 191 *African J. Ecology* 32: 85–87

240. Laws, R. M., 1994k. 'Polar Profile: William Nigel Bonner'. *Polar Record* 31: 67–70

241. Laws, R. M., 1994l. Foreword. In: *Van Someren's Birds II*, L. Van Someren and G. R. C. Van Someren. Douglas, Isle of Man: Aves Publications Ltd., p. 143

242. Laws, R. M., 1994m. Letter from the Master. *St Edmund's Record*, 1993–94, no. 7: 3–4

243. Laws, R. M., 1995a. In: 'Nigel Bonner, Tributes from the Memorial Service at BAS – 22 October 1994'. *BAS Club Newsletter*, no. 33: 21–24

244. Laws, R. M., 1995a. Letter from the Master. *St Edmund's Record*, 1992–93, No. 8, pp. 2–3

245. Laws, R. M., 1995b. 'William Nigel Bonner: 1928–1994' (Obituary). *Marine Mammal Science* 11 (4): 596–8

246. Laws, R. M., 1996a. Preface, pp. v–viii In: *St Edmund's College, Cambridge 1896–1996*, M. Walsh, pp. 104

247. Laws, R. M., 1997. Letter from the Master. *St Edmund's Record*, 1994–95, no. 9: 1–3

248*. Laws, R. M., 1998a. 'The ecology of the Southern Ocean'. In: *Exploring Ecology and Its Applications*, ed. P. Karieva. Sunderland, MA, USA: Sinauer Associates, Inc. (Reprint of no. 125 above)

249. Laws, R. M., 1998b. Letter from the Master. *St Edmund's Record*, 1995–96, no. 10: 2–6

250. Laws, R. M., 1999a. 'Derek Hylton Maling, Signy Island 1948–50'. *BAS Club Newsletter*, no. 41: 40–5. Cambridge: British Antarctic Survey

251. Laws, R. M., 1999b. 'Polar Profile: Derek Hylton Maling'. *Polar Record* 35, no. 194: 259–62

252. Laws, R. M., 2000a. Foreword. p. v. In: *British Polar Exploration and Research: A Historical and Medallic Record with Biographies 1818–1999*, N. W. Poulson and J. A. L. Myres, 2000, pp. xii, 729

253. Laws, R. M., 2000b. 'Sir Vivian Fuchs FRS 1908–1999'. (Obituary) *Norsk Geogr. Tidsskr*. 54: 194–5

254. Laws, R. M., 2001a. 'Return to the Antarctic'. *St Catharine's College Society Magazine*, 2001, pp. 8–9

255. Anon. 2001b. 'Peter Jenkins'. Obituary, *Daily Telegraph*, Saturday 13 October 2001 [edited from a draft by R. M. Laws]

256. Laws, R. M., 2001c. 'Vivian Ernest Fuchs, 11 February 1908–11 November 1999'. *Biographical Memoirs, Royal Society of London* 47: 203–22

257*. Laws, R. M., Baird, A. and Bryden, M. M., 2002a. 'The teeth and age estimation in crabeater seals (*Lobodon carcinophagus*)'. *J. Zool., London* 258: 197–203

258*. Laws, R. M., Baird, A. and Bryden, M. M., (2003a). 'Size and growth of the crabeater seal, *Lobodon carcinophagus* (Mammalia, Carnivora)'. *J. Zool. London* 259: 103–8

259*. Laws, R. M., 2003b. Review of *Encyclopedia of Marine Mammals*, eds. W. F. Perrin, B. Wursig and J. G. M. Thewissen. Academic Press, 2002, pp. xxxviii, 1414. *Marine Mammal Science*, vol.19 (3): 599–606

260*. Laws, R. M., Bryden, M. M. and Baird, A. 2003c. 'The breeding season and embryonic diapause in crabeater seals (*Lobodon carcinophagus*)'. *Reproduction* 126: 365–370

Short Curriculum Vitae

Dr Richard Maitland Laws CBE (1983); *b* 23 April 1926; s of Percy Malcolm Laws (d 1962) and Florence May Laws MBE, *née* Heslop (d 1983). *Educ* Dame Allan's Sch., Newcastle upon Tyne; St Catharine's College Cambridge (open scholarship, res scholarship, MA, PhD, ScD); *m* Maureen Isobel Winifred, da of late George Leonard Holmes; 3 s (Richard Anthony, Christopher Peter, Andrew David); **d** 7 October 2014.

Career biologist Falkland Islands Dependencies Survey 1947–53, biologist and whaling inspector on factory ship *Balaena* in Antarctic 1953–54, PSO Nat Inst of Oceanography 1954–61; Director of Nuffield Unit of Tropical Animal Ecology, Uganda and Univ. of Cambridge 1961–67, Tsavo Res Project Kenya 1967–68; Smuts Meml Fellowship Univ. of Cambridge 1968–69, Leverhulme Fellowship 1969, head Life Sciences Div BAS 1969–73. **Director of BAS 1973–87**, NERC Sea Mammal Res Unit 1977–87; Univ. of Cambridge. **Master St Edmund's Coll 1985–96**, memb Financial Bd 1988–91, memb Cncl of Senate 1989–92, chm Local Examinations Syndicate 1990–94; SCAR: UK memb Working Gp on Biology 1972–90 (chm 1980–86), memb Gp of Specialists on Seals 1972–98 (convenor 1972–88), memb Working Gp on Logistics 1974–80, memb BIOMASS Exec 1976–91; **President of SCAR 1990–94** (memb SCAR Exec 1990–98), hon memb 1996; Food and Agric Orgn UN: memb Working Pty on Marine Mammals 1974–77 (chm 1976–77), chm Scientific Consultation on Conservation and Management of Marine Mammals and their Environment 1976; hon lectr Makerere Univ., Uganda 1962–66, hon memb Soc for Marine Mammalogy 1994, hon warden Uganda Nat Parks 1996.

Bruce Meml medal for Antarctic work RSE 1954, scientific medal Zoological Soc of London 1966, Polar medal (1976, second clasp 2001);

foreign memb Norwegian Acad of Science and Letters 1998; Hon Fell: St Catharine's Coll Cambridge 1982, St Edmund's Coll Cambridge 1996; Hon DSc Univ. of Bath 1991; FZS 1960 (memb Cncl 1982–84, vice-pres 1983, sec 1984–88), FIBiol 1973 (vice-pres 1983), **FRS 1980** (chm Interdisciplinary Scientific Ctee on Antarctic Res 1988–93).

Author of numerous research publications in scientific journals, as well as books and reviews, as detailed in previous pages.

Acronyms and Abbreviations

BAS	British Antarctic Survey
BAT	British Antarctic Territory
BC	Base Commander
BIOMASS	Biological Investigations of Marine Antarctic Systems and Stocks
BM	British Museum, Natural History
CCAMLR	Convention for the Conservation of Antarctic Marine Living Resources
CCAS	Convention for the Conservation of Antarctic Seals
CDW	catcher's day's work
CRAMRA	Convention on the Regulation of Antarctic Mineral Resource Activities
CSAGI	Comité Special de l'Année Geophysique Internationale
CTD	Sea chemistry and temperature at different depths
DES	Department for Education and Science
FAO	Food and Agriculture Organization of the United Nations
FCO	Foreign and Commonwealth Office
FIDS	Falkland Islands Dependencies Survey
Fid	A person who was employed by FIDS or BAS
FRS	Fellow of the Royal Society
HE	His Excellency
ICSU	International Council of Scientific Unions
IGU	International Unions of Geography

IGY	International Geophysical Year
IH	International Harvester
INACH	Chilean Antarctic Institute
IUBS	International Union for Biological Sciences
IUGG	International Union for Geodesy and Geophysics
JIC	Joint Intelligence Committee
KEP	King Edward Point
MOD	Ministry of Defence
NERC	National Environment Research Council
NUTAE	Nuffield Unit of Tropical Animal Ecology
OBP	Offshore Biological Programme
PG	Preparatory Groups
RA	Royal Artillery
SAS	Special Air Service
SBS	Special Boat Service
SCAR	Scientific Committee for Antarctic Research
SGBS	South Georgia Benthic Survey
SJ	Society of Jesus (Jesuit)
SSN	British Nuclear Powered Submarines
SOBS	South Orkneys Benthic Survey
SPA	Special Protection Area
SPRI	Scott Polar Research Institute
SSSI	Site of Special Scientific Interest
VHF	Very High Frequency
VLF	Very low Frequency
UCLES	University of Cambridge Local Examinations Syndicate
URSI	Union of Radio Science Institutes
ZSL	Zoological Society of London

Index